REASON AND SPONTANEITY

For Der Pao and Dawn

This book is published in association with the
Institute of East Asian Philosophies, Singapore

REASON AND SPONTANEITY

A. C. GRAHAM

CURZON PRESS

BARNES & NOBLE BOOKS

First published 1985
Curzon Press Ltd: London and Dublin
and
Barnes & Noble Books, Totowa, NJ, USA

ISBN
UK 0 7007 0172 9
US 0 389 20510 9

Library of Congress Cataloging in Publication Data

Graham, A. C. (Angus Charles)
Reason and spontaneity

1. Ethics.   2. Values.   3. Reason.   4. Spontaneity
(Philosophy)   I. Title
BJ1581.2.G672 1985   170'.42   84–12358
ISBN 0–389–20510–9

Printed in Hungary

Contents

Preface

There are many ways of philosophizing, and one of them is to start from a simple idea with wide ramifications, and follow them through to the end without reserve. The idea of this book is that we men of reason have been misunderstanding the relation between reason and spontaneity. The point is not that we ought to be allowing more room for spontaneous insight and impulse in our lives, an accusation which just or unjust belongs to a different issue, but that we have never come fully to terms with the thought that even our most deeply considered choices of ends are often (might it be always?) choices between goals which are themselves spontaneous.

Although conscious of being less rational than the eighteenth and nineteenth centuries supposed, we are not yet accustomed to thinking of ourselves as primarily spontaneous beings, whose intellect, even if we happen to be philosophers, is in the conduct of life doing nothing else but choose between the directions in which we find ourselves being spontaneously pulled. But if we learn to do so, which is not as great a humiliation to the rational man as he may suppose, many problems reveal themselves in a new light, first of all the relation between fact and value. It has long remained unquestioned that to decide how to act it is not enough to be aware of things as they objectively are. But if it is indeed the case that the basic choices are between conflicting spontaneous pulls, the balance of which shifts with changing awareness of self and situation, then the mere obligation to be aware of things as they objectively are will commit me to prefer the goal to which I am drawn when most aware. This suggests implications which we shall follow without the least humility wherever they may lead, through the themes of egoism and altruism, pleasure, creativity, the sacred, the relation between science and poetry, and between rationalism and irrationalism. A simple idea defines itself most clearly when exposed to a rapid display from all angles.

1

THE GROUNDING OF VALUATION

1.1 'Be aware' as first principle

Since in the last decades of the twentieth century all valuations are in question, let us start by imagining a manner of life in which I do without them altogether. Let us suppose that, when invited to judge actions or persons, I appeal only to what is, never to what ought to be. Facts appear solid, values fluid; there are firm reasons for accepting, if only provisionally, scientific laws of nature, none for submitting to canons of taste or to the moral law. Should I criticize another or myself, it will be for failure to take account of facts, for insufficient awareness of the conditions and consequences of a choice. If I respect your opinion in the arts, it will be because you are especially intelligent, more than usually perceptive of colour contrasts and harmonies, rhythms and vowel sequences, the shades of meaning of a word, the motives of a character, the ring of authentic or false feeling; we shall not argue over tastes. As for morals, I shall have on this policy to refuse to condemn even Hitler's genocide, although I might permit myself to sneer at it as stupid, because the theories about the Aryan race and the Jewish conspiracy which inspired it were fantasies. However little I care for the way you live, I shall concede that as long as you get your facts right, sense flavours and textures with accuracy and discrimination, think out the implications of your choices, are not deceived about your desires and ambitions, you may do as you please.

As long as I stay confined to this moral nihilism, the single unquestioned imperative will be to act intelligently, and in particular to be aware of objective conditions, of those obstinate facts about external difficulties and my own limitations which thwart my efforts unless I recognize and adapt myself to them. In general I shall recognize what is, not what ought to be; but certainly I *ought* to be aware of what I am trying to do, why I want it, how to do it, whether it can be done. In addition to all the rationally established facts I formulate in the indicative mood, there is the imperative to respect them, expressed in injunctions of varying generality imposing varying degrees of obligation, 'You ought to know that', 'You should have had more sense', 'You had better check that', 'You were wrong to overlook that', and sometimes directly in the imperative mood, 'Face facts', 'Know thyself', 'Think what you're doing'. As the most suitable to sum them up provisionally let us pick 'Face facts', a roughly formulated injunction which carries with it its own punishments for disobedience, without any need to appeal to God, philosophers or the police. If I were to question its authority, and find a nurse to look after me, I would no longer be doing anything on my own responsibility, and problems of valuation would in any case no longer concern me. Since temptations to inattentiveness, prejudice, wishful thinking, are as strong as moral temptations, there are

1

times when 'Face facts' imposes itself as the most rigorous, the most unwelcome of imperatives. However, it is unlike a prudential or moral imperative in that it tells me only how to prepare for a choice, not how to choose. 'Face facts' does not tell me what to do about the facts to be faced. A book of ethics does not have to spell it out, any more than a book about mathematics or zoology has to include the reminder 'Read me attentively, intelligently'.

If I could be nothing but a witness and tolerant judge of others, this ethical nihilism would be a fully rational mode of life. But I am myself an agent; there remains the question of how I make my own decisions. The assembling of facts merely sets the stage for asking the question 'What shall I do?'. To choose, I have to judge that here and now, for me, one alternative is the better, and to make my choices consistently I have to add to 'Face facts' other principles to which I ascribe an imperative force, and ensure that they are logically compatible. But although codes of more or less articulated principles are a practical necessity for everybody, they seem to hang in a void without anything to support them. Certainly, once committed to a personal code, I can make value as well as factual judgments about your conduct; but if your first principle is 'Do as you would be done by' and mine is 'Care only for yourself', it seems that there is no objective test by which one of us can convince the other that he is right, as there is for an issue of fact. My temptation is to try to make my other imperatives as unimpugnable as 'Face facts' by rooting them in fact. But how can the advice 'Do this' or the decision 'I will do this' derive its authority from a purely factual claim, whether theological ('The creator of the universe commands this'), sociological ('It's the law', 'It's the custom') or psychological ('I desire it')? To suppose that it can is an assumption long ago undermined by Hume, that one can infer from 'is' to 'ought', from purely descriptive premisses to a prescriptive conclusion. To some extent I can evade the issue by letting spontaneous inclination take its course, without allowing thought to intervene, so that my action is not chosen but caused; but I am not an instinctive being like an animal, I have to choose, and on the position we are considering all imperatives are ungrounded, except such as may be derivable from 'Face facts'. I may be tempted to offer the spontaneous inclination itself as reason for my choice, and say I shall do it because I want to do it; but in examining myself objectively I see that a fact about my wants and likes would be directly relevant only to a causal explanation of my actions, and could be used in deciding what to do only as I use any other objective facts. This, admittedly, is a hard saying, and may well stir a first inkling that there must be something fundamentally wrong with the approach which has brought us to this point. There is surely something very odd about insisting that I need more than the fact that I love cats and hate dogs to decide which to have about the house. However, once granted that one cannot infer what to do from fact alone, there seems to be no flaw in the argument. It appears then that in the last resort, with all the facts before me, and all my ungrounded principles logically ordered, I still have no grounds upon which to choose. It is not that I have no reason to submit to the moral law and can do as I please; I am left with no reason even to do as I please. I can be rational about everything except the point which most immediately concerns me, how to conduct my life.

This is the conclusion which many, approaching by this or similar routes, have come to see as inevitable, after the successive failures to prove that principles of conduct can be grounded in the existence of God, or in Kant's Categorical Imperative validated *a priori* like 'two and two make four', or in the biological facts of evolution or the psychological facts of human needs. It leaves a gap at the very centre of the knowledge which the rational procedures of the sciences are continually expanding, with nothing to fill it except deduction from principles themselves ungrounded, or habit, or religious or political emotion, or the Existentialist's anguished leap in the dark, or doing as one pleases, or as convention or fashion pleases. To live by ungrounded values, which even if organized as rationally as a science have only an inward coherence without external support, has come to be widely accepted as the quintessentially modern condition. Nothing forbids me to dramatize the crisis by saying that the individual has found a new sense of his dignity in the knowledge that he is wholly free to choose, with the sole responsibility for his choice. But would I be doing more than playing with words which sound agreeable to me, 'dignity', 'freedom', 'responsibility', to describe what could still just as well be called nihilism? All that I can honestly say is that after collecting the facts I do decide one way or another, without having any reasons which will satisfy you if you do not share the same standards.

But is this conclusion as inevitable as it has come to seem? It so happens that another growing tendency in contemporary thinking has been undermining the whole approach which leads to it. It no longer seems as obvious as it used to that I can detach myself from my interactions with other things, observe them objectively, and arrive at facts about them wholly independent of my own reactions and decisions. In the sciences of course the possibility of pure objectivity has been a convenient and fruitful assumption, which has only recently run up against its limitations. At the sub-atomic level however physics does now have to take into account the effects of the observer on the particles he observes. Why should the assumption of a perfect detachment be retained in ethics, where it amounts to the transparent fiction that I can, so to speak, stand outside myself, withdraw to a point of observing Ego witnessing unmoved even my own emotions? When I obey or defy 'Face facts', my welcoming or resisting of the facts is itself a psychological process in causal interaction with spontaneous inclination; on the one hand emotional bias distorts judgement, on the other desire or aversion veers with additional information. Certainly I cannot deduce which goals to pursue from the facts to be faced; but will it not be a causally necessary condition of obeying 'Face facts' that I let myself be moved, at least incipiently, in the direction in which the facing of the facts would cause me to move? Suppose for example that I am a smoker who has just heard about the dangers of lung cancer. Some of my friends have been frightened into no longer wanting to smoke, others have faced the facts but are reconciled to being fonder of smoking than they are afraid of cancer, but I myself yield to the temptation to smoke although convinced that I *ought* to abstain. Does that 'ought' depend on some other imperative than 'Face facts'? No doubt if I cannot break out of the convention of thinking *as though* I were a detached Ego contemplating unmoved both the possible consequences and my fear of them, it will seem that I can have no reason to stop smoking unless I recognize some further imperative such as 'Take care of your health'. But if I am not misled by this convention, it will in my own case be sufficient grounds for choice that it is the impulse to abstain which prevails when I am fully aware of the danger. The sight of a photograph of a cancerous lung causes me to shrink with disgust from the very thought of smoking; a few hours later the physical craving revives, obliterates the memory, and causes me to smoke again. Pulled between the conflicting impulses, I *ought* to resist the craving which dulls the awareness which moves me to abstain, because for me that is a causally necessary condition of obeying 'Face the fact that you might get cancer'.

Let us imagine, as the first dawning of objective thought, a child wanting another helping at dinner, remembering what it is like to be sick, and telling himself what he has often been told by his mother, 'Don't, or you'll be ill'. Up to this moment he has always behaved as spontaneously as an animal, surrendering to appetite and vomiting; now for the first time he makes a considered choice. (We describe as 'spontaneous' all activity which is not the result of a considered choice.) What will be the logical form of his thought? A common answer would be to fit it into some form of the practical syllogism:

Shall I eat it or not?
Another helping will make you sick.
You don't want to be sick.
Therefore don't eat it.

But here we run up against the difficulty that this formulation appears to derive a prescriptive conclusion from two factual premisses. One might avoid the objection, following R. M. Hare,[1] by interpreting 'You don't want to be sick' as itself prescriptive, a logical imperative equivalent to 'Don't get sick' disguised by the grammatically indicative form. This would involve claiming that whenever one rejects practical advice by repudiating the presumed end, in the words 'But I don't want that!', one is declaring 'I don't recognize any imperative to do that'. Yet the end would be repudiated even more strongly by a 'But I don't feel the slightest inclination to do that!', which is unmistakably expressive of a spontaneous revulsion. On closer inspection one sees that this interpretation of 'want' misplaces the centre of imperative force in the child's situation. He does not require an imperative to make him avoid the sickness from the thought of which he already shrinks in nausea; what he has to force himself to do is hold on to the fact that sickness is the likely outcome of yielding to temptation. Under the pressure of this unwelcome fact, he is being spontaneously pulled between the revulsion when he remembers and the greed when he forgets. In taking this first step to rational choice, the single imperative which imposes itself is none other than 'Face facts', which has exerted its authority from his first recognition of the obstinate resistance of external circumstance to his desires. The form of his thought will be something like this:

Overlooking the fact I find myself moved to eat, facing the fact I find myself moved to refrain.

In which direction shall I let myself be moved?
Face facts.
Therefore let yourself be moved to refrain.

From this illustration is may be seen why, for choosing a course of action, 'Face facts' may be the only imperative required. The child's greed is obstructing awareness of consequences the facing of which would cause him to refrain; therefore to let the impulse to refrain prevail over the impulse to eat is a causally necessary condition of obeying the imperative. If he succumbs to temptation after all and suffers the consequences, it would be to the point to say 'You should have known better' or 'You ought to have had more sense', reproaches which derive their authority from 'Face facts'; but it would be irrelevant (and exasperating) to say 'You shouldn't have made yourself ill like that', on the authority of the 'You don't want to be sick' of the practical syllogism interpreted as 'Don't get sick'. From the imperative to refrain on this occasion the child may advance, as he observes the situation recur in his own or others' experience, to his first general principle:

Overlooking the fact that too much will make one sick one may be moved to eat, facing the fact one is moved to refrain.
In which direction should one let oneself be moved?
Face facts.
Therefore one should let oneself be moved to refrain.

We might formulate his newly discovered principle as 'One ought not to eat too much', but very probably it would be first encountered by him as 'Sensible people don't eat too much'.

While the first formula (the practical syllogism) served choices of means, the new formula whether in particular or in general form serves choices of ends. The motions in causal interaction with the facing of facts are incipient motions towards goals, spontaneous desires or aversions, and to prefer one inclination in the light of 'Face facts' is to choose its goal as an end. At first the prevailing inclination will issue immediately in action, but with increasing rationality the child will learn to suspend action in order to take further goals into account. Later still he may train himself to eradicate the desire or aversion itself, releasing himself from one causally necessary condition of facing facts, so that the formula is no longer directly applicable; but that will be in the service of other ends, and unless he can discover some new way of validating them these too will be spontaneous goals selected from the rest by thinking within the frame of the same formula. He will also learn to clarify his ends; originally he saw no further than immediate goals, the satisfaction of hunger and relief from nausea; later he conceptualizes the nourishing of the body by food and the danger to health of over-eating, and it is towards or away from these that he finds himself spontaneously pulled.

Of the new formula, we may observe
(1) When particular, it applies 'Face facts' to a choice without introducing any other universal imperative. When general it ordains a standard, which however

has not more but less authority than the particular choice, since it depends on a generalization about everyone's reactions in a recurring situation, which is as vulnerable to exceptions as any other generalization. The generality of the standard will in most cases be local; few standards are as firmly rooted in the universal constants of human nature as the child's 'One ought not to eat too much'.

(2) It applies no more nor less to the most personal and transitory goals than to the most general and long-term.

(3) It does not require any principle for weighing spontaneous inclinations, for example a hedonist principle by which vomiting is to be avoided as unpleasant. One is simply moved in one direction or the other in greater or lesser awareness. If we are to use the metaphor of weighing, in choices of means the agent is the weigher, but in choices of ends he is the arm of the balance itself.

(4) There is no need for any criterion for the relevance of facts which is not implicit in the formula itself. The 'fact' of the first premiss covers all and no more than the facts awareness of which would modify spontaneous reactions to the issue in question; 'Face facts' will be applicable to the issue only within the scope of this information. The test of relevance will be whether awareness of a fact does act causally on spontaneous inclination. That the dish is tasty and that another helping will upset the stomach are relevant facts because they do modify inclination; that it is a rainy or a sunny day and that the wallpaper is yellow or white are irrelevant because they do not move the child in either direction. (If it so happens that yellow wallpaper does take away your appetite, then for you it *is* relevant.)

(5) Different though it is from the practical syllogism, it resembles it in that its conclusions are always revisable in the light of further information, which imposes itself as relevant whenever it does turn out to alter spontaneous reaction.

It is time to look more closely at the imperative for which we have so far been getting along on a rough formulation, 'Face facts'. Since we are using it for choices of ends, we cannot treat the awareness it prescribes simply as a universal means to our ends whatever they may be, which is what the admonition suggests in ordinary discourse (with the implication 'If you don't you'll suffer for it'). What we require is a formulation of that universal imperative to take into account in choices which imposes its authority whenever something is recognized to exist, whenever it confronts us as not illusory but real. Let us reduce it to two words, 'Be aware', and define 'aware of X' as prepared to take X into account in choices. (We shall similarly use 'intelligent' of the general disposition to take things into account.) We put it in the grammatically imperative mood in order to show up starkly its difference from factual statements, but also to leave room to interpret it according to circumstances as the strong 'One ought to be aware of this', or as 'It is a good thing to be aware of this', or in diminishing degrees, as the prospect of something coming within one's range of choice becomes remote, 'Other things being equal, it is better to be aware of it than not'. Allowing this latitude, we may claim 'Be aware' as an imperative both universal and valid *a priori*, since it would be inconsistent to say of anything that it exists yet is irrelevant to any possible choice. Although one can speak also of being aware of the value of something, it will be essential to confine our usage to awareness of the existing, of persons, things, events. The theoretical rigour of the formulation will not however exclude the practical possibility that, as a matter of psychological fact, awareness of something may interfere causally with awareness of something else, so that a local unawareness may be a necessary condition of obeying 'Be aware'. We may now refine the grounding formula as it applies to particular choices:

In awareness of everything relevant to the issue (= everything which would spontaneously move me one way or the other), I find myself moved towards X, overlooking something relevant I find myself moved towards Y.
In which direction shall I let myself be moved?
Be aware.
Therefore let yourself be moved towards X (= choose X as end).

We shall not linger over what we mean by choice, which even when narrowed to considered choice is a concept with blurred edges. To accept responsibility for a choice, I may judge it sufficient that I was closely attentive to the object before responding in one direction or the other. In this vague sense animals likewise choose, and are aware and intelligent by our definitions. It is convenient to limit considered choice to humans, assuming a definition of 'consider' which requires the operation of verbal or other symbols, and to use it as the criterion for distinguishing the deliberate from the spontaneous. But unless I talked out the issue with others, or wrote it up in my diary, it may be far from clear even to myself whether or not I did verbally formulate the alternatives.

Identifying as unquestionably spontaneous whatever cannot even on the most indulgent interpretation be ascribed to considered choice, what will be the place of spontaneity in our model of the rational man? Let us say that in the first place man is a creature responding intelligently or stupidly to his surroundings, much as an animal does. The activity which his reason can criticize and partially direct was not initially chosen by him, it is spontaneous; the physical processes of birth, breathing, digestion, orgasm, death; the emotions; the desires and aversions which are independent of his principles and may conflict with them, irrespective of whether he thinks of them as innate or as socially conditioned; dream, reverie and fantasy; ecstasies of love, mystical illumination, intellectual discovery, artistic creation and contemplation. Rationalists and moralists have always been at least a little uneasy about admitting that so much that they most value comes out of the vast area of human behaviour which shares the spontaneity of physical events. Physical events are caused, human action is willed; causes determine effects, the will is free. To the extent that activities are spontaneous it appears that they belong to the realm of the caused (which in the case of biological process is obvious enough), and that he is a free agent only to the extent that he learns to direct them. For many people there is something terrifying in the thought that in a universe in which man is so insignificant in comparison with the unreasoning forces of nature, most of his own organism belongs to or wants to defect to nature.

Unlike an animal, man can halt his incipient reactions, reason about his situation, and respond more intelligently in the light of increased understanding. But since he can think only of a few things at a time, the routine function of his noble

gift of reason must be to correct spontaneous reactions and keep them running
in an intelligent direction. He breathes, digests, lifts an arm, takes the next step,
without thinking how to do it, and if bad health forces him to analyse and choose
in such peripheral matters he is sorry to be distracted from his central concerns.
He knows too that there are activities in which he is most intelligent when he is
most spontaneous, in which to think may even be dangerous; the ski jumper or
the tightrope walker cannot afford to hesitate and reflect. While still learning, to
swim or drive a car or speak a foreign language, he does have to think out what to
do next, but it is when he comes to trust his own reflexes that he will have mastered
the skill. Not that when apprenticeship is past he will do these things thoughtlessly,
but in this context 'thoughtless' means not 'unreasoning' but 'heedless'. A driver
is sensitive to minute shifts in the pressures on his hand and in the rhythm of the
engine, with an intensity of concentration which when tiring he sustains by an
effort of will; but most of the time he does not ponder alternatives, apply principles,
or make decisions, his hands are as though moving of themselves. Among the
various intelligent activities of the rational man is the analytic thinking which
criticizes the rest, which exposes clumsiness in driving, a weak line in a verse,
ineptitude in an intuitive estimate of character. For 'Be aware' this analytic
faculty will be the final court of appeal; nevertheless, there are all sorts of ways
of being aware. Once we come to terms with the very limited although crucial
place of analytic thinking among the varieties of intelligent behaviour, we draw
from 'Be aware' the corollary 'Reason as much as and no more than will assist
awareness'. For agents in complex and quickly changing circumstances, that
'no more than' will be as important as the 'as much as', until the time comes to
judge in retrospect, when they can analyse and revalue without reserve.

'Be aware' will recommend that spontaneity be intelligent irrespective of any
purpose it may serve. If a car suddenly swerves round the corner while I am standing in the middle of the road, the right thing for me to do is to jump for the pavement as spontaneously as a cat. Without time to think, the only alternative would
be to stand paralysed by shock, unaware of what is happening to me, or be aware
of the danger but too confused to know how to escape in the instant available.
'Be aware' will prefer the intelligent to the stupid reaction, irrespective of any value
set on self-preservation. Even if it happens that I have made a firm decision to
commit suicide, and have been wondering for weeks how to cheat the insurance
company, the failure to jump would accord with my intention only by chance.
It would be highly intelligent to take in the situation instantaneously and choose
to stand waiting for death; but that would be not a reaction but a deliberate act.
After the jump, no doubt I might simply regret not having died, but only if it no
longer matters to me how I die, only if I am past caring about the value of my
acts.

Granted that 'Be aware' suffices for some choices of ends, it does not necessarily follow that it suffices for all. Let us try a rearguard action to confine its scope
to peripheral cases. I concede that it will do for judging in retrospect the spontaneity beyond the margins of my rationality, as when jumping like an instinctive
animal for the side of the road, and for such primitive choices as the child's refusal
of another helping; but I continue to insist that at the centre of me I differ from

the child in having escaped being restricted to choice between spontaneous goals. But when and how did I make this escape? The most rigorous deduction of new ends cannot release me, as long as it was from spontaneous goals that the ends from which my system grew were themselves originally chosen. A stream of spontaneous desire and aversion continues to pour into the centre of me, and I never cease to choose new ends from among its goals. Indeed, as far as my self-interest is concerned, on what principle could I choose as an end sufficient in itself something which I do not spontaneously want? For morals we wait until the next chapter, but there will be the same dependence on spontaneity whenever I choose on behalf of someone else what I think he himself would want in his own interests. Rational people do in general pursue, and at their more moral help each other to pursue, what they want or supposedly would want in fuller awareness of themselves and their conditions, and in unmasking self-deception they recognize the genuine want by its spontaneity; the liberal and rationalist tradition even tends to reject as irrational any prescription of religion or custom which requires us to act otherwise.

Here it may be advisable to point out that we are not advising the rational man to be any more spontaneous than he already is, merely inviting him to continue reasoning about means, ends and principles as before, with his mind at rest about that little puzzle about passing from 'is' to 'ought'. We wish also to persuade him that once he takes fully into account that his ultimate goals are spontaneous (*are*, not ought to be; what they ought to be is intelligent as well as spontaneous), he will require no first principle other than 'Be aware' for choosing between them. The spontaneity even of the most transient whim or velleity never ceases to pull towards or away from awareness. The same applies at every level of involuntary or semi-voluntary behaviour, in falling asleep or waking, health or sickness, interest or boredom, welcoming a scent or recoiling from a bad smell, snapping up a useful fact or closing the mind against an awkward one, or in any kind of creative or contemplative ecstasy. Simply to like or dislike, be attracted or repelled, feel pleasure or pain, involves a quickening or a shrinking from awareness, a point which we shall be looking at more closely in the chapter *Awareness and pleasure*. Expansion and contraction of awareness may be interdependent, so that 'Be aware' would not, for example, pronounce waking good but sleeping bad; when exhaustion is blurring awareness one can go so far as to say 'You *ought* to go to sleep', although only for the sake of waking with refreshed awareness tomorrow. One can conceive the theoretical possibility of an all-embracing ethic in which every moment of every life is in principle evaluable by its degree of awareness, by how intelligently one is acting or reacting. In such an ethic, my rational ends at any one time would be the goals, whether of long-term ambition or of momentary caprice, to which I spontaneously tend in the fullest awareness then available, and all my deliberate acts would be means to these ends.

We may arrive in sight of the same conclusion, near enough to see the possibility of rooting all valuation in a single principle of awareness, by an approach from the opposite direction. My deliberate actions are means to ends, and are defended in debate by proving them adequate to the ends. However, to go on justifying ends by further ends will involve me in an infinite regress unless I arrive at a terminus in something that I do for its own sake. Although moral philosophers tend to treat aesthetics as a poor relation of their own discipline, it is in aesthetics that we arrive at the central problem of evaluating the activities which we pursue without thought of serving a purpose, in particular the one traditionally regarded as not merely good in itself but in some mysterious way improving to the agent, the contemplation of beauty. But an object contemplated for its beauty alone spontaneously attracts the spectator and rouses him to expand and intensify his awareness of it; and however much or little trust he may put in the formulation of aesthetic standards, he evaluates it by his reaction at the unsustainable height of concentration when he is responding to all his information at once. By this approach too we find the starting-point of at any rate one kind of valuation in choice of the spontaneous reaction in obedience to 'Be aware'.

It is now time to call attention to an incongruity in the conception of the rational man from which this chapter started. Why did I introduce myself as a sceptic about values but not about facts? A consistent sceptic would doubt even his senses until reason approves them. It was indeed from this position that the philosophical tradition of modern Europe began. Descartes refused to be sure even of the reality of the external universe until he had proved *a priori* to his own satisfaction that he was not dreaming it. However, most of us now admit that reason unassisted by observation can never break out of the closed circle of logic and mathematics. We are content to acknowledge ourselves beings which sense their surroundings like the animals, but with the power of reason to criticize and to guide the senses. Kant, approaching morals with the same demand for certainty, was radically sceptical about not the reality but the value of spontaneous inclination, and convinced himself that he could start from a Categorical Imperative wholly detached from it. His demonstration nowadays satisfies us no more than that of Descartes. We find ourselves compelled in practice to start from inclination as from perception, questioning inclinations like perceptions only when they conflict, without reason having authorized the initial step. But does not this suggest that we have only to learn the same lesson over again? Without perception and inclination, reason has nothing to engage with; when it does have them to engage with, it can criticize and guide. In assuming that it may be rational to be a sceptic about value alone, we had stopped at an uncomfortable halfway house between philosophy and common sense, between the pure thinker who doubts everything and the plain man who questions neither what he sees nor what he likes or dislikes.

To some temperaments it may seem that in crediting myself only with a capacity to choose between reactions which themselves are not chosen but caused, I would be representing myself as something less than human. But what could be worthier of my human intelligence than to discriminate between and interrelate the parts of a painting or musical composition with the concentration of a mathematician solving a problem, yet respond to them with the immediacy of a dog pricking up its ears? Suppose that I am sitting by a bowl of fruit; my hand hovers over a pear, then a peach catches my eye; their distinctive flavours revive in memory and pull against each other, then my hand moves over and picks out the peach. Let us assume nothing but a causal connexion between the imagined tastes and the motion of the hand. I responded like a monkey to what I saw and smelled, but in full awareness of the two flavours, in obedience to 'Be aware'. Could I in fact have chosen in a manner more worthy of my dignity as a rational agent? It will be said perhaps that I should have combined some principle of conduct with propositions about the flavours. But I do not even have a vocabulary to describe the distinctive tang of a pear or a peach. The best I could do would be to say 'I like peaches better', but quite apart from the logical objection to deriving 'Choose the peach' from this psychological statement, reliance on a generalization about my preference could get me into a habit which would dim my awareness of the tastes, until I fail to notice that I no longer like peaches as much as I did, or that at this moment I hanker after a pear, so that the abortive try at rationalization would make my choice *less* intelligent. Or suppose that I am eating escargots for the first time, and cannot bring myself to forget the disgustingly slimy look and feel of snails in the garden. You reproach me for being stupidly repelled by a taste of which I have never dared to become fully aware. As a gourmet you certainly think of yourself as a product of high civilization, as far above the animal as a scholar or scientist is. Perhaps I am myself no gourmet, and think of food as a matter in which the rational man can excuse himself from making a fully-considered choice. However, if I do think of myself as making a considered choice, can I deny the justice of your reproach? If I reply that in choosing between flavours it does not matter whether or not I confound a present taste with remembered sight and touch, whether I respond to reality or to illusion, I am renouncing rational discourse altogether.

The question now arises: can that rational animal Man ever become more than an animal which criticizes its own spontaneous tendencies in the light of its awareness of itself and of external conditions? Perhaps I think it beneath my dignity to let myself be carried on the spontaneous flood, employing my divine gift of reason only to navigate on the course of greatest awareness. I wish to be wholly responsible for my acts, to be master of my fate; I shall make my own choice of ends, distance myself from my own reactions and learn to manipulate them like external events. There is something paradoxical about this aspiration to lift myself out of nature by the use of reason, since I cannot without setting arbitrary limits to reason forbid the sciences of physiology, psychology and sociology to reincorporate me into nature, as a phenomenon in principle explainable and predictable like everything else. However, the escape from spontaneity has long been a philosophical ideal, at its most intransigent in Sartre's *Being and nothingness*, which treats even emotion as a matter of choice, to the point of denying the distinction between genuine and willed feeling.[2] The ideal would indeed be attainable if a self-contained system of imperatives could be re-established on foundations other than 'Be aware'. Philosophers have of course done their best to do so, by deducing *a priori* a Categorical Imperative, or by deriving imperatives from theological, psychological or sociological premises at the cost of blurring the line between 'is' and 'ought'. It is now widely recognized that all such attempts have failed, yet it continues to be assumed that the rational agent has somehow pulled himself up by his bootstraps out of reach of his own spontaneity. This is to mistake the will for the deed. If the scope of reason is confined to refining and systematizing imperatives and deducing them from each other, how can it ever change their relation to the spontaneous?

2*

I may try to shrink myself to an infinitesimal point of thinking Ego to which all spontaneous process is external, but the spontaneous is always springing up at the centre of me, thrusting me forward or dragging me back, and it is only at the periphery that I can take full control of it. Nor is it sensible to wish that it were otherwise, since raptures, aesthetic, erotic, intellectual, mystical, in which the spontaneous floods the whole of consciousness, can lift us to heights of awareness beyond our ordinary capacities. They can also delude us of course, and the obscured line between revelation and illusion is a distinction to cling to as best one can, to be clarified by reason in retrospect or not at all. The subjective conviction of heightened awareness is so treacherous that to exempt it from the critical tests of reason is to put oneself at the mercy of chance. But if I insist on forcing the spontaneous towards an end which I already deem rational, I remain imprisoned within a circle of old concepts, reason goes on doing the same kind of sums, there can be no novelty except the discovery of unnoticed implications of the familiar. In poetry such a transport is evoked by a pattern of words (selected by the poet perhaps with the most intense thought and effort), which stabilizes it and allows me to evaluate it at leisure. The reader of a poem may find himself 'responding' (a word as fully at home in some dialects of literary criticism as in Behaviourist psychology) with an extraordinary expansion and enhancement of awareness. To a degree unknown in any other use of language he finds himself not only attending to what is said but simultaneously hearing the words as textures of vowels and consonants, noticing rhythm, rhyme, assonance; meanings refuse to be tied down, disclose nuances and associations of which he has never been conscious; sights and sounds which he has never heeded become sensuously precise and vivid in imagination; emotion assumes a peculiar lucidity, undisguised by what he habitually feels or has been taught that he ought to feel; truths about life and death, which he follows social convention in systematically evading, stand out as simple and unchallengeable. Or the poem might be one which has the opposite effect, lulling him in established habits of perception and feeling, or fascinating with some novel and appealing fashion in self-deception. A literary critic devotes much of his space to analysing such effects. We may raise, although this is not yet the place to answer,[3] the question: does he need any aesthetic standards which cannot be treated as implications of 'Be aware'?

Among the wildest of the ecstatics who float themselves on the spontaneous, comparable only with the poet, lover or mystic, is the man of reason possessed by a new insight. When a routine problem arises he perhaps assembles the information and pursues his inferences to the conclusion almost as tidily as he would on paper. But on other occasions, to use a phrase of Nietzsche,[4] 'a thought comes when "it" wants, not when I want', explodes and opens out too fast and in too complex ramifications to be disciplined, takes bold analogical leaps in defiance of logical rigour; the problem on which it centres is obscure, defining itself in the process of being solved, and as he struggles to formulate it the thought is running in another direction, yet he yields to the flow out of a vague intimation that it will circle back; for the final effort to force the argument into a coherent and publicly testable form—the only assurance even for himself that he is illumined and not deluded—he waits until the time comes to complete it on paper. Even for philosophers, one suspects, it is less the philosophy than these episodes that give meaning to their own lives. It is curious that thinkers should explore the logic of rational conduct without coming to terms with this phenomenon at the very centre of their own experience. It has after all become a commonplace that the creative imagination of the philosopher, mathematician or scientist is not much different from that of a prophet or poet; what distinguishes him is how he treats his findings in retrospect. A great formula has been known to appear to a scientist ready-made in a dream as though he were a Siberian shaman, but unlike the shaman he accepts it not on the authority of the dream but because afterwards it satisfies his most stringent tests. But if even in the sciences rationality is no more than the capacity to criticize the spontaneous, where can we expect it to be anything else?

As for the slogan that man is master of his fate, no doubt it has its uses in combating a fatalism which could contract still further the limits within which he can influence the spontaneous by reason and will. In insisting on these limits, we are not concerned with the philosophical problem of whether there is free will at all, but with the evidence of common experience that although you can choose to think about a problem, be considerate to your wife, distribute pamphlets for a cause or pray for forgiveness for a crime, you cannot by mere exertion of will hit on a new thought, love your wife, have faith in the cause, or repent the crime. Someone may ardently desire to create, love, believe, repent, but if the hope is fulfilled it will be because of a spontaneous process of maturation or crisis of conversion, which reason and will can coax but not force. He can only work to prepare the ground and let the change happen of itself or not at all. (Not that we are denying the importance of making such efforts for uncertain gains.) There is nothing essentially new in thus narrowing the scope of will; most of mankind throughout most of its history seems to have taken it for granted that they were moved by forces from beyond them and mysterious to them, which might lift them above or drag them below the capacities of which they might presume to be in command (in Christian theology, the unpredictable visitations of divine grace assisting a will otherwise impotent to resist the Devil), and in the present century, ever since Freud demonstrated that the same conception of man could be translated from a religious into a psychological language, we have found ourselves thinking our way back to it. The man of reason is becoming reconciled to admitting that the function of his reason is critical, that it is not itself the initiator of what it judges to be best in him. He can make this concession without allowing any limits to the scope of reason as a critical tool. Is this perhaps the only conception of rationality which is viable in the late twentieth century? A rationalism which imprisons in systems of means and ends, in which the ends are both disconnected from spontaneity and without rational foundations, resting on nothing, summons up irrationalism as its nemesis.

1.2 Awareness and morals

Is it possible to build a coherent ethic on the principle of awareness alone? We have still to try it out on relations between persons. But having started from a basic-ally simple idea, let us see how far it can take us. Its interest, as will already be clear, is that it offers a prospect of closing the gap between fact and value, bypassing the issue of whether or how one can draw prescriptive conclusions from descriptive premises alone: it affirms the apparently naive claim that to know how to act I have only to be sufficiently aware of myself and my surroundings. To come to terms with it demands an abrupt shift in one's conceptualization of the rational man, which runs against resistance from one's vanity, from a certain ideal of human dignity perhaps, but above all from habit. In the abstract it may not be too difficult to acknowledge that the thinking, desiring and feeling which seem more intimately myself than my bodily motions are spontaneous, and also volun-tarily controllable, in much the same proportions as the physical process of breath-ing, and that there has never been a moment of choice when I was not already being spontaneously pulled by them in the directions between which I chose. However, in abstract thinking it has always been our habit to assume the role of Ego perfectly isolated from spontaneity; and even when in theory we have learned to distinguish the play-acting from real life, we are still liable to slip back into thinking as though the agent applying 'Be aware' were indeed an Ego unaffected by inclination veering with awareness. As long as the habit clings, to derive evaluations directly from 'Be aware' will *feel* like making an indefensible leap to value from fact.

However, let us assume that the habit is broken. So far we have been presuppo-sing a single agent responding to a present situation and trying to guide his sponta-neity by reason. Submitting to 'Be aware', he attends closely to his situation and to his own reactions, and instead of trying to infer from principles how he ought to respond, discovers how when most aware he does respond, and perhaps surprises himself by an impulse contrary to social convention or to his own self-image. Then 'Be aware' entitles him to choose its goal as end and find means to it; and if the situation is a recurring one, he can generalize the choice by formulating a rule, like the child advancing from 'Don't eat it' to 'One ought not to eat too much'.[1] On this basis he may by all means erect a system of imperatives logically interrela-ted with statements of objective fact, and elaborate it to any degree of complexity he pleases, but to confirm or correct it he has always to return to subjectivity, to his own spontaneity in the concrete situation. His choices of ends require no appeal to principles, not even any verbalization, only the discerning of conflict between inclinations and self-alerting to the situation, after which, whether instantaneously or after protracted exploration, one inclination spontaneously prevails. It will be a choice of ends, for example, even if forgotten a moment later, when he chokes back an erupting laugh at a slip by an important man, the choice being between a momentary and a long-term goal, the latter of which the other man could jeopardize. But although he sacrifices the transitory for the long-term, the latter are not differently or more solidly grounded; indeed they are in danger of becoming rigid and brittle if they are not continually being enriched, modified and eroded by local and temporary reactions. Above all, however deeply he commits himself to a long-term end, it must never be allowed to outweigh 'Be aware'. There will always be the possibility that his spontaneous preferences will change with wider information or finer perceptiveness, and to retreat from awareness in order to cling to a highly-valued end will be one of the great offences against 'Be aware'.

What happens when I extend this approach from myself, as I am here and now, to other persons, places and times? Clearly I cannot get along entirely on factual information, any more than I infer from the mere facts how to act here and now. If all valuation starts from choice between responses, it will extend beyond the here and now only if I am spontaneously reacting to situations outside the here and now. I have to simulate perception of situations not present to my senses (that is, imagine them) in order to discover how I would respond, and incipiently simulate other persons (that is, empathize them) in order to discover how they respond; I have to explore how things look and feel from different viewpoints. Suppose that I have a sudden impulse to settle when I retire in the village where I was born; but reality breaks in, I recognize that I had better remember it not as a nostalgic vision but as I indeed saw it before experiencing the city, admit to myself that it will have changed beyond recognition, try to anticipate living in it not as I am now but as an old man who no longer easily makes new friends, try to see myself through the villagers' eyes as already a stranger who may no longer deserve a welcome. To decide, I require not only facts but awareness of how it is likely to feel passing my declining years in that village, and for that I must try to achieve independence of my personal and present viewpoint, reduce it to equality with other viewpoints. My whole understanding of the human world requires that in thought and imagination I am constantly shifting between and responding from different viewpoints, here or there, remembered or anticipated, individual or collective, my own or someone else's, hypothetical, fictional, or simply indefinite; it is only in action that I have to settle in a present viewpoint, whether personal ('I') or social ('We'). The different viewpoints, although not of course equally informative, are equal in the sense that whether 'Be aware' obliges me to take one of them into account depends on its relevance to choices, not on its nearness to 'here', 'now' or 'I'.

Now a crucially important consequence of basing an ethic on 'Be aware' will be to extend to value the neutrality as to spatial, temporal and personal viewpoints which is claimed for fact. I make myself aware of a three-dimensional object by synthesizing what I perceive from here with what I imagine from there, of a continuing event by synthesizing what I perceive now with what I remember from past and anticipate from future viewpoints; and in either case 'Be aware' obliges me to let myself be moved from the different viewpoints, as a causally necessary condition of becoming aware from them. In choosing between the goals towards which I spontaneously tend, I may find myself being excited more strongly by what I perceive here and now than by what I imagine from other viewpoints, so that for example a present amusement obliterates consciousness of a future danger. Then 'Be aware' prescribes awareness from the future viewpoint, and letting myself be moved to avert the danger. Now awareness of other persons similarly depends on synthesizing perception of their bodies with imagining and feeling from their viewpoints, and awareness of myself on synthesizing imagination of my body from other viewpoints with perceiving and feeling from my own; otherwise I would become, to vary Ryle's dictum that the mind has been commonly conceived as 'a ghost in a machine', a ghost in the company of machines, no longer aware that I resemble other people in the respects in which they resemble each other. 'Be aware' therefore prescribes the same neutrality for personal as for spatial and temporal viewpoints; it refuses a privileged status to 'I' as to 'here' and 'now'. But if 'Be aware' requires me to be aware both of you and of myself both from your viewpoint and from mine, it requires me also to let myself be moved towards both your goals and mine, as a necessary condition of becoming aware from either viewpoint. We may therefore propose as a specialization of our grounding formula:

In awareness from all spatial, temporal and personal viewpoints which are relevant to the issue (= viewpoints from which I do find myself spontaneously moved in one direction or the other) I find myself moved towards X, overlooking a relevant viewpoint I find myself moved towards Y.
Be aware.
Therefore let yourself be moved towards X (a goal which may be here or there, now or then, yours or mine).

Here the prospect of building an ethic on spontaneity and awareness brings about an unexpected shift of the burden of proof. Moral philosophers are accustomed to start from the individual pursuing his own ends; at once the question arises 'Why should I prefer anyone else's to my own?', and until it can be answered the advantage lies with the egoist. The moralists—as it seems to many of us who have worried over this question—either shirk the answer or botch it. But if we start from the conception of the rational man who disciplines his spontaneity by an awareness independent of viewpoint, then it is for the egoist to explain why he claims priority for responses from his own viewpoint. An egoist who tries to ground his ethic in 'Be aware' would have to break down the analogy between personal and other viewpoints; and to do so he could not appeal to the most obvious difference, that while 'here' and 'there' are exchanged by the agent's movements, and 'now' is continuously changing into 'then', he remains to himself unalterably 'I'. That 'Be aware' requires one to perceive or imagine from all relevant viewpoints is wholly independent of whether the viewpoint to which one is confined in perceiving is freely mobile, carried forward by time, or permanently fixed.

The first question which an egoist might raise is why it should be assumed that I cannot be aware from another's viewpoint without being moved towards his goals. The other perceives, I merely imagine; he suffers, I merely simulate his distress by letting myself be moved by what I imagine. He himself is moved to relieve his distress, but why should my imaginative simulation move me to do the same? This objection, it will be noticed, assumes a difference between the emotion and the simulation corresponding to that between perception and imagination. But to simulate a feeling is to feel similarly, just as to simulate a process of thought is to think similarly. When trying to guess where someone went when I missed him at the airport I do not imagine his thoughts, I try to imagine his situation as someone like him would see it, and think; if he tells me he has just learned he has cancer I may hear in imagination the doctor's grave voice, but I do not imagine the fear, I feel the chill of it; if I see him cut his finger I do not imagine the pain as something objective before my 'mind's eye', either I look on as though the knife were cutting through cheese or I incipiently wince. Provided that an object is conceived to be real, reactions to it are the same in kind whether one happens to be perceiving or imagining it; and if in the latter case one reacts less strongly, that is because one is also less aware of it. If I explore in imagination a coming danger, I cannot simulate my future fear without already being afraid, and moved to avert the danger. Here the analogy of personal to temporal viewpoints plainly holds. That being moved by imagining from a sufferer's viewpoint does draw me towards his goals is sufficiently shown by my impulse to shrink from imagining, as painful in itself, and liable to draw me into action against my own interests. If there is such a thing as a simulation in the same relation to suffering as imagination to perception, it is in response not to a real but to a fictitious situation; it is the emotion of the actor revelling in the part of a tragic hero.

The egoist might raise a further objection: granted that I do indeed suffer from a sufferer's viewpoint, I generally feel very much less from other viewpoints than from my own; then will not the inclinations I choose in obedience to 'Be aware' tend to be self-centred, even if they do not quite fulfil the requirements of a pure philosophical egoism? But how strongly one feels has nothing to do with the argument. Even in making oneself more aware in preparation for a choice, it will be enough that one can identify which would be the relatively stronger inclination in the fullest attainable awareness; there will be no need to experience it in its full intensity or to prolong it after the choice. In the case of temporal viewpoints this point will be easily conceded. My fear of a remote danger may be almost driven from mind by current emotions; but to decide to take precautions I need no more than the faint tremor as I glimpse what the consequences of neglect would be like, I do not have to maintain the stimulus to action by living in constant terror until the danger has passed. Similarly, it may take no more than a momentary pang of empathetic distress to convince me that if I could become as aware from the sufferer's viewpoint as from my own I would be spontaneously moved to help him even to my own cost. That will be sufficient to oblige me to choose the inclination which I felt increasing *pari passu* with intensifying awareness, after which choice there will be no need to go on agonizing over his plight, which might even impair my efficiency as a helper. I can recognize the choice as right (as I would the choice to prepare for coming danger) however strongly I am inclined to shut off the brief glimpse in order not to be distracted from present and selfish goals. Superficially it may seem reasonable to prefer a firmly-held end to a faint altruistic stirring which is easily dismissed. But in the course of developing our case we have found no grounds upon which I could have validly chosen my present ends except that they are the ones to which I spontaneously tended when most aware; on what grounds then could I persist in preferring these ends to a further advance in awareness which would undermine them?

The egoist might now appeal to the difference between awareness and attentiveness. Granted that 'X exists' or 'X is real' implies 'Be aware of X' (= 'Be disposed to take X into account in choices'), it certainly does not imply 'Remain attentive to X'. But it is only while attentive to someone's suffering that one is spontaneously moved to help him. The egoist might concede that, since in choosing means to his own ends he has to try to predict others' behaviour, he does find it a practical necessity at times to imagine from their viewpoints at the cost of transiently feeling himself moved in altruistic directions. However, after attention lapses he can retain his insights into another person, and use them in choices of means, without abandoning his long-term egoistic ends for the altruistic goals to which he briefly felt himself drawn; he can therefore claim to have obeyed 'Be aware' without ceasing to be an egoist. But the point is not whether or not attention is sustained, but that it is when most attentive that one is taking most information into account. Although awareness outlasts attention, it is by attending that one arrives at, maintains and renews it. Even if it is only for one moment that a spasm in your face draws my attention to the intensity of your pain, a glimpse from which I flinch back into insensibility, it is during that moment that a choice between my conflicting pulls to help and to ignore will be made in fullest awareness.

What is called the 'moral sense' is on this account being able to recognize that if, even against my present will, I let myself become aware of how someone in trouble feels, I would be moved to help, and that I ought not to close myself to this awareness. It depends on the act of viewpoint-shifting, which we must now consider more closely, remaining always on the lookout for loopholes through which the egoist might slip. To 'put myself in your place', to 'see your point of view' and 'understand how you feel', is not a moral but a cognitive act, but of what sort? Is it inference by analogy? If so, it would seem to be no more than a logically disreputable form of reasoning to which I have to resort until the scientific study of behaviour puts more rigorous methods at my disposal. Certainly simulation by shifting to other viewpoints is a kind of analogizing, the active kind which makes myself like instead of recognizing as alike. But analogizing is an operation deeper down in human and animal behaviour than any kind of inference. Pavlov's dog analogizes to previous occasions when it learns to expect its dinner as before when the bell rings as before, the ape simulates when it 'apes'. Man too has a mechanism of mimicry which goes back to the baby in the cradle answering its mother's smile, older than any utilization for learning how others feel or how to pick up skills or even for play, and which can get out of control in neurotic echolalia and echopraxia. The language in which he makes inferences itself built its vocabulary by similar naming of the similar and was learned by mimicking other speakers. The imagination without which he would be imprisoned in 'I' and 'Now' is a simulation of perceiving which analogizes to what he has already perceived. Analogizing, including simulation, is already involved even in the organizing of sensations as perception. I see a man up on the hill, but when as the minutes pass he does not move it occurs to me that what I am looking at must be a stone. It is not that I inferred from the resemblance in shape that it was a man, until I began to doubt I was not thinking about it at all. Being a man myself, the similarity by which I recognize as a man must be not only to others previously classified as men but to myself; I assume, and when close enough to read expression and gesture simulate, thought and emotion like mine, turning his observed behaviour inside out. It is not that I am inferring information about him by analogy; without the incipient mimicry I would not be perceiving him as a man, would be seeing him as an automaton only outwardly resembling myself. It appears from Jean Piaget's child psychology[2] that perception has been inseparable from simulation right from the start, and that instead of learning to project my inwardness on to other persons I had to unlearn the habit of projecting it on to the rising sun or a bouncing ball. Even after leaving behind this 'animism', it is still by their relative resistance or permeability to insight through simulation that in relating things to each other we relate them also to ourselves as inanimate, vegetable, animal, human.

Moral philosophers often ignore empathy as though it were an irrelevance outside their province, a matter for psychology perhaps rather than philosophy. But analogizing, as we shall be arguing more fully in a later chapter,[3] is an operation too fundamental to thinking to be escaped in philosophy or anywhere else, at any rate outside logic and mathematics. It is part of the spontaneous process which reason guides; inference is indispensable to criticize and correct its spontaneous assimilations and differentiations, but can never abolish them and start again from logically impregnable foundations. Wittgenstein and Ryle have taught us that no kind of philosophical argument is exempt from the danger of vitiation by concealed analogies. Why should I assume that in combining imperatives with propositions about other persons I can afford to ignore, while taking for granted the analogizing on which the mere use of a common name depends, the operations of assimilating to and differentiating from myself without which the propositions would not even have their full meaning? Such a sentence as 'He feels sad' would be unintelligible without assimilation to my own feelings; and although 'He is sad' is interpretable as a dispositional statement about behaviour, in the manner worked out in Ryle's *Concept of mind*, someone who did not know that it entails 'He feels sad' could not be said fully to understand it.

The impossibility of becoming aware of another's inwardness without a readiness to let myself feel as he does is plain when someone tries to communicate what is inside his head. When an emotionally articulate speaker wants to convey to me, not the fact that he is sad, but in what way and to what degree, his language becomes rhythmic and metaphorical, pulls me to his viewpoint to visualize his situation, becomes a poetry which infects me with his melancholy and a rhetoric stirring me to help him, and afterwards perhaps I find myself regretting having committed myself to an action in his interests rather than my own. He does not describe his emotions, he calls them up; if anything is described, it is the situation which excites them. Imaginative writers know, as an important item in their craft, that the way to convey emotion with most lucidity and particularity is to choose the apt words, not for the emotion itself, but for the image or scene which activates it. Nor does their command of verbal symbolism, the only medium in which one can even pretend to be describing inward states objectively, give them any advantage over painters and musicians. The media through which the sharers of a culture refine their insight into what goes on in each other's heads are the arts in general, through which the most aware evoke in their audience the look and feel of things from their own viewpoints (in the case of the drama and novel, of multiple inter-acting viewpoints), in fixed forms available to be explored at our leisure.

As long as I remain detached from you, I see your actions as aids or obstacles to mine, as means to my ends. But in so far as I achieve awareness from your view-point I feel the pull towards your goals, and even when I resist, I do so very much as I push away inclinations of my own which are dangerous to my long-term ambi-tions; a choice between your goals and mine belongs among my choices of ends. To the extent that inclinations from my own viewpoint harmonize or conflict with yours, the interaction moves me in new directions for or against you and your goals, to sympathy or antipathy, love or hate, pity or cruelty, gratitude or revenge. These passions are disinterested, in the sense that they excite me to help or harm you as in yourself attractive or repulsive to me, irrespective of further advantage to myself; they treat you not as means but as end, if only as a negative end. Thus to love or hate you, it may not be enough that your actions in your own interests make all the difference between success and failure for my highest hopes; but it may be enough, even if nothing you do has any bearing on my projects, that in being drawn to or shrinking from your viewpoint I feel myself in touch with a personality of which the total pattern attracts or repels my own.

Indeed, it is the disinterested character of the reactions which is the criterion for being aware from other people's viewpoints. In general, whether someone is shifting viewpoints or not, the test of whether he is aware of the look and feel of something, not merely of the facts about it, is whether he takes it into account in choices of ends as well as of means. (Ends sufficient in themselves, it will be remembered,[4] include for us anything chosen however briefly for its own sake, even if it is only lazing in a deckchair in the sun.) You demonstrate to me your awareness of the *fact* that water is boiling hot by pouring it over tea-leaves, your sensuous awareness of the heat of the bathwater by preferring to linger long after you are clean but get out when it turns cold. Are the people in the room aware of the redness of the roses in the bowl, or merely of the fact that they are red? The wife, who prefers red roses to white, and has just put them in place of the white roses by her chair, is aware of the redness. The husband who bought them to placate her may not be aware of more than the fact that they are red (the wife too, come to think of it, if she was only signalling forgiveness). Similarly, if I treat someone's urgent need of money solely as an opportunity to buy cheap from him, you may well doubt whether I am aware of more than the fact that he is in trou-ble, and try to rouse me from my callousness: 'How would you feel if I did that to you?' But if I sympathize and help, or gloat and take opportunities to add to his difficulties, in neither case with any prospect of advantage to myself, you can be sure that I am indeed aware of how he feels.

The disinterested passions compel me to see from other viewpoints, but also blind me to the equality of viewpoints. The range of my sensuous and emotional awareness reveals monstrous gaps when compared with my awareness of fact, and extreme disproportions, as in the distortions of pride, anger and jealousy. The envious man is obsessively drawn to see through his rival's eyes, the cruel man is as sensitive to a sufferer's feelings as the compassionate; and both are disinterested, in that it does not matter to them whether any injury they do is of benefit to themselves. In choices of means, I may pay severely for failing to recognize the equality of personal as of spatial and temporal viewpoints, if for example I lose awareness of the fact that a competitor's need and determination is as great as mine; but in choosing between our ends, nothing compels me to feel the pull of his inclination equally with mine, other than a recognition that it is illogical to shut my eyes in one case to what I am forced to acknowledge in the other. To the extent that I let myself be moved spontaneously in and out of perceptual and emotional awareness, it is likely to be my own ends, and those of persons whom I love or hate, which determine most of my choices of ends. But in spite of the fact that I am more attentive to my own affairs than to yours, the disproportion of awareness is not necessarily in my own favour. In any intimacy between a stronger and a weaker personality the weaker is inclined to yield even when he has the means to prevail, from a compulsion to see through the eyes of the stronger. It is no mystery that a child can feel compelled to to judge himself from his father's viewpoint, although it may seem so if one uses Freudian language and starts puzzling about what it could mean for an instinctive egoist to 'introject' the image of his father. In the complex interactions between myself and the countless others with whom I am remotely or directly engaged, my self-awareness and the self-regarding inclinations which it generates may occupy only a small part of my field of awareness, and not for any moral reason; I feel myself spontaneously pulled towards admiration as well as pride, submission as well as power, masochism as well as sadism, judging myself from other viewpoints as well as judging others from mine. In the swing between extremes, it can seem almost a matter of chance whether a man bursts out in self-reproach or in righteous indignation, in suicide or in murder. Above all, for emotional as well as for factual awareness, others have the weight of numbers on their side. For most people the dread of being surrounded by contemptuous or accusing eyes (a dread independent either of the awe of moral authority or fear of practical consequences) is a weightier factor than all but their most basic needs. 'Be aware' in morals is a warning, not only against sheer insensibility—to be aware and responsive in some degree from other viewpoints is in any case a practical necessity of living in society—but against the distortions and disproportions of awareness, including those demanded by one's society.

However many facts I know about another person I can treat him as pure means, but I cannot be perceptually and emotionally aware from his viewpoint without letting his inclinations interact with mine and affect my ends. The question arises whether there is any such thing as a specifically human goal which is fully detachable from influences from other viewpoints. There are pre-human ones of course, food, shelter, orgasm. But is there any major passion excited by interactions between persons which is not a blend of reactions from multiple viewpoints? A man may pursue power simply as a means to employ others for his own purposes, but someone with the true passion for power will betray, by exceeding any rational design to control those useful or dangerous to his ends, that he does penetrate deep enough inside his subjects for the exhilaration of sensing their wills tense against his own and yield. It would be self-contradictory to say that Stalin treated all men as tools—for exercising power over men. Even pride, the most self-centred of passions, implies that one does see oneself from other viewpoints and care whether one is admired or despised, even to the point perhaps of valuing respect by others above self-preservation. It would seem likely that more people get themselves killed out of pride than sacrifice themselves for any moral end. But unless it is possible to escape being moved from other viewpoints, our selfishness cannot perfect itself to its theoretical absolute except in such circumstances as a tooth-and-claw fight for survival. Instead of asking 'How do we ever unlearn our native egoism?' we must ask 'How near to a true philosophical egoism do we ever succeed in getting?'

Our ordinary selfishness in practice is relative, a matter of tending to put reactions from our own viewpoints first. We may define 'egoism' as the principle of acting only for the goals to which one inclines from one's own viewpoint, and suggest two directions from which it might be approached. One is by reducing awareness from other viewpoints to a means to the ends from one's own. This is at its most practical in empathizing sufficiently to collect useful facts about a person but closing oneself to sympathy; it is at its purest in vanity, basking in awareness from other viewpoints as long as it is of oneself. The other course is to withdraw altogether from the awareness, towards a liberation from emotional entanglements in an amoral indifference for which others are no more than means. Both defy 'Be aware' by adapting awareness to present ends, instead of adapting ends to increasing awareness.

The most extravagant possibilities of an egoism which both enhances and distorts awareness spring from the appetite for power. To start from myself, I cannot choose between reactions without having some control over them; to choose not to be burned I must at least have the power to withdraw my finger from the flame. This power is my personal sovereignty, on the one hand freedom from domination by others, on the other self-control when threatened by the rebellion of disruptive desires. As I enter into interactions with others, I become aware from their viewpoints and respond in favour of their sovereignties as of my own. But I also discover both reactions of my own which are in their power, and reactions of theirs which are in mine, so that the drive towards sovereignty urges me, either to dominate, or to let myself be drawn to the viewpoint of the stronger and submit. The assurance of power is in having compelled against spontaneous inclination. In my own case it is by self-denial, by acting against my own inclination, that self-control is confirmed and strengthened. Therefore the drive to sovereignty can generate the supremely irrational impulse to act *against* the inclination in fullest awareness, against in sadism the other person's, in masochism one's own. 'You shall *not*, because you want to. I do this, because it hurts you'. The challenge, as in Sade, is in the abyss of unreason it opens up; it could as well be, and easily becomes, 'I do this because it hurts *me*'. Here there is none of the numbing of awareness characteristic of plain selfishness. The enjoyment of power over another is fed by imagination from the viewpoint of his resisting and suffering self. There is an inflation of pride, through intensified awareness of one's own power by seeing oneself through the subject's eyes. There is also a simple desire to enhance one's own well-being by widening the contrast with another's distress; and this too attracts towards his viewpoint, since it is only in awareness from other personal or temporal viewpoints that one's well-being is experienced as relative, arousing envy of another's happiness or nostalgia for one's own in the past. Whereas pity has to overcome a reluctance to be drawn into subjective awareness of another's suffering, cruelty welcomes it. But the awareness although sharpened is also twisted by the appetite it serves. To the extent that awareness from multiple viewpoints is equalized, it is of the pleasures as much as the pains, and moves one to help the other rather than oneself when his need is greater. But cruelty in intensifying awareness contracts and withdraws it from the pleasures, even from pains not inflicted by the sadist himself. The pains themselves, since he is aware of them only in order to be assured of his sovereignty, remain on the boundaries of an awareness always centred on his own reactions to them. In the case of an only moderately cruel man, the intensification of the pain beyond a certain point will suddenly switch him to the equalization of viewpoints, and his pleasure will lapse. But the cruellest experiences the victim's pain however great as less than his own enhancement of power however small, so that the suffering of a victim who is being crippled for life may be deliberately empathized by the torturer, but as less than his own titillation, which he may have forgotten by the time he goes home to lunch.

Sadism is not an inherently egoistic drive, rather it is the assertive phase of a drive which may also be submissive even in the same person. The lover of power is attracted to the viewpoint of the strongest, the one who can, even if he graciously refrains, force others to act against their wills; he may himself achieve power, or fantasize it, or in consciousness of impotence prefer to look down on himself through the eyes of real or imaginary conquerors. Since in practice power concentrates, greater the fewer the contenders, the last of these solutions has strong attractions as a more generally attainable second-best. The powerful are forced to strain towards an absolute always beyond reach without which they are insecure; but for the security of an absolute subjection, abjection, it seems that one has only to let go. Nothing illustrates better the fluidity of viewpoints by which we can swing towards and away from egoism, and how little it has to do with morality. Even Hitler, whose life and ideology glorified an untrammeled lust for power, surprises by his docility under discipline as a corporal in the first World War, and the little reported about his sexual tastes suggests that they were masochistic.

As for the drive towards egoism by withdrawing from emotional awareness, in competitive conditions it appears reasonable to detach oneself from the joys as well as the troubles of others, on the calculation that love or trust is likely to be betrayed, and any generous action may be utilized against oneself. How far can I proceed in this direction?

A consistent egoism quite unsullied by altruism is a philosophical abstraction. Suppose that I try to act consistently as an egoist, indifferent to any effect on others which is not a means to an effect on myself. Another person is happy or unhappy; I can use his good mood perhaps to charm a concession out of him, or take advantage of a time when he is distracted by trouble to steal a march on him; but I shall not be pleased or displeased by emotions which do not touch my interests. I shall be incapable of kindness, pity or cruelty. I shall not be grateful for a benefit, although I may return it in the hope of future benefits; similarly I shall not avenge injuries except as a deterrent to future injuries. I may seek to control him, if he is potentially useful to me; but I shall be betraying my principles if I begin to enjoy the sensation of another resisting and yielding, if I develop a taste for power for its own sake. A good reputation will be merely a means to winning what I want from others; I shall care nothing for the respect or contempt of people who cannot help or harm me, and find no pleasure in the prospect of millions seeing my face on television or reading my books after I am dead. I shall associate with others when they are useful to me, but without feeling either friendliness in their presence or loneliness in their absence. I shall treat my own family in the same way, desregarding the fiction that my children are in some mystical way an extension of myself. Nothing in sex will concern me except the pure physical pleasure; I shall be incapable of love, of Don Juan's pride of conquest, even of caring whether the woman is pleased or bored with my company. I shall reject all arts and entertainments which depend on participation in the feelings of other people, whether these people are real or imaginary, whether I am watching a game or watching a theatre. All my pleasures will be solitary, even when I happen to be in company; I shall not be exhilarated simply because the people around me are enjoying themselves, nor depressed because they are in low spirits. Clearly all this is not going to be much fun, but my aim is egoism and not hedonism. Successful hedonists are, for short periods, very sensitive to the feelings of those with whom they talk, drink or make love, postpone the question 'Am I getting as much as I am giving?', and do not revert to egoism until the party is over.

This journey towards egoism is not a progressive liberation of the desires from moral restraints, but a step-by-step renunciation of everything we desire except food, raw sex and a few bodily comforts. Its destination is a state near to apathy, emptied of most of the strongest and most dangerous human appetites, and therefore relatively harmless. Admittedly most of us become egoists in a struggle for mere physical survival,—starving men fighting for food, drowning men climbing into an over-weighted boat; but it does not follow that we can become egoists from principle in conditions where basic human needs are satisfied. The egoist, like the puritan, must inhibit his immediate response in obedience to a principle: 'It is happening to him and not to me, I have no reason to care.' A person who approaches anywhere near this ideal affects us, not as the natural man freed of civilized restraints, but as cold and inhuman, rational to the point of emotional impoverishment. The man who does not use his reason to weed out his emotions is not an egoist; he is selfish and generous, kind and cruel, grateful and revengeful.[5]

It is time to take account of that difference between perceiving from 'Now' and 'I' and imagining from other viewpoints which we have so far put aside as irrelevant.[6] Although one can respond with some awareness to remote or hypothetical situations, and evaluate them *sub specie aeternitatis*, everyone's actual choices of ends are of course confined to his own present and future and to his effective scope of action. But there is something more to be said about the focusing of attention on the present and oneself. Suppose we have a hedonist who says 'Live for the present, why bother about the future?' and 'Live for yourself, why bother about other people?', two maxims which once again assimilate temporal and personal viewpoint-shifting. It might not be just to press philosophical objections, since it is obvious that a rhetorical question does not commit him to ignore even the most imminent of coming events. This hedonist tends to live for the moment, because if one is constantly distracted from present experience by designs for the future nothing will ever be fully enjoyed. Similarly he tends primarily to heed his own sensations, because pleasures from other viewpoints are pale and shallow compared with those from his own. Now we have already made the point that the weakness of a premonitory or sympathetic reaction compared with experience which is present and mine is no objection to acting on the former rather than the latter.[7] Nevertheless, one does not have to be a hedonist to agree that a person is somehow impoverished by living too much for the future or for other people, and 'Be aware' can show us why. Imagination from other viewpoints depends on my having already perceived something analogous from the then present and my own, and is undernourished if I was distracted at the time by consideration of the future or of others. This ultimate dependence becomes obvious to me whenever I make a mistake about others by supposing them to be like myself. The intelligence and sensitivity by which some people draw rich implications from quite narrow experience would have nothing to work on if they had not plunged deep into that experience. A society of extreme altruists, each devoting most of his attention to the welfare of others, would not be the ideal community it might seem; since each would be poor in self-awareness, he would be still less aware of the actual needs of those he was trying to benefit. The same would apply to a Utopian society projected by thinkers too remote from the people of their time to pay much attention to their behaviour in real circumstances. To know how to live for oneself and for the present when a choice involving sacrifice for others or the future does not arise will be indispensable to learning to make such choices in sufficient awareness.

This line of argument supports, as beneficial to all, a certain kind of individualism, which is not of course the same as egoism. True egoism, as we have described it, is conceivable only under conditions of conflict in which only the pre-human ends remain. Individuals in interacting either harmonize or conflict, and there is no reason to suppose that any enlargement of awareness would either reconcile all conflict or expose all harmony as illusory. The development of co-operation or conflict has its own momentum, and there are limits to the extent that rational effort can influence it. When the swing is from co-operation to conflict, the modification of one's ends by reaction from another's viewpoint will tend towards hate, revenge or cruelty rather than love, gratitude or pity; by an effort to see from his viewpoint one can resist the tendency, but at the extreme point of escalation one's ends narrow to the survival of self or kin, and the other and his destruction are reduced to means to it. One no longer has to hold on to any specifically human end, because the circumstances allow only a single and pre-human end, survival. Admittedly a society cannot without self-extinction dissolve into units smaller than minimal families, so that an untrammeled egoism is possible only under limited conditions. But given these conditions, egoism is not only possible, it may be permitted by 'Be aware'. It is not that in desperate circumstances we discover ourselves to be natural egoists and throw off moral restraints, it is rather that morality no longer applies. Two shipwrecked men in a boat have only enough food for one, so that one of them must die if the other is to live. One of them would not mind sacrificing himself if he thought that the other is of more use to humanity, but sees no evidence of it. He would be willing to draw lots as to who jumps over the side, except that he is sure that the other, if he lost, would go back on his word. He would rather fight in the open than wait to murder the other when he falls asleep, but is so much the weaker that to fight without an advantage would amount to suicide. In such a pure case of one man's gain being the other's loss, what forbids him, even in the fullest awareness from both viewpoints, to act on the inclination from his own? 'Be aware' has become irrelevant, morality has lapsed.

However, even if we cannot blame him for murdering the other in his sleep, we might respect him more if he did put himself at a disadvantage by clinging to one of his last disintegrating scraps of morality. Without any ends at all for which to survive life would be, in the strict sense of the words, not worth living, and on this boat a few decencies preserved without regard for consequences would be the last ends left which he values for themselves. The reduction of the other to means and of his own ends to survival, itself no more than a means without ends left to serve, would be tolerable, if at all, only because the variety of human ends will open up again for him if he ever gets to shore. As a variation on the same theme, let us amuse ourselves with a science-fiction possibility. Suppose that in the future it becomes possible to predict others' behaviour more efficiently by observation and computation than by the always hazardous venture of trying to fathom the mysteries of the human heart. (This assumes the behaviourist position that what is experienced subjectively as thought and emotion is identical with the behaviour, incipient as neural process as well as overt as bodily movement, which objectively is perceived by the senses.) Let us say that, although not trapped in a fight for survival, we are all still caught up in the ordinary competitiveness of business, social gamesmanship, and marriage. It is becoming less useful to enter into each other's feelings, more and more convenient to consult one's pocket computer. In competition it is to my advantage to feel for others as little as possible, an advantage which outweighs my dread of a growing isolation. Gradually I get out of the unscientific habit of trying to read other people's faces, and come to see the bodies from which personality has faded as the automata which for scientific explanation they already are. In the middle of a still most active social life I am being drawn into an absolute solitude in which I cannot even entertain myself with the motions of the teleonomic mechanisms on stage or screen, and making love is equivalent to copulating with a perfectly lifelike mechanical doll. Everything and everyone is drained of value except as means to my own dwindling and at last exclusively pre-human ends, and I myself am equally a means in the eyes of everyone else, as I am forced to recognize whenever an automaton interacting with me reaches for its own pocket computer. If finally I become wholly submerged in this solipsism there could be no other rational ethic for me than egoism. But it would not be the egoism imposed temporally by external necessity on the two men in the boat. We should all be vaguely conscious of a disaster brought about by ourselves, a universal mutual degradation, and would be making feeble intermittent efforts to restore contact and rehumanize each other.

Egoism, then, is no more than a terminus towards which interacting individuals are pushed by competition. But with the glorification of competition by capitalism it has come to seem natural to think of ourselves as fundamentally egoistic. Several fortuitously converging considerations have encouraged this faith in the primacy of egoism.

(1) When desires disrupt co-operation their spontaneity is evident, when they support it nothing proves that they were not instilled in the first place by moral training.

(2) To the man of reason, that as a physically and mentally distinct person he should look after his own interests seems self-evident like a geometrical axiom, that he should care for others seems to require proof like a theorem.

(3) The tradition of scientific explanation is atomistic; if the study of social behaviour, human or animal, is to become a science, the simplest approach is to start from individual organisms as the atoms.

The first point does not establish that people are spontaneously more inclined to conflict than to co-operation, merely that the latter tendency does not prevail absolutely. As for the second, we have undermined its apparent logic by approaching from the opposite direction; what is self-evident is that a person should prefer his reaction in fullest awareness, what would require proof is a claim that the awareness should be from all spatial and temporal but only one personal viewpoint. The reversal has a further consequence. As long as we start from the conception of a rational agent, it appears easy to decide whether an inclination is egoistic; it will be so if its goal by the agent's own standards is beneficial to himself. But if one starts from the spontaneous inclination itself, the question arises whether it makes sense to call it egoistic before it has been chosen in terms of the agent's own standards for the beneficial. Even granted that everyone, for example, finds pleasure beneficial, to judge an inclination egoistic because achievement of its goal gives the agent pleasure would be vacuous, because whatever his goals he will be pleased if he succeeds, sorry if he fails. With the breakdown of faith in the fundamental rationality of man we no longer ask, for example, whether the drives of Freud's Id and Super-ego are to be classed as egoistic, or see a puzzling self-contradiction in masochism. Nietzsche already made the point, and as a philosopher who was willing to call himself an egoist his witness is especially interesting:

As every drive lacks intelligence, the viewpoint of 'utility' cannot exist for it. Every drive, in as much as it is active, sacrifices force and other drives: finally it is checked; otherwise it would destroy everything through its excessiveness. Therefore: the 'unegoistic', self-sacrificing, imprudent, is nothing special—it is common to all the drives—they do not consider the advantage of the whole ego (because they do not consider at all!), they act contrary to our advantage, against the ego: and often *for* the ego—innocent in both cases![8]

There is however one kind of inclination which may legitimately be classed as inherently egoistic or altruistic, the biological drive either to self-preservation or to preservation of offspring or others. Here we do not have to ask by what standards the agent estimates benefit, since no one can be benefited if he does not survive. At this biological level the evidence is unequivocal; there are drives both to preserve self and to sacrifice self for others, and the latter cannot be derived from the former. It seems indeed that in Darwinian terms egoism cannot be primary, in spite of the fact that genetic traits will survive only if they favour their carriers. Natural selection is of traits favourable to the survival, not of individuals.

but of successive generations. Egoistic traits may be expected to survive if they benefit also the descendants which inherit them, to be weeded out if they benefit the individual at the expense of its offspring (for example, cannibalizing its brood, or long outlasting its reproductive powers); altruistic traits will tend to survive if they benefit kin which are also transmitting them (in particular, the mother's protection of her young), to die out if they give the advantage to strangers which are not. Darwinism destroys the presumption that a separate organism functions primarily to preserve itself (as do simpler homeostatic systems which do not reproduce); it shows me that even at the biological level my spontaneity only secondarily and partially serves myself, and invites the reflection that behaving consistently to my own advantage became conceivable only with the clarification of my viewpoint in contrast with others, which in turn implies that I have been assuming other viewpoints from the beginning of self-consciousness.

But although Darwinian natural selection seems plainly to deny primacy either to egoism or to altruism, it is interesting to notice that nearly everyone has preconceptions which hinder him from coming fully to terms with the evidence. On the one hand one rather likes to find examples of animals helping each other, out of a confused feeling that it will somehow strengthen human motives for altruism to know that the lower creation can be altruistic too. On the other hand it would be so much simpler for explanatory purposes if animals did behave like the rational egoists of classical economics. Here both the second and the third of our considerations encouraging faith in the importance of egoism come into play. Since Mother Nature does not teach morality, how would brute beasts ever learn to be unselfish? Moreover, as interpreters of animal behaviour we have our own convenience to consider; to dissolve species (and human societies too, as in classical economics) into uniformly egoistic atoms offers much the best prospect of finding simple laws to apply to them. A remarkable illustration of the explanatory convenience of egoism is the concept of the 'selfish gene',[9] through which the rational egoism which is so difficult to find in the hopelessly illogical world of men is finally tracked down in our ultimate genetic constituents. The mechanism of natural selection can indeed be beautifully expounded in a metaphorical language which treats organisms as designed by their constituent genes in accordance with the mathematics of games theory to serve the egoistic projects of each of them. Yet it is plain that the selfishness of a gene can have nothing whatever in common with human egoism. A gene, for purposes of the theory,[10] is a segment of genetic material divided off as best suits the investigator, who needs a unit small enough to be treated as identical through successive generations; it has no self with which to be selfish. Even if it had, the selfhood would be in the replicas of the gene scattered over different bodies; that the gene, analogous though it is to species rather than to individual, has to be taken as the unit, is precisely because it is more useful for explanation to speak of the selfish gene than of the altruistic replica. In any case, if one insists on anthropomorphizing the gene, it behaves not selfishly but in utter disregard of its own interests, either doing the same thing over and over again or, by mutation, doing something else quite arbitrarily, and passively allowing itself to be favoured or eliminated by natural selection. It does indeed seem touchingly human in its irrationality, as unegoistic as according to Nietzsche we should all be if we surrendered completely to our drives. The geneticist's language is no more nor less metaphorical when he calls the gene selfish than when he depicts it as though itself working out the solutions in games theory by which he is explaining its survival.

To respond always with full awareness would be to become equally aware from all relevant viewpoints and react with sympathies and antipathies as impartial as those with which one reads a play of Shakespeare or novel of Tolstoy. Then one would no more require moral standards than that 'Vengeance is mine, I will repay' which Tolstoy put under the title of *Anna Karenina*. In practice however awareness is unequal, variable, uncertain, with impassable limits even in the case of self-knowledge, so that we can never take the full measure of our reactions from all viewpoints; like the child wondering whether to risk another helping at dinner, we require an 'ought' whenever we are losing sight of the reaction at an unsustainable height of awareness. We still remain then, for moral as for prudential questions, at the position that imperatives can serve only for judging between spontaneous reactions. Certainly duty can pull against one's strongest inclination; but could one recognize the force of a moral imperative without feeling some inclination however slight towards the course which it commands? It appears reasonable to claim that a man without the capacity to put himself in another's place could not *understand* a moral appeal (even if he should happen to be a law-abiding man who accepts commands and prohibitions on external authority), just as someone incapable of shifting temporal viewpoints could not understand an appeal to his future interests. On the present analysis, moving to the viewpoints of other persons is not in itself a moral act, any more than is temporal viewpoint-shifting, so that a reduced capacity for either is not a moral but a cognitive defect. It may be noticed that insensibility both to moral appeals and to appeals to one's future interests, imprisonment within both 'I' and 'Now', are often combined in the same person, and that the combination is widely accepted as the strongest criterion for classing him as 'psychopathic' and exempting him from moral judgment. The psychopath, even so, falls far short of the ideal of philosophical egoism. His sympathetic feelings are shallow and transient rather than absent altogether, and if he had no insight at all into how things look to others he would never learn how to manipulate them. A criminal psychopath would not want to kick someone's face in for the fun of it unless he had at least an inkling of what it feels like to the victim. Someone for whom it really is of no concern whether others enjoy or suffer is schizophrenic; he is no egoist, but one whose imaginary viewpoints are disconnected from the real people around him.

The argument of this chapter bears a superfical resemblance to familiar attempts to base morality on the claim that human beings are naturally unselfish and behave egotistically only out of ignorance. But our approach has by-passed all questions about the goodness or wickedness of human nature. My spontaneous recoil from awareness of others' troubles (or of future danger to myself) is no less or more natural than my impulse to sympathy or cruelty (or to avoid or irrationally court danger) when I do become aware; it is as pointless to ask whether human nature is selfish or unselfish as whether it is improvident or far-sighted.

1.3 Awareness and pleasure

Throughout our argument we have never questioned that there is a logical gap between 'is' and 'ought', indicative and imperative, fact and value. Even without insisting on the strict claim that inference from fact to value is logically inadmissible, a claim which since Hume has been a commonplace, and after G. E. Moore's analysis of the Naturalistic Fallacy was for some time an orthodoxy,[1] it has been convenient to stay out of range of standard criticisms by showing that we can get along well enough without resorting to this kind of inference. We do not intend to abandon this policy. However, we have already noted in passing a complication in the case of psychological facts.[2] What would commonly be taken as a characteristic example of the Naturalistic Fallacy is ethical hedonism, the doctrine that we ought to do what gives most pleasure. There is something decidedly odd about objecting to it that the mere psychological fact that one alternative is more pleasant than another cannot by itself be a reason for choosing it. The gourmet, presented with a difficult choice between two dishes, ponders which will please him more as in other circumstances he might weigh conflicting moral demands, decides which one tempts his palate, chooses to order it without even being conscious of making a second decision, let alone one which requires a logically different kind of support, and afterwards perhaps is disappointed by the dish and regrets having chosen wrongly. It seems to be a matter of ordinary experience that in such circumstances we *do* accept the psychological fact as sufficient reason for making a choice and for retrospectively judging it right or wrong.

Suppose that I am hoping to discuss some urgent problem with a friend, and ask,

'Will you be in tomorrow afternoon?'
'No. I am going to Regent's Park.'
'Do you have to? Why?'
'I want to go to the zoo.'
'Why, at a time like this?'
'I want to take another look at the gibbons.'

My friend is not simply explaining why, for good or bad reasons, he did decide to go to the Park (as he might after the event, in which case it would be no objection to his explanation that when he got there the zoo turned out to be closed); he is defending his decision to go to the Park rather than meet me at his house, and I can still try to change his mind. I may object on a point of fact ('There are no gibbons there now') or by appealing to some other end or principle ('You ought not to put that problem off any longer'). In any case, his chain of reasons remains unsupported unless he can answer one more question:

'Why do you want to look at the gibbons?'
'For the fun of it. I just like gibbons.'

Whatever reply I find for that one, obviously it is not going to be

'I'm afraid you're making an illegitimate leap from fact to value. Irrelevant psychological information about yourself only confuses the issue.'

His answer was not merely acceptable, it was final, in the sense that he need give no further justification of his decision, and if I still wish to object the burden of proof has shifted to me. I may continue to look for factors which will outweigh his prospects of enjoyment at the zoo. Or I might suspect too much vehemence in his insistence that he loves gibbons, and suggest that he is deceiving himself, that visiting the animals has become a habit without much joy in it. But if I do admit his claim to enjoy them, and still persist in the inquisition ('Why do you like gibbons?'), the logical nature of the question will have changed. I shall merely be requesting information about a taste which puzzles me, not demanding a further reason without which the whole string of answers will prove to be baseless.

We may look at this example from another angle. The chain of argument, up to the penultimate stage, is of the kind which supports a hypothetical imperative: 'If you want to look at gibbons ... go to Regent's Park'. It justifies the decision to go to the Park as a means to see the gibbons. However, the formula is not usable in a practical situation unless the end is either supported by a principle or further end, or else is anticipated as enjoyable in itself. The mere fact that I have set myself the end X, with Y as a necessary means to it, and without conflict with other prudential or moral considerations, does not guarantee me from being mistaken in doing Y (Anyone who supposed that it did would indeed be guilty of the Naturalistic Fallacy without appeal.) If for example I am pursuing X in the expectation of enjoying it, but when I get it am disappointed, or seem to enjoy it yet afterwards come to recognize that only habit or a false idea of myself or susceptability to persuasion made me suppose I was enjoying myself, then I was mistaken in doing Y. Every choice of means, however well argued, proves groundless with the discrediting of the end, yet that I did not have the fun I expected is itself no more than a fact. We are thus led back to the same problem as before; although the fact of taking X as end does not justify the decision to do Y, the enjoyment of X which does complete the justification is itself merely a psychological fact.

Indeed a hedonist would be unnecessarily cautious if he were content to defend his grounds of choice as no better nor worse than those of other ethical schools. It may be a theoretical difficulty to him that logically imperatives are derivable from other imperatives but not from psychological or other factual statements uncombined with imperatives. Yet in practice justification by an imperative does not benefit from this logical advantage, is very much open to doubt (indeed invites it, without a first principle such as Kant's Categorical Imperative to save from appealing from imperative to imperative in an infinite regress), while the appeal to pleasure does not seem vulnerable to ethical scepticism at all. To say, as I pull my hand back from the flame, 'I have no reason to shun pain', is no more than playing with a verbal formula of doubt; it does not open any abyss under my feet like 'I have no reason to obey moral imperatives'. The most radical possible objection to the argument from pleasure is not scepticism but the counterclaim that pleasure is evil, which condemns as wrong any choice in favour of the enjoyable. We may imagine an ascetic who consistently chooses the sour instead of the sweet apple, in order to mortify the flesh. But should he ever lose faith in the principles behind his asceticism, and fail to put other principles in their place, he will not find himself living in a void without grounds for preferring one apple to another. He has always recognized the sweetness of an apple as a reason for choosing it, although a sinful one; with the lapse of the standard which condemns it, it asserts itself as the only relevant consideration. The hedonist has a privileged place in ethics; his is the case which stands if every other falls.

As our first example of deciding on hedonistic grounds we took a choice between two dishes.[3] It is similar to an instance discussed earlier,[4] of choice between a peach and a pear, in which the spontaneous preference for the peach in full awareness of the flavours was approved on the authority of 'Be aware'. Now it must be confessed that no one in that situation would be likely to justify his choice by saying 'In recalling the tastes I found myself spontaneously moved to take the peach'. It may be noticed too that our analysis rather simplified the relation between awareness and spontaneity, taking account of the awareness only up to the rousing of the impulse. It did not make it clear that the impulse to take the peach is a continuing reaction in awareness of its anticipated taste, so that I have chosen rightly only if I continue spontaneously to welcome the awareness right up to the savouring of the juice on my tongue, in other words if I do relish it, enjoy it. If then it would seem artificial to analyse and describe the whole process when asked the reason for my choice, is that not because I already have the vocabulary of pleasure to name it? 'I enjoy X' entails 'In becoming aware of X I am drawn towards it, I approach it with sharpening awareness of it'. The natural justification of my choice between the fruit would be something like 'The peach looked delicious', which conveys the full information that I expected to be responding in accord with 'Be aware' until the last trace of the flavour faded from my mouth.

To return to the enjoyment of looking at gibbons, it will be agreed that it is not an activity separate from looking at them, not an end to which looking is the means (as looking is the end to which visiting the zoo is the means). Nor is it simply looking at them with no further end in mind, which might be the listless action of someone who can think of nothing else to do. An obvious difference is that one who is enjoying the sight of the gibbons will be intensely aware of their small black faces and long black fingers showing up against white fur, of their swift agile leaps and the poise of their immensely long arms at the moments when they balance perfectly still. He would of course be equally or more aware of a nagging toothache, but there is the further difference that while he would shrink from awareness of the pain, in this case he wants to sustain and enhance the awareness just as he wanted to come to Regent's Park in the first place, and can be judged to want it by the same kind of tests, for example his reluctance to be dragged away from the cage. The quickening of awareness in pleasure and the shrinking from it in pain are spontaneous, as I discover whenever I suffer, or deliberately resist a temptation, or try to enjoy some cultivated entertainment which bores me. The connection between enjoyment and a spontaneous welcoming of awareness is logically necessary, for it would be contradictory to say 'I intensely enjoyed the sensation, but I had to make an effort to be much aware of it.' It can be recognized even in such an extreme case as enjoyment of sinking into sleep. As long as I was forced to stay awake I shrank from any stimulus to sensation; now I relax and welcome the fading sensations until they are extinct, and for a few minutes will notice impressions of which I am normally unaware, such as the twilight images on the edge of consciousness.

Enjoying, we spontaneously welcome awareness; bored and listless, we cannot without effort summon it up; disliking, we withdraw from it; suffering, we recoil from it but cannot escape it. The differences, it is important to notice, are in the spontaneous tendency, not in the actual degree of awareness achieved or suffered. Local pleasures and pains may be very much alike in both intensifying awareness and contracting it to themselves; but the difference remains that pain forces itself on awareness against our spontaneous resistance. The experience of tragic art confirms that the relation of pleasure and awareness is two-way; if a welcoming of the sharpest awareness of things from which we most deeply recoil, without any reservations of the sort of 'This hurts but it is good for me', can make even the fate of Lear or Oedipus enjoyable, it would seem that there can be no involuntary quickening of awareness without joy. Of course this imaginative feat is possible only because we watch the tragedy secure in the knowledge that we shall be ourselves again when the curtain goes down. Detachment of a situation from its anticipated consequences allows many such mysterious transformations of anguish into joy in memory, imagination or the arts. Danger, as an experience which especially enlivens awareness and is unpleasant only in relation to consequences, is especially rich in possibilities of becoming enjoyable. The imagination of danger keeps us immersed in a story; the adventurous court it in actual life; the unadventurous relate with gusto how they were carried off to hospital with an undiagnosed and probably fatal illness, as a vivid patch in an otherwise uneventful life.

We may notice too that since pleasures tend to fade unless varied at every recurrence it is difficult to distinguish in practice between the man who lives for pleasure and the man who lives for new experiences. The former perhaps will repeat a pleasure until exhausted, the latter lose interest as soon as he is fully aware of its nuances, as though suspicious of the tendency of pleasures, like pains, to contract awareness to themselves. For him apparently, although no moralist, the answer 'I enjoy it' does not quite settle the matter. Pleasure interests him only as long as its quickening of local awareness contributes to his overall awareness. Approaching from another angle, there is at least one answer which has the same claim to finality as 'I enjoy it' (finality in the sense that no further reason may be demanded, although other reasons may outweigh it). Most such answers imply enjoyment, even 'I am interested in it' (which at least suggests the prospect of happy hours of observing, reading, thinking); but 'I am curious about it' is neutral as far as enjoyment is concerned.

'I want to find out about it.'
'Why?'
'No reason. I'm just curious'.

The search has the same prospects of satisfaction or frustration as any other purposive activity. At the other extreme, 'I dislike it' turns out to be highly questionable when it implies diminished awareness:

'I don't like to think about it'.

This answer would be fully acceptable only if the speaker is fully aware of his situation and can do nothing at present to ease it. Otherwise, he has provided both a reason which is in our sense final and a counter-consideration which outweighs it.

It can now be seen that the argument from pleasure draws its imperative conclusions, not directly from psychological fact, but from psychological fact combined with the imperative 'Be aware'. Examining myself, I find spontaneous inclinations and aversions, which I express by 'I want/don't want'. From the mere fact of wanting more or less or not at all or the contrary I can derive no imperative for choosing between my wants. But as soon as I say 'I enjoy/like/desire', even 'I want' spoken with a certain stress, something new enters; I convey the further information that with awakening awareness I am stirred to approach, and as I approach awareness quickens. However local and limited the awareness to which the words testify, I have identified a spontaneous reaction to which, since it is provisionally approved by 'Be aware', it is rational to seek means as an end good in itself; if you disagree, the burden of proof has shifted to you, to make me aware of something overlooked which will redirect my response. Conversely, to say 'It hurts' conveys the information, not merely that I spontaneously flinch from the sensation, but that I am sharply aware of it. In the light of 'Be aware', the spontaneous recoil from the object in becoming aware of it will be the right reaction; but the suffering, as a spontaneous shrinking from awareness itself, will be bad, just as pleasure, as a spontaneous welcoming of awareness, will be good. 'I enjoy it' and 'It hurts' testify of course only to awareness of the immediate stimuli, and will always be outweighed if enlargement of awareness changes the response. This analysis lifts us above such complications of hedonism as having to measure degrees of pleasure or distinguish the higher from the lower. Estimating awareness no doubt raises its own problems, but at least it can be conducted in terms of the things of which one is made aware. It may be difficult to explain why a few minutes spent reading fourteen lines of Shakespeare should be a higher pleasure than reading an equivalent length of a James Bond story, but the analyses of literary criticism elucidate how in the former case one is living those few minutes in intensified awareness with an extraordinarily extended span, from the texture of the words sounding in one's inner ear to the remotest implications for the living of one's whole life.[5]

Here a difference emerges between becoming perceptually and emotionally aware and becoming aware of a fact. In deliberate action, 'Be aware' obliges me to take account of any fact relevant to achievement of the end, which may require an exertion of will to resist emotional bias and acknowledge the facts whether I like them or not. Any obscuring of the world as the known facts show it objectively to be betrays a weakness in me. In the case of the spontaneous goals from which the ends are chosen, the same neutrality would be theoretically conceivable; it is possible to imagine a being immune from pleasure and pain, who is moved towards or away without either welcoming or shrinking from awareness. However, that is not how we are constituted. Even in obeying 'Be aware', the objects which with arousal of awareness draw me towards them also enhance awareness of themselves, the objects which repel also numb awareness of themselves. 'Be aware' does of course recommend a sensibility open rather than closed to new impressions, but even the most greedy for new experience cannot embrace joy and suffering with equal fervour, there is always a bias in favour of the enjoyable. In my universe of smells, the nuances will be much more finely discriminated in the scent of flowers than in the stench of carrion. That there must be such an imbalance follows from our consistently maintained position that the rational man can never rise above his spontaneous inclinations, merely learn to choose rationally between them. Our spontaneity is such that even in obeying 'Be aware' attention is drawn from the dark side of the world towards the light. If our constitution does not altogether submerge us in wishful thinking, that is because pain and misfortune force themselves on attention from outside. It is perhaps a physical impossibility to be as aware of a bitter as of a sweet taste, but a toothache relentlessly pulls wincing sensibility to itself. An impartially distributed awareness would presumably require an optimum ratio, with enough trouble to stimulate without overwhelming, and enough joy to prevent morale succumbing under too much pressure. Blake in *The marriage of heaven and hell* sums it up: 'Joys impregnate. Sorrows bring forth.' The thinker who most boldly exploits this psychological tension is Nietzsche, who in the exuberance of his thought always strains to seize the most sombre truths without losing the momentum of his 'gay science'. But even the most abstract thinker does not wholly escape the need to impregnate thought with joy. The logical structure admittedly is independent of the desires of the thinker, but the drive behind it is an enthusiasm, or an obsession to rid himself of an intolerable burden; at the point when we notice there is no more joy or stress in his thinking, that it has become a routine, we begin to be afraid that his creative phase has passed.

Suffering happens, is not chosen, is a 'misfortune'; shall we say that, since by nature attention quickens only as a function of the organism striving towards its goals, the optimum of internal and external stimulation to awareness can be only a matter of chance? To choose suffering for the sake of the stimulating effects of running away from it is indeed a paradox. Suffering can make its full contribution to my awareness only if I do *not* pursue it in advance, even though its value may be appreciated in retrospect. I cannot will the disappointment of my highest hope, in the expectation that the catastrophe will make a new man of me, because it is no catastrophe unless I am fully committed to the hope. Still less can I will the death of someone I love on the calculation that the bereavement will be a rewarding experience. Nevertheless, it does seem that there is an impulse of curiosity which can correct the chance relations of internal and external stimuli by choice of a painful experience simply as a means to equalize one's awareness of the light and the dark. It is in a sense a perversion, by which instead of attending to situations in order to respond to them intelligently, one treats awareness itself as an end. Since the awareness from which we recoil is constantly being forced on us by pain or misfortune, no doubt many or most people can take every opportunity they have to avoid the unpleasant without being in any danger of becoming more aware of the bright side than the dark. However, among the lucky or sheltered it is common enough for someone to have the uneasy feeling that he is living too comfortably, might find himself unprepared to cope if his present security were to collapse, lacks adequate understanding of miseries outside his experience. Such a person might, with the full sanction of 'Be aware', deliberately choose the unpleasant alternative, to live for a while in a jungle or a slum. But after the initial choice, which is exceptional in treating awareness itself as an end to which hardship is the means, he will not be taking suffering as an end; to force himself to accept it passively would insensitize and brutalize him instead of enhancing awareness. Once in his jungle or slum he will learn by trying like anyone else to make the best of his circumstances.

To cultivate awareness of fact one goes to the sciences, of sensation and emotion to the arts; and we expect the latter, in sharpest contrast with the former, also to give pleasure. Not that this stops the tragic artist from coaxing us into awareness of the normally intolerable, taking advantage of ways in which things terrible in experience become agreeable in imagination. But one can hear the naked cry of agony in Greek tragedy only because its conventions are elaborately designed to distance the events from our own affairs, to show only noble personages speaking eloquent and musical language. A realistic genre has less obtrusive conventions, but still has always to recognize that it can never evoke as real unless the audience welcomes rather than shrinks from the awareness. We can be well aware in the abstract of the horror, misery and emptiness of much of life, but is there any such thing as an intense imaginative vision of life, however pessimistic, which is not in some sense pleasing? We shall not go into the variety of psychological mechanisms which convert terrible actuality into pleasing imagination, but there is one of them, sado-masochism, which demands attention because it explains why tellers of harsh truths so often offend not only our sentimentality but our moral sensibility. The difficulty of becoming vividly aware of the worst without having a positive taste for it may be illustrated by listing underminers of eighteenth century faith in human perfectability who have earned our thanks by laying the ground for a view of life reconcilable with the trenches, bombs and concentration camps of our own era—Sade, Maistre, Baudelaire, Dostoevsky, Nietzsche, Freud. Except for Freud, whose impersonal style does not reveal him, all of them flaunt a pronounced sado-masochistic sensibility. In their own ways, do they not all see the world through rose-coloured spectacles? The morally estimable act of exposing to us the worst in ourselves nearly always has something morally equivocal about it. The name which stands chronologically first in the list is eloquent in itself; and Nietzsche is explicit about the underlying cruelty (in which he includes cruelty to oneself), not only of tragic art and religious self-denial, but of the pure appetite for truth, for its own sake and at any cost.

Consider finally how even the man of knowledge, when he compels his spirit to knowledge which is *counter* to the inclination of his spirit and frequently also to the desires of his heart—by saying No, that is, when he would like to affirm, love, worship—disposes as an artist in and transfigurer of cruelty; in all taking things seriously and thoroughly indeed there is already a violation, a desire to hurt the fundamental will of the spirit, which ceaselessly strives for appearance and the superficial—in all desire to know there is already a drop of cruelty.[6]

But sadism, as we have noticed, in intensifying awareness also distorts it.[7] Even if Nietzsche is right that cruelty is at the root of tragic art, the serious artist knows that he must transcend it. It is, after all, only another kind of sentimentality, drowning the painful scene in the self-indulgent feelings of the onlooker. The point may be illustrated by the different treatments of violent death in art and entertainment. Sadism suspends awareness that death comes to all of us, by exploiting the death of another to intensify one's own consciousness of life and power. A traditional device for drawing us beyond the possibility of sweetening by sadism, right to the viewpoint of the dying man, is the death speech, at its starkest when Agamemnon cries offstage that he has been struck his mortal blow. As it happens, the film which in 1930 began the Hollywood gangster cycle, *Little Caesar*, ended memorably with Edward G. Robinson dying in the gutter with the words 'Mother of God, is this the end of Rico?' But it is notable that this convention, universal in tragedy, never established itself in the crime film. There violent death is spectacle; one has the sense of killing but not of dying. The spectator has come for blood, but did not buy his ticket to be reminded of his own mortality.

It is time to consider or reconsider certain fundamental questions about awareness. We defined it as being prepared to take into account in choices, and have throughout treated it as the fluctuating disposition to take the look and feel of things into account in choices of ends and the facts about them in choices of means. In presenting the imperative as both universal and absolute (and without yet even discussing why there are so many situations where common sense or common decency oblige us to violate it!), we are not far from the claim traditionally put in metaphysical terms, that Good is identical with Being.

It will be objected perhaps that it is too late in the day to try to re-establish our crumbling values on 'Be aware', since the True is already sinking into the gulf which has swallowed the Beautiful and the Good. When even measurements of space and time have proved to be relative, and the sub-atomic world to be as insubstantial as the realm of Platonic ideas, is it perhaps time to recognize that each of us lives in his own reality? If so, 'Be aware' is no securer than any other proposed foundation of morals; better settle for the Assassins' 'Nothing is true, everything is permitted'.[8] However, one may well draw the opposite lesson from modern science and art. For physics there is only one true measurement from any one position, and it can be more accurate than ever before; writing and painting communicate look and feel from a viewpoint with more sophistication than ever before; with a Cubist vision which constructs reality from the different facets exposed from different angles one is better orientated than ever before. The more complex technology becomes the more depends on getting the facts exactly right. If there is indeed the same relativism in physics and in morals, should not one individual's choice in his particular situation be as unimpugnably right or wrong as his measurements of distance and duration? In any case, there is no point in letting the great abstractions Truth and Reality divert us into epistemology and metaphysics, since such questions have no relevance to the application of 'Be aware' in the conduct of life. If I happen to be pondering them when about to cross the street, and the green light has changed to yellow, 'Be aware' resumes all its authority; never mind that at another level of discourse physics dismisses colour as subjective, unreal. When thinking how to act, I am in the world of common sense where something either is or is not, and where it is a matter of course that I can be in touch with it through highly subjective impressions. If the thought comes into my head that a careless remark has just hurt a friend or made an enemy, 'Be aware' awakens and exerts its force even if I cannot even tell what nuance of expression in his apparently untroubled face set off this vague disquiet.

Why have we chosen to say 'aware' when philosophers generally say 'know'? Philosophy has an incorrigible bias towards thinking of knowledge in terms of the verbally formulable, the proposition, the logical grounding of which has nothing to do with such psychological questions as whether the knower is being acted on causally by things which the proposition is about. Consequently, the enterprise of building an ethic on the imperative 'Know' could hardly be understood except as an attempt to deduce principles of conduct from the propositions known, vulnerable to standard criticisms of the Naturalistic Fallacy to which we have offered no answer. To give this impression would ensure shipwreck on a reef which we shall in any case be lucky to avoid, the indifference of the reader who takes it for granted that we are trying to deduce imperatives from the *facts* of which one ought to be aware, and assumes in advance that there has to be a flaw somewhere, hardly worth the trouble of locating, as in a new proposal for a perpetual-motion machine. The substitution of the word 'aware' may not be enough to dislodge so strong a preconception, but it should help. Awareness, although aided by propositional knowledge, is primarily of the concrete situation, to which one cannot attend without being causally affected, so that to have become aware of it at all one must already be responding to it in ways which vary with the range and degree of awareness. Knowing, on the other hand, is not a matter of degree, either one knows or does not. Whether my knowledge that I shall some day die, that a nuclear war is likely sooner or later, that alcohol will kill me, that another person is suffering, does move me in one direction or another, depends on the extent of my disposition to take these things into account in choices, on awareness which may spontaneously vary from one moment to the next and be sustainable only by an effort of will. I may well know how I *would* react if I could remain consistently aware of what I know in the abstract, yet yield to the opposite reaction, so that 'I see, and approve, the better: I follow the worse' (Ovid's *Video meliora proboque, deteriora sequor*). A further objection to 'know' is that knowing a proposition to be true is independent of viewpoint, so that there would be no possibility of an imperative 'Know' proving like 'Be aware' to be relevant to morals. The moral consequences we have drawn from awareness of how someone else feels could not be derived from the mere knowledge that he is suffering and needs my help.

Of what does one have to be aware? Since one cannot be aware of everything, 'Be aware' will of course be unusable without tests of relevance. When someone is said to act or react with 'full' or 'sufficient' awareness—qualifications which recur in our argument without further explanation, with no doubt irritating frequency— it is implied that he is aware of everything relevant to his choice of means or ends. It will perhaps be said that, although there may be no inherent difficulty in establishing criteria of relevance to choices of means, the vagueness of 'Be aware' for choices of ends reduces it to meaninglessness as our proposed 'first principle'. But this is almost the reverse of the case. Deciding what facts are relevant to a choice of means may be very complicated, and that the difficulties deter nobody from admitting his obligation to take account of them testifies to the irresistible authority of 'Be aware' in practical decisions. But to judge something relevant to the choice of a spontaneously emerging goal as end, it is enough—as we have insisted from the first—that awareness of it does in fact act causally on the spontaneous inclination. For a person insensitive to visual impressions the pattern on the wallpaper he is buying may seem not to deserve close scrutiny; but if the room he has papered begins after a while to depress him, it has turned out that the pattern was relevant to the choice after all. Whenever in relation to a loved person, idealized place or personal indulgence I find myself pushing out of mind some disagreeable thought, its relevance (as distinct from its importance) is not in doubt; it is enough that it does spontaneously move me against what I have decided for.

We must insist too that the authority of 'Be aware' is independent of practical advantages and disadvantages. Admittedly such corollaries as 'Face facts', which we introduced at the very start of the discussion in the first chapter,[9] do support their authority by the urgency of factual awareness in choices of means. Without doubt it is the obstinate resistance of facts blocking the way to goals which has taught mankind such awareness as it has. However, choices of means, taken by themselves, encourage only an awareness mixed in advantageous proportions with illusion and insensibility. The utility of believing that, however many setbacks my cause may suffer, God or the historical process is ultimately on my side, an effectiveness demonstrated throughout history by so many religious and political movements, is only one example of the practical value of delusion. Or again, for the ruling class or race against which such a movement rebels, as long as its authority is secure there are very strong practical advantages in thinking of its subjects as incapable of governing themselves, happy and carefree in their poverty, innately inferior in intelligence, out of work only if lazy, loyal and grateful for all one has done for them unless misled by irresponsible agitators; it is only when they start to be dangerously restive that it becomes practically useful to understand their motives and capacities better. Our application of the principle of awareness to morals implies that the pursuit of any selfish end exerts strong pressures to close oneself to awareness from other viewpoints; indeed, if full awareness were required for the intelligent choosing of means, our thesis would invite the rejoinder: 'If "Be good" follows from "Be aware from all viewpoints", why does not the urgent need to be aware of the people with whom we deal compel us all to be moral?'[10] However, if X is there, it is there whether I take account of it or not. If a thing is objectively so for one choice of means it is so for another; it is a contradiction to estimate the capabilities of a subject class or race in one way when they are tractable and in another when they are not. If it is so for choices of means it is so for choices of ends; and it is one of the greatest temptations to irrationality that nothing compels us to acknowledge in the realm of ends what we cannot afford to deny in the realm of means. There is no obstacle at all except a respect for logical consistency to weighing facts justly when a mistake can cost money but refusing to extend the same standards to the historicity of Bible narrative, or to shutting one's eyes to the use of Einstein's relativity in work on the atom bomb while publicly denouncing the theory as Jewish science or bourgeois idealism.

But in recognizing the authority of 'Be aware' as absolute we run up against that imbalance of the organism in the direction of what pleases it, by which it spontaneously expands awareness in one direction by contracting it in others. The involuntary expansions and contractions have the consequence that to hold on to the most aware response it may be a practical necessity to numb oneself to a local awareness which distracts from it. The compromise involves some danger of overlooking factors relevant to a choice, so that in principle one would be better off without this weakness of the flesh. The obvious example is the surgeon with his ruthless but healing knife. He is best imagined as an old-fashioned sawbones before the invention of anaesthetics, carving away placidly while an assistant holds down the screaming patient. When someone protests at his callousness he says 'Would you rather my hand shook?'. In the last resort his conduct is in accord with 'Be aware', because he would be acting the same if he were capable of full awareness both of the goal of saving life and of the temporary anguish he is inflict-ing, but being merely human he would lose sight of the goal if he let his mind dwell on the pain. But suppose he is told about the new discovery chloroform, and says 'I've no time for such newfangled nonsense'. Then one could say 'You've forgotten what it must feel like'; this time he *ought* to be aware of the pain.

The question might be raised whether a surgeon's callousness is after all even a local violation of 'Be aware'. We have defined awareness as the disposition to take into account in choices,[11] and we have always insisted that although a capacity to recall a feeling is necessary to continuing awareness of it, a constant maintenance of the feeling is not. A surgeon who immediately welcomed news of chloroform could reasonably claim always to have been aware of the pain although he had disciplined himself not to heed it. In one's own case it is perhaps always theoreti-cally possible to withhold attention without losing awareness. But that 'Be aware' does allow the judgment that a person can be better off locally unaware is plain enough in dealings with other people. If someone is critically ill, what well-disposed person will choose the moment to tell him that his business has crashed and his wife has gone off with another man?

There is some danger that founding an ethic in 'Be aware' may encourage ruinous excesses of truth-telling like the events in Ibsen's *Wild duck*. However, a consequence of so extending the scope of the imperative is that it becomes relevant only to the logic of value judgments, and has no direct bearing on how far a creature adapted to heed only what pleases it can push towards awareness against the grain of organic functioning. Our choice of 'aware', as a philosophically uncorrupted word which can help us to approach philosophical problems from a different angle, does have something to do with its recent currency in the valua-tions of ordinary discourse, as when someone is said to apply abstract principles without being aware of other people as persons, or to have lost by too exclusive concentration on the uses of things awareness of the colours of dawn and the scent of the flowers. But having turned awareness into the universal test of value we cannot, as perhaps would most habitual users of the word, take the side of perceptual and emotional awareness against the abstractions of philosophy and science. Our concern is rather to break away from the stale confrontation of reason and spontaneity which has persisted since the Romantic Movement, to invite the man of reason to admit that he never has had any ends which did not spring from his own spontaneity, and the intuitive and impulsive that no insight that flashes from theirs can be acknowledged as objective truth until it survives the ruthless justice of reason.

Factual awareness is a theoretically simple matter of weighing the evidence without regard for what flatters our hopes, and the requirements of 'Be aware' are straightforward and stringent. But as for perceptual and emotional awareness, lacking which we would have no motive to bother about facts, without pleasure or hope it simply fades. Then how far forward can one press in submission to 'Be aware'? Let us leave the last word to Nietzsche, whose cruel intelligence is quickened only by the taste of bitter truths.

Something might be true although at the same time harmful and dangerous in the highest degree; indeed it could pertain to the fundamental nature of existence that a complete knowledge of it might destroy one—so that the strength of a spirit could be measured by how much 'truth' it could take, more clearly, to what degree it *needed* it attenuated, veiled, sweetened, blunted and falsified. But there can be no doubt that for the discovery of certain *parts* of truth the wicked and unhappy are in a more favourable position and are more likely to succeed; not to mention the wicked who are happy—a species about whom the moralists are silent...[12]

1.4 Decision and principles

It is tempting to think of all decision after the analogy of the choice of means, which is the most easily analysed type. In it we know ourselves to be rational agents detached from spontaneity, judging on objective grounds what will serve our ends. A man is getting ready to travel. He considers taking an early flight because it is the quickest, doubts whether it will give him time to prepare and settles for the quickest later flight; he wants to be bothered with as few suitcases as possible, starts packing the biggest he has, finds the lock broken and chooses another. Any spontaneous pull to which he yields (for example, a proneness due to laziness to exaggerate the difficulty of getting things done in time for the earlier flight) will merely bias his judgement; in the pure choice of means you *either* choose rationally *or* surrender to the spontaneous. This kind of decision fits the model of a 'weighing' of considerations; we may think of the man as piling items pro and con on opposite sides of a balance and making his judgement after one side goes down.

However behind these choices of means there was a choice of ends. Let us suppose a less hurried traveller who is flying to Bali with the intention of staying, who wants the life he expects in Bali not for some business or educational purpose but for its own sake, as his vision of the Good Life. Let us make him a highly intelligent but intuitive and responsive young man not much interested in abstract principles, the very antithesis of a philosopher. Certainly he expects to be happy there, but even if we were to claim that his ultimate end is pleasure we should be using 'end' in another sense than when we say that his flight was the end to which booking the ticket was the means, since to enjoy living in a place is not an activity separate from and subsequent in time to living there. But why did he choose to live in Bali rather than England? On the analogy of a choice of means we might suppose that he would choose in terms of principles which are behind his ends as the ends are behind his means, and as before would resist as bias all spontaneous inclinations in either direction. But very obviously our traveller's decision would not be at all like that. He has seen the Peliatan dancers on tour, hung his walls with posters of that photogenic island, bought records of gamelan music. He begins to find himself day-dreaming about Bali. Reveries of palms and frangipani flowers, terraced ricefields, cockfights and shadow plays, interrupt his work by day, at night he dreams of brown graceful women naked to the waist. He takes to reading about Bali, and is impressed by the evidence that its culture is unique in the degree to which art is part of ordinary life and folk art is fine art. Insensibly wish becomes want, arousing and tugging against a reluctance to leave his home country which was inactive as long as he was merely fantasizing. He begins to ask himself realistic questions. To what extent is a romantic yearning for a lost Eden making him idealize the island, and on the other hand how much of his caution is inertia and fear of the new? Does he want to live where he would always be seen as a stranger? Would gamelan music come to bore him if there were not much else to listen to? He considers money, climate, health, Indonesian politics, whether nowadays the women still bare their breasts, whether he could learn the languages of the island. He takes a holiday in Bali, the spell intensifies, the practical issues clarify. Now it becomes urgent to decide, but frivolous or weighty considerations keep pulling him in one direction or the other. Finally, when he has taken in all the information he can assimilate, after a dramatic 'I *will* go' or after waking one morning knowing that the problem has solved itself in his sleep, he applies for his visa, resigns his job, packs his bags.

Throughout the whole sequence, from the first musings to the final decision, he has been reacting spontaneously to what step by step he has been learning. He has done an enormous amount of hard and soft thinking, but most of it about the stimuli to which he is responding, and the rest about whether he is being honest with himself as to how he is responding. We have deliberately presented him as never at any point appealing to a principle of conduct. Shall we say then that he has drifted spontaneously through the crisis without ever making a rational decision as to whether to go or not? Suppose that when asked his reason he replies vaguely 'I'm going to seed in England, I'm sure life will be more interesting there'. When life gets more interesting one is more responsive, more aware of one's surroundings and what one is doing; his answer, inarticulate as it may be, has behind it the authority of 'Be aware'. Obviously there are other aspects of intelligent behaviour, some of which Bali may discourage; perhaps a time will come when he tells himself 'I've run away from a big world to a little one, I was wrong'. But let us assume that when we question him he proves not to have overlooked such dangers. We see that he has not simply yielded to the stronger of two pulls, as would be the case if, for example, he never overcame a fear of being uprooted which he judges cowardly, and ever after said to himself 'I ought to have gone'. He has resisted both pulls until he has assembled all the information he thinks relevant, the test of relevance being whether it does in fact strengthen one pull in relation to the other. His final decision is in favour of whichever proves stronger, but the stronger for perhaps no more than the brief spell of fullest awareness in which he decides, afterwards to be panic-stricken at having committed himself to a choice which none the less he still knows in his heart was right.

What would a rational decision to live in Bali be like, if this is not one? It will be suggested perhaps that, instead of simply feeling himself pulled between a thirst for new experience and a dread of losing his pension, a rational man would ponder conflicting principles, 'It is good to welcome new experience' and 'One ought not to risk one's pension', and judge between them by deducing from more general principles combined with verbally formulated facts about Bali and himself. But, even assuming its feasibility, this would be a grossly stupid way of going about the business, reducing the whole delicate operation to a clumsy manipulation of crudely simplified formulae. In the first place, we are no longer in the realm of choice of means, where all relevant information can be presented in verbal descriptions (supplemented on occasion with mathematical symbols and diagrams). To decide whether to live in Bali you have to imagine the conditions with as much sensuous and emotional vividness as possible, and will learn more from photographs, music records, documentary films of dance, impressionistic writing, the talk of enthusiastic or disillusioned people who have been there already, than from strictly factual propositions. It might be that the traveller after a prolonged deadlock sees a picture of Bali on a magazine cover as he is walking past a newspaper stand, thinks 'I *must* go there', the decision is made, and from then on he never wavers. Is he being irrationally swayed by a fleeting emotion? Apparently not, for he has been thinking hard for months and his decision is now solid. His visual impressions have been fading without his knowing it, and with their reactivation stale information has suddenly sorted itself out into a new and firm pattern.

In any case, what kind of general principles would be of help in judging between 'It is good to welcome new experience' and 'One ought not to risk one's pension'? The rational man may contemplate them and give more weight to the former, and more still perhaps to 'Art should be a part of ordinary life', but these are not the sort of principles which he will profess to have interrelated in a deductive system. Whatever he may think he is doing he can only be discovering, like our romantic traveller, but perhaps much less aware of what he is doing, that in the last resort his desires outweigh his fears. To revert to the metaphor of weighing, in choices of means the traveller would be the weigher, but in this choice of an end he is the arm of the balance, and when the information is assimilated the impulse to go prevails over the reluctance to take the risk as the arm goes up or down when the balance is fully loaded. If the glimpse of one more picture could turn the scales and leave them steady, that is a proof that the traveller is a very sensitive instrument indeed.

It must be admitted that in deliberately excluding considerations of principle we are crediting the traveller with a rather narrow kind of intelligence, acute though it may be. Even for those of us who admit that he has made a rational choice on this occasion, it remains surprising that he has benefited so little from experience, that he has never made, or let God or society make for him, any previous decisions on general issues which could be of help to him. Thus his conduct very well illustrates the maxim 'Look before you leap'; and if his final decision was made when the trend of circumstances was making it harder to leave home, he might well have recalled 'He who hesitates is lost'. However the general decisions formulated as maxims are themselves about how to act in a recurring situation and have no independent authority; they do not pre-decide particular issues, each of which will have its peculiar features. The rational way to employ such conflicting prudential principles would not be to deduce from more general principles which of them applies to the present case. It would be to let one maxim remind him of the treacherous limits of his information and the other of unconsidered consequences of delay, and try to fill both gaps in his awareness before letting himself be moved in one direction or the other. The maxims would serve only to guide him towards fuller awareness of the present situation.

If we proceed from prudential to moral imperatives, will the conditions of the choice be fundamentally changed? The traveller, we now discover, is a young man whose ailing parents want him to stay within reach. Society imposes an obligation to look after his parents, as a debt owed to them for his upbringing, and owed to society for passing on to his children the obligation to do the same for him. Such an obligation seems to be a factor different in kind from any considered so far. As an external pressure, if only one to which it might be politic to submit, it certainly is different. But what would transform it from an externally enforced to a moral obligation? On the present argument, the recognition that in widening awareness, exploring from his own former viewpoint as child and future as old man, and generalizing to the viewpoints of all, his spontaneous dislike of the obligation as a hindrance to himself turns to approval of it as beneficial to all. But then 'One ought to look after one's parents' derives, like 'Look before you leap', from a general decision following the same procedures as his particular decisions, and it too can claim no stronger authority. In a particular situation it will bind him only to heed, in addition to its other features, everything taken into account in the general situation. As a moral imperative, far from being incommensurable with his previous considerations, it merely adds others similar in kind; he now has to see things from his parents' viewpoint as well as his own, consider their health and resources, ask himself how much they have done to arouse his gratitude or his rancour, whether his staying would really do them any good, whether he can get on with them without quarrelling, and add all this to the information which he must assimilate before he lets the needle of his internal compass finally settle in the direction of Bali or of home.

There remains a further complication. To act on or defy a socially established rule has effects on all who benefit or suffer by its observance. To disobey one's father in traditional China would violate the filial piety integral to the whole system of mores and be seen as a threat by all; on the other hand when the young of such a society begin to question the code and assert themselves against the old, they see a disobedience as a blow struck for all of them. Assuming a social code rather nearer to the Confucian than to our own, the man who wants to go to Bali might choose to obey his parents although convinced that to stay in England is both to his own disadvantage and of no real advantage to them. However, if it is a moral decision rather than mechanical conformism or a prudent surrender to social pressures, the case remains fundamentally as before, but with an added layer; he now takes account, not only of the effects on his parents but of the damage to the community as a whole of any successful disobedience. Here it may be as well to shift from filial piety to what for our society is the more straightforward issue of theft. A rich and aged relative, who has little use left for his wealth, refuses to give him the money he needs to go to Bali (he has at last made up his mind), but there is an opportunity to steal it from him. He would be doing little or no harm to the old man. But from the viewpoint of any property-owner, an unpunished theft is a danger, increasing the chances of being robbed himself. The most deeply spontaneous, the gut reaction, from every viewpoint except that of the destitute, or of a criminal ready to pay for the advantage of robbing by the risk of himself being robbed, or of the kind of anarchist who acclaims private theft as a blow to the oppressive institution of private property, is of being threatened. Seeing from the viewpoints of the many, the traveller therefore recognizes the force of the general imperative 'Thou shalt not steal'. How is he to measure it against 'Look before you leap', 'Care for your parents', and such other imperatives as he has been picking up on the way? In the same manner as with the rest of them, by taking into account the increased danger to property-owners, minute but replicated for each of them, in awareness of which from their viewpoints he reacts against theft. This might not stop him reacting still more strongly in favour of theft, from the viewpoints of all who as an anarchist he believes to suffer from the institution of private property; but otherwise he has to put the danger on the same side of the scales as the slight loss to the old relative, against the great gain to himself. Treated as an instance of the Utilitarian calculus, the whole increasingly complicated operation would no doubt be quite unreal. But all that we are requiring of him is that, widening his viewpoint from himself to the comminity, he has taken account of the communal effects of theft, before, as himself not the weigher but the balance, he allows himself finally to settle against or in favour of taking the money. In that final settlement he can be influenced by, without necessarily even remembering, every relevant experience throughout the whole of his life. We conclude then that choice even by the most responsible moral agent, however closely it resembles a pure Kantian decision for principle against inclination, is rational only if its fundamental procedure is that exposed to view by our unintellectual, intuitive romantic deciding whether to flee to Bali. Obviously there are issues for which the pondering of moral principles will from the start play a much bigger part than the one which confronts the traveller. But there is no issue for which simply to deduce from socially prescribed principles combined with factual propositions would be anything but a mechanical conformity; I know *why* I should do the prescribed thing only if, at least at my moments of fullest awareness from other viewpoints, I feel moved to do so.

This analysis shows up a further difference between choices of means and of ends; the former start from facts publicly testable by objective criteria, the latter from the look and feel of things tested privately and subjectively, by assuming in experience or imagination the relevant viewpoint in the fullest awareness available, and discovering how one does respond. Choices of ends, as of means, are debatable in terms of public tests (of whether things are in fact as the agent imagines them, whether his reactions as observed in his behaviour are as he feels them to be), but can take account of public observations only to the extent that they are subjectively confirmed. To speak of private testability runs the risk of being misunderstood, of seeming to claim that there are truths—the most important truths—which are accessible only to an infallible private intuition. But that is not at all what we have in mind. Let us remind ourselves of the grounding formula for choices of ends:

> In awareness of everything relevant I find myself moved towards X, overlooking something relevant I find myself moved towards Y.
> Be aware.
> Therefore let yourself be moved towards X.

That I find myself or let myself be moved implies consciousness of being moved. However strong the objective evidence that I do want X or Y, I can take these wants into account only if they pass my private test, if subjectively I do feel them. The point then is not that the subjective impression is infallible but that without it no choice of ends can arise, very much as no choice of means can arise without highly fallible generalizations about causal connexions. If others point out to me that I always shirk opportunities to get something which I earnestly insist that I desire more than anything else in the world, I shall be persuaded to relinquish it as an end only if on reflection I am forced to admit to myself that I do not feel about it as strongly as I supposed. Let us imagine that the traveller has at his disposal a computer, far ahead of present possibilities, into which—we assume the behaviourist position—is continually fed all, and much more than, his own information about himself and his situation. After provisionally deciding to go to Bali he consults this oracle: 'How would I react if I had all your information?', and gets the answer 'You would stay at home'. Does 'Be aware' now require him to act on the advice of the computer? Not immediately, for to do what he would be moved to do if more aware, without trying to become more aware, would be a direct defiance of the imperative. He would obey it by consulting the computer for the information he has missed. Then, as with fuller information he feels himself being moved in the opposite direction, he can say to himself 'Ah, now I see why I ought not to go'.

In the case of means, I can take many of the facts on trust from experts, even leave the choice itself to experts; but in the case of ends, however humbly I listen to advice, the decision remains my own. It might be that a friend says to the young man who is thinking of living in Bali 'You don't really believe that nonsense, you're playing at being Gauguin'. Without being offered a particle of evidence to support the accusation the young man sees in an instant that it is true, and abandons the whole project. But he has not taken the word of a wiser man on trust, his private test has confirmed it for him. Certain individuals stand out as more perceptive, sensitive, far-seeing than the rest of us, and we recognize their value judgements as maturer than our own; but they differ from experts in that we can learn from them only how to evaluate more maturely ourselves. I cannot choose something as an end simply because a wiser man tells me I would want it if I understood myself better, because I cannot choose ends at all by inferring from facts about my inclinations; the choice of an end is nothing else but the spontaneous settling of inclination in one direction or other, and the honest or self-deceiving interpretation of its goal. Any goal of mine which I have allowed to be chosen for me by others, even if I think of it as an end in itself, can only be serving as a means to something else which my private test does confirm as wanted for its own sake. If I run after the goals which I see everyone around me running after, I reduce them to no more than means to the well-being of feeling at one with the many. If I think I am going mad, and let a psychiatrist make my decisions for me, the goals I borrow become means to keep out of trouble and recover my health.

By now a consequence has emerged which has been implicit from the first in the whole enterprise of grounding valuation in awareness, that Good has now the same claims to objectivity as Truth. In whatever sense it is to be recognized as an objective fact that I am now responding in awareness of more factors than before, my reaction will likewise be objectively better than before. In the early stages of our argument, before the possibility of an egoistic interpretation was excluded, this implication had only a limited interest. Even granting the absurdity of Hitler's racialist theories, it would be possible to credit him with realistic goals (to exploit a political scapegoat, to depopulate Eastern Europe for resettlement) for which he could massacre Jews and Slavs in as full awareness as theirs when they flee or fight. The massacres would not be right from his viewpoint and wrong from theirs, he would be objectively right to kill and they to resist being killed; the parallel would be to two contenders for a job both being right to apply in the eyes of all, not to each thinking himself right to apply and the other wrong. But with the recognition that 'Be aware' prescribes responding from all relevant viewpoints, the judgement changes to condemnation of the massacres as objectively wrong, on the grounds that to be moved against Hitler and on behalf of his victims would be the reaction of anyone, including Hitler himself, who responded impartially from the viewpoints of both. Whether one names this position absolutism or relativism may be left to the reader's discretion, but it is neither the absolutism which ascribes unconditional authority to universal standards ('It is wrong to take human life even in self-defence') nor the relativism which is neutral between judgements of a particular act ('You think Hitler was right to massacre them, I think he was wrong. Let us agree to differ'). It implies that objectivity is to be sought, not by trying to root judgements in absolute standards, but on the contrary by treating all standards as provisional in order to get behind them to the reality of the concrete situation and the authentic response of the individual.

The very considerations which make many so anxious to establish that value judgements are objective, a sense of the urgent social need of common rules, disquiet at the anarchic consequences of everyone doing as he likes, have had the effect of raising irrelevant doubts about that objectivity. As long as attention is diverted to supposedly universal standards and the differences of opinion and taste which undermine them, it seems that all value slides into the subjectivity from which factual judgements are exempt. But if we begin from situations in which the community does *not* find it necessary to impose standards, we find, in the very simplest cases, full confidence and agreement in evaluating, untroubled by worries over differences of taste. If hesitating between a peach and a pear you languidly inspect, sniff and fondle the fruit before deciding for the pear, and eat it

slowly with a look of bliss, no one who has left behind the absolutism of childhood ('Anyone can see that a peach is nicer than a pear') will doubt that you made
the best possible choice between the flavours; the rightness of the choice, and the
objective fact that in the fullest awareness of the two flavours you were spontaneously moved to take the pear, are two sides of the same coin. The case of the traveller to Bali is vastly more complicated, his deciding reaction having been influenced by an indefinite series of accessions to his awareness from the viewpoints of
parents and community as well as from his own. But acknowledgement of increasing complication and uncertainty is not a retreat from objectivity; doubt or
acceptance of a supposed historical fact or law of nature likewise depends on
accumulation of evidence which can never be complete. There is even a special
affinity between evaluation of a choice of ends and one kind of factual judgement,
prediction of that choice. An observer would follow the same procedure in judging the traveller's choice right or wrong and in predicting that choice, except that
in the former case the question is how the traveller would react in fullest awareness, in the latter how he will react in his actual awareness. The possibilities both
of prediction and of evaluation will of course be limited by the observer's own
range of awareness. He has himself, let us say, spent a couple of disillusioning
years in Bali, so that he fully understands the considerations which tempt the
young man, but has the advantage of fuller information. He is thus qualified to
predict that the other like himself will go and will be disappointed, and is proved a
true prophet by the event. He sees too that the other should from the first have
known better, as he himself should (he has come to understand that in retrospect),
and therefore judges that they both made not only an unlucky but a bad choice.
The young man's disillusionment when it comes confirms, not only the observer's
prediction, but the superiority of his evaluation over the young man's, although
not necessarily its correctness. As with a question of fact, the more informed
judgement could be the mistaken one. There might be a third person wiser than
either who is living happily and fruitfully in Bali, and remembers that both of them
came with unrealistic expectations. However, in being always revisable in the light
of new information the judgement still remains on a par with acceptance of a
historical fact or a law of nature, which likewise never escape the possibility of
being discredited by new evidence. There will be only one right decision in the
unique circumstances of each unique one of the three travellers, as there can be
only one right prediction of it.

   We may push the parallel between evaluation and prediction a little farther.
When the complexities of circumstance defeat analysis, and we grope for the best
prediction or choice attainable, we do not doubt that there is a better founded
prediction or better informed choice which no one perhaps will be lucky enough
to hit on. There can be unestimated value in the same sense that there can be
unknown truths and unmeasured dimensions. We shall ignore the epistemological
issues, and certainly are not proposing to Platonize values as eternal entities on
another plane of reality. However, in the world of Orwell's *1984* there may be
people who although sure that the events abolished by official historiography did
happen, are not so sure that the experiences treasured in memory keep the value
which official propaganda degrades; they might be happier for the assurance that,

in the sense that it remains true that an event happened even if universally forgotten, an experience remains good even if in universally shrinking awareness there
will never again be anyone capable of appreciating it. In ordinary affairs, for which
we aspire only to the best choice on the available information, the only assurance
we need is that each veering of spontaneous reaction with expanding awareness is
objectively a change for the better. Everywhere individuals, communities and cultures respond differently to similar situations; their reactions are always criticizable in terms of awareness, including awareness from each other's viewpoints;
at the ideal limit of awareness each would still respond differently, yet rightly even
by the judgement of the rest.

It has been commonly assumed that in controversy even if we could finally
agree on what is objectively so, the moral debate has not yet started; you can still
find good what I find bad, and unless we discover common principles from which
to argue, the debate can never begin at all. But the present argument has led to the
opposite conclusion; when we reach agreement, by public tests, on what is objectively so—which includes how we do respond when we see the situation as it is—
the debate is over. (If my private test convinces me that I do not want what you think
I want, I assume error in your reading of me the public tests, which I must expose or
leave you unanswered.) Where we may feel at a disadvantage compared with moral absolutists with fixed standards is not in the claim to objectivity but in the sense
of certainty. The awareness on which valuation depends is that on which we act
in ordinary life, seldom treatable by the strict methods of proof of the sciences.
Our understanding of each other is adequate enough for the small change of moral
discourse, leaving us in no doubt of how most people feel about being murdered,
robbed, raped or cheated, but the more sensitive the valuation the less confidently
it can be made. We cannot hope to recover that certainty about good and evil
upon which in the ethical religions salvation itself depends. But outside a religious
context, why should I ask for a certainty with which I dispense in every other field
of life? What matters is that I need never question that there *is* a course which is
objectively the best for me, and that when most aware I am nearest to it.

What if the critic of a choice lives in another society with a different moral
code? Those who simplify moral judgement to the application of standards would
assume that he has either to impose his own code or to accommodate himself to
the other. We affirm on the contrary that he has to see every code including his
own as criticizable in terms of 'Be aware'. If you grew up in a society which is
strange to me, I have first of all to acknowledge that its customary approvals and
condemnations are as spontaneous in you as are your more personal reactions.
I have to acknowledge too that since you ought to be aware from your fellow's
viewpoints and incline towards their benefit as well as your own, and ought also
to be aware that individuals cannot benefit themselves or each other by community
without agreeing on common rules, the rules you follow in acting towards your
fellows should be those of your community and not of mine. If I myself joined
your community, I should be obliged to adapt myself to your code, even if my
spontaneous approvals and disapprovals did not change. Up to this point, 'Be
aware' instructs me to judge individuals by their own code, not my own. However,
it no more obliges me to apply without question your standards to you than mine

to myself. A standard is acceptable on the authority of 'Be aware' to the extent that, when most aware of the recurring situation to which it applies from the viewpoints of those affected by it, one is spontaneously moved to act as it pre-scribes—which is what makes the standard *feel* right. But would you and your fellows spontaneously so react if you could break through traditional assumptions to a fuller awareness of the recurring situation? Would you so react to the particular situation which confronts us now, if you were not applying the standard mechani-cally? If the prescribed action affects others outside your community, would you so react if aware from their viewpoints? This last question is crucial; if the con-dition is satisfied, different codes may prescribe different behaviour within the so-cieties they organize yet still be reconcilable, never contradicting each other's judge-ments of the same person or action.

The ethics of the universal religions take a different course in pursuit of objectivity, seeking to break out from the limitations of local custom by submitting to stand-ards acceptable from the viewpoints of all mankind. But on the present approach the search for universal standards is irrelevant to the objectivity of right and wrong; it is in the nature of standards, which must alter with changing conditions and vary in stringency and applicability to particular cases, to be both a help and a hindrance to discovering the objective worth of a particular act. A socially accept-ed code, whatever its pretensions to universality, will in practice be moulded not only by 'Be aware' but by the ubiquitous 'We are better than you' and the equally mindless 'You are stronger than we are' which can cow us into doubting our superiority. No amount of reflection on first principles will stop a Christian from assuming that the morality demanded of women, which in Islam he judges to be imposed by the physically stronger sex in its own interests, is in his own religion true to the equality of the sexes before God; not until women become conscious of and vocal about their own interests does he appreciate that the difference from Islam has from the very first been only one of degree. Although the sociologists and anthropologists are too polite to mention it, social codes in general, including in these changing times whichever one was brought up in oneself by the preceding generation, can be seen from a sufficient distance to have been in large part shaped by gross delusions about the cosmos and about man, and by a brutal ignorance of everyone outside one's own people, sex and class. We are not denying that in the case of an alien culture one has less right to criticize than in one's own, out of lack of experience of what it can be like to live in it. However, if a people sacrifices all strangers to the sun, because it will burn out unless nourished by human blood, it would be unduly humble to think that they have as much right to their opinion as we have. If they learned a sounder astronomy and a clearer insight into how things look through the eyes of strangers, they would act differently, and better, because in greater awareness. What can be said for them is that if the High Priest is acting in the fullest awareness at present attainable by his people, it is right for him to perform the sacrifice, just as it would be right for a Western onlooker to try to dissuade him; he is not like a Nazi who has voluntarily shut himself off from the knowledge of biology and history and the personal sensitivity attained by the culture of the Weimar Republic.

Here a question may be raised as to just what we mean when we think of ourselves as plunged by the twentieth century into a chaos of relativism. In relativism, so it is said, every valuation is debased to 'a matter of taste', on which anyone's opinion is as good as anyone else's. Yet even in cuisine, from which the metaphor of 'taste' comes, people who take food seriously do not think of their preferences as relativistic in this sense. They do give weight to the judgements of the most aware, those who have educated themselves to discriminate between flavours most accurately. Not that I have to make the same choices as someone I acknowledge to be more discriminating, since my differently constituted palate may react differently, but my own choice will be better informed if I heed nuances which I would have missed if he had not pointed them out. We also generalize about the taste of the discriminating and set up standards, useful as guides as long as one does not credit them with greater authority than a considered choice which violates them, but not without the suspect motives and tyrannical pretensions of standards in morals; if you show signs of food-and-wine snobbery, I had better when listening to your recommendations take care to distinguish what I sense on my tongue from an affected taste. There is an objectivity behind the subjectivity of our preferences which entitles you to recommend to me a dish which you do not choose yourself and which I have hitherto been repelled by, but may come to like if I can forget my prejudices and for the first time attend closely to the flavour. This is just the objectivity which is to be claimed in general for the good; what is good for me now is not necessarily good for you or for me at other times, nor even what I now spontaneously prefer, it is what anyone would spontaneously prefer for me if sufficiently aware from my present viewpoint. If this is relativity it is like Einstein's, by which it is not that you can make any measurement come out as you please, but that from any spatio-temporal viewpoint you can estimate what will be the right measurement from any other.

In the fluidity of contemporary values we do indeed sink into a relativism for which your opinion is worth as much or little as mine whenever we lose faith in awareness itself, and surrender to irrationalism. But to the extent that rationality continues to prevail, we have long since been submitting all codes to 'Be aware', without noticing that this imperative is creative of values as well as destructive. We may be nostalgic for the security of those old standards which have been dissolved by changing conditions and needs, and by the opening up of viewpoints which have only lately become articulate, of women, working-class, blacks, Third World, homosexuals. It may seem that if we succeed in adapting our values to such disturbances instead of losing them altogether, it is because we still retain some vestige of a Christian and liberal moral tradition, a memory of 'Do unto others...' at the roots of social habit, which saves us from the collapse into competing egoisms into which deepening conflicts are perpetually driving us. This supposition is mistaken, according to the argument of this book; the imperative to become equally aware from different spatial, temporal and personal viewpoints is independent of moral traditions and habits, and we need not doubt that under any conditions spontaneity will continue to channel itself in selfish or unselfish directions with inequality or equality of awareness. In so far as the fear of relativism is of it becoming even for the most aware a matter of taste whether one is selfish or unselfish, compassionate or cruel, the fear is misplaced. However, the consensus about the value of particular reactions which we have declared theoretically conceivable is not practically attainable in times of perpetual and world-wide interaction, conflict and change. The danger is of a breakdown, in the disorientation of excess of information, the compass needle going wild as multiple pulls drag it hither and thither, and then a self-defensive shutting off of information and lapse into irrationalism.

1.5 Analogizing

Traditionally it has been assumed that thinking, whether about value or about fact, has to be fully detached from the spontaneous, which engages with it only as emotion biasing judgement. We have argued that for questions of value reason cannot achieve this independence. That the same is true of questions of fact is a conclusion that lately has become increasingly difficult to resist. There, however, the spontaneous currents which reason navigates are not inclinations but those analogizing processes already discussed briefly in an earlier chapter, with particular reference to simulation.[1]

The sciences were at one time supposed to generalize from observations by a logical operation called induction, claimed to free them from dependence on the merely analogical thinking which prevailed in the mediaeval proto-sciences, and which regrettably remain for the time being indispensable in dealing with everyday problems. But this involved a misunderstanding of analogizing. It is not that on the borders of logic there is a loose form called argument from analogy, but that all thinking starts from a spontaneous discrimination of the like and the unlike, and tendency to group the similar in categories and expect similar consequences from similar conditions. The problem, as with inclination in the case of questions of value, is whether reason ever quite lifts itself out of reach of spontaneous analogizations, or whether its function remains limited to organizing, criticizing and choosing between them. The difficulty in establishing a clear break from analogization arises at all stages, in defining terms and in observation as well as in induction itself. The similarities between things called by the same name are indefinite and fluctuating; one tries to pin terms down by definition, so that they can be used for strict inference, but Wittgenstein showed that in the vocabulary of natural languages the similarities are 'family resemblances', by which A may be like B in one respect and B like C in another, but A like C in neither, so that it is useless to look for common characteristics by which to define the word which names them all.[2] It seems too that analogizing is so deeply involved not only in thinking but in perception that there is no hope of escaping from it by isolating pure observations from which induction can start. Thus it has been shown experimentally that, because we all expect playing cards to fall into familiar sets, a briefly exposed black four of hearts will be perceived as a red four of hearts or black of spades.[3] This effect can vitiate scientific observation, as when seventeenth century experimenters, familiar with the concepts of post-Galilean mechanics but not of electrostatic attraction and repulsion, regularly reported observing chaff falling as though by gravitation, or mechanically rebounding from the electrified bodies which attracted them.[4]

Above all, there is the doubt as to whether induction itself is more than a logical fiction to justify the generalizations which regularly spring from spontaneous analogization. In everyday affairs we formulate a generalization when we find ourselves beginning to expect consequences as before to follow when conditions are as before. It is not clear that one has to postulate anything more than a reaction like Pavlov's dog learning to anticipate its dinner whenever it hears the bell. This is not to deny that it is an intelligent reaction, and that the sense of when to trust the analogy between present and former situations is in some individuals very intelligent indeed, but there is nothing in that to distinguish it from the other insights and hunches by which we instantaneously synthesize similarities and differences too fine and complex to be analysed before a change in the situation obliterates them. There has been a long resistance to accepting that, in spite of the logical stringency with which laws in science are formulated, interrelated and tested, their origin has never ceased to be the same. To establish laws of nature without analogizing would be possible only if there is indeed a logical operation for inferring from the particular to the universal, which induction is supposed to be. But it has never been shown that induction is logically more respectable than a formalized argument from analogy, indeed that induction from some particulars leading to deduction of others is anything else but a roundabout argument from analogy.

The admission that laws of nature cannot be established by induction became possible only with Karl Popper's demonstration that they are sufficiently assured by a continued failure to refute them, the rationality of a claim depending not on its origin but on its success in surviving criticism.[5] Strictly universal statements (such as 'All men are mortal') are in principle unverifiable and are tested by trying to falsify them, while strictly existential statements (such as 'Unicorns exist') are in principle unfalsifiable and tested by trying to verify them. This solution induces vertigo if one thinks in terms of a self-contained realm of observation and inference; does it mean that the most you can say of Einstein's physics is that it has not yet been refuted, which can be said equally of 'Unicorns exist'? But it no longer seems so queer if one thinks of rationality as starting not in inference from observations but in the testing of spontaneous expectations, just as in our theory of valuation it starts from choice between spontaneous inclinations. My expectations from analogy with the past, like a dog's, are sometimes realized, sometimes disappointed; if the mechanism were not often effective it would not as it evolved have been spared by natural selection; but I, as a rational being, want to be able to judge when it is reliable. To sort out which expectations are sound or unsound, a procedure to falsify the unsound (as with universal statements) will be just as effective as one to verify the sound (as with the existential).

It is from the chaos of spontaneous analogizing that creativity breaks into the ordered but closed realm of analytic thinking. Nothing prepares for the glimpse of a new analogy. When a thinker unravels previously unnoticed implications of a familiar idea, one seems stupid to have missed them oneself; but anyone who discerns a similarity which runs athwart the current categories, a poet by metaphor or a scientist by a new model or paradigm, can strike us with astonishment and awe, as a genius whose spontaneous flash illuminates what no logical operation within the frame of accepted concepts could have disclosed. Donald Schon has shown how the displacement of a concept by analogizing not only initiates new thoughts but also, by changing the concept itself, forces one to rethink the old.[6] He discards the assumption to which most of us still cling (if only because the ground seems to melt under our feet if we think otherwise) that we can clearly distinguish the literal and metaphorical uses of a word, fix the literal by definition, and leave the metaphorical to the poets. Schon argues that it it is time to recognize that scientific as well as poetic language is riddled with metaphor, that there is no clear line between literal and metaphorical, and that a perfect system of mutually definable terms is not even conceivable outside logic and mathematics. One of his most striking illustrations, highly relevant to our own use of the term 'view-point', is the constellation of visual metaphors embedded in cognitive vocabulary. I am presumably using words literally when the metaphor is a matter only of etymology ('insight'), and feel still more confident of it when the etymology belongs to the Latin ancestor of the word ('intuition', from *intueor* 'gaze at'). I am also rather confident of speaking literally when I say 'It was enlightening' or 'I discovered that ...', since 'enlighten' and 'discover' are not commonly used directly of lighting up or unscreening; but what of 'It was illuminating' or 'I uncovered the fact that ...'? When I speak of 'seeing' or 'showing' a truth which becomes 'apparent', of 'lucid', 'clear' or 'obscure' ideas, of 'points of view' or 'aspects of a situation', of 'shedding light' on a matter or 'being in the dark' about it, my language becomes more and more plainly metaphorical. Nor is it quite obvious on second thoughts that even in the most literal usages the visual metaphor is wholly dead; however accurately 'insight' may be defined in a dictionary, could I handle the word with any confidence without being guided by its grammatical and seman-tic affinities with 'sight'? No doubt many users of the word 'introspection' are unaware of its Latin etymology (from *introspicio* 'look within'), yet they are surely influenced by its affinities with 'inspect', 'spectator', 'spectacle'; otherwise, why do they claim to introspect entities as not physical but mental because not extended in space, treating introspection as analogous with sight, which reveals spatial extension, rather than with hearing, smell or taste, which just as much as conscious-ness of love or anger, hope or fear, exhibit temporal change without spatial extension? Even if one does think of self-consciousness as perceiving one's own activities rather than heeding them (as one also heeds the perceived), there is no obvious reason why one should not be perceiving as thought and emotion what to the eye would be neural process, just as when, with the same experience of temporal change without spatial extension, one hears as sound what one would see as vibrations.

The analogizing of knowing to seeing may pervade the concrete experience of coming to know, in the mystic's vision flooded with light; or it may be explicit in parable, as in Plato's of mankind misled by illusory appearance as prisoners in a cave who see only the shadows on the wall. Or it may set the direction of a programme of research, as when the Gestalt psychologists extended their prima-rily visual concept of 'insight' into a *gestalt* (literally 'shape') from perception to thinking. A very striking example of a philosopher dominated by the visual metaphor is Descartes, of all the one who made the most radical attempt to break away from the preconceptions of common experience and establish knowledge on purely rational foundations. He must have supposed himself to be using a language absolutely purged of metaphor when he wrote at the grand climax of the *Discourse on method*

...And having noticed that there is nothing whatever in this 'I think, therefore I am' which assures me that I say the truth, other than that I see very clearly *[je vois très clairement]* that to think it is necessary to be, I judged that I could take it as a general rule that the things which we conceive very clearly and very distinctly *[que nous concevons fort clairement et fort distinctement]* are all true...

The words are easily accepted as an appropriate dress to clothe a perfectly abstract thought, yet throughout Descartes' philosophy, as Schon says, 'it suggests itself that intuition is displaced seeing; the "clarity and distinctness" of ideas is a displaced clarity of objects; and the light of reason is a displaced theory of the eye, the eye of the mind, containing covertly the ancient doctrine that the eye projects its own light'.[7] Nevertheless one can hardly hope to discuss knowledge in a language any less metaphorical than Descartes' (I have myself a few paragraphs back analogized not only to seeing but to 'glimpsing' and being 'illuminated' by a 'flash', not only to clarity but to drawing a 'clear line'). It appears impossible to detach oneself from the visual analogy sufficiently to criticize it, without finding another to put in its place or balance against it. Among other metaphors there is a rich cluster based not on sight but on touch, some likewise submerged in Latin etymologies ('conceive', 'apprehend', 'comprehend', from *concipio* 'seize together', *apprehendo* 'grasp', *comprehendo* 'grasp together'), others overt ('be in touch', 'grasp' something, 'catch on' to it, 'get the point', 'feel' that it is 'palpably' true). The two sets of metaphors have persisted side by side, not only in the West since the ancient Greeks, but in other civilizations as well (Chinese *ming* 'bright' is the ordinary word for the enlightenment of the sage, which is often compared to a mirror reflecting things exactly as they are,[8] while *te* 'get' is used of insight; 'I've got it!' says the disciple to his master as he catches on to the Tao). Metaphors of grasping call attention to the active process of thinking rather than to static and distinct thoughts, and make it easier to understand that we interpret and organize rather than passively reflect. The contrast between the tactile and the visual metaphors makes it plain how the latter encourage assumptions very characteristic of Cartesianism, that the clear and distinct ideas reflect things unaltered in the mind like brightly lit objects in front of our eyes. As for 'aware', its associations are with the cognate 'ware', 'beware', 'wary', 'warn'; the analogy is with putting oneself on guard against a peril, a vigilance imposed by pressing need or by duty. It predisposes us to think of coming to know, not simply as active in itself, but as inseparable from reacting to the object and acting in reply.

A seminal influence in this style of thinking has been Gilbert Ryle's exposure of the category mistake, which implies that the most logically organized case may crumble because it turns out to depend on unnoticed analogies. To pick once again examples relevant to awareness, philosophers have often argued on the assumption that since an observer cannot be mistaken about what he sees or hears (although he may mistakenly suppose that he has seen or heard it), or a thinker about what he knows, there must be infallible operations by which to arrive at this certainty. Ryle points out[9] that in being impressed by the certainty of the seen and the known, one is assuming that seeing and knowing are analogous with looking and thinking, so that it becomes a problem how they escape the fallibility of these operations; he invites us to shift 'see' and 'know' to the category of achievement verbs such as 'find' and 'cure', which are related to 'seek' and 'treat' as 'see' and 'know' to 'look' and 'think', but do not tempt us to suppose that there are infallible methods of discovering lost articles or restoring to health. This approach has radical implications:

(1) Theories about perception and knowledge which it has seemed possible to prove or disprove *a priori* turn out to depend on concealed analogies; with the exposure of the analogy their foundations collapse.

(2) Neither the old nor the new analogy is logically derived; the former is rooted in habit, the latter emerges by a flash of insight.

(3) Once the new analogy is recognized, it can be compared with the old and shown to be more adequate, in that it dissipates previously insoluble problems. The choice of the new analogy is not arbitrary, but neither is it justified by a rigorous proof; by the conceptual readjustment problem-solving becomes easier.

(4) One escapes the old analogy only by submitting to another; the role of logic, even when it is suspected that there is something wrong at the foundations of the argument, is confined to applying and criticizing concepts thrown up by the spontaneous process of analogizing.

In the sciences it is a commonplace, not at first sight disturbing, that physics began by simulating Euclid's demonstrations in geometry, and that the inverse square law of gravitation became the model for another in electro-magnetism, that 'waves' of sound or light are suggested by waves on water, and the genetic 'code' by language. But Thomas Kuhn has argued that even the concepts and laws become intelligible in practice only as components of a disciplinary matrix which he calls the 'paradigm', in which the scientist learns to apply them through concrete instances of problem-solving which serve as models in approaching new puzzles. Observation and reason, far from establishing results on independent foundations, are guided by the paradigm, simulate the observation and reasoning in the exemplars. Not of course that the reasoning is invalid, or that the paradigm itself cannot be questioned when it is sensed that something is going wrong; indeed it is its destiny to lead eventually to intolerable anomalies and be replaced by another. But Kuhn insists that scientists never abandon a paradigm until they have found another, even at the cost of that supposed blasphemy against the spirit of science, the saving of hypotheses by *ad hoc* modifications when they conflict with observation.[10] Nor, when a more viable alternative does appear, are they necessarily much bothered if it reopens issues peripheral to the main line of advance which seemed to be already settled. The new paradigm must pass critical tests to survive, but it is born as spontaneously as the metaphors of a poet:

Paradigms are not corrigible by normal science at all. Indeed, as we have already seen, normal science ultimately leads only to the recognition of anomalies and to crises. And these are terminated, not by deliberation and interpretation, but by a relatively sudden and unstructured event like the gestalt switch. Scientists then often speak of 'the scales falling from the eyes' or of the 'lightning flash' that 'inundates' a previously obscure puzzle, enabling its components to be seen in a new way that for the first time permits its solution. On other occasions the relevant illumination comes in sleep.[11]

That all thinking is grounded in analogization shows up especially clearly when we try to come to grips with the thought of another civilization. The concepts which it assumes as self-evident, until persistent failure to solve a problem calls attention to them, appear to an outsider as strange metaphorical structures to be examined and re-examined as he learns to find his way around the conceptual scheme. To take an example from my own professional field, sinology, the first Christian missionaries in China were confronted with the Neo-Confucian cosmology, for which the universe is composed of something called *ch'i* and ordered by something called *li*. *Ch'i* is a universal fluid out of which bodies condense and into which they dissolve. At its densest, as in a stone, it is inert, but the more tenuous it is the more freely it moves, for example as the air we breathe; even the void is *ch'i* at the ultimate degree of rarification. Inside the denser *ch'i* of the living body flow more rarified currents which circulate and activate it, moving freely as breath, less freely as blood. The concrete meaning of the word in ordinary language is in fact 'breath', and the alternations of breathing out and in are the paradigms for the *ch'i* in its active phase moving, expanding, rarifying as the 'Yang', and in its passive phase reverting to stillness, contracting, solidifying, as the 'Yin'. This duality accounts for the generation and alternation of opposites throughout nature, light and dark, moving and still, male and female. Since *ch'i* occupies the place in Chinese cosmology corresponding to matter in ours, Westerners took a long time to grasp how very different it is from what we understand by matter. Early in the present century S. Le Gall was still translating *ch'i* by *matière*. A passage by the Neo-Confucian Chang Tsai (1020–1077), translatable as

The assembly and dispersal of the *ch'i* in the *T'ai-hsü* ('Supreme Void') is like ice congealing and melting in water

is rendered by Le Gall

'La condensation et les dispersions *des atômes* [my italics] dans la T'ai-hiu peuvent se comparer à la fonte de la glace dans l'eau'.[12]

Although Chang Tsai's comparison with water shows clearly that the *ch'i* is a continuum and not an aggregate of atoms, the analogy with matter is so deep in Le Gall's preconceptions that he assumes the component atoms to be implicit in the word *ch'i* of the Chinese text. A reader asking the important question 'Is there atomism in Chinese philosophy?' would find the wrong answer embedded in an actual quotation from a Chinese philosopher.

As for *li*, it is pattern, structure, order; the concrete uses of the word are for veins in jade and the grain of wood. The *li* as a whole is the cosmic pattern which lays down the lines along which nature and man move, which harmonizes opposites with complementary functions, Yin and Yang, ruler and subject, father and son, and alternates day and night, birth and death, the rise and fall of dynasties, in regular cycles, diverging downwards to the minutest detail of texture and converging upwards to the unity in which everything is interrelated. The *li* is not obeyed or defied like a law, one goes either with or against the grain of it, as in chopping wood. Le Gall translated it by *forme*, thus by the choice of two words remoulding the whole Neo-Confucian cosmology after the analogy of Aristotelian form and matter. J. Percy Bruce chose for his equivalent 'law', and so incorporated into the Neo-Confucian terminology itself the wrong answer to the question 'Are there laws of nature in China?', a misunderstanding which Joseph Needham in elucidating the concepts of Chinese science had to analyse at length.[13] But to think of Le Gall and Bruce as making mistakes which we now avoid would miss the whole point. There are no exact equivalents for *li* and *ch'i* among our concepts, and there is no way of approaching them except by breaking out from or awakening to one analogy after another.

Approaching this cosmology, it is natural for an outsider to suppose that the Chinese can think only concretely, after the analogies of breathing or the veins in jade (a supposition encouraged by misunderstandings of Chinese script as a kind of picture-writing), while he thinks abstractly; that the Chinese are wrong and he is right (for is not the universe in fact composed of matter obeying the laws of nature?); that the Chinese are trapped within an unchanging conceptual scheme while he is free to go wherever reason bids. However, to take the first point first, the Chinese concepts appear concrete to us only because the inquiring outsider, unlike the insider who habitually thinks with them, needs to fix his attention on their metaphorical roots. He is much less conscious of the metaphors behind his own 'matter' and 'law', which however he must rediscover if he wants to explore the differences to the bottom. He himself thinks of matter after the analogy, if not actually of the timber which is the concrete meaning of Greek *hulè* and Latin *materia*, at any rate of the 'materials' utilized in making an artefact; and the usage of 'matter' has behind it a larger model, of a universe created by God for a purpose, from which the transparently metaphorical 'laws of nature' also derive. Indeed we no longer employ the word with full assurance, or are confident of what we mean by philosophical 'materialism', now that we are forbidden to think of atoms as little balls out of which a universe could be constructed; twentieth century physics has less substantial entities which would slip through one's fingers. As for the metaphor of 'law', its persisting power is evident whenever someone, pondering the determinist thesis that even his own actions are 'bound by', are 'subject to', 'obey' the laws of nature, finds himself thinking as though he ought to be conscious of his own resisting will, as he is when submitting to human laws.

Secondly, there can be no sense in insisting that the universe *is* composed of matter and not of *ch'i*. The former concept had a crucial historical advantage at the birth of mechanics; Western thinkers approaching things as materials which stay put until the craftsman or builder reaches for them, would not have started trying to measure how the inert is moved by external forces if they had been thinking in terms of inherently active *ch'i*. The advantage however is accidental, and brings with it difficulties of its own; assuming that matter, unlike *ch'i*, is inert until moved, it took some time to arrive at the thought of inertia as either rest or uniform motion in a straight line. The concept of *ch'i* was not without local advantages, predisposing the Chinese to think of blood as circulating and of the earth as having condensed out of a more fluid state (hence the fossil sea shells found up in mountains). Nowadays, with the boundary between mass and energy abolished, the advantage might be said to have passed to *ch'i;* yet it would be absurd to suggest that the Chinese have been proved right, since the advantages and disadvantages depend on which problems happen to be current. There can be no right or wrong, true or false, for the primary stock of concepts from which thinking starts; they reflect classifications of the similar and the different guided by past needs, and the inherited categories prove themselves useful or misleading in the course of putting them to service. The concepts of each civilization, like the soil of its homeland, have been cultivated by a long tradition of directed effort, but in the last resort are not invented but given.

Thirdly, there is no difference in kind which entitles us to think of the concepts of civilizations other than our own as static and imprisoning. (There are differences in degree, for the unprecedented acceleration of Western civilization since the fifteenth century does indeed make all others seem static by comparison.) The Chinese cosmology based on *li* and *ch'i* goes back only to the Neo-Confncian movement of the Sung dynasty (AD 960–1279), a conceptual revolution which can itself be understood in Kuhnian terms as a response to the breakdown of an older paradigm. The concepts themselves have an earlier history on the margin of the philosophical tradition, and were changed in being drawn to the centre. In the older Chinese cosmology Heaven ordains by its decree everything which man must accept as unalterable by his actions, the nature he is born with, the moral rules he should obey, the changes of fortune and the day of his death. Confucians ever since Mencius (fl. 320 BC) were very much concerned with the problem that if, as seems evident, there is evil in the nature which man receives from Heaven, to do evil in accordance with one's nature would seem to have the authority of Heaven. During the intervening 1,500 years, even in the periods of least philosophical activity, we find Confucians debating whether human nature is good, or bad, or mixed, or neutral, or good in some and bad in others.

Ch'eng Yi (1033–1107) and Chu Hsi (1130–1200) solved the problem to the satisfaction of later Confucians by changing the paradigm. Heaven, its decree, and other related concepts, were reinterpreted as different aspects of *li*. Man's basic nature was identified with the *li* which, to the extent that his *ch'i* is permeable by it, patterns his behaviour in the moral order which belongs within cosmic order. His basic nature, then, is morally good. The *ch'i* however varies in density from person to person, and the line that I should follow may be hard to discern through the turbid obscuring *ch'i* of which I am composed. The individual's congenitally imperfect constitution is commonly described as his nature, but is not to be confused with his basic nature. The effect of disciplining and training myself morally

5*

is to refine my *ch'i* to a perfect transparency; then the *li* show through and it becomes effortless to live in accord with my nature.

In the arts it has become over the last century not the exception but almost the rule for the innovator at the crucial time of forming his style to find something in another culture from which he can learn, an influence not superficial, as in eighteenth century chinoiserie, but radical (the Impressionists and the Japanese woodcut, Debussy and the Javanese gamelan, Frank Lloyd Wright and Japanese architecture, the Imagists and Japanese and Chinese poetry, the Cubists and African sculpture, Henry Moore and the Mexican Chac Mool, Brecht and Chinese theatre, Artaud and Balinese dance). When Fritjof Capra claims the same kind of affinities between twentieth century physics and Indian and Chinese philosophy (although not the same direct influence), one is at first inclined to demur. There can be no significant relation between a hypothesis in our physics and a superficially similar idea in a tradition which never developed the procedures of mathematization and controlled experiment. But that would be to miss the point. Capra's parallels are between not hypotheses but concepts, for example the *ch'i* and the quantum field [14] Whatever one thinks of his comparisons, there is no difficulty in conceding in principle that physicists breaking with Newtonian concepts would be struggling to unlearn distinctions and assimilations which other cultures will never have made in the first place, so that the fundamentally different conceptualizations even of a pre-literate culture might illuminate him. In the changing conceptual frame inside which a science progresses, it would be as out of place to look for progress as in the styles of an art.

2

VALUATION AND COSMOS-BUILDING

2.1 The languages of means and ends

It has long ceased to be a novelty to say that language, even in its scientific uses, does not afford a point-by-point representation of reality, true on a simple correspondence theory of truth, but adjusts us in complicated ways to the things with which we interact. But there remains an unexamined assumption that, even if we are to take the role of doers rather than pure observers, at any rate it must be as men of reason acting deliberately on things to realize ends. Here, as with our approach to the grounding of valuation, our changed view of the relation between reason and spontaneity demands a shift of perspective. The agent in the first place reacts spontaneously, and it is only after choosing ends from his spontaneous goals that he can choose means to them and act in order to achieve them. It is at the second stage that he comes to distrust the uncertainties of spontaneously intelligent behaviour, and test and control it by reason. The kind of language which is at its most intense in poetry, which excites him to react intelligently instead of equipping him to act rationally, ought then to have the same function in choices of ends as the language of science in choices of means. But if scientists have dropped their pretensions to mirror nakedly a world disguised by the pretty conceits of the poets, a fundamental question arises: why should I any longer allow their language special authority as a vehicle of truth? The language which in questions of means draws me nearest to reality might in questions of ends only push me further away, the reverse of the case of trying to use poetic language to solve practical problems. If how the world looks to me varies with how I interact with it, it is no longer clear that there can be any point in asking whether I see it more as it is—rather, shifting from a visual to a tactile metaphor, am more in touch with it as it is—when acting or when reacting, when thinking or when feeling.

   With the coming of relativity and quantum mechanics, the mad sayings of physicists striving to translate their formulae into the inappropriate medium of words have come to be as remote from common-sense description as those of Zen monks or of King Lear on the heath. Nevertheless, the tendency, even among complainers about the spiritual vacuity of the scientific description of the world, is to have reservations only about its completeness, and try to paste on additional information which keeps peeling off, about God, mind, free will, and value, for which it is supposed insufficient to claim a mere 'poetic truth'. The approach we are considering would allow us to avoid such compromises. Let us explore the possibility that science and poetry are not simply languages suitable among other things for dealing with questions of means and of ends respectively, their whole difference is in being structured to evaluate, in one case as means, in the other as ends. If so, we can stop looking for breaks in the fabric of scientific fact where there might be room for little leaks from the realm of value. Poetic language will be wholly adequate for the valuation as ends of the same things that scientific language is wholly adequate to value as means.

Science and poetry will then be two specialized offshoots from the language, neutral as to ends and means, which describes and narrates. 'The cat sat on the mat' could be used indifferently either to answer the practical question 'Where was the cat?' or to evoke a pleasing picture of furry Pussy by the fire to amuse the child learning to read. Spoken in a real situation, it might provide someone with both a self-sufficient end, the sight of the cat as pleasing in itself, and a means to it, to go to the room where the mat is in the hope that the cat is still there. Detached from context, it provides both a potential end, a sight pleasing or disturbing to lovers or haters of cats, and a potential means, usable not only for seeking out or avoiding the cat but for an indefinite number of other purposes as well. However, even in this specimen of undifferentiated language, the internal rhyme is a first step to structuring the sentence to please the imagination rather than convey a fact. It picks out the image-evoking and, by their affinity in sound, image-fusing words 'cat', 'sat' and 'mat', while distracting attention from the connectives which organize them to make a statement of fact. A phrasing directing attention to the fact rather than to the image would have no use for the rhyme but would specify details helpful in utilizing the information, for example, 'At 5 o'clock the cat was sitting by the dining room fire'. The undifferentiated language includes general as well as particular statements. Thus 'All men are mortal' is relevant to choices of means, such as deciding it is time to make a will, but also to choices of ends, such as to enjoy life while you can, or pursue a goal which will outlast death. In this case it would be when thinking in terms of ends that one might rephrase, in search of concreteness and immediacy, for example to the Biblical 'All flesh is as grass'.

Proceeding from here, we have to keep our usages for 'means' and 'end' firmly parallel. Something will be a self-sufficient end to me, or (to risk deceptive Kantian echoes) end in itself, if I pursue or avoid it for its own sake as spontaneously attractive or repulsive to me, and judge it good or bad irrespective of consequences. It is a means to me if I pursue or avoid it for its consequences, irrespective of immediate attraction or repulsion. Anything may in principle be treated as end, as means, as both at once; deciding between two jobs is a choice of means of support, but also, to the extent that I consider whether the work is interesting, I shall meet stimulating people, travel to new places, the choice of a mode of life as an end in itself. Although we shall generally be dealing with positive means and ends, obstacles as well as aids will come under the heading of means, and the disliked as well as the liked under that of ends. We shall apply both terms primarily to the reaction or action, but also to the object. The axe as well as the chopping would commonly be recognized as means, and by analogy the warm Mediterranean as well as the swimming and sunbathing count as ends for the holiday-maker; and we need not be too particular about distinguishing the car from the act of driving either as means to travel or, for the car-lover, as self-sufficient end. It is important for our case to insist that ends as we understand them do not have to be exclusively, or even primarily, the long-term goals which give conscious direction to a life. Just to interrupt a train of thought for a moment to enjoy the moving pattern of shadow on the back of a transparent leaf in the sun is on the present account a momentary submergence in an end in itself.

We have admitted that the undifferentiated language of description and narration does attain that truth irrespective of means and ends which is claimed, wrongly as we believe, for science, and for poetry as well when it takes the form of dogmatic religion. But it is neutral in the sense, not that it flawlessly mirrors things as they are, without reducing them to means or ends, but that it allows us to treat them as either or both indiscriminately. The two specialized languages have developed to unravel the confusion. Let us start with an open mind as to whether one or other of them might turn out after all to be the nearer to a neutral truth, and see how far we can make them run parallel.

(1) The language of poetry treats as ends, of science as means.

EL (Ends-language). 'How should I respond to X as an end in itself?' = 'How *do* I respond to X when most aware of it?' The answer, different for different individuals (hence 'subjective'), will demand a language which sharpens awareness of the aspects to which one spontaneously reacts, in the first place its look, sound, smell, taste, feel. This language does not affirm or deny, or it does so only incidentally in evoking a response.

ML (Means-language). 'For what could one use it, by what bring it about?' = 'What are its effects and causes?'. The answer, the same for different individuals (hence 'objective'), will demand a language which can affirm or deny causal connexions. In this language I may objectivize even a response of my own, and affirm that it is caused by the object in conjunction with objectivized factors in myself.

(2) An ends-language synthesizes in a concrete whole, a means-language analyses and abstracts from the whole. Here we need a minimum of two components, let us say A regularly followed by B.

EL. One's reactions to an event are modified by anticipation of any consequences and recall of any conditions to which one reacts otherwise. To respond in awareness one has therefore to synthesize in their interdependence A, B and any other related factors, so that the response to each is modified by the responses to the rest.

ML. That A is regularly followed by B suggests that it is usable as a means to B (= is a cause of B), a possibility which may be tested by manipulating A to see how B is affected. To do this A and B must be distinguished from each other and abstracted from their circumstances, including one's own response.

(3) An ends-language particularizes, a means-language generalizes.

EL. To respond in awareness of one occurrence of A and B, one has to ignore whatever A and B have in other circumstances but not now, and synthesize them in a concrete whole which will be further differentiated from all other wholes by every addition made to it.

ML. In establishing that manipulation of A regularly affects B, the regularity is stated as a general law, and A and B treated as the same at each recurrence and abstracted from particular circumstances.

(4) In an ends-language one defines ostensively, in a means-language by substitution of symbols.

EL. In a language which stimulates awareness of the concrete look and feel of things, a colour word, for example, will be inactive unless one can recognize the colour when one sees it. Substitution of other symbols would be useless unless they in their turn were ostensively definable.

ML. Propositions can be combined to make inferences only if their crucial symbols are mutually definable. But the ideal of full mutual definability is attainable only in the artificial symbolisms of logic and mathematics, within the sciences therefore only as far as they are mathematized. A generalization that foam on a liquid will be white is not deducible from other propositions as long as 'white' is definable only ostensively. The owner of a fashionable bar who gets the idea of dying the foam on his beer puce, maroon or magenta might think it could be done after a little trial and error. But since colour theory is mathematized, with the absence of light as black and the mixture of all wavelengths as white, it would be simpler to deduce that light of all wavelengths will become mixed when reflected in all directions from the spherical bubbles, and therefore foam will be white. This deduction could be made by a man born blind who cannot define colour words ostensively.

(5) To show how to respond in awareness of a new particular, an ends-language analogizes; to show how to use it, a means-language applies laws.

EL. By metaphors which compare as synthesized wholes the new particular to others of which one is already aware, one is moved to react in accordance with the similarities and differences of which they make one aware.

ML. By bringing the new particular under an old law, one deduces its causes and effects.

(6) Ends-language is most widely informative through the representative instance, means-language through the general law.

EL. The most representative particular instance is the one which, having the widest range of similarities to others, can be a metaphor for them all. A tragic hero is such a metaphor, and so is the tragedy itself.

ML. The most general law has the widest application to particulars.

(7) An ends-language clarifies the subjective factors in becoming aware, a means-language the objective.

EL. One is made to imagine an object in heightened awareness, stimulated to attend to it for its own sake, and freed from the habit of heeding only the useful, from emotional confusion, bias and self-deception, and from the interests which blind to other viewpoints. Whether the object exists, and if not whether it resembles the existing sufficiently to be an instructive metaphor for it, is a question outside the language, which does not affirm or deny (as noticed under Point 1 above).

ML. One weighs the objective evidence for the truth of propositions, irrespective of willingness or reluctance to accept them.

(8) As to whether what is said has to be taken into account in choices (let us not waste effort over the words 'reality' and 'truth'), in the case of ends-language it is tested subjectively and privately, by experience or imaginative simulation; in the case of means-language, objectively and publicly, by experimental replication.

EL. One confirms, within the limits of one's information, that the object would appear so, and that this is how one would feel about it, by assuming the same viewpoint and being moved to the same response. The test is private, in that it is binding only for myself, a point which has nothing to do with infallible intuitions or with public unobservability.[1] If there is a consensus against me I may doubt myself, re-examine my feelings, suspect that with maturing awareness I shall come to react like other people, and that it will turn out that after all they were right. But at my present level of awareness I can only stick to my authentic response and guard against being overawed into falsifying it. However, each person's awareness from his own and others' viewpoints is subject to public tests, including behavioural tests of whether he or they are responding as he supposes. Granted our claims for the objectivity of value judgements,[2] the results of conflicting private tests will converge with increasing awareness from multiplying viewpoints, and if we could achieve full agreement on the objective facts would be identical in all whose interpretation of their private feelings coincides with the public evidence of their behaviour.

ML. The testing which in ends-language must be private must in means-language be public. That manipulation of A does regularly affect B is confirmed by the experiment of repeating the manipulation. The test is public in the sense, not that it is publicly available (although this is of course a necessary condition), but that if binding for one it is binding for all. Since the effects of a manipulation are independent of who performs it, my own experiments have no privileged status.

(9) An ends-language systematizes a cosmos by synthesizing the harmonious or conflicting reactions to things in larger and larger wholes, a means-language by subsuming propositions about things under wider and wider laws.

EL. The reactions to interrelated things as self-sufficient ends will either harmonize or conflict. They may be structured from an individual viewpoint within the limits of a self-contained work of art, but if one reduces to more and more simplified patterns there is no necessary terminus to their expansion short of a poetic or mythic cosmos in which everything is pure end, good in itself or bad in itself, whether structured from an individual or from a social viewpoint.[3]

ML. A cosmos organized to expose the potentialities of each thing as means is that of science.

At the final stages, the two extremes of language can be seen to run parallel in their relation to and divergence from the elementary truth of 'The cat sat on the mat' or 'All men are mortal'. At the earlier stages it was not in question that the object to which one responds does exist, and that at every trial B follows A. But at Stage 6 the possibility of fiction arises with both the representative instance and —only a little less obviously—the general law. As far as exemplary persons are concerned, it is nowadays easily comprehensible that the hero or anti-hero in whom the widest variety of people see similarities to themselves and from whom consciously or unconsciously they learn how to see, feel, and act, is as likely to emerge from drama or story as from life. But the ability to take fiction seriously without confusing it with fact has not always been a commonplace. For much of the past, acknowledged fiction has been treated as light entertainment, and all models found in sacred narrative assumed to be historical. Dream, hallucination, poetic imagination, being independent of the will, seemed intelligible only as true or deceitful revelations from beyond. Narrative poets seem to have taken their imagination for a vision of events as they actually happened; Homer, and the other earliest Greek poets, appeal to the Muses, not to infuse them with eloquence, but to prime them with the facts.[4] Anyone brought up (as I was myself) to believe in the great myth of the Garden of Eden as literal truth, written down by a divinely-inspired historian, has himself lived and thought within the same cultural assumptions. That a law of nature might, like a myth, perform its functions without being literally true, is a more recent and not yet fully assimilated idea. It did not compel attention until physicists got used to playing such tricks as treating electrons for some purposes as particles and for others as waves. Yet at the very beginnings of modern science in the sixteenth century it was an open issue whether the earth indeed revolves round the sun or the Copernican theory is no more than a fiction useful for calculating the positions of the planets. Why should we have to insist on the truth even, for example, of Newton's First Law, that a body if not acted on by external forces remains either at rest or in uniform motion in a straight line—a motion which whenever observed does have a force sustaining it? In what sense is a law about events which never happen any less a fiction than an instructive story about people who never lived? Granted that the law is indispensable for economical explanation and prediction, economy is only a human convenience, and there is no reason to expect the universe to be simple rather than complicated. The law is at the foundations of a system by means of which calculation arrives at accurate results; but to suppose that every component of the system must have something corresponding to it in reality is no better than presuming that since one cannot count things in irrational numbers no sum which includes them could work out, or that every word in a sentence must have its counterpart in the state of affairs, assumptions which in the past history of thought have had to be painfully unlearned like that of the historicity of myths.

We may push the parallelism further. At Stage 1 we acknowledged ends-language as subjective and means-language as objective, which is the most obvious consideration which can lead one to think of a scientific description as true and a poetic description not. However, there was the further difference that ends-language particularizes while means-language generalizes. Thinking in ends-language, we do advance to generality and objectivity as we grow used to treating viewpoints as fluid and equal. The converse, that even in means-language description of particulars is subjective and relative to viewpoint, would have seemed absurd throughout the reign of Newton's physics, but is basic to Einstein's. When Milton in *May morning* writes

> Now the bright morning star, day's harbinger,
> Comes dancing from the East...

his description of the rise of Venus is affected not only by his position as earthly observer for whom morning and evening stars are different phenomena, but by his joy at the coming of spring and eagerness for the dawn, and by associations special to his culture and himself which make him think of the planet as like a harbinger, as though of an army or royal train, and its rising as like a dance. A description of the event observed by Milton deduced from the laws of planetary motion by a physicist would escape subjectivity on all these points. But the physicist's account would be limited to spatio-temporal measurements, which are all that remain of those 'primary qualities' which once seemed to be firmly located in the object and independent of the observer (Locke for example enumerated five of them, solidity, extension, figure, motion and rest, and number). With the Special Theory of Relativity these measurements too turned out to be relative to the observer. Granted that disagreements over the times and distances of Venus will be negligible for observers who do not travel nearly as fast as light, so are disagreements over colour among people of normal sight, divergences over morals in a homogeneous community, differences in imagining the rise of Venus among conventional poets drawing on a common stock of clichés. At either extreme of language, objectivity is approached only by co-ordinating descriptions from different viewpoints, in the one case analysing and in the other synthesizing. The conflicting measurements of distances and durations by travellers at different speeds do not worry the physicist, because analysis and abstraction have arrived at laws of nature in conjunction with which the measurements are mutually derivable. In the case of the changing shape of an object viewed from different angles, the escape from subjectivity is through synthesizing, so that one recognizes it from an unfamilar direction without having to make geometrical calculations. Similarly, in synthesizing viewpoints, you might guess without my telling you that something which is bad from yours is good from mine, even discern that something I now think is bad I would with greater awareness see to be good from mine. To describe a particular thing as good or bad, beautiful or ugly, is as much and as little subjective or objective as describing it as 13.74 metres long. Thinking of the descriptions as different in kind may turn out to be no more than a historical accident, in an individualistic and scientifically progressive culture already familiar with diversity in taste and morals but not yet with speeds approaching that of light.

A language of means is committed to affirm or deny causal connexions, therefore it is confined to living verbal language and to the artificial symbolisms of logic and mathematics. But a language of ends, which at its minimum has only to make us perceive or imagine and respond, has at its disposal every kind of symbolism, words, pictures, theatre, music, dance, even mathematics in the shape of numerology. A language which can excite a reaction valued for itself has of course all sorts of applications, entertainment, advertisement, propaganda, ritual. But for an ethic derived from 'Be aware' its supreme function will be to evoke a response justified as an end in itself by its heightening of awareness. Since the works most highly valued for themselves are commonly dignified by the name of 'Art', we must decide how 'Be aware' relates to aesthetic standards. Although such standards are variable, and even more variably named, something will be gained if it can be shown that the value of, let us say, unity within variety, truth to nature, authenticity of feeling, spontaneity, clarity and vividness of imagery, detachment, pleasure, affirmation,[5] can be derived directly or indirectly from the principle of awareness. This will entitle us to recognize the arts as the repository of publicly available examples of what we understand by an aware spontaneity. Generally speaking, our episodes of fullest awareness are transient and elusive, and the detail cannot be fixed in memory; only the artist knows how to use words, notes or brushstrokes to stimulate and control them, and in shaping them for himself he puts them on record for the rest of us. The goals to which he spontaneously tends in his heightened awareness are available to reader or spectator as potential ends, which will become actual to him too if his own viewpoint is close to the artist's; their role corresponds to that of causes in the sciences, potential means which become actual if he is pursuing the ends which they serve.

We may start with a term common to criticism of the arts and to the title of this book, spontaneity. If ends are to be chosen or rejected from among the goals of spontaneous tendency, the work which is an end in itself must in the first place be spontaneous, not intellectually constructed like a scientific or philosophical study. Not that the spontaneity is a virtue in itself; to take it as the main test of value would assume a highly questionable idealization of Nature inherited from Romanticism. Nor is it to be equated with a full surrender to automatism, as in early Surrealism. The writing and reading of a text may demand intense intellectual effort, only provided that it never ceases to be an ultimately synthesizing process for which analysis is an aid but not a substitute. It will be enough that there is a certain line of growth independent of the author's will, a direction to which he is faithful even if characters get out of hand and the story runs counter to any intended moral or political message. One assurance to him of not having missed it is that a word, sentence, episode, however carefully pondered, can assume new meanings and dimensions in retrospect to the author himself. As for the reader, he may have to think very deeply before being satisfied that he understands difficult writing, but the thinking is not about how he ought to feel, in coming to understand he discovers how he does feel, and perhaps surprises and alarms himself. However much he may learn from critics, to let them tell him what to feel, disguising from himself his own boredom, moral revulsion or supposedly vulgar enjoyment, would be to turn his back on an opportunity to throw off preconceptions and renew his ends by returning to the spontaneity from which they are born, in an awareness enhanced by the artist beyond his own normal capacity. Any standard or convention which can be cited against him has itself, so we have argued,[6] had the same origin, and deserves acceptance only if reconfirmed by this reversion to spontaneity.

To approve the spontaneity of a work of art will then be to single it out from the commonplace mass of the artificial and derivative as one which has at any rate distinguished itself as being approachable as an end in itself whether positive or negative, which can move us in a new direction either for better or for worse. In certain circumstances it might be reasonable to claim that conventions have become so sterile that any breakthrough into spontaneity is better than none, wherever it may lead. However, there always remains the question whether spontaneity is tending towards enhanced or diminished awareness, which on the present thesis must be the final test of whether the work is good or bad. An art begins, shall we say, with the discovery that manipulation of an exciting shape or sequence of sounds hits on preservable or repeatable patterns which enhance the effect. To the extent that the effect pleases, it draws one spontaneously into deepening awareness of the object, and the response distinguishes itself from the commonplace as positively good, a withdrawal from projects into present experience of spontaneity in heightened awareness. However, the merely pleasant implies only a localized awareness, which may shut off awareness of anything beyond it. To do more than amuse, the work will have to enlarge awareness of one's world and of oneself, which is to tell the truth in one or other of the specialized senses in which the word 'truth' is applied to the arts. In the first place there is truth to oneself, the sense specified by 'sincerity' and 'authenticity', words which commend self-awareness and warn against self-deception. For our ethic, it is crucial: all valuation starts from how you *do* react when aware, and to confuse it with how you suppose that you *ought* to be reacting poisons valuation at the source. In this usage truth has nothing to do with mimesis, and even the emotions roused by music can be judged true or false. At the level of sensation, the arts break down the habit of noticing only the practically relevant, and restore the plenitude of the response when the senses are open to what normally eludes them. The value of the vivid and distinct image in poetry derives from this sharpening of awareness, not from its accuracy alone, which is why, however accurate it may be, becoming a cliché erodes the effect. As for 'truth to life', 'truth to nature', whether a novel or drama illuminates the constants of human nature or the detail of contemporary trends, it does so not by telling new facts, but by forcing us to imagine concretely situations we know only in the abstract, or to see all sides of an issue which involves us personally.

Here our enterprise of restating commonplaces about the arts in terms of awareness may help to clarify why 'truth', however vaguely the word may be used in the arts, is generally understood to be something more than, for example, a portrait being a good likeness. Looking at a portrait by Rembrandt, in the first place the eye is attracted by the pattern of paint on the canvas, which compels an awareness of minute distinctions and remote relationships of line and colour of which the spectator is hardly capable in gazing at a natural object, by the force of a highly synthesized design in which impressions harmonize and reinforce each other instead of conflicting and confusing like accidental phenomena. The intensity of awareness of a pattern of brush strokes enriches awareness of things outside it, on the one hand of the contrasts of light and shadow in nature to which Rembrandt is so sensitive, on the other of images which the configuration resembles—firstly, for those who knew him, the figure of the sitter (and one would expect that after praising the likeness they would see more in the man himself than they had noticed before, as from his self-portraits we see more in Rembrandt), then, for any viewer, of a coherently characterized person, of a human type, of Man in general. That what matters is not some abstract truth embodied in the work, but an intensified awareness radiating out from the instance in a web of analogies, is especially clear when it is impossible to pin down the theme of a work. It is not that Kafka was writing stories about the frustrations of bureaucracy, the destiny of the Jew, the isolation of the individual in an atomized mass society, or the anguish of knowing oneself judged by an unfathomable but unquestionable authority, one's father, the state, God, but that he created an imaginative structure rich in analogues, from a point of vantage from which to see especially far and deep into seemingly disparate situations.

Following this line of argument, it can be seen that a piece of writing, painting or music will most clearly exhibit its fidelity to 'Be aware', its right to stand as positive end in itself, if it fulfils certain other of the traditional conditions of a work of art. In the untidiness of daily life there is no certain limit to the factors which, if we were aware of them, might alter a response provisionally accepted as a self-sufficient end. To escape the possibility of revision requires a self-contained system in which responses are modified by each other but by nothing outside. But the system which most educates in an aware responsiveness will also be one in which the responses adapt to the widest range of factors. This then will be one which has the 'Unity within variety' of an organic whole, in which according to Aristotle the parts 'are so organized that if any part is displaced or removed the whole is disjointed and disturbed'.[7] In novel or drama 'Be aware', since it admits no privileged viewpoints, will forbid self-identification with a favourite among the characters, not excluding a first-person narrator. This self-elimination is for aesthetics 'detachment' or 'impersonality', but as a renunciation of egoism it also has a moral dimension. On the argument of this book, to think morally is to synthesize one's reactions from the viewpoints of all involved. If so, when the subject of a work of art is human relations, there will be no difference between being aesthetically successful and being moral. A person in a story is real to the extent that one is aware of the action from his viewpoint, and the reader responding from the viewpoints of solidly realized persons, in awareness higher than is ever attainable in the confusions of life, is sustaining for a few hours and in an imaginary situation a degree of moral sensitivity beyond his usual capacity. Granted that he needs to be on the lookout for disproportions in awareness which do injustices to the characters, these as infringements of 'Be aware' are not only moral but aesthetic faults. Then it is no proof of immorality if an author moves me to sympathies in conflict with what I suppose to be my highest standards. If he indeed obeys 'Be aware' he is more moral than my standards; by throwing me back into a spontaneity which dissolves conventional judgements, at the same time opening my eyes from previously unexplored viewpoints on to unfamiliar situations, he returns me to the roots of morality and restores the power to revise standards in the light of fuller awareness. He does not even have to persuade me that he is consciously moral at all. Anyone who is impatient of an explicit moral in a story, and persuaded that a writer best expresses his moral vision by showing his characters in their situations without taking the side of any of them, might at this point ask himself why he has come to take for granted this apparently paradoxical position, and whether he has a better justification for it than ours.

To treat the arts as morally instructive or dangerous is not at time of writing a fashionable line. In the absence of agreed standards, is it not an impertinence to preach or condemn? But the point of interest for us is precisely that there can be morality in art without the support of standards. Nor is the claim that the arts provide a moral education, for those who want it, discredited by their lack of moral effect on those who do not. It is felt by some that it ought to be impossible to go back on the moral vision of the masters once it is comprehended, so that when the commandant of a concentration camp turns out to have a taste for classical music it comes as a disappointment that understanding of the arts does not, any more than belief in God, change people who do not want to be changed. But this is to forget the precariousness of awareness outside the realm of means, where it is forced on us by the obstructiveness of circumstance. Aesthetic awareness is, not of obstinate facts which once grasped go on nagging if one tries to ignore them, but of transient webs of image, thought and emotion so intricate and extended that the detail is fading from memory the instant attention moves elsewhere. The highest states of awareness are the ones hardest to sustain, the ones which leave us freest to learn or ignore. In fiction no doubt I have learned to maintain impartiality towards characters without identifying myself with a favourite, but in ordinary life I *am* identical with the favourite. There is no need to be surprised that in practice the pressures of an English department, or rivalries of an artistic clique, or vanities of any circle which includes the arts among the weapons of gamesmanship, make it almost a matter of chance whether the mind expands or contracts under the influence of great literature.

This approach to the arts leads back to where it began, to spontaneity and its relation to pleasure. As the arts come to engage more deeply with misery and catastrophe, they move far away from entertainment, yet for reasons explored already[8] there has always to be some stirring of attraction to coax forward into responding to what ordinarily would repel awareness. The bored reader of a science book can make an effort of attention, but exertion of will to get through a novel is worthwhile only if it revives at least intermittently that spontaneous quickening of awareness without which one is not responding fruitfully. How it is that an artist can transmute anguish into pleasure may be a psychological puzzle, but in the last resort one does enjoy Hopkins' 'Terrible sonnets' and Goya's black paintings, or else gets nothing from them. The inviolability of the pleasure principle is not a peculiarity of the aesthetic, it applies to ends-language in general. The ordinary motive for manipulating symbols to excite a response without further purpose is to entertain, and what is glorified as art is a kind of entertainment somehow felt to do one more lasting good. It may seem curious to suggest that even a religious or civil ceremony is subject to the pleasure principle. Yet to the extent that a rite is expected to nourish attitudes valued for themselves, adoration, faith, hope, repentance, civic pride, martial spirit, fellowship, you prove yourself a full participant by your joy and zeal, and visible boredom is read as a sign of being irreligious or unpatriotic.

We have discussed the dilemma in requiring awareness of an uncomfortable world from creatures, such as we are, who are naturally adapted to be vividly aware only of what pleases them.[9] A consequence is that, although aversion to an unwelcome fact is conquerable by will, the imagination of an evil can spontaneously intensify only if the work is either affirmative, opening up a hopeful possibility, or else morbidly negative, masochistically depressing or sadistically exciting. As with the spontaneous in general, the alternative to being lifted up is to be dragged down. To insist that great art is affirmative may seem an evasion of the worst in life. But the choice is not between affirmation and recognition of things as they are, but between the pleasures of affirmation, the pleasures of negation, and silence. The tradition of high art always acknowledged a tract of life beyond its range, in which indeed it tended to include the entire life of the common people. That the socially unmentionable can after all be assimilated was proved by nineteenth century Naturalism. But there always remains an uncomprehended chaos of apathy and meaningless pain outside the reach of art. Samuel Beckett, who gets as far into it as anyone, still fertilizes it with humour, word-music, an ineradicable Irish charm; and when these dry up, he bores.

It appears then that the points on which critical debate centres are those where it can be shown that a work directly or indirectly sharpens or dulls the capacity to respond with awareness. Does it follow that the value of a work can be publicly demonstrated by showing how it enhances awareness or indulges unawareness? Such a demonstration is persuasive, even meaningful, only for someone already spontaneously reacting to the work; critical comments are verbiage to people who happen to be unresponsive to the art in question. There always remains then the necessity, having assimilated all publicly available information, of referring judgement to the private test of how I myself do respond. The arts provide the clearest illustration of Point 8 of our differences between the languages of means and of ends, that in the former confirmation is public but in the latter private. The obligation to judge for myself is in no way reduced by unanimity among qualified judges. Consensus in the arts, although often incomplete and transient, is sometimes more stable than in the sciences; Shakespeare's reputation as the greatest writer in English, which was consolidating about the time of Newton, has survived through all later changes of fashion to outlast the reign of Newtonian physics. Nevertheless, in case of conflict between majority judgment and my own, only the latter can affect the spontaneous preferences behind my choices of ends. There is no parallel in the arts to a scientist dismissing his own observations as mistaken because the observations of others have consistently failed to confirm them, and proceeding to act on a hypothesis supported by theirs. I may suspect that there is more to a writer than I can yet see, as everybody else seems to think so, and should I be a lecturer in English, give him more space in a course than he seems to me to deserve, but he cannot influence my underlying attitudes to things until I do begin to catch on to him. If my subjective feeling conflicts with valid public tests I am wrong; but only if my feeling does alter to accord with the public tests can I know that I was wrong.

Turning now to the language of means, it is most transparent when a thing designed for fighting, sitting down or knocking in nails is named by its function 'sword', 'chair' or 'hammer'. But utilization as means requires a corpus of knowledge about the possible uses and disadvantages irrespective of their relevance or irrelevance to present ends, for example of constituents of the hammer also usable to make other things and neutrally named 'wood' and 'iron'. Within this corpus it will be necessary to speak of the sword-thrust and the wound without regard to whether the piercing of flesh was intended or accidental, and treat them both as potential means to an indefinite variety of ends, that is, as causes. When the corpus reaches the stage of Newtonian science the whole universe can be seen as a complex tool, a machine, intelligible to the extent that one can take it to pieces and find out how it works, with all causality as a 'mechanical' relation. As long as scientific ideology remains deistic, causes can even be identified as the actual means of the divine watch-maker, ultimately serving the actual end for which he started the universe ticking; and it remains plausible to think of a cause as exerting force to impel an effect, after the analogy of those causes which are human acts. But with the discarding of God as an unnecessary hypothesis, the ultimate end lapses, and we are left with a pure system of potential means at the disposal of man. With the disappearance of any rational agent other than man, it comes to be seen that to choose cause A as a means you do not have to think of it as pushing effect B, it is enough to know that you can predict B from A by applying a law of nature. With the further recognition that there need be no necessary connexion between A and B, only a statistical regularity, thinking in terms of cause and effect becomes as dispensable as thinking directly in terms of means and ends. As the analysis of relations increases in sophistication, it becomes possible to pursue it as a purely theoretical activity, in indifference to its practical applications. The Newtonian cosmos is a beautiful machine, and the pleasure of appreciating how the parts of the universe fit together always remains the supreme instance of that joy which makes some people seem happier pulling their cars to pieces than driving them. A car is none the less designed as a means to transport, and the relations which fascinate disinterested seekers of truth are between things as they have been conceptualized in the process of learning how to use them.

This account of the matter will not be welcome to everyone. It will be agreed that post-Galilean science has always been linked with technology, and deserves the credit for the accelerating material progress of the last few centuries, even that its spread throughout the world testifies less to a universal hunger for truth than to the promise of new goods and above all the threat of new weapons. But why has modern science such tremendous practical effectiveness? Surely, it may be said, because of its uniquely rigorous procedures for establishing objective truth, which clear away all confusions of emotion, distortions of perception, mystifications of poetry and religion, to reveal the world as it really is. This may seem simple enough, but one may still ask whether the truths of science are to be conceived as true answers to what are ultimately questions of means, which is all that we are claiming, or some kind of deeper truth on which the answers depend. To suppose the latter would be to take an unthinking turn into metaphysics which science can hardly countenance. After all, it did not achieve its great takeoff until it abandoned the Aristotelian search for Being and reduced its questions from 'What is it?' to the more modest and practical 'How does it work?'

Can it be seriously maintained that the truths of science have that neutrality as to means and to ends which we admired in 'The cat sat on the mat'? There could be no more striking asymmetry; as far as ends are concerned, a scientific cosmos is utterly empty of value and meaning, and is muddled instead of improved if you try to introduce them; yet in relation to means, it is as though it were deliberately designed for man's convenience. It will be said perhaps that this is simply how the universe has turned out to be—nowhere a trace of that value with which religions glorified it, everywhere that infinitely extendable web of causal relations where every new discovery adds to man's power. Why not accept it as our fortune that we find ourselves in the one respect deprived, in the other more prodigally favoured by the order of nature than pre-Galilean man ever suspected? But the asymmetry is not something which has emerged with the discoveries of science, it has been implicit in its procedures from the start. The sciences systematize knowledge of how to predict from, and retrospectively explain by, preceding conditions. There may be no *a priori* reason why our explanatory-predictive apparatus should have turned out so successful, but obviously that apparatus has nothing to do with evaluating things as ends in themselves. If explanatory-predictive science is mistaken for the systematization of knowledge in general, then of course it will seem that the cosmos (like the corpus of the knowledge) has no place for ends, yet as a storehouse of available means is arranged (again like the corpus) exactly as we would wish it.

'The cat sat on the mat' is unspecialized description independent of both ends and means, and can serve as well for inferring that there was only one cat, and that it was not in the garden, as for imagining the sound of its purr and the feel of its coat. Scientific description is fundamentally different. It has methodically eliminated all the sensible qualities for which one might contemplate a thing for its own sake, and in physics succeeded in narrowing itself down to spatio-temporal measurements fitted to its mathematized explanatory-predictive laws. Back in the seventeenth and eighteenth centuries philosophers still took it for granted that such a description can and must convey an 'idea' in the sense of a mental picture, divested of colour and other secondary qualities, but still visualizable as a geometrical figure. It was assumed that the unimaginable would be the unrecognizable for observation, therefore for science the unreal. But in due course even visualization had to be discarded as a hindrance to non-Euclidean geometries. With this step the abstract idea as such comes near to being a contradiction in terms, an image abstracted from everything imaginable. The breakout from this impasse may be dated from Peirce's review of Berkeley's works in 1871. Against Berkeley's principle that nothing of which one cannot frame an idea can be real, Peirce declares mental pictures irrelevant to science, and lays down the Pragmatist test, 'Do things fulfil the same purpose practically?', later clarified as

Consider what effects, that might conceivably have practical bearings, we conceive the object of our conception to have. Then, our conception of these effects is the whole of our conception of the object.[10]

But in science this amounts to saying that every symbol for a concept derives its whole meaning from its relevance to choices of means. The principle of asking of a term in scientific language only how it is applied in practice has outlasted Pragmatism; it is in poetic language that we still take the side of Berkeley and insist on the sharply distinct image. It has not been sufficiently noticed that to take this step is in effect to renounce all pretensions of science to strip the object of all its human associations in order to expose its naked reality. Science simply transfers the object from one human interest to another; in detaching it from emotion, perception, imagination, from all reactions which can be self-sufficient ends, it attaches it indissolubly to the deliberate actions which are means to them.

There is another direction from which we may approach the problem and reach the same result. We go to the sciences to learn what will happen under given conditions. Often the conditions are simpler than will occur naturally, so that they have to be artificially contrived and controlled, in experiment or in the designing of a machine, in order to get the intended result. In other cases the natural conditions are relatively simple and out of reach of human interference, so that the prediction of consequences becomes prophecy, for example of the planetary motions. The issue then may be reduced to this question: do I resort to the sciences

(1) to predict what will happen if I do this or that, including what will happen anyway whatever I do, or

(2) to predict unconditionally, just as I retrodict the past?

Now it is plain that events which I myself decide or influence by my decisions cannot be predicted from preceding conditions by me, although conceivably they may be by others. For these events I can make only conditional predictions of what will happen if I do this or that, which is alternative A. But if there are circumstances to which only A can apply, B is irrelevant, because it explains nothing which is not covered by that item in A 'including what will happen anyway whatever I do.' Information about what will happen if I do this or that is precisely the information required for choices of means.

With scientific progress and growing mastery over nature, there is a continuing transfer of events from the prophesiable to the decidable, so that each agent's blind spot for unconditional prediction expands indefinitely. No doubt for some time to come we shall go on being sure that the sun will rise tomorrow, as a recurring event outside man's control. But in the early 1940s, before it was certain that there could be a nuclear explosion without an uncontrollable chain reaction, there must have been physicists who were in real doubt as to how much longer there would be an earth revolving round the sun; perhaps mankind will never again enjoy more than brief respites from that thought. It is also theoretically conceivable, on a more optimistic forecast, that mankind will some day become a community of voluntarily co-operating individuals so well informed and sensitive to each other that there will no longer be any irrevocably predictable events for anybody, only the results of harmonized decisions how to act or to refrain from action; mankind would approach the omniscience and omnipotence of a God who does not predict but decides. This flight of fancy suggests another test between A and B. On Position A, science will have been perfected as a tool for choosing means. But Position B leads to the paradoxical conclusion that since with every advance in control over natural events science undermines its capacity for making more than hypothetical predictions, it loses in relation to the future its proper function of discovering truths.

Position B is implicitly deterministic, Position A is not. Determinism of the old-fashioned sort, which has me bound by chains of cause and effect, and pushed from behind by causes when I suppose myself to be pushing towards goals, is no longer viable in any case. A modern determinism, confined to the claim that all macroscopic events including my own actions are unconditionally predictable in principle, runs up against the difficulty that even in principle there can be no observer in a position to make the predictions. Such an observer would have to carry in his brain full information about a certain span of the duration of every-thing, and therefore be more complex than the universe around him, which is a contradiction. He would also have to withdraw from all action. Granted that an agent can progressively remove events from the influence of his own choices and so increase their predictability by refraining from interference, there remain at least two barriers to reducing himself to the condition of pure observer. The first, already recognized by Marx in his *Theses on Feuerbach* of 1845, is the observer's interaction with others in society. The sociological analysis becomes a conservative or radical influence on the society analysed, the straw poll anticipating the election affects its outcome, the form of the anthropologist's questions contaminates the tribesman's conceptualization of his myths and rites. The second barrier, Heisen-berg's discovery, is at the sub-atomic level where the particles of the light used to observe will jolt the particles observed, and has necessitated a new physics (in-comprehensible to innumerates such as myself) in which the observer has to include himself as agent in the account of the observation. Scientific progress might conceivably, as we noticed, extend man's powers as agent until there remains nothing predictable unconditionally, but the reverse, his reduction to a pure observer in a deterministic universe, has ceased to be even a theoretical possibility.

May I rest assured then that my actions are ultimately unpredictable for others as for myself, and therefore I enjoy free will? The present argument does not quite touch the traditional problem of whether there is free will, what it is and whether it matters, and it may be as well not to get involved in it. Our position certainly allows the possibility that my behaviour might be fully predictable to a detached observer of a higher order of complexity than man. Perhaps some day earth will be invaded from outer space by androids of superhuman complexity to whom humans and their interactions will appear as simple and in principle predictable as billiard balls to us. Such beings, let us say, can understand me subjectively by simulation, but disdain to do so, and prefer to explain and predict the motions of so elementary a creature as they would of an automaton. Then I would have to admit that I can be reduced to pure means, wholly manipulable for ends other than my own. Nevertheless, my chosen ends, although mere means to his own ends for the android, would remain ends for me. It would be a humbling experi-ence, but it would not be the annihilation of all value which many see in every kind of materialism, positivism or determinism. On the contrary I would be humbled because the androids are my superiors, who react with an awareness beyond my comprehension; what could I do but hail the coming of the *Übermensch* and resign myself to going the way of the dinosaurs?

If science is to be understood as the thinking, not of observers, but of agents acting upon nature and each other, each agent will be applying the laws of nature to explain, or conditionally or unconditionally predict, events which he objec-tivizes as potential means, including the outermost of his own thoughts and emo-tions. At the core of him, not objectivizable by himself nor describable by him in scientific language, is the spontaneously emerging, the source of his ends. At this centre he is reachable by the language of poetry but not of science. Let us say that I am thinking rationally, as I suppose, about the probable consequences of someone's act, and notice with surprise the angry pounding of my heart. The anger is driving me towards a vengeful act which, as I begin to devise means to it, I perceive to seem acceptable as an end only because I am seeing things out of proportion. In asking myself why I am so angry I objectivize the emotion, and recognize it not only as a disadvantage in the present situation but as a self-indulgence to which I am prone which can in general endanger ends which demand a cool head. Thus a reaction of my own, in being transferred to the realm of means, is externalized as one of the causally interrelated phenomena which I analyse in the language of means; I attend to its causes and effects, worry perhaps that it is visible to and exploitable by others who know my weaknesses. With this, my own reaction can itself become a stimulus to further reactions of mine, such as alarm or shame at my lack of self-control, emotions which can afterwards be objectivized in their turn.

As material for science my objectivized anger belongs in the first place to psychology, but in that all sciences aspire to the state of physics, the ideal would be to identify it as a commotion in my nervous system, and provide a mathematized description of the neural event. In theory I can admit that even the innermost reactions which for ever elude objectivization by myself might be analysed as neural process by other agents. It may be that some day we shall be able to cast on a screen magnified images of regions of each other's brains, and read them as we read each other's faces, but following the most intimate thoughts and feelings— an enhancement of empathy beyond the hopes of the most sensitive and intuitive, made possible by technology. At the same time, let us imagine, each of us has access to strings of mathematical formulae which can be applied by others to observations of himself to predict in given circumstances everything he will do. It would then be quite obvious that the scientific description is a symbolization usable only in choices of means. A description of a simulable activity, state or disposition ('He glares/he is angry/he will start throwing things about') enables one both objectively to observe and subjectively to simulate. But I cannot sub-jectively simulate the content of a mathematical formula. I could consult my own personal formulae to learn peripheral things about myself, for example to explain or predict the consequences of some ailment or temperamental weak-ness which is getting in the way of my plans. But when choosing my ends, I could use only the screen, to project and imagine myself into the brains of others whose ends I am weighing against my own, I could not consult my personal formula to predict my own choice. This is not because the decision is a mental event beyond the reach of science. It is simply because my own decisions are not predictable by myself, except by provisionally deciding in advance; others may consult my personal formulae to predict how I will decide if they do this or that, but if I were to attempt a prediction myself the result of my computation would in turn become a fact relevant to my choice but not yet taken into account when the computation was made. The formulae then would be usable precisely to the extent that I or something about me is being treated as a means. To protest that the scientific description is an unrecognizable portrait which reduces me to pure means would however be a misunderstanding. An explanatory-predictive formula is not a portrait of me at all. To feel degraded would be to assume just what is here denied, that a scientific formula applying to me is the one and only true description of me, and that if it is complete my subjective impression of myself must be an illusion.

There is another feature of science which betrays its exclusive relevance to choices of means; it cannot be tested privately, only publicly. We noticed[11] that a statement is relevant to means only if testable publicly, to ends only if testable privately. In the case of human behaviour at least we expect a true statement to satisfy both tests, and if we fail to reconcile them are not committed to one rather than the other. That someone glares and throws things about is evidence of his anger which is the same for all observers, that in my incipient simulation I feel the anger surge is a test binding for myself alone. If the second test fails I might say, 'I don't think he's angry at all, he's putting it on', and try without success to translate into a publicly testable form my unalterable conviction that his gestures *feel* exaggerated. To the extent that sitting is conceived as an act, not a mere physical process, even 'The cat sat on the mat' is not fully testable by me without some shadow of simulation of the cat feeling the warmth of the fire and curling up on the rug. But science, which takes such pride in admitting only the most strictly tested results, is not simply mistrustful of the reliability of private tests, it aspires in human behaviour as elsewhere to the mathematized description which, not being subjectivizable, cannot be privately tested at all.

In the case of events already past, in which I can no longer intervene, it may seem that science does inform me of no more nor less than the objective truth of what did happen. But let us consider the manner in which science judges the reality of such past events as interest it, which is as remarkable and in some respects as alien to common sense as the rules of evidence in law. Outside the sciences, we do to some extent infer from general principles that something will, may or cannot happen, but only as one of many approaches—seeing for ourselves or listening to witnesses, comparing their testimony and scrutinizing its contradictions, estimating their opportunities for first-hand observation, their intelligence, motives, honesty and so forth. In human affairs at least, we do not suspend judgment until an event is replicated under the same conditions, circumstances being too complex to be perfectly replicated at all. In one discipline, history, the criteria for weighing testimony are so well developed that the status of a science is sometimes claimed for it. But in the mathematized disciplines which have a stronger claim to the name of science, physics being the exemplar, repeatability is all-important. One retrodicts what did happen as one predicts what will, on the grounds that under the given conditions it always must. There is strict inspection of the procedures of the observer, which have to conform to stringent standards, but not of his character or motives. Although scientists have as strong motives for faking results as ghost-hunters and spoon-benders, and sometimes do, there is no need for them to scrutinize each other's honesty with the suspiciousness of historians and lawyers on a perpetual lookout for bias and falsehood, because results which turn out to be unreplicable are inadmissible even if presented in good faith, but if replicated are acceptable even if the discoverer turns out later to have tampered with his figures (as for example the geneticist Mendel is thought to have done).[12] On the other hand if one cannot identify conditions under which a reported phenomenon will recur, it is against the rules to accept it on the testimony of witnesses however reliable, even if one is a witness oneself. Now it may be admitted that in the case of the past, unlike the future, there would be no objection in principle to assuming the role of pure observer of a deterministic universe, able to retrodict all past events by applying the laws of nature to present observation, and dispense with fallible human testimony. But this perfection, even assuming determinism, is not practically attainable. To narrow the rules of evidence to this point is to give up all claims to discover the truth about the past beyond the range of events retrodictable in practice by current explanatory-predictive laws—that is, in the last resort, events directly or indirectly relevant to the choices of means which have guided the development of the science.

It will perhaps be said that this self-restriction is a consequence of renouncing all but the strictest canons for judging truth, and that other kinds of knowledge show their inferiority by their vulnerability to the personal failings of witnesses. But when one speaks of the rigour with which the laws of nature are established, the comparison is with the rules-of-thumb of practical experience, which have also won a conditional acceptance by a repeated confirmation of expectations, but fall short of the strict delimitation of conditions and consequences required by scientific experiment. The rigour is for the sake of practical effectiveness and has only an oblique relationship with objective truth. When it comes to particular events, whether the Vikings discovered America, what was decided behind the doors of a ministry, what the accused did on the day of the crime, most of the evidence differs from evidence acceptable in physics not in rigour but in kind. In the sense in which history is claimed by some as a science, physicists can be very unscientific about the historicity of particular events. An example is that surprising phenomenon, the scientist who, even in the infidel Soviet Union, approaches Biblical narrative like a fundamentalist, as though the Victorian rumpus about the Higher Criticism had never happened. The point may be illustrated, perhaps rather unfairly, by a careless turn of phrase of the physicist and mathematician John Taylor. Referring to the stories in *Genesis* about intermarriage between the Sons of God and human women breeding giants before the Flood, and of the destruction of Sodom and Gomorrah by fire from heaven (as though by nuclear bombing), when Lot's wife was turned into a pillar of salt, he remarks that they are 'difficult to explain rationally without calling upon some intervention of beings from outer space'.[13] For the historically-minded reader a more obviously rational explanation would be that the documents are at least a thousand years later than the later of the supposed events, and that since well back in the nineteenth century critical readers of the Old Testament have not felt firm ground under their feet until somewhere about the *Books of Samuel*. If a man trained to intellectual rigour sees tales of giants born of demigod fathers, and of miraculous punishments from heaven, as explicable only as distorted reflections of physically possible events, without taking any account of the date or authorship of documents, external or internal evidence of historicity, or the different styles of myth, legend and history, it is because the discipline in which he is at home encourages him *not* to weigh testimony. At this point one may ask why a historian meticulous in getting his facts right should want to insist that he is practising a science not an art. It is precisely because historians try to discover, with all the evidential procedures at their disposal, what actually did happen, that history cannot be a science on the model of physics. It really does have objective truth as its first concern. It tells us whether, when or where the cat did sit on the mat, information as available for choices of ends as of means, and has equal possibilities of specialization as art or as science.

The insistence on repeatability in scientific procedures is itself an indication that concern for testing facts is secondary. The obvious reason for demanding the replicable is not truth but usefulness; when you experiment to satisfy yourself that the matches in a damp box do light when struck, the purpose is to ensure that you can rely on them to work. If you tell me that the matches in a certain box ignite only occasionally, and sometimes without being struck, without further delimiting conditions under which the ignition may be observed, I have no reason to doubt your word, only the utility of the matches. Similarly in the sciences, where only the event replicable under clear conditions can support or discredit an old law or be the foundation of a new one, there is nothing to be done with the unreplicable except ignore it, not necessarily as unreal, but as unusable. A persisting failure to identify conditions under which an observation is repeatable does in some cases establish a presumption of non-existence (the Loch Ness monster should have turned up by now after half a century searching one lake), but the demand for repeatability is not limited to such cases. For many centuries sailors reported sightings of the creature now identified as the giant squid, but it has existed for science only since the nineteenth century when specimens were found on shore and it became possible to say, 'If you want another look, this is where you go.' In the future perhaps all specimens will be lost and the rigour of standards of observation will be so tightened that twentieth-century descriptions will no longer be acceptable as evidence; then the giant squid will officially cease to exist. It is like the box of matches which may be somewhere round the house but is usable only if one knows where to put one's hands on it. For the sciences, as for the law, there are facts of which one does not take cognizance. One may imagine an anthropologist alone in the jungle watching with amazed delight a living australopithecine walk past and disappear in the trees. Returning to civilization, he can only add one more to the intermittent reports of ape-men seen in out-of-the-way places; it has no place in the text-book he is writing about the origin of man. Its significance for him will be as an end in itself, the most marvellous experience in his career. Shall we say that privately he knows something not yet known publicly? That is not quite the point. As he gazes at the ape-man he may be hallucinating, but to raise that possibility is to doubt his own sanity, his own capacity to judge between aware and unaware reactions, and therefore to choose between ends. He cannot put off the decision whether to believe his own senses until observations of australopithecines, as of the giant squid, become repeatable under controlled conditions. In relation to choices of ends it may be necessary to commit oneself to something of which in choices of means one cannot yet take cognizance. The same issue of ends would arise if the witness were a friend whose honesty and sense he has learned to trust. He cannot just postpone deciding whether to go on taking the man seriously; with the friend as with himself, the acceptance or dismissal of the claim is a judgement of the witness both as a savant and as a man. The point, it may be necessary to stress, is not that I cannot doubt the evidence of my senses, but that if I am to make choices of ends I must either trust it or consider putting myself in the hands of a psychiatrist. Here it may be noticed that, in the refusal to take cognizance, the languages of means and of ends in their opposition can once again be seen to run parallel. In ends-language it is a commonplace that the intelligent man does not take cognizance of abstract truths not yet 'proved' by his own experience. As Keats said of Wordsworth: 'We find what he says true as far as we have experienced and we can judge no farther but by larger experience —for axioms in philosophy are not axioms until they are proved upon our pulses'.[14] Here the taking into account of a truth is relative to the development not of a scientific discipline but of an individual life, in which there is no point in paying lip-service to some abstract truth before the time is ripe—to take Keats' example, 'no man can set down venery as a bestial or joyless thing until he is sick of it, and therefore all philosophizing on it would be mere wording.'

The extreme case of the scientifically unusable, and one which shows up the oblique relation to factual truth very clearly, is the 'Fortean phenomenon', the reported event which the followers of Charles Fort add to their collections, as not only unexplained but for current science inexplicable. When a scientist refuses to look at Forteana, as having nothing to do with real science, is he necessarily denying that the events happen? Until recently no doubt this would have seemed an absurd question. It was taken for granted that laws of nature are discovered once and for all, and entitle us to pronounce an event physically impossible whatever the testimony of witnesses. But according to Kuhn's philosophy of science[15] explanation is restricted by the limits of the current paradigm, and always collides with problems soluble only by a paradigm switch. If so, we should not be surprised now and then to run up against events which by current standards are physically impossible. Fort himself used this argument as long ago as 1919, in terms of a philosophy of science which, when detached from its monist metaphysics, looks very like a partial anticipation of Kuhn's.[16] Yet a scientist aware of this complication would still be entitled, even obliged, to dismiss Forteana as not his business. Their collision with the laws of nature is too general, they are not replicable exceptions to specific laws, usable in correcting them. If the reports are true, there is something wrong with his paradigm, but he knows that already; he accepts it not as perfect but as the best available. Even if it happens to be time for a conceptual revolution, there are better ways of preparing for it than the study of a pure anomaly, out of all relation with the available explanatory laws. As to whether the thing actually happens, any curiosity the scientist may feel he has to satisfy off duty. He will have to think like a detective rather than a scientist, in the same position as we all are when general considerations making us reluctant to accept an astonishing report clash with concrete evidence that it is true.

Forteana arouse strong prejudices, perhaps the strongest of all, on the one hand the yearning to restore value to the realm of mere fact and the delusive hope of doing it with one more fact, on the other the practical need to exclude the impossible. We could not choose means at all without narrowing possible courses of events within manageable limits, by rules-of-thumb which the sciences replace by more dependable laws; if the impossible happens, what are we to trust? Reports of queer phenomena are no doubt unrivalled for their profusion of error, self-deception, fantasy and fraud. However, unless our present conceptual frame fits reality much more completely than we have any right to expect, it would be surprising if none of reported phenomena embarrassing to current science turns out to be well grounded, and explicable within some future paradigm. One for which I personally find the evidence rather persuasive is Spontaneous Human Combustion (SHC), the destruction of a human being by fire of unknown origin which can be so hot that it reduces even the bones to cinder, yet often spares the extremities and does little or no damage to the surroundings. We are concerned of course not with its genuineness but with the relevance of the testimony to choices of means and of ends. In the eighteenth and early nineteenth centuries it was scientifically respectable, and explained by the supposed inflammability of the fat in obese alcoholics. But by the time that Dickens used it for the death of Krook in *Bleak House* (1853), it was ceasing to be credible. In terms of the science of the time the fires were inexplicable, and the absence of damage to surrounding objects physically impossible. There were experiments in soaking obese rats in alcohol, but they failed to ignite. SHC was dismissed as a legend, and medical journals generally took no cognizance of the cases reported in the newpapers and collected by connoisseurs of the unusual. However, apparent cases of SHC have never stopped, and since an unexplained death requires an inquest, expert examination, photographs, they are among the best documented of Forteana.[17]

The concept of SHC is unusable in science, because it has no explanatory and predictive power. But when one is not doing science, is that necessarily a bad thing? If one insists on an explanation, then on present knowledge there seems to be only one way of accounting for a body totally destroyed by fire in an unburned room, that the remains were brought from elsewhere after the burning of the corpse, by someone who very probably murdered the victim. What if one could be faithful to the best scientific knowledge of one's time only by condemning a man who on the other evidence seems innocent? In 1725 a landlord in Rheims was condemned to death for the murder of his wife, but the verdict was reversed after the hearing of evidence of similar cases of SHC. In 1850 in Darmstadt, after a protracted *cause célèbre*, with conflicting testimony on SHC by the experts, a footman was condemned for the murder of the Countess von Görlitz, but sentenced only to imprisonment and soon released on parole. In 1951 at St. Petersburg, Florida, the ashes of a Mrs Mary Reeser, and of the chair she sat in, were found in a room which beyond a diameter of $4^1/_2$ feet showed only slight damage (such as soot-blackened upper walls and ceiling, melting of electric fittings). Dr Wilton M. Krogman, called in as a specialist in the effects of heat on cadavers, was fascinated by the mystery, and established that the body was more completely consumed than it would have been after eight hours in a cremation furnace at 2,000 degrees F, although one foot and its slipper remained intact. He rejected the possibility of SHC (of which at first, since it does not exist for modern medicine, he knew only the fictitious case in *Bleak House*), and eventually settled for the only visible alternative, that improbable as it seemed someone murdered Mrs Reeser in her room during the night, took the body away, burned it, brought it back, and tampered with the room as a mystification, in time for the discovery early next morning. On this occasion no one was arrested, but it is instructive to imagine oneself as a juror in such a case. Let us suppose that the only alternatives are SHC and murder by the man in the dock, and there is no other serious evidence against him, but experts from the science departments of universities agree that SHC is long discredited. One would know that many similar cases have been reported, and that there is no more or less reason for assuming a murderer and an apparently purposeless mystification here than in any of the others. A scientific judgement for or against SHC is temporary and provisional, and follows an arcane procedure which excludes most of the evidence on which one acts in ordinary affairs. Its effectiveness as a research procedure is beyond doubt, but in a court of law to behave as though one were doing science would be to play games with a man's life or liberty, which are not means but ends. There might be a juror who when doing science refuses to take account of SHC, as without explanatory power, yet while on the jury admits this as a possible case of SHC, rather than be committed to an implausible explanation by which a man could be fortuitously destroyed.

Although a statement in neutral language may be accepted as true on private tests alone, it has no place in science and is relevant only to choices of ends, as long as there are no criteria for testing it publicly. This point may be illustrated by the pretensions of psycho-analysis to be a science, which can be rejected without necessarily denying that its doctrines are true. Freud explains neurosis, dream, art, religion, on the one hand by unconscious desires, on the other by a system of repression, displacement, projection and other operations causally relating the desires to observed behaviour, the whole conceivable as a mechanism inside the nervous system. There is no reason in principle why all this should not someday be publicly tested, with unconscious patricidal urges located as neural impulses which, should any father be willing to offer himself for the experiment, could be shown to eventuate in his murder when the obstacles which block them are surgically removed. For the present, however, the only supposedly verified prediction to which a Freudian can appeal is that people who come to understand themselves in these terms do throw off their neuroses. But apart from doubts as to whether psycho-analysis does achieve a significantly high rate of cures, belief in psycho-analytic doctrine might be therapeutic without its being true; successful treatment by ritually casting out a devil is not nowadays taken as proof of the devil's existence. The Freudian has therefore to depend on the private testability of his claims. Certainly many people do become conscious of forbidden desires, and of their own resistance to acknowledging them, and sense of release and well-being when they do, and learn by experience that Freudian techniques such as dream analysis stimulate this process of self-discovery. But however much they learn from Freud, which items in his or his rivals' systems they accept or reject is uncontrolled by objective tests.

Does all this make Freud just another witch-doctor? Many who for this reason deny that psycho-analysis is a science seem to think so. However, we are not always doing science when we seek truth. There may be something in my heart which I am glad that no one else can see, and which I am tempted to treat as though, being invisible to everyone else, it is not quite real. In such a case I am hardly in a position to congratulate myself on my scientific rigour in refusing to accept what remains publicly untested. 'Be aware' requires me to admit the truth to myself; whether others of whom it is true admit it to themselves too is their own business. La Rochefoucauld's 'In the adversity of our best friends we always find something which does not displease us', offered to us as an aphorism without proof, is just as testable as a quasi-scientific tenet of Freud, which is to say that it is tested privately. You can take it or leave it, in the light of insight into yourself and into others whose viewpoints you assume. If you accept it, you have an explanation, much in the Freudian style, of why for example we make a joke of our best friends' more trivial misfortunes. But if for this maxim public testability does not matter, it is because its relevance is rather to ends than to means; it illuminates a secret reaction which one would like to repudiate, not as frustrating projects, but as unworthy of oneself. Similarly Freudianism, in committing its claims to truth to private tests, shifts its ground towards becoming an answer to questions of ends. In theory the analyst is a physician like any other, and the real or illusory self-knowledge is induced as a means to cure the patient's fear of spiders or of getting trapped in lifts. But what he offers is nothing less than a total spontaneous re-orientation in the light of the profoundest self-awareness, which judged by 'Be aware' is one's reconstitution as a better man; as for the neurotic symptoms, the patient is assured that any less radical treatment would merely replace them by others. The attraction of psycho-analysis compared with publicly tested and arguably more effective physical treatment of symptoms is that implicitly it promises not mere resumption of normality but a breakout from emotional blockage, renewing the power to respond with awareness in new directions—an evangelism which becomes explicit in the heirs and rivals of Freud from Jung onwards. Consequently its influence nowadays is less among psychiatrists than among writers and intellectuals, who originally tended to deride it as crude scientism.

As for the private sorting of psycho-analytic claims convincing or unconvincing to oneself, it involves the moral struggle characteristic of inquiries into truth or falsehood in relation to ends. Acknowledgement that at bottom one shares the patricidal and incestuous urges of the Oedipus Complex (as more than a now commonplace abstraction) presents itself as an ordeal, a step in growth, an initiation into the great modern quest for a radical honesty; if you can admit that of yourself you ought to be able to admit anything. Am I refusing to remember because the thought horrifies me? Or have I deluded myself that I remember what Freud put into my head? A decision on either side is a commitment which condemns all who disagree as being either afraid of the truth or too suggestible to the voice of the guru, so that if confused with a decision on a matter of scientific fact it is in either case liable to be come self-confirming. It is characteristic of Freud's kind of inquiry that the sufferer in whom he first recognized the Oedipus Complex was himself, in the self-analysis of 1897 after his father's death, in which he struggled with the meaning of his dreams and childhood memories, and that one's admiration for the personal courage of the feat is almost independent of one's opinion as to the significance and universality of the pattern which he recognized in himself. In

reading his reports to Fliess on the progress of his self-analysis one comes suddenly on the great illumination:

> To be completely honest with oneself is good practice. One single thought of general
> value has been revealed to me. I have found in my own case too falling in love with the
> mother and jealousy of the father, and I now regard it as a universal event of early
> childhood, even if not so early as in children who have been made hysterical. [Similarly
> with the romance of parentage in paranoia—heroes, founders of religions.] If that is so,
> we can understand the riveting power of *Oedipus Rex*, in spite of all the objections raised
> by reason against its presupposition of destiny.[18]

Freud like La Rochefoucauld universalizes his insight, rightly or wrongly sure
that on this point he can see all men after his own likeness. It is a bold commitment,
at the opposite pole from science; and his right to challenge us by risking it
remains the same whether everyone or no one confirms it by his own self-examination.

2.2 Man and nature

In the logical gap between 'is' and 'ought' there seems to be implicit an irreconcilable divorce between man and Nature. But is it perhaps, as the previous chapter
might suggest, that the divorce is only a projection of a reconcilable difference,
between treating Nature as means at the disposal of man, and as end in itself?
Since the experience of divorce from Nature reached its critical point in the Darwinian theory of Natural Selection, let us approach the question of man's apparent
uniqueness and solitude from the pure Darwinian position, using as textbook the
biochemist Jacques Monod's superbly lucid *Chance and necessity*.[1] Our dichoto-
mization of poetry and science has given us a strong bias in favour of Darwinism,
since we cannot allow purpose or value to trespass from the language of ends into
the language of means. Whether or not one insists on explaining evolution entirely
by Natural Selection, it remains the classic explanation in terms of causality and
chance alone. By 'Nature', whether or not distinguished by the capital letter, we
understand the spontaneous in general, everything which is independent of human
choice including the undeliberated in human behaviour, irrespective of whether
it is genetically or socially conditioned.

In his final chapter Monod presents uncompromisingly a conception of man's
place in the universe which many find inevitable, the only one that he finds compatible with a full commitment to post-Galilean science. It is that man must acknowledge his absolute isolation, and abandon for ever that 'Old Covenant' by which he
supposed himself allied to an animistic Nature which ordains the rules by which
he should live. It happens that I am sympathetic not only to Monod's conclusions
about evolution (not that I am qualified to criticize them), but to his general
positions that teleological explanations have no place in science, and that no
Christian, Marxist or other prescriptions for action can be derived from facts
about the cosmos. Among positions peripheral to the main argument, I share also

his sense of the importance of subjective as well as objective approaches to know-ledge, and his identification of the former as an incipient or overt simulation of observed behaviour. But I hope to show that if we subjectivize with the same consistency as Monod objectivizes, and take care at every step that the subjective has its counterpart in the objective, everything that he has to tell us turns out to lead to a very different conclusion, and even restores a part of that despised Old Covenant.

In speaking of language as subjectivizing or objectivizing, we can avoid commit-ment as to how far it is neutral or has specialized in the directions of poetry or science. A subjectivizing language, whether poetic or not, is highly metaphorical, not as a stylistic decoration but inherently, and the farther one departs from man the more treacherous it becomes. Any discussion of the relation between man and nature, Monod's included, supplements the objective descriptions of science by subjectivizing language, if only in dealing with man himself. But if one is to subjec-tivize at all it must be done consistently. That imposes its own discipline, which Monod appears to me to neglect.

To start off in Monod's own objectivizing language, I must allow myself to be described, for purposes of explanation and prediction, as a 'teleonomic system', a system in which movement towards a goal, its 'project', is wholly explicable by physical laws; the simplest examples are machines designed to return to a constant state by negative feedback. Ordinarily I would be content to explain the behaviour of any human being, as of myself, by the goal itself, the type of explanation called 'teleological'. But all teleological explanations of the functional adaptations by which a teleonomic system fulfils its project, in terms of the project itself treated as its 'purpose', must, if we are not to revert from modern to Aristotelian science, be excluded in principle; it must be assumed that, as can already be shown in the case of the simplest teleonomic systems, its processes when not deterministic are statistically random. (In this language 'it' is the only pronoun available to refer to myself.) For reasons which emerged in the last chapter,[2] there is no need to object to any of this, but I had better remind myself that I cannot pursue this adventure in language when I am making choices, I still have to say 'Shall I?' and 'I will'. The reason for this limitation is not merely that too little is known of the more complex systems for an objective description in detail, so that a more primitive language which explains and predicts in terms of purpose remains indispensable until the gap is filled. I cannot limit my life to describing objectively my own activi-ties and explaining them in retrospect, and to apply laws to predict my future choices (as distinct from provisionally deciding in advance) is in principle impos-sible for me. I have to look forward to goals and act in order to attain them, and to do so I require a subjectivizing language, in which I use 'purpose' for what the objectivizing language calls 'project'.

As a teleonomic system, I resemble other men, and in varying degrees resemble and differ from animals, plants, and cybernetic machines. A simulative function, very highly developed in the human teleonomic apparatus, enables me to assume the viewpoints of other persons and in progressively reduced degree of less similar things, and speak of them in the subjectivizing language I apply to myself. Indeed, for Monod the enlarged capacity to 'simulate experience subjectively so as to anticipate its results and prepare action'[3] is the most distinctively human property of the brain and the precondition of language, as well as of creative thinking in the sciences themselves.

I am sure every scientist must have noticed how his mental reflection, at the deeper level, is not verbal: it is an *imagined experience*, simulated with the aid of forms, of forces, of interactions which together barely compose an 'image' in the visual sense of the word. I have even found myself, after lengthy concentration on the imagined experience to the exclusion of everything else, identifying with a molecule of protein. However, it is not at that moment that the significance of the simulated experience becomes clear, but only when it has been enunciated symbolically. Indeed, the non-visual images with which simulation works should be regarded not as symbols but, if I may so phrase it, as the subjective and abstract 'reality' offered directly to imaginary experience.[4]

It should follow from Monod's account that since in the subjectivizing language I call the project of my own organism 'purpose', I have when not doing science the theoretical right so to call the project of any animal or vegetable, right down to the molecule of protein, which is a teleonomic system like myself. In speaking in the name, not only of biochemists, but of all scientists, Monod seems even to entitle me to subjectivize, if I can, inanimate process in general. The commonsense assumption that to a limited extent I can read the cat's thoughts, see the world, through its eyes, as though it were human, is quite modest compared with Monod's. Is then everything subjectivizable in principle? To say so will be precisely as acceptable or unacceptable as to say, following Monod without reserve in the other direction, that in principle the composition of *Hamlet* would be fully analysable by a superhuman intelligence as a teleonomic process in Shakespeare's nervous system.

Knowledge through simulation is not scientific knowledge, merely substitutes for it, as a second-best, in fields such as human affairs not yet accessible to rigorous procedures. Monod himself, in his moments of being a molecule of protein, relinquishes the objectivity of science, but recovers it in returning to himself to formulate his insights in verbal and mathematical symbols. Ideally, we cheerfully concede to Monod, it should be possible to eliminate animistic descriptions even of human behaviour, which could be treated exclusively as the motions of teleonomic systems. But all this does not touch the crucial point, which Monod seems to miss, that subjectivization is only secondarily a resource for exploring questions of fact. For myself as agent, it is the only approach to the core of my own deliberate behaviour, which I do not predict or explain (though others may), but decide in relation to ends, and which can enter my own objective knowledge only when already past. If, as Monod recognizes, I have as companions in my loneliness in this supposedly alien universe other humans huddling beside me, it is because in classing someone as human, by assimilating to and differentiating from other persons and things, as myself human I have subjectively to assimilate him to myself, see from his viewpoint, react for or against his goals. But one cannot introduce subjectivity into Monod's universe without turning the whole of it inside out. It is a continuum in which the demand to submit everything to the same laws forbids the drawing of uncrossable lines, between human and animal, or animate and inanimate, so that to allow subjectivity, ends, value, at any point—which for each person is himself—is to let them spread throughout.

The manner in which subjectivizing and objectivizing approaches run parallel in opposite directions shows up especially clearly in the animal kingdom, as a region intermediate between human and inanimate, equally accessible from either. As far as explanation and prediction are concerned, one has to be on guard against analogies with man which become more treacherous with increasing distance, and the prospect which still seems so remote in human affairs, of replacing subjectiviz-ing language by a sufficiently sophisticated behavioural explanation, is already within reach. If you wish to explain the birds' dawn chorus, you nowadays have to forget that you sing in the bath on a sunny morning, and instead attend to the behaviour of these teleonomic mechanisms as they fulfil the project of marking out and defending their territories. Approaching from the other direction however, having extended subjectivization from man to other beings, I shall be friendly, sympathetic or angry with a dog much as with a man, a fellow-feeling to which increasing ease in dispensing with subjectivization for explanation and prediction remains entirely irrelevant. I am drawn into subjectivization for the same reasons as with man; I recognize something as a bird or a dog by assimilating to and dif-ferentiating from other things, including myself. From the assumption that like myself the animal feels comes the possibility of, for example, being deliberately cruel to it, and of judging the cruelty morally wrong, as though it were human. This opens a breach in Monod's wall between man and the alien world around him, which seems impassable only if one is inconsistent in assimilating and differentiat-ing, leaving oneself out of the comparisons in the case of everything but man. In so far as the Old Covenant is an entitlement to subjectivize the things with which we interact, feel ourselves in conflict or accord with them, aspire to order our relations with nature as with man, belong in a cosmos as in a community, then, far from it being discredited by science, it becomes impossible to deny it without inconsistency. It would be beside the point to object that cosmos likened to community is a false analogy, on the grounds that things other than man do not co-operate voluntarily as we do in society. Individuals who choose to co-operate voluntarily may still feel alien to each other; the sense of belonging which is strongest in the family results not from choice but from spontaneous interactions which at their most basic are the same as in animal families. As for rationalizing the subjectivizable, the function of the intellect, we continue to insist, is not to forbid and usurp the place of analogizing—which would be to destroy its own foundations—but to criticize it, and forbid, for example, likening natural forces to ourselves to the extent of trying to move them by prayer and sacrifice.

In analogizing it is important not to be frightened by accusations of animistic thinking. If animism is the attempt to explain a thing's motions rationally by postu-lating a mind controlling it, we repudiate it absolutely, excluding from science even animistic explanation of human behaviour. Subjectivization, as we understand it, does not imply crediting myself with a mind and then inferring by analogy that another person or thing has one too, which it would be reasonable to call 'animism'. Subjectivization is simulation in order to explore similarity to and difference from myself. Preceding and underlying analytic thought there is an uninterrupted process which guides reactions to the not yet known by assimilating to and differentiating from the already known, with simulation as one of its modes. It is a synthesizing process which can sort out relevant similarities and differences with great sensitivity but is liable to mistakes which can be located only by analysis. When one meets language which looks animistic the question is not whether the object concerned has a mind but whether the analogy exceeds its implicit limits. The metaphors it throws up may be misleading, or just practically irrelevant; no one reading 'The mountain rises . . .' is going to act on the assumption that the mountain itself lifts like the eye following its curve upwards. But when the Futurist Marinetti exemplifies his 'intuitive psychology of matter' by the resistance to pressure of a strip of steel,[5] he could develop in his support a well-structured analogy between the strip snapping or rebounding and human behaviour under the stress of circumstance. A person anticipating the moment when a strip bending in his hands will snap is not inferring from the laws of physics but guiding expectation by the synthesized influences of every precedent however long forgotten, of things more or less like this strip giving under pressure more or less as it does, and if somewhere among the merged influences in the discerning of the coming moment is a 'This is when *I* would snap', the likening to oneself is as legitimate as the rest. The analogizing, too complex to be fully unravelled by analysis, turns out to have been sound if the expectation is fulfilled. As Marinetti himself knew well, although science and technology have no room for animism in theory, in practice the handling of machines encourages simulation of the inanimate. It can take quite complicated forms, with immediate analogies to oneself successfully co-ordinated with others which mediate through the already subjectivized. If a driver is at some level thinking of the car as a woman submissive to his mastery, the engine throb as a heartbeat, a bump as a shock to his own extended body, as his metaphors betray, he proves the soundness and coherence of the superficially contradictory analogizing by his success in manoeuvres which do not allow him time for analytic thinking. The man of intellect, in the operations which he leaves to intelligent spontaneity, tacitly admits that responses are quickened by simulation. The efficacy of the driver's submerged analogizing is as immune to philosophical objections to animism as to moral objections to his male chauvinism. It goes wrong only when it strays beyond the limits of the analogy, as when the driver kicks his car in exasperation, as though he could frighten it into starting again. Then the analytic intelligence comes into its own, exercising its purely critical function.

Granted that metaphor which analogizes the inanimate to man is easily pressed to assimilate too far, and when intellectualized breeds animistic beliefs, its function, as of simulation in general, is not to assimilate everything else to ourselves, but to explore subjectively both where they resemble and where they differ from us. When someone starts to explain and predict physical phenomena by the wills of personal beings it is time to examine the limits of analogy, by analysing differences in an objectivizing language; but the differences are already implicit in a sensitive subjectivizing language which balances, against similarities to man, similarities to things which are even more remote from man. Consider for example this description of pines in a New Mexican landscape by D. H. Lawrence, at first sight flamboyantly animistic:

That pine-tree was the guardian of the place. But a bristling, almost demonish guardian, from the far-off crude ages of the world. Its great pillar of pale, flaky-ribbed copper rose there in strange callous indifference, and the grim permanence, which is in pine-trees. A passionless non-phallic column, rising in the shadows of the pre-sexual world, before the hot-blooded ithyphallic column ever erected itself. A cold, blossomless, resinous sap surging and oozing gum, from that pallid brownish bark. And the wind hissing in the needles, like a vast nest of serpents. And the pine-combs falling plumb as the hail hit them. Then lying all over the yard, open in the sun like wooden roses, but hard, sexless, rigid with a blind will.

Past the column of that pine-tree, the alfalfa field sloped gently down, to the circling guard of pine-trees, from which silent, living barrier isolated pines rose to ragged heights at intervals, in blind assertiveness. Strange, those pine-trees! In some lights all their needles glistened like polished steel, all subtly glittering with a whitish glitter among darkness, like real needles. Then again, at evening, the trunks would flare up orange-red, and the tufts would be dark, alert tufts like a wolf's tail touching the air. Again, in the morning sunlight they would be soft and still, hardly noticeable. But all the same, present and watchful. Never sympathetic, always watchfully on their guard, and resistant, they hedged one in with the aroma and the power and the slight horror of the pre-sexual primaeval world. The world where each creature was crudely limited to its own ego, crude and bristling and cold, and then crowding in packs like pine-trees and wolves.[6]

Lawrence is not humanizing the pine, he is evoking an impression of its remoteness from man much stronger than we could derive from any objective botanical description. Certainly he ascribes 'will' to the pine, sees it as a 'guardian', as 'assertive', 'alert', 'watchful'. If he were explaining vegetable properties by human motives (its trunk is so erect in order to assert itself, its cones are so hard in order to resist us), he would indeed be indulging in an obselete, animistic kind of science —as he sometimes does when he is writing as a confused thinker rather than a true seer. But he starts from the continuity of self with tree only to make contrasts. The trees are 'strange', as he twice says; in answering his implicit question, 'What would it feel like to be a tree?', he shivers at the uncanny contact as he intrudes into a mode of being disturbingly remote—not absolutely alien, for there is no discontinuity of kind—from human and animal sexuality. The human is counterposed with mineral analogies, a pillar of copper (described by an adjective fusing mineral and animal, 'flaky-ribbed'), glittering needles of steel, a flare as of fire, with bridging comparisons with animals antipathetic to man, the wolf and the snake; if he mentions will and assertiveness it is to call them 'blind will', 'blind assertiveness', emptying them of consciousness; the trunk suggests the erect penis only to be contrasted as 'passionless, non-phallic'. The bald sentence at the start, 'That pine-tree was the guardian of the place', had invited us to think of a sacred tree guarding the house. It is indeed sacred to Lawrence, as is everything which he senses as intensely alive, but in its sacredness it is so inhuman as to be 'almost demonish', and it guards only itself.

It will be objected perhaps that all through this argument we have been missing the main point; the simulator of the tree is trying to discover how it feels to be a tree, and unlike a man a tree doesn't feel. But the elusive question of what is or is not conscious has nothing to do with the matter. What one takes as a behavioural test of consciousness is a matter of convenience; it may be judged expedient to confine consciousness to man, as the sole user of language, or allow it to the chimpanzee and orang-utan because they recognize themselves in mirrors, or to the dog barking in its sleep as though dreaming, or to anything which sleeps and wakes, or moves freely unlike the vegetable, or is alive, is teleonomic at all. The more or less arbitrary choice of a criterion can have nothing to do with the question how far away from man one can risk analogizing to oneself. Here personal view-point-shifting once again runs parallel with temporal.[7] To simulate the experience of a time when by behavioural criteria one was unconscious is to recall a dream. To say, 'If a tree is unconscious you can't subjectively simulate it' makes as little sense as to object to the reporter of a dream, 'If you were unconscious you can't be remembering what was going on'; 'If you can simulate a tree it must be in some sense conscious' is like 'If you dream you are in some sense conscious while asleep', an elusive philosophical thought which one may or may not suppose worth pursuing. To think in this way betrays that one is trying to objectivize the subjective experience of conscious behaviour without sacrificing its subjectivity, as some kind of light which comes on again inside one's head on waking in the morning, and supposes that at the stage of evolution when, by one's preferred behavioural criterion, consciousness began, the inward lantern was lit for the first time. But that light is invisible to science even inside such complex teleonomic mechanisms as you and me. Even if I claim to perceive it in myself by introspection, and take the logically unsatisfactory step of inferring its presence in you by analogy, it remains pointless to ask how far back it can be traced in the evolutionary scale, whether to dogs, crocodiles, fish, amoebae, the mineral world before life began, or whether it has yet flashed inside an electronic computer; I am crediting my own fellow men with the glow of consciousness only because of their similarity to my-self, and what degree of similarity am I to take as sufficient evidence? The only test to which the analogizing is subject is success or failure in anticipating behavi-our; and granted that success in anticipation diminishes with distance from myself, at any rate the owner of a cat or dog learns what to expect by much the same combination of observation and simulation by which he comes to know his friends, and Monod to know a molecule of protein. When as I move down the scale it is the increasing unlikeness to man which impresses me, I can appreciate that too only if, like Lawrence, I make an effort at understanding which stops short at a 'blind will' somewhere 'in the shadows of the pre-sexual world'. It is all very well to say that science ruthlessly exposes man's isolation in an alien universe, but the fact is that it has nothing whatever to say about the relation between man and the universe except that it hopes some day to prove that they are united under the same laws, and its language evokes no feeling at all of the remoteness of nature from man (having nothing to do with feelings anyway); it is on poetic language that we depend to measure the distance.

Even in religion, where metaphor insists that it is fact, analogizing serves not only to assimilate but to differentiate the divine from the human. Rudolph Otto showed how religious sensibility unobscured by rationalization is intensely aware of the otherness of a *numen* or Godhead which breaks out of the limits of the per-sonal and the moral.[8] This sense of otherness is essential to any religion which genuinely serves to relate man to a universe the laws of which are so foreign to his reason and his morality, and does not dwindle into a fantasy of supernatural encouragement for human ideals and hopes of defeating death. The imagination of sacred presences in or beyond nature therefore shows the same tendency to balance human against animal and mineral analogies that we noticed in Lawrence. The neat dictum that man created God in his own image is true without qualification only of humanistic ages. The anthropomorphism of classical Greece and Renaissance Italy reflects a failing sense of the numinous; Venus de Milo is not a goddess but an idealized woman. Real gods have elephants' heads or six arms. Even in Christian imagery it is by no means true that the sacred has human shape and that the animal is reserved for the obscene and diabolical. Christ is the Lamb of God, the Holy Spirit descends as a dove or as tongues of fire, angels have wings, the four evangelists are depicted with the faces of lion, calf, man and eagle of the Four Zoa who, 'full of eyes before and behind', surround the throne of God in *Revelation*, and the Egyptian Anubis found a place for himself in Byzantine art as the dog-headed St. Christopher. Christ and his saints, although their former life as men on earth sets a limit to taking liberties with their form, are as much mineral as human, with gold-leaf halos as inseparable from them as their faces; and they look most sacred in the Byzantine mosaics, as severe inorganic patterns of coloured stones. (The vegetable kingdom is seldom allowed much share of the god, as though man knows instinctively that his affinity to the mineral through the animal bypasses the vegetable, as on the evolutionary tree.) John of Patmos, the finest visualizer of sacred beings in the Bible, confirms that the mineralized look does not come only from artist's materials, as in the very first he sees:

...and his head and his hair were white as white wool, white as snow; his eyes were like a flame of fire, his feet were like burnished bronze, refined as in a furnace, and his voice was like the sound of many waters; in his right hand he held seven stars, from his mouth issued a sharp two-edged sword, and his face was like the sun shining in full strength.[9]

In subjectivizing, I understand other things to the extent that they resemble myself. The analogies in radiating outwards become increasingly remote, the familiar words from human experience such as 'purpose', 'knowledge', 'power', 'struggle', 'altruism', 'selfishness', become more and more obviously metaphorical, as far as the outlying which objectively still presents soluble problems but which subjectively is a mystery which I no longer try to penetrate. Thus I may humanize animals and plants by imagining them as, like ourselves in harsh conditions, 'competing in a ruthless struggle for survival'; but I can risk this Darwinian metaphor only as long as I remember that no more is implied than that, without their for the most part knowing of each other's existence, one's gain works out in games theory as another's loss. To take the argument a step further, if I can 'put myself in the place' of an individual animal, I can do the same—although with still greater risk of misunderstanding analogies—with the network of super-systems and sub-systems around and within my organism. For some purposes the whole branching tree of replicating and changing individuals through successive generations may be conceived as a single super-system, the biosphere. Communities may be seen as thinned-out organisms, different only in degree from the concentrations of cells which are their individual members. Some readers who have followed us thus far will no doubt want to draw the line at systems other than individual organisms. But the crossing of the line is ceasing to look fanciful, even seems likely eventually to become a practical necessity, in the case of robots, especially since they have incorporated organic molecules. An eco-system is itself a teleonomic system which is subjectivizable, a point illustrated by the fascinating speculation of J. E. Lovelock, that the entire biosphere with its atmosphere, oceans and soil is to be seen as a single eco-system with a homeostasis like that of an organism, 'a self-regulating entity with the capacity to keep our planet healthy by controlling the chemical and physical environment'.[10] Here what matters is not the validity of Lovelock's argument (which I am incompetent to judge) but the way it exemplifies the possibility of subjectivizing inanimate systems. His evidence is strictly physical, not metaphysical, for example that the survival of life requires a temperature constant within narrow limits, which has somehow been maintained through the 3.5 aeons of its history, as though by a negative feedback like that which regulates body temperature. But he notes that in physical terms it is difficult to arrive at a definition of the living which would exclude eddies in a stream, hurricanes, flames, self-regulating machines, and this comprehensive super-system too: all come under the heading of 'open or continuous systems able to decrease their internal entropy at the expense of substances or free energy taken in from the environment and subsequently rejected in a degraded form'.[11] Nor is there a firm definition of intelligence which would entitle us to deny it to any self-regulating system, in the sense that to survive it must 'interpret correctly information received about the environment'.[12] Lovelock named his super-system 'Gaia', after the Greek Earth goddess (following a suggestion of the novelist William Golding). The choice of name was something more than poetic playfulness:

I felt also that in the days of Ancient Greece the concept itself was probably a familiar aspect of life, even if not formally expressed. Scientists are usually condemned to lead urban lives, but I find that country people still living close to the earth often seem puzzled that anyone should need to make a formal proposition of anything as obvious as the Gaia hypothesis.[13]

As for sub-systems within the organism, they must be postulated if everything subjective is to be credited with an objective counterpart, as hypothetical equivalents of such subjectivized but spatially unlocated entities as the self, God, gods, devils, the multiple souls of some mythologies and the multiple personalities of psycho-pathology. Here we can make the same sort of use of Freud as we made of Lovelock. Freud showed in principle that the reasoning and choosing self, and the God whose voice is heard as conscience, and the irrational and amoral urges in rebellion against both, could have as objective counterparts a trinity of sub-systems in the organism, Ego, Super-ego and Id, and be causally explicable by their mechanical interactions. For reasons mentioned earlier,[14] we do not accept Freud's objectification of the inward drama as a genuine scientific hypothesis, because although in principle it is publicly testable he was unable to show how it could be tested in practice. But simply to conceive the theoretical possibility has altered the way we see ourselves. Formerly the only alternative to the subjectivizing language in which gods are analogized to men, and therefore separate from men, was an objectivizing language which simply abolished them. For the pre-Freudian style of rationalism, there is none of me but Ego, God either exists outside the organism or is a figment of the imagination, and it is a hard problem to understand how I can desire irrationally without having reasoned incorrectly; I am obliged to forget the ancient knowledge that my organism can be driven by forces other than my will and inhabited by selves other than me. But Freud's identification of God as the Super-ego alters the terms of the case. The Super-ego is not a figment of the Ego's imagination but an equally autonomous formation from the same processes, with the same ontological status. With this change Freud transforms the gods from fictions into 'psychological realities' like our own selves, and entitles us to think of the mythic, not as never having happened, but as obsessively recurring and dominating life, imaginary only in that instead of being overtly re-enacted the deed is generally incipient, repressed. The re-estimate of the self as no more nor less real than the other subjective entities which it precariously dominates is unaffected by doubts about Freud's general doctrine, since it is backed by a variety of previously unassimilable evidence that we are unstable formations out of forces which dramatize themselves as interacting persons in dream, fantasy and fiction, and can overwhelm the self in ecstasies of divine possession, or in Dickens taken over in amateur theatricals by Bill Sikes; or can split it in multiple personality, or obliterate it in Peter Sellers the actor without solid identity outside his roles, or in any fully achieved conformist with only a social self. This shift of perspective is one reason why Freudianism, in spite of its precarious status among psychiatrists, won such a firm footing in literary circles. Precisely because of the clarity and rigour with which he organizes a few basic concepts, the rationalistic Freud gives a much solider meaning to the claims of the poetic and mythic to be real than does the mystical Jung.

Our present line of thought is leading to the perhaps unexpected conclusion that to be meticulous in subjectivizing only what objectively is found scientifically respectable will result, not indeed in the return of the gods, but in something very like that supposedly even more primitive consciousness which feels itself surrounded and pervaded by different degrees and configurations of the personal, semi-personal and impersonal. If we are to risk such challenges as that the God of each religion is as real as each self which defies or bows down to him, we shall have to be careful to distinguish this imputed 'reality' from what theists commonly understand by the existence of God. In general, the question of the existence of God becomes, on the present approach, the question whether or how far subjectivization of cosmic order can validly analogize it to an order imposed by human intelligence and purpose. As for the God of a particular religion, he acts only through the organisms in which he was culturally implanted, more or less identical in all of them, as different copies are the same book, and it is only by the error of locating him externally that he comes to be credited with omnipotence and eternity. He will die with the last believer, or the last atheist in whose unconscious he still lurks. We generally have to be on watch for unnoticed metaphor, but the apparent oxymoron 'God is dead' is more literal than we think. It is worth considering, however, whether we have as much right as we suppose to be confident in distinguishing the real and the imaginary beings who appear to be confused in so much of the literature of the world. In Homer and the Old Testament, so impressive for a psychological realism which post-Renaissance man lost for centuries, everyone takes the fluidity of the self for granted, feels powers from beyond him aiding or thwarting him in the spontaneous ebb and flow of energy and confidence, and assumes that whenever, as we say, he is 'not himself', a god has possessed him with benign or malign intent; reading them, one may well ask whether among these unindividuated persons and personified forces the god does not have just as much claim to historical existence as the man. We might ask too whether, for example, to say that Julius Caesar 'lives again' in some later conqueror is as transparent a figure of speech as it seems. It would be a considerable over-rationalization to think of later imitators simply as individuals who chose to follow his example. Caesar is a persona which grew up in and possessed the man who bore the name (Shakespeare has him referring to himself in the third person even in private conversation with his wife). That potent image does 'live again' in the admirer whom it vampirizes.

It is time to return to Monod. As a teleonomic system, I subjectivize my project as will or purpose, and there is a project for every such system, for Lovelock's Gaia too if she exists. Might it be that in turning Monod's world inside out we shall return to that idea he despises of a cosmic purpose realized through evolution? But we had better be careful; Monod's world subjectivized is coming to look unexpectedly primitive, the vision not of evolutionary progressivism but rather of that pre-rational and pre-moral sensibility from which religion and mysticism start. Let us push forward on the principle that we have the right to subjectivize whenever and only when we can translate into Monod's objectivizing language. According to Monod

> But it is only as part of a more comprehensive project that each individual project, whatever it may be, has any meaning. All the functional adaptations in living beings, like all the artifacts they produce, fulfil particular projects which may be seen as so many aspects or fragments of a unique primary project, which is the preservation and multiplication of the species.[15]

As for the evolution of new species, it is by statistically random mutations. However, of the enormous variety of occurring mutations, natural selection eliminates all but the few which 'do not lessen the coherence of the teleonomic apparatus, but rather strengthen it in the orientation already assumed...and that is why evolution itself seems to be fulfilling a design, seems to be carrying out a "project", that of perpetuating and amplifying some ancestral "dream".'[16]

By this account, the evolution of species is like that of automobiles and aeroplanes, with a direction set in the one case by chance, in the other by designers' wills, acting within limits imposed by the structural orientation. Under 'chance' Monod does not exclude the theoretically predictable fall of dice, but he explains mutations by accumulations of quantum perturbations which are unpredictable in principle. 'Chance *alone* is at the source of every innovation, of all creation in the biosphere'.[17] The line of development has at every stage a narrow range of possibilities, but the one realized seems inevitable only in retrospect. Consequently there can be no question of subjectivizing the evolutionary process as the unfolding of a cosmic purpose.

Destiny is written as and while, not before, it happens ... The universe was not pregnant with life, nor the biosphere with man. Our number came up in the Monte Carlo game.[18]

In the first of the quoted passages it seems clear enough that if I can speak of my own organism's project as my purpose, then the project which goes on replicating an organism's structure is also subjectivizable as purpose—one that everyone recognizes under some name or another, let us say the will of Life to reproduce itself. We could allow ourselves the luxury of the metaphor that when a mother animal dies to save her young, Life is sacrificing the old for the sake of the new. But Monod firmly forbids us to account for evolutionary change by crediting Life with a progressive, as distinct from a conservative purpose. Rather, it seems that Life breaks with its routines much as a man does, selecting from chance circumstances what accords with his potentialities, in a direction which becomes plain only in retrospect. This is not the working out of a purpose, although it may be the discovery of a 'purpose in life'. Applying Monod's objectivizing language to myself, it is the play of chance circumstances and my orientation as a teleonomic mechanism which set off the spontaneous episodes of high awareness which I judge good in themselves and which, if repeatable, become ends to which I choose means. Evolution has so far had two supreme events of this kind, the origins of life and of man. Monod does not think of these as inevitable once the general conditions for them are ready. He suspects that coincidences so complex may be unique, of near zero probability. Twice over, immeasurable consequences have flowed from conjunctions which may never happen anywhere else in the universe, might never have happened in the history of the universe—to the subjective imagination, unheralded creations of new value. As such they are predecessors of the creative thoughts and acts of men, still more complex conjunctions of teleonomy and chance which are also unique. In the future or elsewhere in the universe there could be other such events, as unimaginable by us as human reason would be to an animal.

We need not scruple to use the noun 'value' as though of an objective quality of such epiphanies. If 'Be aware' is the ultimate imperative, there can be no more evident good than the birth of awareness itself and its elevation to a new level by reason. Nor would there be much point in asking whether there could be value before there were men to evaluate, any more than whether things had dimensions before there were men to measure them. With life and man as ends in themselves, we must also find good the teleonomic projects which maintain and reproduce them. As for the evolution of new forms, set off by chance mutations within the limits set by structural orientation, this too will be judged by 'Be aware'. An advance in awareness could either assist or threaten survival, as in human affairs, where to be intelligent enough to see the other man's point of view, or know that there is more to life than making war or money, are not advantages in highly competitive conditions. A line will be progressing or degenerating according to whether the adaptations favourable to survival increase or reduce awareness. The line which leads to man has so far been progressive, but the Second Law of Thermodynamics ensures that in the long run all lines are likely to regress and certain to come to an end. Such an evaluation in terms of awareness is fundamentally different from the simple-minded application of Darwinism which, treating intelligence as a means to survival, grades by survival value; that should oblige anyone who takes it seriously to prefer the unicellular organisms which alone have proved capable of living out unaltered the entire course of evolutionary history. More complex organisms survive at the expense of their rivals by proving better adapted to conditions in which their very complexity makes them more vulnerable; man himself, by becoming intelligent enough to discover how to exterminate himself, puts himself in danger of dying out in a ravaged world which he bequeathes to the insects.

One obvious difference here from the doctrines of evolutionary progress criticized by Monod (of Herbert Spencer, Engels, Teilhard de Chardin) is that, although this version of evolution allows the reading of purpose into natural process as the will to conserve, it greets the new, the creative, as the bounty of chance. Evolutionary progressivists have never been able to tolerate this thought. The chance event is the uncaused, unusable for prediction or explanation. They would despair of life itself as meaningless unless they could scry in its evolution a purpose analogous to man's. But to insist that the origins of life and of man must serve some purpose reduces them to means, with a merely instrumental value which will turn out to be illusory if by some unfortunate accident the cosmos fails to achieve its pre-ordained goal. The origin of a wholly new end is by definition *not* the working out of a purpose, and whether to ascribe it to chance or to causation becomes an issue only when one turns it round to search it from another angle for its possibilities as means. What is so disturbing about ascribing an event to chance, unless one is thinking of it as a means slipping out of control? Whatever one evaluates in the present as good or bad in itself was once qualitatively new, subjectively unanticipatable like the sweet or bitter flavour of a never yet tasted fruit, the astonishing gift or stroke of chance, which is why childhood seems to many in retrospect like a continuous panorama of marvels which diversion to practical interests finally emptied of its magic. An unanticipated eruption of high value where there was none, of tendency, direction, end, springing from fortuitous circumstance (as in awakening love or in intellectual or artistic creation) can have a miraculous quality which tempts us to look for a miracle-worker to give the credit for it. But where are we conscious of supposedly supernatural powers as numinous or daemonic, if not in the experiences they are called in to explain? The Surrealists were the first fully to accustom themselves to the thought that the sense of the 'Marvellous' needs no other origin than the generation of new value by 'Objective chance'.[19] The Darwinian account of the origin of life and of man as chance events, far from devaluing them, makes them the supreme instances of value at its moments of creation.

A second difference from evolutionary progressivism is that Monod's consistently Darwinian account forbids us to deduce standards of valuation from the supposed upward direction of evolution. I myself have to make my choice between ascending and descending lines. To the extent that Monod means by the 'Old Covenant' the assurance that norms by which to conduct our lives are somehow written into nature, whether as the decrees of God, a law of universal progress, or the Hegelian-Marxist dialectic, we must agree with him that it is entirely discredited. It has always depended on an unauthorized move from 'is' to 'ought'. One cannot infer that it is good to love and to bear children from the factual proposition that to do so contributes to the self-conserving project of the biosphere (subjectivizable as Life's will to renew itself). But if you do love and bear children, you do serve that purpose; and if, when most aware from the viewpoints of living things in general, you spontaneously approve of the perpetuation of life, 'Be aware' will entitle you to recognize the purpose you serve as both superhuman and good. That sense of dedication by a marriage rite to a life-renewing purpose which is beyond the social, beyond the human, or of love and desire as irresistible power from beyond, possession by the god Eros, is fully justified within a subjectivized vision of Monod's world. But the belief that to act rightly puts one in harmony with a will beyond man's is one part of that Old Covenant which Monod holds to be discredited, the part which offers the security of knowing that you belong to a cosmos wider than and comprehending human society.

The conclusion that a human being belongs within a cosmos as within a community is indeed implicit in the whole enterprise of replacing teleology by teleonomy, since it can deal with society itself only as another teleonomic system. Let us test how propositions about community and cosmos run parallel. By 'cosmos' we understand the super-system beyond society, the ecosphere and biosphere, Gaia if you like.

(1) *Community*. It is a false jump from 'is' to 'ought' to infer what ought to be from the fact that society prescribes it.

Cosmos. It is a false jump from 'is' to 'ought' to infer what ought to be from a supposed fact about the direction of cosmic process (as divine will, progress, the dialectic).

(2) *Community*. I feel myself to belong to a community to the extent that, rather than merely recognizing objectively that its shaping of me serves its project, I subjectively feel myself spontaneously drawn to its goals. This is a fact about me, which I do not necessarily approve; but as a rebel I still carry my background with me, as an outsider meticulously observing the forms as I try to get myself accepted in another society I betray myself as foreign by every involuntary gesture.

Cosmos. I feel myself as bonded with other living things within the biosphere to the extent that, rather than merely recognizing objectively that its shaping of me serves its project, I subjectively feel myself spontaneously driven towards the goals of Life, towards self-preservation and reproduction. This is a fact about me, which I do not necessarily approve; I may feel degraded by the union of my flesh with another person and with past and future generations which proves me kin to the animals, and pursue through celibacy an anti-vitalistic ideal, or I may train myself to indifference to death, but in either case against the grain of my physical constitution.

(3) *Community*. A community's spontaneous adaptations may serve its own survival more intelligently than the designs of its members, as the body may be wiser than the mind which overworks it ('The fainting fit was Nature's way of telling you to slow down'). Nevertheless, it is only by their reason that individuals can deliberately assist its functioning, as medicine assists the body.

Cosmos. An eco-system's adaptations may serve its own survival more intelligently than the designs of its only rational members, who for reasons of their own are chopping down all the trees. Nevertheless, its rational members are the only ones which can deliberately assist its functioning, by for example irrigating barren land.

(4) *Community*. 'Be aware' requires me to choose that spontaneous inclination, rooted in nature and modified by society, which prevails when I am most aware from all viewpoints in the community, whether or not it accords with the accepted norms. A society is only relatively intelligent, and each individual is a point at which its intelligence is rising or declining.

Cosmos. 'Be aware' requires me to choose that spontaneous inclination, rooted in nature and modified by society, which prevails when I am most aware from the viewpoints of the living in general. Gaia is only relatively intelligent, and each individual is a point at which her intelligence is rising or declining.

In what sense can one think of awareness as extendable to the viewpoints of everything living? Experiencing from a universal viewpoint would be a possible interpretation of the mystic's oneness with everything, but having no first-hand knowledge of this state I cannot profitably discuss it. In any case, for a parallel to the sense of participation in a community, one can get along with something more modest than an illumination of universal oneness. Morally, we are already at the universal viewpoint as soon as we can think of the extermination of a species as a disaster, irrespective of any consequences for man. A somewhat more difficult demonstration is fully reconciling oneself to human mortality. As long as I divorce man from nature I see death only as a brutal fact, which I accept because I must, the most telling illustration of Nature's indifference to man. I may at the same time know well enough that it is the shortness of individual lives which allows the rapid turnover of generations necessary for biological and cultural evolution, and ponder the debated question of whether appeal to the advantages of mortality for the adaptability of species is a legitimate Neo-Darwinian explanation of its universality in other than unicellular organisms. All this at best elucidates why my cruel doom by the laws of nature is inevitable. However, you might well ask me where I would be if evolution had never got properly started, why I think my own or anyone else's death is more important than the rise of new species, the advance of civilization. I should have to acknowledge in the abstract that from a wider perspective it is all to the good that some day I shall die. This is to place myself in relation to the cosmos as an offender does in relation to society if, instead of professing innocence or lamenting his bad luck in getting caught, he recognizes the authority of law and the justice of his punishment. Subjectively, then, reconciliation with disaster which on a longer view is beneficial has the same kind of moral significance in relation to cosmos as to community.

The subjectivization of Monod's scheme, it is important to remember, allows the imputation of purpose only to the teleonomic, to Life by all means but not to Nature, and the purpose in the last resort is the system's own preservation. The goddess Gaia reigns only over one planet, and she is a conservative. It may be possible to push the expanding circles of the systems farther than Gaia, even conceive the universe as a single system, but already at Gaia such metaphors as 'purpose' and 'intelligence' have weakened in appositeness in receding from man. The outlying must be for normal consciousness an abyss of otherness, whether or not it is plumbable by the mystics. In Nature, let us say, there can be direction but not purpose. But it is direction which, as the structural orientation of the living, renews purpose by enriching value through the play of chance. I shall have struck roots going right down into Nature if, underlying all present goals, I am sensitive to a deeper orientation and to the range of possibilities of my future growth or decay. In retrospect no doubt my life will reveal a pattern to which accident has contributed like chance mutations to the orientation of an evolving species. Even in the present I may have a sense of moving forward which is independent of the success or failure of ambitions and enterprises, provided that I remain on an elusive line along which I am learning, growing, which can be lost by a false step, a wrong marriage or choice of career. This is not like the Providence of a personal God, more like the Tao of Chinese philosophy, the unprescribable course of heaven and earth on which the sage moves with unerring spontaneity. It is a 'destiny' as Monod uses the word of a line of evolutionary change: 'Destiny is written as, and while, not before it happens'.[20] I have other possible destinies, which might if I am unlucky include one which realizes my worst potentialities and none which realizes my best. Which of them I live out will, to the extent of my rationality, be affected by my choices, but I can choose between them directly only when I glimpse them in advance. I could deliberately refuse a malign destiny; I could also discover in retrospect that I have betrayed my highest destiny without knowing it.

Here, once again, a consistent subjectivization of the universe of modern science revives a kind of sensibility which, when it intrudes into explanation and prediction, is rightly dismissed as pre-scientific. Sharing in the projects of teleonomic systems, structural orientation selecting from the riches of chance, are concepts which, if you turn them inside out, give a sense to religious or superstitious intimations of being moved by beneficent or baleful powers towards goals which transcend the human, or guided by subconscious influences which are sometimes wiser than ourselves. It may be as well to exemplify the point by experience of a kind which does not fit too easily into conventional frames of religious or mystical interpretation. Thus in many lives there are occasions when a recollected fantasy, dream or piece of writing seems in retrospect to have presaged later events, without any relation to conscious designs. Freud as a medical student in Vienna, not yet inclined to psychology, indulged a fantasy of having his bust in the university aula and inscribed with a line of Sophocles about Oedipus, 'Who divined the famous riddle and was mightiest of men'. Many years later he became 'pale and agitated ... as if he had encountered a *revenant*', when his disciples presented him with a medallion depicting Oedipus answering the Sphinx and inscribed with the identical line, which had occurred to them independently as suitable to the discoverer of the Oedipus Complex. (Ernest Jones, who tells this story,[21] had the bust put up 80 years after Freud imagined it.) André Breton in his *L'amour fou* is excited by the discovery in an automatic text of his from eleven years earlier of an apparent pre-enactment of a current love adventure.[22] The interest of such anecdotes is not as cases of precognition for psychic research; there is no premonition in any case, and the correspondence is not always as striking to disinterested parties as to the person involved. Many such prefigurings must pass unnoticed because the destinies they prepare are unrealized. If Breton had written down his conception of an ideal encounter, and deliberately sought out opportunities for it, no one would be in the least surprised if within eleven years he happened on a much more precise and detailed fulfilment of it. The fascination is in catching a retrospective glimpse of a subterranean trend in line with the course of external events, already encoded in spontaneously erupting imagery long before it surfaced, in the sense of having been guided by a submerged intelligence not quite recognizable as one's own. Not only was it sensitive to a deeper impulse, a more consistent direction, it scanned the external opportunities in advance. In such a correspondence there is assurance that one's ends are not artificial concoctions of will and reason but spring from sources deeper than oneself, belong to a scheme larger than oneself. It becomes easier to understand that, in a culture where hallucination arouses awe rather than fear of madness, the hearing of voices and pondering whether they come from angels or from devils would be a wholly suitable way for Joan of Arc to discover her mission, not just an unreliable and now obsolete way of making up one's mind. Prefiguring images occur also to others sensitive to the undercurrent which one man will discover as his destiny. To take Hitler as the most spectacular modern instance of a man living out a destiny, pre-Nazi German literature and cinema abound in evil hypnotists who in retrospect seem like distorted dreams of him, such as the stage mesmerist and Fascist Cipolla in Thomas Mann's *Mario and the magician*.

We have arrived by Monod's route at conclusions very different from his. He writes that scientific objectivity 'ended the ancient animistic covenant between man and nature, leaving nothing in place of that precious bond but an anxious quest in a world of icy solitude',[23] and that

If he accepts this message in its full significance, man must at last wake out of his millenary dream and discover his total solitude, his fundamental isolation. He must realise that, like a gypsy, he lives on the boundary of an alien world; a world that is deaf to his music, and as indifferent to his hopes as it is to his sufferings or his crimes.[24]

But why should one teleonomic system feel lonely in the company of others, in the middle of the inanimate universe to which all of them are presumed to be bound by the same laws? Monod continues to speak *as if* he and the rest of us had minds distinct from our bodies, to be mentioned in undertones when raising the issues which touch us most deeply, although only the body as teleonomic system may be officially recognized. His underlying assumption is that all language is one, and has the simple function of telling the truth; he conceives the hard lesson which science has taught us, not in methodological terms, as an imperative to describe with uncompromising objectivity while one is engaged in explaining and predicting, but in ontological, as a metaphysical doctrine that 'nature is objective',[25] and 'objective knowledge is the *only* source of real truth'.[26] In spite of the value he puts on subjective simulation, he never comes to grips with the problem of how to speak without confusing the subjective and objective modes. 'A world that is deaf to his music, and as indifferent to his hopes as to his crimes' is highly personifying language; a piece of paper or a brick wall is not deaf to music or indifferent to crimes. This is not a trivial point, for to suppose that Monod is simply decorating his scientific thought with a little of the rhetoric pardonable on solemn occasions would be a fundamental misunderstanding. There is no other language in which Monod could have talked about the divorce from nature; as Lawrence's pines illustrate,[27] one cannot show how different something else is from oneself without trying to penetrate a subjectivity foreign to one's own. By speaking as though the universe is alive but refuses to notice us, Monod betrays that subjectively as well as objectively our difference from the rest of nature can only be one of degree.

In objectivizing I assimilate myself to the external, in subjectivizing assimilate the external to myself; either approach is legitimate, but they must not be confused. While subjectivizing, one has the full right, if that is how one sees it, to display the past and future of evolution and entropy as a tragic panorama. Over millions of years Nature turns a smiling face towards man, afterwards over millions of years will slowly turn away. One may regard Nature, or God if one prefers a stronger personification, in any number of ways, as mysterious, holy, benign, capricious, prodigal or cruel, overwhelming man by its vastness or yielding to him as its Faustian conqueror. The one conception which is to be excluded absolutely is the one which to so many seems inevitable, a 'world of icy solitude', in which man lives in 'fundamental isolation'. That starts from a basic confusion of approaches.

2.3 Cosmos-building in the language of ends

It is commonly assumed and widely regretted that modern science has finally demolished that comfortable sort of cosmology which shows man his place in the world. But the arguments of recent chapters require a change of perspective. The cosmology of post-Galilean science triumphed by restricting its scope to questions of means. But to organize phenomena in a cosmos is equally important in answering questions of ends. In thinking out choices of means, I find the world around me intelligible to the extent that I can predict what will happen in given conditions, by applying laws of nature tested by the rational tradition of science. But before choices of means arise, I am already responding for or against from different or changing viewpoints, and find the world intelligible to the extent that I know what harmonizes with or conflicts with what, so that my reactions adjust to the interactions of the rest. This more basic order emerges from a synthesizing which is not only spontaneous but at its roots unconscious, and even when not institutionalized by religion or made articulate by poets, it is latent in the metaphors of speech and the symbolism of dreams. To the extent that older cosmologies tried to answer the same questions as modern science they are indeed discredited. But their weakness was in not yet having learned to confine themselves to questions of ends, as science has to questions of means. In principle each of us could have two symbolic systems, perfectly corresponding, for objective and subjective approaches to the same universe. What cannot be done is to combine them as one. There can be an account neutral as to means and ends, but that will neither value nor explain, will be the bare description or narrative of 'The cat sat on the mat'.

We noticed that while means-language is primarily verbal, ends-language embraces every medium which can directly stimulate spontaneous motions, and that, even when it is likewise verbal, affirmation and denial have only a secondary place in it.[1] A society may be seen as relating itself to its cosmos through the entire range of its customary symbols. Its myths and rites spring from process which, granted that it is the better for being rationally guided, betrays its fundamental spontaneity when it gets out of control, in the images of hallucination or in the repetitive compulsions of neurotic ritualism. When symbolizing verbally, we are tempted to assume that the essence of cosmos-building for ends, as for means, is the affirming of propositions, the truth of which gives meaning to the image or rite, but in practice a ritual may be seen to keep its vitality through historical or cultural changes, however differently it may be interpreted. In distinguishing cosmos-building for means and for ends, we are not suggesting that science is to be rivalled by another verbalized system which is distinct but equally coherent. That would give verbal symbolism a priority which would be deserved only if it were indeed telling truths like those of science, and refutable by science. But cosmos-building for ends, even when its medium is words, adjusts spontaneous motions to the interrelations of objects without having to affirm or deny, and if it needs help from reason, it is not for support but for critical guidance. Intellect cannot establish the foundations of such a cosmos, nor can it demolish them. The pre-rational sources of the cosmos-building impulse never dry up, and continue to fertilize the metaphors of verbal language even as reason is discrediting the affirmations derived from misreadings of them.

Those who hanker after a truth inclusive of both fact and value complain that scientific description is incomplete, and try to locate the source of value in something it leaves out. To the extent that they recognize the spontaneity at the bottom of their own valuations, they conceptualize it as cognitive, as intuition of that something left out. Yet even the existence of God, if treated as a fact somehow overlooked by science, can seem to authorize moral judgments only if one takes an illegitimate step from 'is' to 'ought'; the fact, if it is a fact, that an almighty being created me and has ordained how he requires me to live affords no reason other than fear for obeying him, unless I already assume him to be good. In building a cosmos of ends, there is no advantage at all in trying to introduce entities unknown to science. We have conceded that there are cases where for choices of ends one might reasonably accept something ahead of scientific demonstration, even a Fortean phenomenon if personally one finds the evidence strong enough,[2] but even if it is a fact it remains only a fact. The fascination of queer events is only too easily mistaken for the intimation of a higher reality just out of reach, entitling one to condescend to scientists as spiritual inferiors because they remain sceptical. But this is a futile displacement of the sense of the Sacred on to fortuitous odds and ends of unexplained phenomena. Even if they all turned out to be real after all, once proved they would lose their mystery and settle down comfortably in our desacralized world, with the yeti in the next cage to the giant panda, visitors from outer space like any other tourists or invaders, telepathy proving its utility for communicating with submarines. They would not even have to be explained, any more than hypnotism, which was once as uncanny and as suspect to the rationalistic as other supposedly supernatural performances, but since the nineteenth century, when its replicability under controlled conditions came to be accepted, just another fact which will be explained some day.

We may go so far as to claim that in cosmos-building for ends it is a disadvantage of words that their message even looks like fact, is mistakable for fact. Words can help to relate one to a cosmos only by acting on the nerves as directly as the rhythms of music, dance, ritual or controlled breathing; indeed, it is significant that so many of the most rational people, unable to take any mode of language but their own quite seriously, do give music an importance in their lives out of all proportion to such effects on them as they can verbalize. They are none the less at a disadvantage in depending exclusively on a medium which cannot be related to verbal language at all. The man of reason cannot altogether dispense with words in finding his place in a cosmos, but he is safest if he puts his trust in the use of words least confusable with his own, that of poetry. He may even be recommended, as the perfect assurance of not pulling some intellectual sleight-of-hand at his own expense, to help his cosmos to define itself by following the Surrealists in exploring through automatic writing the indistinct myths latent in the twilight images on the edge of consciousness.[3]

An ends-cosmos being subjective, the one which is right for you may be wrong for me. My own will relate universe and mankind to my civilization, my society, myself; it has to be true to the structural relations which I view up a single perspective, my own, but if I insist that it is better than some other (which on the present account I have the full right to), that can only be as in judging between works of art, on the grounds that one exhibits a greater range and depth of awareness than another. Post-Galilean science does, for the present at least, seem in contrast to be unique and culture-free, changing of course, but within a unified tradition of research whether West or East. But on the Kuhnian approach to science it seems that in the last resort the difference must be superficial. The successive paradigms with which scientific thinking goes on adjusting to recalcitrant problems were at first culture-bound, and there is no reason to suppose that they have ever ceased to be, so that it is imaginable in theory that traditions starting from different conceptual schemes might adapt themselves equally successfully without ever becoming the same. Not that we are likely ever to see a demonstration of the possibility, because once science was revolutionized by mathematization and controlled experiment in a single culture it spread too fast for the 'discovery of how to discover' to be made independently in another. (The centuries through which the

Scientific Revolution has been diffusing from the West, although long by its own accelerated timescale, are brief in relation to the slow changes of pre-modern cultures.) If the possibility were indeed realized, we should have to analyse to co-ordinate basic concepts as we synthesize to co-ordinate viewpoints. However that may be, we have to accept without reserve that ends-cosmologies have the subjectivity of individual visions in the arts, to be transcended, not by syncretism mixing the supposed elements of truth in all of them, but by interrelating them like sightings of the same object from different directions, and evaluating them, like more and less informative angles of vision, in terms of 'Be aware'. In an unstable age it may be a natural weakness to hanker after the security of a single true religion, but dogmatism is not objectivity, it is a self-blinded subjectivity, and to have a variety of views available to be co-ordinated like the angles of viewing an object, far from submerging us in subjectivity, is the only escape from it we have. Besides, contemporary cosmos-building for ends has to be fluid, ready to adapt itself to scientific changes of mind. One can no longer count on lasting for centuries on the same vision of the origin and end of the universe. Whether in terms of means or of ends, the same world is being interpreted, and there has to be an ultimate agreement with science on the plain question of what happened or will happen. The spontaneous formation of one's ends-cosmos has a bias, whether nobly or meanly motivated, towards what ought to have happened, not what did happen, and needs science to guide it. One knows by the hard experience of centuries that whenever there is conflict between science and men's finer feelings on such purely factual issues as whether our earth is the centre of the universe or man is descended from the beasts, it is always the scientists who are right.

A means-cosmos appears as ordered to the extent that processes are explainable and predictable, an ends-cosmos to the extent that they are mutually relatable as harmonious or conflicting. In an ends-cosmos one judges something good or bad in so far as in subjectivizing things in awareness of their interactions one spontaneously reacts for or against it. The changed conception of the relation between reason and spontaneity which is the subject of this book explains why rationality need not uproot us from cosmos any more than from community. It is by the harmony or conflict of one's own spontaneity with the rest that one is drawn into the interactions of cosmos (which put in other words is the tautology that only the natural in man can belong to nature). But the spontaneous may be judged either good or bad, and there can be deliberate acts to influence the interactions in favour of the good against the bad. These we class as not practical action but ritual. The simplest example would be prescribed manners the scope of which is limited to effects on society. An etiquette differs from a useful convention like driving on the left or right of the road in that for those who share the values of a community it contributes to the whole quality of life, while to the misfit it is meaningless, burdensome, imposes a mask which distorts his true identity. It affects the relations between people by influences of a subtlety and intricacy which eludes analysis, so that one gets only crude or vague answers if one asks the conformist what good some formality does or the rebel why he resents it, or asks where it came from or why all of a sudden its power has begun to fail and it is withering away. Prescribed action which influences the interactions not only of a community but of its cosmos would be, let us say, the repetition every spring of a fertility dance followed by the ploughing and sowing. Let us assume ideally primitive people whose whole thinking about their place in the cosmos is synthetic, not analytic. They are not yet in the habit of thinking of the crops as being grown simply as a means to their self-support, rather they assume that within the cosmic order it is proper that the grain should grow in its season just as it is proper that man should eat it. Their customary labour in the fields is itself a ritual, unlike their practical actions for private ends. The dance and the sowing guide and focus the spontaneous mutual influences of nature and man; the work helps the crops, the crops feed man, the rhythm of the dance revitalizes communion between the dancers, stimulates their own fertility, energizes them for the work. How the dance and the sowing act so benignly on man and nature, like the influence of manners in our own society, is understood only imperfectly, so that the dance is supposed to fertilize not only the dancers but the soil. When these villagers come into contact with our own civilization, the ritual quality is soon drained from labour by the habit of analysing its effects, reducing it to means. The dance, with its more elusive effects, remains a ritual until they are educated to analyse its psychological effects and defend it as socially useful; then the villagers will no longer be living in their cosmos of ends.

Shall we say that the cosmos we have sketched has been dissolved by rational criticism? No, by falling into a habit of analysing rather than synthesizing, as more useful in choices of means. Rational criticism would take a different direction. The structure of this cosmos has turned out to be analysable as that of a society inside an eco-system, a structure which it partially distorts. There is indeed an interaction of man, sun and water, dance, fertility, work, but it does not include direct action by the dance on the fertility of the soil. If the ritual should happen to include prayer and sacrifice to the sun, one could object that, although solar energy certainly is the source of power in the eco-system, one cannot win favours from the sun as from a powerful man. The objection is not quite that the sun is not a god but a ball of fire,—an insufficiently precise way of putting it—but that the subjectivizer's analogization to himself has turned out to be misleading when pushed so far beyond the human. The pattern of cosmic interactions from the perspective of man, as it is being brought to light in the present century, above all by the new discipline of ecology, surpasses in intricacy and must supersede anything conceivable by our villagers or by any other pre-scientific cosmos-builders. But ecology as a science does not impose more than an abstract recognition of the interdependence of man and other beings on the plane of means. I may be well aware of the complex interactions within eco-systems, as within societies, and of the dangers of tampering with them too freely, yet remain an outsider objectivizing them all as means to my ends. It is when I subjectivize other beings, as the villagers do the sun, that the ecosphere turns into a cosmos like theirs, in which all life is valued for its own sake, and for its continuing possibilities of evolution even if mankind should vanish from the earth. If I find myself speculating about what goes on in the whale's enormous brain, or listen with a shudder of awe to recordings of his uncanny songs, the shock at the thought of his possible extinction is independent of any ill effects on man.

As an instance of the advantages, even as a guide for subjectivization, of the objectively testable findings of the sciences, we may take a by-product of Michel Gauquelin's investigation of that Babylonian-Hellenistic pseudo-science astrology, which as a relic of an obsolete culture proving itself perfectly at home in the metropolitan life of the late twentieth century is as remarkable as the Mafia from feudal Sicily. The researches of his team confirmed that there is no statistical relation between astrological prediction and the realized course of a person's life. But he also chanced on the surprising result that an unexpectedly high proportion of great physicians were born at either the rise or the culmination of Mars or Saturn, information quite unknown to traditional astrology, and later he found similar correlations between success in other professions and birth under other planets. The explanation which he favours, on the reasonable assumption that fitness for a career is to some extent genetically determined, is that different planets have effects on the onset of labour which vary with the genetic constitution of the child. This would put the phenomenon among many remarkable examples of the sensitivity of organic growth to celestial influences (possibly through effects on the geomagnetic and other fields), such as the breathing inside a hen's egg or the metabolic activity of a potato varying, even in a uniformly lighted laboratory, with sunrise, sunset and moonlight.[4] If Gauquelin is right there is indeed a planetary influence, but not on personal destiny, merely on time of birth.

This is not what has traditionally been understood by astrology, but it does have a bearing on a feature of astrology which deserves more sympathy than its predictive claims. Contemplating Gauquelin's conclusions, and assuming for the moment their still contested validity, it startles me to think that *my* birth too may have been hastened by a planet. In the celestial cycles I have my widest view of order in the cosmos: my birth was the moment of my emergence as a separate being: all at once, between these extremes crucial to my orientation, an influence is seen to have passed. It speeded up the process which made *me*, not just the shape of my nose but the way I have chosen to live. If I were a physician, to check the records and find that I was born at the culmination of Saturn would suggest that my choice of life was not arbitrary but fulfilled my true potentialities, which derive from the same forces that revolve the planets. In subjectivizing I am stirred to analogize too, discover an unsuspected kinship with the unhatched chick and the potato. This sense of participation in the cosmos is one of the attractions of astrology, the one which wins it acceptance as a substitute for religion. Yet nothing in the artificialities of astrology carries the authority, vividness and precision of this insight sparked by the subjectivization of a scientific hypothesis.

The advantages over astrology do not include permanence; such an illumination quickly fades. In astrology on the other hand the sense of participation is renewed daily by the ritual of reading a 'What the stars foretell' column, consolidated by acting on the prospects it opens up, nourished by fellow-feeling with any stranger who can tell you his zodiacal sign and shares your hope in the coming Age of Aquarius, intellectually buttressed by assurances that 'Science has been forced to admit that there is something in astrology', for which even Gauquelin's refutation can be adduced as support. Gauquelin's findings, even if they win general acceptance, are hardly likely to become rooted in our culture as the traditional and discredited influences of Jupiter, Mercury and Saturn have been by the currency of the words 'jovial', 'mercurial' and 'saturnine'. A cosmos of ends has to grow in the first place from relations with persons, things and places close at hand, if insights from remote studies are to take root in it.

An individual's cosmos of ends begins in the spontaneous interactions of family and home out of which personal identity first emerges, and it continues to be shaped largely by the metaphor of the family, all the way to the trinities of religion and politics, Father, Son and Holy Spirit; Liberty, Equality and Fraternity. Our primitive village may be presumed to be the ideal organic community in full harmony with nature, interpreting its bond as kinship by blood, unalterable because biological. Most of us today however are not lucky or unlucky enough to live in such communities, but in vast webs of loose, pluralistic and overlapping organization; for a modern state to pose as an organic community can only be a sinister pretence (Nazi Germany, with its imagery of Blood and Soil). If however, as we claim, individuals exercise their rationality primarily in choosing between spontaneous inclinations, we certainly cannot think of society as an association of rational individuals pursuing their own interests and co-operating for their mutual benefit; we have to think of it as constituted in the first place by their spontaneous interactions, and as approaching rationality to the extent that they choose rationally between its spontaneous tendencies. The ends of society, as of individuals, will be chosen from spontaneously emerging goals. Society will be part of a cosmos of ends only where man submerges in nature, that is to say where it is being temporally or lastingly shaped for good or ill by the interacting spontaneities of its members.

One's actual society can belong within one's cosmos of ends only in so far as it is configured by this spontaneity of ends rather than by what one might call the automatism of means. There is a clear difference of kind between trends found good or bad in themselves, for example towards greater or lesser personal freedom, communal fellowship, creativity in thought and the arts, sensitivity to other persons, refinement in pleasure, and those trends against the will of all, of which the most obtrusive contemporary example is the pressure on competing states, each of which would rather be fighting with muskets against an enemy with bows and arrows, to excel their rivals' nuclear armaments, so that all are forced step by step in the direction of mutual annihilation. Our rational institutions, since they function as means through their causal relations, have a mechanics of their own which tends to alienate them from the ends they are designed to serve. Marx analysed social evolution as a process by which religion, morality, law, the state, and above all the market, emerge as independent forces 'alien' to the wills of all, culminating in the transition from feudalism, in which economic relations are not yet wholly impersonal, to capitalism, in which even the capacity for the work by which man can realize his potentialities becomes a commodity to be sold for self-support ('Life itself appears only as a means to life'),[5] and gluts, slumps, unemployment and destitution result from the interactions of individuals yet happen against their wills like natural catastrophes. At the extreme of 'alienation'[6] society appears as a self-moving apparatus in which everyone is trapped, and each person's actions as alien to himself in that they impose themselves as means to further means up a vista in which he sees no ends recognizable as his own. Whether in pre-capitalist or capitalist times, the community fully shaped by the spontaneity of ends has no doubt always been an ideal set in the past or future, although with an actual nucleus of spontaneous fellowship in the imperfect present, even if no wider than the circle of one's kin and friends.

Historically it has been conservative thinkers such as Burke and Maistre who have understood the spontaneity of society, while revolutionaries (with exceptions such as the anarchists) have put their faith in its rational reconstruction. Spontaneous relations have been interpreted, by those who approve them, as permanent relations of subordination, 'natural', 'organic', like those of the limbs to the head in the biological organism. But this assumes social fixity, and confinement to a few by economic shortage of the resources and leisure for cultural advance, assumptions undermined by accelerating industrial revolution. In recent centuries the individual has on the one hand discovered his freedom to criticize rationally the ends of traditional society, on the other has been caught up in the automatism of increasingly complex means. In so far as he now experiences the spontaneity of ends, it is less and less in a stable inheritance from the past, more and more in the shifting interactions of his contemporaries, at the extreme of volatility in the swings of fashion. The industrial revolution having once been launched, it would seem to leave us no escape from the mounting automatism of means unless it does fulfil its apocalyptic promise, universal abundance and leisure releasing us all from the pressure of means. Then, presumably, the whole business of life will be to discover what we really do spontaneously desire, and co-operate or compete to enjoy it; there could be a wholly fluid society submerged in cosmos, its changing harmonies and conflicts following the spontaneity of ends. An automated world of universal plenty does indeed seem as likely an outcome of technological progress as universal destruction. Marxism expected it to mark the passage from socialism to communism (and, equally dubiously, the end of conflict), but as it has turned out the nearest approach to it we have seen has been in capitalist California. Since every so far known form of social organization has presupposed the need of the majority to work for a living, we have little to go on but our hopes and fears in imagining what life could be like after so fundamental a change. Only at the height of affluence in the late 1960s, when many of the young felt for a while the burden of looking for a job lifted from their shoulders, did we catch a tantalizing glimpse of the careless good and motiveless evil which would be possible in such a world.

We cannot live without organizing some kind of cosmos of ends; if the forces in us which shape it fail, the universe of science itself turns into its inverted form, alien, meaningless, valueless. To dismiss the shaping processes as irrational, instead of learning to criticize them rationally, is a self-stultification. Let us consider a kind of thinking on which Lévi-Strauss tried the structuralist approach,[7] the systematization of scientifically irrelevant correspondences which organizes the world-pictures not only of pre-literate but of many literate cultures, and in the West still survives in occultism. We would see it as an elaboration of the pre-logical patterning by assimilation and differentiation which in guiding spontaneous reactions also provides the categories from which analytic thinking starts. Thus traditional Chinese thought organizes its cosmos as a system of interacting components, in the first place pairs classified under the active and passive principles *Yang* and *Yin*, as shown in Table 1.

Table 1

The Supreme Pole (T'ai-chi)

Yang	*Yin*
Light	Darkness
Day	Night
Above	Below
Man	Woman
Hard	Soft
Hot	Cold
Moving	Still...

At a lower level the system correlates sets of fours and fives as shown in Table 2.

Table 2

	Yang			*Yin*	
Five Phases	Wood	Fire	Earth	Metal	Water
Four Seasons	Spring	Summer		Autumn	Winter
Five Colours	Green	Red	Yellow	White	Black
Five Directions	East	South	Centre	West	North
Five Virtues	Kindness	Manners	Truth- fulness	Duty	Wis- dom...

In both series, the vertical correspondences are of mutually stimulating members, the horizontal sequences are of conflicting members which give way to each other in turn in recurring cycles. Consequently, the corresponding sequences interact harmoniously as long as they move in time with each other. The moral and ritual applications are, for example, that the Emperor's ceremonial robes should be green in spring, red in summer, and so forth, thus helping the seasons to come at the right times; and that since kindness corresponds to spring and duty to autumn, he should put off pardons to spring and punishments to autumn.

One may be tempted to read the system as proto-science pretending to explain why fire is red and stretched to explain why men ought to practise the five cardinal virtues. (It was on this assumption that the term *wu hsing*, here translated by the increasingly current 'Five Phases', was until recently generally translated 'Five Elements'.) It will then seem that what the Emperor has to do is inferred from false or artificial analogies together with a gigantic leap from 'is' to 'ought'. But this would be to detach man from the system of harmoniously interacting agencies of which he is one; granted that the cosmology did also provide the theoretical foundation for the Chinese proto-sciences, its basic function is to maintain one's spontaneous rhythm in accord with nature. The Emperor does not have to infer anything by analogy. Spring directly stimulates a warm and kindly mood in him, just as it does the growth of wood and green. There is a natural rhythm by which his temper changes from benevolence in spring to sternness in autumn, and to forgive or punish at the wrong times would disturb that rhythm and weaken his capacity to balance kindness and duty. His deliberate ritual acts harmonize his own spontaneity with nature just as, in the choice of colours to affect the seasons, they are conceived to harmonize nature with man. It will be objected perhaps that such complications as wars, famines and the wiles of his eunuchs and concubines would upset the annual rhythm in any case. Certainly the meagreness of such a scheme must impose extreme simplifications. Yet if we consider what is left of our own traditional seasonal festivals, it appears perfectly comprehensible that someone should feel that to miss the reunion with the family at Christmas is not just a disappointment, it is an interruption of his rhythm damaging to the sense of security which he annually renews by going back to his roots.

To suppose this kind of thinking foreign to us would be profoundly mistaken; it is influencing us all the time through the vocabulary of the English language. The classification of races as white, black, yellow, brown and red fits their complexions hardly better than the Five Colours fit the Five Phases and the Four Seasons; many of the yellow people are to the eye whiter than many of the white, and American Indians are red only because the brown people live in Asia and Polynesia. Of especial interest are series of pairs of the Yin-Yang type. The cliché 'golden sun' may seem to stand by itself, sufficiently accounted for by the sun's colour and glory. But we have also the 'silvery moon'. Sun and moon, gold and silver, have a parallel grading in value, not as good and bad, but as best and second-best. Thus 'silvery hair' suggests not senility but a dignified old age surpassed in value only by youth with its 'golden hair', as the Silver Age was surpassed only by the preceding Golden Age. There are other pairs which do contrast as good and bad, such as

White	Black
Day	Night
Joy	Gloom
God	Devil
White man	Black man

Here one appreciates how serious such hidden structures can be, for this one functions to equate the black man with night and the Devil, deep in the thinking of people not necessarily conscious of discriminating between races. Should we conclude that all such analogizing is dangerous superstition? But the racialist application is a fallacy exposable inside analogical thinking. Compared with the opposition of the colours white and black, human races are highly similar, variations of the species whose skin colour is among the least significant of their differences, being without inherent relation to any other. It would take a very primitive racialist indeed to insist when challenged that the black man really is evil because he is the colour of night; such a claim would be superstitious because it is wrong analogizing, not like rejecting black as the colour for a bride's wedding dress, rather as though one were to refuse to heat the house with coal because it is the colour of the Devil, which would indeed be superstition. If we recognize that all valuation starts from applying 'Be aware' to spontaneity, it becomes plain that to criticize such analogizing there is no need to introduce a moral principle from outside. 'Be aware' is here at the basic level where it begins, as 'Be aware of similarities and differences', where for a reaction to be the right one it is enough that the analogizing which guides it is sound.

Such schematism must always be going on incipiently in the perpetual stream of analogizing at the back of analytic thinking. Analogizing has to synthesize very complicated patterns of similarity and difference, and very fast, often much faster than the unfolding of any rational thought. It must therefore be grouping the different under the similar, in the beginnings of a scheme which would resolve all distinctions in an ultimate One like the Chinese *T'ai-chi*, as analysis aspires to subject everything to the same laws. In the Chinese cosmology such a schematism is overt and fully evolved. Are we perhaps making a mistake in driving the process underground, instead of letting it flourish side by side with scientific thinking? A racial implication would then be overt and criticizable, like the implication that man is above woman in the Yin-Yang scheme. We should be grateful, not condescending, to modern poets such as Yeats who are fascinated by occultist systems.[8] As those most responsible for the health of the language, it is their business to expose and revalue a culture's submerged patterns of metaphor.

It is only in the last century that Western science has become confident in dealing with the complexities of systems of interdependent parts, with living organisms above all. The Chinese in juxtaposing the harmonious and separating the conflicting had no choice whatever but to lay out their cosmic order as a symmetrical table of correspondences. Modern cosmos-building has of course broken with such artificial schematism, and with the elementary conception of interaction by which the colours of the Emperor's robes can affect the seasons as the seasons affect the crops. Nor can we share the assumption of a conservative culture that stasis is good and disturbance bad; we would think of cosmos rather as changing pattern lifting towards new value, with increase of awareness as the test. The interest of the Chinese correspondences is in the assumptions underlying them:

(1) All things interact, including the spontaneous in man.

(2) There is an order which juxtaposes the harmonious and separates the conflicting, a cosmos. If the order is disturbed there is chaos.

(3) It is man's duty by his deliberate acts to maintain cosmos and resist chaos.

But these are principles which in essence remain valid in all cosmos-building for ends, however modern. The ecosphere when subjectivized becomes an ends-cosmos like that of China or any other pre-industrial culture, in which the natural cycles which are the concrete evidence of order in the universe, day and night, the phases of the moon, the seasons, birth and death, rather than being analysed to predict recurrences for the timing of action, are synthesized as rhythms with which to keep in step. To sense a recurrence as a rhythm is to simulate by incipient motion, and adjust one's other motions to it as spontaneously as to one's pulse and breathing. To sleep at night and wake with the day is a response to rhythm inherited from our animal ancestors; a modern city-dweller, who might smile to hear that the Chinese Emperor should pardon in spring and punish in autumn, will very likely, when starting for the first time on the night shift, feel queasy with forebodings of coming damage to his metabolism. He will probably also have some feel for the city itself as responding to the rhythms of day and night, with a spontaneous self-ordering which sets limits to rational planning, and for metaphors of the city as asleep or waking, its centre as a throbbing heart, traffic as circulating in its arteries. He will also, in spite of his consciousness of living in an age of accelerating change, be organizing time by the cosmic rhythms of the centuries and decades of the Christian era. Under a compulsion to think in chronological cycles, no different from that which periodized time in the cosmologies of Mayas and Hindus, we find ourselves visualizing history as though everyone changed from wigs and knee breeches to beards and frock coats in 1800 (there must be many who, like myself, have for much of this century had a secret hankering, absurd as it may be, to last until the year 2.000, in order to catch a glimpse of what the world will be like in the third millenium AD). An assumption, which by setting a rhythm with which to keep in step is to some extent self-confirming, that the culture of the present breathes in phases of ten years counted from the birth of Christ, makes it seem entirely acceptable that, for example, a reviewer in the London *Times* on 26 October 1982 should write of an art exhibition called *Zeitgeist*:

The choice of moment for the show is spot-on : far enough into the Eighties for us to have some emerging idea of what the decade may be like, but early enough to claim precedence as the first confident artistic declaration on the subject.

A cosmos of ends has events which originate, change or destroy it, narrated in myth. The mythopoeic imagination never dries up, but since we are nowadays habituated to treat the spontaneity which is the source of ends as an irrelevance, hindrance, or distraction from the rational pursuit of means (which is to be in the state called 'alienation'), it has come to be confined to the dream and fantasy from which it starts and to the leisure activities, art and play; it gets itself taken wholly seriously only by adopting a protective colouring of science, as in Marxism and Freudianism. In tradition-bound societies, although hardly in our own, mythopoeia is above all the imagination of origins, in relation not to means but to ends. In a cosmos of means, to know the origin of something is to know the means of making it; whoever can give the first full account of the beginnings of life will have the prescription for manufacturing living tissue in the laboratory, indeed could confirm his hypothesis only by doing so. The rationalizing habit of mind, acting on the universal disposition to imagine others to be like oneself, tempts us to suppose that mythic cosmogonies are premature attempts at scientific explanation. But the need which a myth satisfies is like, not a scientist's curiosity, but a foundling's for the names of his true father and mother. The reactions which relate me to others in a cosmos of ends have grown spontaneously, even if with rational guidance; if I am curious about origins, it is in order by returning to them to recover the most basic in myself, community, mankind, nature, and so renew or redirect present reactions by starting again at a point where I or we were firm on the right path. The unthinking interplay of insight and impulse which binds a community, at a level deeper than collaboration on rational projects, depends on common influences, of descent, homeland and upbringing, and has traditionally been maintained by rites periodically recalling and celebrating common origins. A cosmology of ends does not analyse and explain by preceding conditions, it synthesizes and subjectivizes the origin and its outcomes as an ancestral tree, in which each can recover his proper line of growth by going back to the common roots, for example by re-enaction as rite of a primal deed narrated in myth. When a culture becomes literate and, in *Genesis*, the *Theogony* or the *Kojiki*, knits together the discrete events by which universe, mankind and community became as they now are, the principle of organization is not causal or even teleological, but simply genealogical, the tracing of lines of descent from the first gods and men to the tribes and the royal houses of the present. Myth presents without explaining an act which shaped some part of cosmos out of chaos, or marred it with some flaw such as sin or death, and manifested itself as good or ill simply by being done.

Mircea Eliade's theory of myth,[9] the one more or less followed here, exhibits a curious structural parallelism with Jacques Monod's of evolution. According to Eliade, the dweller in an archaic cosmos lives the whole of his significant life as the re-enaction of the exemplary deeds narrated in myth which shaped the order of things at the beginning of time. For generation after generation men go on repeating the primal acts just as, for the biochemist, their bodies go on replicating the genetic model fixed at the origin of the species. As for the primal events themselves, they simply happened, like species coming about by chance mutation. Here no doubt many will protest. What greater contrast could there be than between draining events of value by a Darwinian explanation, and sacralizing them as the exemplary acts of gods and heroes, even without crediting them with reason or purpose? Yet we have already, in discussing Monod, undermined this apparently obvious distinction.[10] Evolutionary changes which are advances in awareness will, simply by according with 'Be aware', be good in themselves irrespective of whether or how they can be explained. They appear subjectively as qualitatively new, unanticipatable outbursts of value like the primal events which shape a sacred cosmos, irrespective of whether objectively they are attributable to causation or to chance. Similarly, in *Genesis* God does not create in order to fulfil some purpose, he simply declares 'Let there be. . .', then sees that it is good; the Hebrew cosmos was made for no other reason than that it is good in itself. Mythology in general, to the extent that it escapes intellectualization and moralization, is conspicuously free of any modern worry that the cosmos will lose all meaning if its great constitutive events came about by whim or chance.

Let us take an example on which to try out this approach. Theorizing about myths, especially when detached from social context, is at best highly subjective. However, since we are approaching cosmos-building for ends as a process still active in ourselves, it need not much matter whether my envisaging of a mythic scene illustrates modern or ancient mythopoeia. I shall therefore pick at random from an encyclopedia the first short myth which strikes my imagination, and treat it as though it were a literary text, without even asking how much may be missing from the abstract. This one is from the Chibchas or Muisca of Colombia.

According to the Chibchas the human race was born from a woman who appeared on the shores of Lake Iguaque holding a child in her arms. Later they were both changed into snakes, and disappeared into the lake, for which reason the Chibchas made offerings to it.[11]

The myth subjectivizes the origin of man as each person remembers his beginnings, as a child in his mother's arms. Where did the woman come from? Was there a father? Pointless to ask. Looking backwards, this is the place where you stop. However, a little amateur psycho-analysis is perhaps in order. Beyond the image of the mother, the lake stirs remoter intimations of a pre-human womb out of which everything came. By a logic intelligible in dreams, the ancestress and her child assume the phallic shape of snakes and by plunging into the lake assure its continuing fecundity. So you go to Lake Iguaque, the primordial source, and throw in offerings to renew life in the present.

Shall we say that this myth is one of the many now superseded explanations of man's origin, by descent from or creation by divine beings? The woman with the child appearing beside Lake Iguaque certainly impresses the imagination from the start as a sacred image. Yet there is nothing in the text to say that she is a goddess, and in any case which beings get classified as divine depends on a largely arbitrary choice of criteria from their characteristics in myth. Her apparent immortality might seem to count as such a criterion, since to receive the offerings she would have to be still alive in Lake Iguaque. But to respond to the lake as a vitalizing image of the source of life one does not have to ask whether the snakes are still there; one may react without self-examination or analyse sexual symbols, but to infer that the woman must be immortal, far from being a precondition of revering her as sacred, would be a rationalization, a first step towards desacralizing her. It would exclude another interpretation which enlarges the meaning, as the unravelling of an ambiguity enriches a line of poetry, that our first ancestors went down ahead of us to the nether world of the dead. The effect of perceiving it deepens awareness of something previously outside the range of the myth, that the death of every generation is necessary to the life of its successor. We must conclude that it is not that being about a goddess sacralizes the story, but that her presence in the myth sacralizes the woman.

Let us suppose for a moment that excavations were to confirm that the human race really did originate near Lake Iguaque, and tourists could go on a pilgrimage there, marvel at the skulls and thighbones, and admire the statue of the first mother and child by a Colombian disciple of Henry Moore. The experience would be impressive but to someone haunted by the Chibcha myth perhaps a little disappointing. Would it be because our ancestress has turned out to be just a woman who never turned into a snake after all? That is surely not the point. The mythic quality will drain from any account of the first men if I imagine them as though I were close enough to take a photograph. To place myself subjectively in relation to the first mother and to all who share descent from her, I must have the sense, on the one hand of her remoteness and otherness, on the other of being her progeny, of having drawn my life from her fecundity. Adding to the mere facts does nothing to awaken this sense. But in the myth I am as though looking back into my earliest memories, at an image of my mother no longer distinguishable from dream, and pushing beyond her through the generations to the ancestress whom I share with all mankind, in a primordial age of inexplicable apparitions and metamorphoses.

Although myth comes under our general heading of 'poetry' in opposition to 'science', one sees from this example how it differs from the poem as a fixed pattern of words. Poetry can evoke the most complex and sophisticated response to the concrete detail of peripheral things and ephemeral events. Myth however, in renewing and redirecting my interactions with a cosmos, returns me to the most basic reactions to the most basic events. If, as in the Chibcha myth, or in a dream, the womb-like image of a lake evokes a plunging snake, I find myself back in the pictorial thinking of my childhood, and the childhood of man. Obviously it is a regression to the primitive from which I had better find my way back to the world of reason. But the whole point of myth, on Eliade's interpretation, is in going back to go forward again. The very strangeness to conscious thought reassures me that I am at the level of the pure spontaneous impulse and image out of which sophisticated attitudes have grown, and that the rationality of choices between such attitudes has not detached them from their roots. Just as I embed myself in my own remembered past by thinking myself back into outgrown ignorance and delusion (true information from external sources is as though about a different person), so I discover the uncorrupted power of growth or renewal by reversion to older modes of thought now overlaid by acculturation. To visualize the origin of the sun as modern astronomy reconstructs it does not generate myth because it snaps the connexion with myself as I am now by putting me with all my present knowledge at a viewpoint contemporary with the event. It will perhaps be objected that the initial decision to approach the myth as a modern trusting to his own imagination has made it look more primitive and dreamlike than it would to the Chibchas, rather as the primaeval look of megaliths gains by the accident that, worn down by time, they seem like natural outcroppings of rock only half way to becoming human architecture. But it would seem that in the primitives themselves imagination distinguishes itself as more primitive, infantile, dreamlike, when of mythic beings than of the things of everyday. Australian aboriginals distinguish the time of origins from the present dispensation as the 'dream time'. In Hesiod's *Theogony*, first Void (Chaos) is born, then Earth (Gaia, in person), who engenders Sky (Ouranos); Sky fructifies his own mother Earth but hates their children and imprisons them; Earth gives their son Kronos a flint sickle, Kronos while his father is lying with her castrates him; then Kronos goes on swallowing the children he fathers by his sister Rhea until she deceives him with a stone wrapped in swaddling clothes and he vomits them all up alive. There was surely never a time when a Greek would expect in ordinary life to deceive an anthropophagous father into swallowing a stone in the belief that it was his son, or to see him vomit up all his children alive; even in their most primitive self-orientation they must have been looking back towards the origins of sky, earth and man by reliving the outgrown terrors, lusts and jealousies of childhood. Is it only for a modern taste that the most impressive myths are those endowed with this power to propel a withdrawal which is into both the past and the subconscious, as though calling up memories of a previous existence? It is the simulation of memory that explains that quality of what Eliade calls 'sacred time', of events *in illo tempore*, at the beginning of things yet present, into which each re-enaction in rite is another incursion, like an experience lived again in a recurring dream. That Jung's theory of inherited archetypes has established itself as the most popular intellectual justification for taking myths seriously is a striking testimony to that persisting power.

Myths are in all cultures accepted as historically true, quite distinct from fables and fairy tales. Mythopoeia is indeed the imagination of real and supremely important events past and future, in the sense that the universe, life and man, one's community and its customs and crafts, did have origins and will have an end. What makes the mythopoeic imagination indispensable is, as far as the past is concerned, that among all the simulations by which I view from different angles a cosmos of ends, its simulation of memory is the only subjective path towards our ultimate origins. One's self-orientation in a cosmos has a missing dimension unless one has imagined an answer to a question for which we may borrow the resonant line and a half of Prospero searching his daughter's memory:

> 'What seest thou else
> In the dark backward and abysm of time?'

In practice of course we can return no further than the remotest images on the earliest borders of memory, and repeat and renew the course of growth only from the most basic in self and community. But any personal or social performance of Eliade's 'Eternal Return' is itself only a tiny local surfacing of the whole organism's spontaneous re-enactions of the steps from birth to death of its animal and human ancestors. Apart from the replication of the species, from its origin by mutation, there are several scientific discoveries or hypotheses of recapitulation which have clarified, and for those who not only objectivize but subjectivize, sharpened, the sense of re-living the history of life and consciousness. It appears that I grew to what I now am from being a single cell like an amoeba, had gill-pouches in my mother's womb, barely missed being born with a tail, and in becoming fully human with the acquisition of language passed, according to Piaget's child psychology, through the stages of thought which preceded civilization. The easy convertibility of modern theories of recapitulation into myth is well illustrated by that remarkable anomaly Freud's Oedipal drama, a genuine modern myth backed by the claim to factual truth. Freud invites me to call back the repressed memory of having once upon a time murdered my father and ravished my mother, in imagination, but before I knew the difference between fantasy and fact. This crime is supposedly at the beginning, not of my life only, but of every male's since primordial times, and it is at the origin of man's culture as well as his neuroses. To remake myself I must go back to relive that primal act, and so win the freedom to return to the present by another route, in consciousness instead of ignorance. Thus Freud offers me a story with the genuine function of myth, to take me back to the origins I share with other men, in order to recover the right direction, which for Freud as for us is the most conscious, the most aware. The beauty of the idea is that alone among mythic events this is supposedly both real and recallable to memory, since it is repeated at the beginning of each new life. In *Totem and taboo* Freud even surrenders to the temptation to add a refinement not strictly necessary to his thesis, the image of the primal horde, of the old man who keeps all the women to himself, the sons who band together to murder and eat him, and take their own mothers as wives; and he insists that this was a real prehistoric event, and ponders without coming to a conclusion how the memory of it could have been transmitted in the Unconscious through the generations. After all, as he remarks, if archaic man shared our deepest desires, then not yet having any repressions he would have acted them out.

Static communities are dominated by the myth of origins, but in so far as a society is conscious of its own changes it turns the mythopoeic imagination towards cosmic events in the present and the future. When Oswald Spengler in his *Decline of the west* designated the European since AD 1000 'Faustian' man, he identified the story of Faust's pact with the Devil, in its successive literary reworkings culminating in Goethe's, as the central myth of our civilization. The thirst for unlimited knowledge and power at whatever risk or cost, against which the older versions warn or pretend to warn, becomes for Goethe the essence of man's most heroic endeavour. It is a story which resonates in the imagination of whoever feels equally the promise and the danger which have been implicit from the first in the great adventure of modern civilization. But Faust's revolt differs from Satan's, for example, or Adam's, in that we do not see it as an event at the beginning of our history which later generations re-enact, rather as a movement growing stronger since the Renaissance and only now reaching its climax. In spite of his period fancy dress Faust is alive and well in the present, and getting spectacular results in nuclear physics and genetic engineering.

As for the myth of last things, modern examples would be nuclear catastrophe and the Revolution. Both exert a growing power as it becomes harder to conceive runaway technological and social change as having any other than an apocalyptic outcome. They are not of course mythic to people who think of them merely as possibilities which the rational strive to avert or to realize. They become landmarks in my cosmos of ends only if I see them as issuing from an unfolding destiny, which objectively is one of the trends, not inevitable but independent of rational design, in the interactions of human spontaneity with changing society, economy and technology.[12] Nuclear catastrophe is a cosmic event if you acknowledge the danger of it as the challenge or the punishment for being Faust, for the sublime or criminal daring of having since the Renaissance jumped all bounds to the pursuit of knowledge and power. Similarly, the Revolution is mythic when it takes hold of the imagination, not as a means to realizing a formulated programme, but as an explosion of the interacting spontaneities of all, returning man to nature and regenerating or barbarizing his ends. It belongs not to practical politics but to the visions of anarchism and surrealism, and to a poem such as Alexander Blok's *The twelve*, yet it is stirring somewhere at the bottom both of the hopes of revolutionaries and the fears of reactionaries. To be truly mythic, the Revolution must also be anticipated as the outcome of the sort of trend which the religious would read as divine providence preparing the Millennium. It is a commonplace that a millenarianism religious in origin is still alive underneath the Scientific Socialism of Marx and infuses it with its power. The effect of his theorizing in history and economics is not simply to invigorate Marxists with the assurance that in the long run they are bound to win, it orientates them in a cosmos by declaring that history has a direction and it is the one they are on. Marxism even succeeds in combining the modern hope of progress with the old nostalgia for the Golden Age, by the dialectical spiral which through the Revolution restores at a higher level the lost communism before class divisions began. Marx like Freud tries to objectivize as science what subjectively is myth, and likewise fails to satisfy the conditions for explanatory-predictive science (a weakness which, in human matters, as we noticed in the case of Freud,[13] by no means implies that one's generalizations are necessarily unacceptable). Marxism does make refutable predictions about the deepening crisis and final breakdown of capitalism but triumphantly survives their failure, like a millenarian sect which repeatedly commits itself to the date of the end of the world. As for its practical achievements, of course they are revolutions, not the Revolution. But in revolutions the stage which touches the deepest layer of hopes and fears is the initial overthrow of institutions and transitory reshaping of society by uncontrollable forces, the gallop in an unknown direction which the leaders rough-ride until they are thrown off, the eruption of unimagined potentialities for fellowship and cruelty, sacrifice, creativity and destructiveness. For a time the Revolution descends to earth, soon to be betrayed like Christ as the spontaneity of ends is eroded by the automatism of means.

This is not to deny that the intellectual coherence of Marxism, as of Thomism or Calvinism, is essential to its appeal to rational minds. But although someone with the will to believe may be intellectually convinced by a theology or a political philosophy, God may still withhold the gift of faith, or he may go on reading about the cause without being moved to work for it. In the case of Marxism, it would even be theoretically possible to accept the interpretation of economic and political fact in its entirety and yet decide to defend one's interests as a capitalist as long as possible. With the mind wholly satisfied one can still remain a stranger in the world. One cannot by reasoning alone discover the cosmos to which one belongs, only use reason to guide its spontaneous formation. But one's own cosmos is already incipient, however stunted, inchoate and confused, in images, words, rhythms at the back of the mind even of the most rational.[14]

INTERRUPTION

The sun beneath the coral

After the sunset
    the cells still multiplied in the coral city,
    the pressures in splitting seams exploded brief splendours:
after the lightning
    strata still creaked and settled, displaced the nostalgic statues.
    Dust drained from the aqueducts.
    Then a dorsal fin rose from the quiet sea.

lava in the shadow under the bridge the faces in volcanic flowers remember firesides the man in the water comes up through the floor of the boat THE MAN IN THE WATER COMES UP THROUGH THE SLIPS THROUGH MY FINGERS THE MAN IN THE WATER COMES ALL THIS ABOUT THE DECLINE OF the smoke in the seams uncoils its ammonites a vein quickens in the leaves of the electric skeleton in the sky the stone eyes follow the trajectory of the fossils FUNNY THINGS YOU THE MAN IN THE WATER THE DECLINE OF THE PROBLEM OF where do the parallels of the eddies meet between the stalactites of the hull whose is the cathedral of funnels and sea-birds tomorrow when the epitaph had forgotten its project IF THE END THE REVO-LUTIONS IN ALWAYS THE SAME blood ripples in the marble and sets fire to the dragonfly's wings morning dips the granite of its antlers in the sea-anemones exhales the heliotrope of cascading crystals sings its magnesium into the sand of vulvas DOES NOT EVER COME BACK THE SAME in the lagoon between the houses NOT LONG NOW SLEEP AM LOSING THE bubble in the alcohol rises from the embryo's mouth the feathers of the dusk distend the pearls and black olives antennae of diamond and Carboniferous flora riverbed pebbles in your hair Ophelia WHEN IT BEGINS AGAIN SHALL WE RECOGNIZE warp in the mirror and coelacanth in the mine NOTASLEEP YET METAPHOSE METAMORPSYCHOSE DISLOCUTE THE MUSIC DIS-COMPOSES the praying mantis feeds in the coral of the cenotaph trickle of bitumobabel oleocongelagl

[1]

The extinguished sun journeys below the sea
between the giant fern and the coelacanth.

  Eyes in the mirror study the eclipse in the iris.
        The observatories of ice descend
how many strata, how far down
through breathable night ink of the squid compression of coalseam
has the sap ebbed which quickens
the unseen gardens of the sightless fishes?
A tentacle strokes the window from a dilating star.

The stripped layers of the pearl disclose its seed,
the jewels of the seabed explode as they rise.

[2]

In the shrinking straits between the precipices
where disorient the dismembered sun
at midnight stares from prison windows,
where the Arctic flowers smell of menthol,

    where palaeoliths accrete
        around fatigued steel
            above the uneasy caryatids,
where metal strains to breathe
or thrashes under the trident of the lightning underground,
where the ikon in the apse wears the rings of Saturn
and the stuffing of the hours sifts through insect waists,
where the black galaxies that teem in the lymph
congesting sink slowing the epicycles of the ant's-eggs,

the coral-insect spans the sky as the back of Atlas breaks.

[3]

A hair suspends the blade above the head.
Breath of urgent shadows
minutely quivers the window.
The red of morning has drained away in the gutters.

    The edge drops, slices the wax nape.
    The blood jets streams
    on the roots in the black soil:
    the transfigured ghosts probe the wounds in their hands.

The hero has settled into the saddle, Medusa,
the teats of the earth drip on stalagmites
trickle of bitumen of Babel oleocongelaglute indolengelatharge
behind the glass the wax fingers beckon to the pausing shadows.

[4]

Daylight the honey
    of encephalographs which crawl on the skyline of cities,
breezes the flux
    of rubber lungs in the drained aquaria.
Shadows with their eyes to the glare
walk through the giant fern that warps the pavement.

    Where the stick-insect crooks
    its twig above the houses
    an electric vein quickens.

The lizard in the swimming-pool raises its head.
A seam splits, the smoke
    of a night in Africa
        uncoils its ammonites;
on the faces in the vulcanite the fireflies scrawl.

[5]

The print of the fern grows on the pages of carbon,
the antennae of the Phoenix stir in the amber of the microscope.

    In the coral of the cenotaph
    where the praying mantis feeds
    the eyes of caryatids
    study the trajectory of the fossils.

The blood ripples in the marble and sets fire to the dragonfly's wings.
Fever of sun in the water
    waver of heat in the air
        lava in the shadow under the bridge
            plumes between the pearls and black olives
                riverbed pebbles in your hair Ophelia.

[6]

The spent diamonds sink back into Africa,
the ladder of the white peacock closes its eyes.
The sea is a rumour in the quick of a whorl.

    A bud opens in the lignite,
velvet peels from the branches of the candelabra.
Morning dips its tongue in the plankton,
floats its nova above the dew on the mirror,
explodes its anemone into the caves of pumice.
    The well of the resin   the shock in the amber
may nothing untransmuted return from the nadir of the mine.

    A long wound spreads in the corridor
where a sea-horse climbs the stairs.

[7]

.......a sunset, a lament.......a city accreting out of the sea......the crowds and the banner.......lightning, a veering fissure down a facade.......a statue in the rubble stirred and breathed, it was beginning again, then recollection faded from its eyes....
...the disc of that sun rose from the sea, the city above the beach was always waiting, milk of powdered coral swirled in the receding tide, minute feet from the dripping green of the rockpool tested the clinging grains of a moist white clay.

The level sun at the window, red patches on the varnish. There was a white beach at sunrise and the tide was going out, it was very vivid. There were ruins in it somewhere. Which was the first amphibian, was it the lungfish?

RESUMPTION

2.4 The sacred and the obscene

One deep difference between the rationalistic and the religious is in their conceptions of the moral life. The rationalist thinks of himself as a free agent choosing
in the light of reason, a habit of mind quite unaffected by his opinions on the
issue of 'Free will vs. determinism', and tends to find it puzzling, even as raising
a philosophical problem, that we so often do what reason judges to be wrong.
The religious man on the other hand sees himself rather as a battleground of powers
from outside, with a very limited freedom to follow those he reveres as sacred
rather than those he shuns as abominable, obscene. The difference is no doubt
fading as the religious, on the defensive against reason, likewise come to think of
themselves as self-dependent individuals. But traditionally Christians have thought
themselves capable of good only when strengthened by the grace of God, which
enters them through the sacraments or comes unexpectedly or in answer to prayer.
The extent to which a Christian thinks himself free to resist the temptations of his
corrupted flesh inflamed by the Devil depends on how much predestinarianism
there is in his theology, but until quite recently it was taken for granted both by
Catholics and by most Protestants that to credit oneself with the unlimited power
of choice claimed by the rationalist was to fall into the Pelagian heresy.

Now according to the argument of this book the second of these two conceptions
of man is the more realistic. We too allow reason only the relatively modest
function of arbiter between the spontaneous forces pulling upwards or downwards.
This does not commit us to the Christian interpretation of the spontaneous, in
particular to the doctrine of Original Sin which humbly passes the credit for all our
spontaneously good deeds to God while putting on us the whole responsibility for
the evil impulses roused by Satan. We are not in any case thinking of nature as
good or bad, but of the good and the bad in us as equally spontaneous and requiring reason to discriminate between them. Moreover, as we shall argue, there is an
irresolvable tension between the experience of the sacred and the idea of a morally
good God, which has at last become intolerable and more and more inclines
Christians to retreat from the sacred in the interests of a consistently moralized
religion. Indeed, whether or not the reader thinks the word 'religious' appropriate
to the attitudes of this book is entirely a matter of his own choice of words. Our
approach to the sacred is independent of the question of the existence of God,
in the tradition not of theology but rather of the Surrealist Breton (who pursued
'a certain extra-religious Sacred'),[1] and of his rival the 'atheologian' Bataille (who
did think of himself as 'religious'). We shall explore the opposed experiences of
the sacred and the obscene as phenomena detached from Christian and other
mythological interpretations, against the background of a morally neutral universe.

Our position throughout has been that spontaneous activity may be either less or
more intelligent than the deliberated. In the case of voluntary activities this is a
commonplace; until I learn to swim my spontaneous motions in the water do not
keep me afloat, but once the skill is mastered my motions are spontaneously more
intelligent than when I had to think how to co-ordinate them. But the claim is no
longer a commonplace if we extend it, as psycho-analysts have done, to the
involuntary processes which we conceive, when conscious of them, as happening

to us rather than issuing from us. A psycho-analytic model of the mind leaves one the choice of either striving to understand unconscious desires and draw them into one's system of rationalized ends, or else either shunning them as obscene or surrendering to them as sacred without understanding them. As a professed scientist the psycho-analyst must prefer the former alternative, but even the rationalistic Freud values the irruption of uninterpreted images into the conscious mind when it generates poetry, and for Groddeck, Jung and others the unconscious is in some sense wiser than the conscious. The spontaneous prompting which seems to spring from an intelligence other than and unlike one's own, yet wiser about one's own affairs, may be ascribed to God or to the Muse, or psychologically to submerged but intelligent processes in the organism itself, but the experience is in either case the same. If I cannot shake off the feeling that a dream has told me something important, even if its meaning is not transparent, it has the quality of the sacred for me, whether I think of it as a message from the gods or as a process of pictorial thinking which unfolds spontaneously as I sleep. But it will not seem sacred if I either dismiss it as meaningless or treat its images as not symbols but signs like clouds presaging rain or symptoms from which to diagnose a disease.

In what sense may a spontaneous process in the organism be said to be outside me? Thinkers struggling to relate reason to spontaneity have often been driven into very curious manipulations of the personal pronouns, such as the Freudian use of the 'I' and the 'It' (softened in English by latinizing German *Ich* and *Es* as Ego and Id), the originator of which was Groddeck:

In other words, the use of the word 'I' shuts off essential territories of life. In order to make them accessible, one must at times, but only when necessary and that truly is seldom, put aside the word and the idea of an 'I', and try to proceed without it. It would be well if in its place we could put 'The Universe' or 'Nature', or simplest of all, 'God' ....For this purpose, I have for many years been using the word 'It', and instead of the sentence 'I live', I have trained myself to say 'I am lived by the "It" '.[2]

We have already noticed Nietzsche playing a rather less spectacular trick with the pronouns ('A thought comes when "it" wants, not when I want')[3] but the most famous pre-Freudian example is in Rimbaud's letter to Izambard calling for what he calls an 'objective poetry'.

I want to be a poet, and I work to make myself a *seer* . . . .The sufferings are enormous, but one must be strong to be born a poet, and I have recognized myself as a poet. It is not at all my fault. It is false to say 'I think'. What should have been said is 'I am thought' [*On devrait dire: On me pense*]. Excuse the play with words.

I is someone else [*Je est un autre*]. So much the worse for the wood which discovers that it is a violin, and balls to the insensitive who quibble over what they know nothing about!

Rimbaud *wants* to be a poet, toils and suffers to become one; at the same time he has discovered himself to be a poet, is not responsible for it, it is not his fault. The paradox is concentrated in the words 'One must be strong to be born a poet'. What speaks through his voice is the power which made him a poet, the poetry is objective in a sense which has nothing to do with science, 'I is someone else'. This claim does not imply that the poet writes in a trance which feels subjectively like possession by a god, although Rimbaud himself very probably often did. We understand his 'I is someone else' whenever a poem impresses as impersonal, independent of the poet's intentions in writing it and of his ordinary thoughts and emotions, so that a critic's interpretation seems worth as much as the poet's own. It may well be that the poet put a lot of work and thought into it; one can be sure only that any thinking guided without disrupting a process of crystallization by which it assumed a shape independent of his will.

Let us try to define the situation which drove Rimbaud and Groddeck to do violence to the personal pronouns. We must shun the dishonesty of latinizing the pronouns and pretending that they are nouns (Ego, Id, which obscure the very problem to which their forcing of grammar called attention), but let us indulge in the luxury of starting with a pictorial illustration. Imagine the spontaneous as continually dividing into two streams: from one, which is flowing transversely before my eyes, I select objects as my means: from the other, which is pouring through me from behind and plunging towards the same objects, I choose my ends. The pronoun 'it', in spite of Groddeck, seems fully appropriate only to the former. The latter is rather the 'not yet I', the Pre-ego if you do insist on latinizing. We noticed in chapter 1.2 that subjective understanding is constantly shifting between viewpoints, indefinite, hypothetical, remembered, anticipated, or located in other persons or in groups or in the fictitious characters of a novel; it is only in action that I have to commit myself as to whether a viewpoint is my own. When an impulse or urge which is not yet mine enters me from behind, I am facing towards its goals without yet asking *who* is seeing it in this perspective. To the extent that a viewpoint is indefinite there will be latitude in choosing a pronoun. I may assume full responsibility for what is not yet I and say 'Deep down I do want that', or begin to dissociate myself in various degrees ('My deeper self wants it', 'Something in me wants it'). If it seems truly foreign to me I may say 'I have an irrational urge to···', or else speak as I would of the desires of someone else, using a metaphor from mythology ('Some demon tempts me···') or from literature ('Some imp of the perverse tempts me···'). That imp or demon is a foreboding of the person whom as Dr Jekyll I would call Mr Hyde if the alien impulses were to grow to the point of cohering around a second personality. If I succumb to a desire against my will, I may continue to protest 'I didn't want to do it, but the Devil drove me to it', or I may gracefully surrender ('Nature wouldn't be denied'). It will be remembered that when Groddeck decided on the term 'the It' he had been hesitating over the possibilities 'the "Universe" or "Nature", or simplest of all, "God"'. We do refer to the universe as 'it' but not God ('he') or even Nature ('she'), which may help to suggest why his choice of a pronoun makes one uneasy. The indefinite agent, however indicated, has aims which I am judging in relation to my own ends, which implies some degree of animation if not of personality. But what is 'not yet I', as my deeper self, the imp of the perverse, Eros, Nature, recedes further and further through the dimly human and the animal towards the purely physical. In this progression I at first use 'he/she' but at some arbitrary point will shift to 'it'.

The impulses which are not yet mine may elevate or degrade, tend towards an awareness higher than I can voluntarily rise or lower than I would voluntarily sink. They are mysterious to me, in that they enter me from depths beyond the reach of subjectivization, and any scene, thing or person which stimulates them seems pregnant with the same mystery. In so far as I can analyse the interrelations in causal terms I can dispel the mystery, objectivize the effects on myself and choose the causes as means. However, since I can never wholly objectivize my own self there must remain a blind spot where influences on myself are unanalysable by me, although not necessarily by others—that same blind spot which prevents me from achieving the wholly deterministic explanation of myself which I may admit to be possible in principle.[4] To lose altogether the sense of being uplifted or abased by forces beyond my own range of comprehension would, then, be strictly comparable with losing the experience of free will. Whatever affects me incomprehensibly for good or ill requires me to set it apart and keep my distance, above all when its reverberations are strong enough to shake self-control, foreign enough to threaten identity. If it lifts me above myself without my understanding how, I had better approach it cautiously, in the dread that if too confident of my knowledge I try to force or manipulate it I may fall into unforeseeable dangers, which is to reverence it as 'sacred'; if it debases me below myself, I have to shun it as 'obscene'. In either case there is a shrinking back, yet at the same time an attraction, which is that of being relieved of or escaping the burden of selfhood and strain of self-control by dissolution in something higher or lower than myself (for that 'I' which to reason seems fundamental delimits itself only by a costly effort). Since above and below are judged in relation to one's own values, we may think of the sacred and the obscene as opposite interpretations of the same experience, which is at its purest in the sense of something incomprehensibly other the touch of which would change me, before I know whether it is for better or for worse. The word 'taboo' has this neutrality to good and ill, as to varying degrees have so many ancient words translatable by 'sacred', such as Latin *sacer*, usable also for what is set aside as accursed.

Not only is the sense of the sacred and the obscene reconcilable with the morally neutral universe of science; one can go as far as to affirm that no one who lacks this sensibility, however well he understands the scientific cosmos objectively, has ever experienced it from within. (Many of the scientifically minded will no doubt find this claim unintelligible, but a too exclusive habit of thinking objectively inhibits one from experiencing *any* cosmos from within.) I can get along without the sense of the sacred and the obscene as long as I can keep up the fiction of being pure Ego detached from all interactions, acting on other things but moved only by my own will. But even the current of objective thinking itself is at its most creative when it takes its course regardless of my will, making nonsense of any sharp distinction between what happens through me and what I myself do. Not only the means at my disposal but my goals, needs, tastes, thoughts, character, are being altered continuously and almost imperceptibly by external forces; I establish myself as a responsible agent, not by trying to force them to my will, but by staying on the alert as to whether they are changing me for better or for worse, and in the one case preparing the ground and refraining from interfering, in the other shutting myself off from them. Both belong to the realm of ends, outside the secular or profane, which is the realm of means.

Does acknowledgement of this numinous dread sound a little unscientific? Certainly it has to be suspended as long as I am thinking objectively; then no idea is inviolable because sacred or unmentionable because obscene, and powers subjectively experienced as either demand the same kind of reductive causal explanation as anything else, even though in the thinker's own case it must stop as it nears the blind spot for objectivity at the centre of himself. But in subjective thinking the need for a cosmos of ends, in which the sustaining forces are inviolable and the disruptive shut out, remains the same as ever. Not that our claim that to subjectivize the scientific cosmos revives the sense of the sacred and the obscene is enough to dispose altogether of the old issue of 'Science vs. Religion'. In religions, or at any rate the 'higher religions', even a recognition of something supra-personal and supra-moral in the numinous does not quite dislodge the assumption that an extra-human power which can raise man above himself must be a person like man, possessing in a higher degree the qualities valued in man. They have assumed too that he has an objective existence for all men which confirms the objective validity of the moral code promulgated in his name. But to transfigure, by subjectivizing, the world objectivized by science, in no way entitles us to forget that the findings of science discourage belief in the moral government of the universe, in the existence of any fully personal being other than man (on this planet at least), and in categorizations as sacred or obscene which are absolute, not relative to a viewpoint. To acknowledge as sacred the extra-human which lifts me above myself does not forbid me to analyse it into interacting forces in nature, society and my own organism, which may indeed compose a system more or less analogous to a person, moving in a direction more or less analogous to a purpose, but of course without the full personality of myself and my human peers. The extent to which it is legitimate to animize is finally as irrelevant to the sense of the sacred as of the obscene, which continues to be experienced irrespective of disbelief in the unclean spirits which incarnate it in the religions. As for the issue of 'Absolutism vs. Relativism', our position for the sacred and the obscene will be the same as for good and evil.[5] What is right, or is sacred, for you, may be wrong, or be obscene, for me. Nevertheless, I can make any particular choice in the confidence that what is right or wrong for me would be found so by myself, you or any other observer who correctly judges that the reaction I decide for is or is not the one in fuller awareness. Similarly, any convergence on myself of physical, social and personal forces configured by causation or by chance which moves me towards the choice without my knowing why, will in principle allow only one correct judgement from my viewpoint as to whether to bow to it as sacred or repel it as obscene.

Some may protest that we are missing the crucial point, that the sacred is outside nature, not material but spiritual. But is it necessary to treat the sacred as spiritual in any sense incompatible with the present analysis? We have no intention of denying that human awareness is an advance on animal, and that the thought, imagination and feeling which distinguish me from an animal must be ranked higher than the biological processes which I share with it. In so far as I think of the biological, in particular the sexual, less as nourishing the growth of my higher faculties than as dragging me down into the bestial, I shall experience the demands of the body as obscene rather than sacred. The fear, distrust or hatred of the flesh has been a powerful stimulus, not only to religious consciousness, but, as Nietzsche perceived, to rationality itself; philosophy even at its most secular is an invention largely of celibates.[6] The revulsion from the body may be intellectualized by conceiving the sacred as lifting me against the pull of matter into a more rarified world of spirit. But in pre-philosophical religious consciousness even this tension between soul and flesh is very far from the absolute separation of mind from matter, and of the spiritually from the spatially higher or lower, to which we have been accustomed since Descartes. In the New Testament story, when Christ ascends to sit on the right hand of the Father, in the heaven where he will be joined by the souls of the blessed, a stone has had to be pushed back to let him out of his tomb, and he rises into the air before the eyes of witnesses and disappears behind a cloud. For our own argument, the dichotomy of mind and matter can only be a projection of that of the languages of ends and of means, which have been mistaken for a single language describing distinct realities. We have assumed throughout that Gilbert Ryle in his *Concept of mind* successfully discredited the 'ghost in the machine'; we shall also be showing the influence of Georges Bataille's insights into the affinities between the biological and the sacred. For our purposes it is more useful to classify in terms not of spirit and matter but of ends and means. It is in submitting to the sacred that man discovers his ends, in thrusting away the obscene that he defends them, while his choices of means belong to the realm of the secular.

The kinship in polar opposition of the sacred and the obscene may be seen from another direction in their relation to laughter, an activity as exclusively secular as reason itself. Laughter, as an explosion relieving tension, reveals the cost of sustaining an imposed order, in the burst of sudden pleasure in seeing authority defied, dignity humiliated, designs frustrated, etiquette violated, reason made a fool of, language dislocated, suppressed truths exposed, sexuality and violence let loose, laziness and cowardice indulged. A sound instinct tells us that ribaldry is the healthy reaction to any false claim to reverence. Laughter mocks the sacred which maintains order, sets free the obscene which disrupts it, and in emptying them of mystery in the light of everyday abolishes them both. A moment later the cosmos fits itself together again, readjusted to weigh a little less heavily on the spirit, letting us see the proportions of things with a new clarity. A point relevant to our denial that men are natural egoists[7] is that in these surrenders to license we become, although cruel and anarchic, also less self-centred than when reason is reminding us of our interests. We do it is true use derision to feed our pride at the expense of each other. Nevertheless, laughter is inherently communal, releases tension between individuals as well as inside them, dissipates anger and restores fellow-feeling. Imprisonment in an individual viewpoint is revealed as itself part of the order which constricts us, from which we break out when we join in laughter at our own expense.

In the secularized world of today most of us, including believers in the existence of God, have a much reduced sense of the sacred. As Otto showed in *The idea of the holy*, such words as 'holy', 'sacred', have shed much of the quality he renamed 'numinous', in the course of a process of rationalization and moralization which is much older than secularism. The Christian, whose ends are both moral and rooted in his experience of the sacred, naturally expects his God to embody his own highest moral ideal. Yet the sacred, in its otherness from everything human, bursts out of all categorizations as moral, personal or rational. It is of the essence of pagan gods to be capricious, and of the Father who accepts the death of his own innocent Son as atonement for the sins of the world to be incomprehensible in terms of human justice. Paradoxically, the sense of the sacred deepens the nearer we come to recognizing, with science, the amorality and impersonality of the cosmic order; it becomes shallower the more we are assured that the universe has been made for our convenience by a God for whom the closest analogy is ourselves at our presumed best. As for the obscene, unclean, abominable, it does remain part of the living experience of modern man. Rationalism, which abolishes the sacred, still tacitly recognizes the danger and fascination of forces of dissolution which promise release from the strain of submitting to reason. Although the word 'obscene' has a very narrow and trivial application in modern English, and the taboo on the unmentionable has to a great extent lapsed, the shunning of the obscene, unlike reverence for the sacred, can still be understood by all without any effort of historical imagination.

Without wishing to seem frivolous, I would suggest that it is by reviving in imagination the horror of the sexual and excremental in its full Victorian splendour that we can find the most direct access to that pre-moral experience which is distinctively sacred. The impurity of 'foul language', of a 'dirty joke', is just that pollution which is washed away by a sacred rite, by lustration or baptism. Swearing, which by formulae like those of incantation or prayer both conjures with the unclean words and desecrates the holy ones, demonstrates that they have a similar though opposite potency. Victorian books replaced them all by hyphens, and that there was a time when the holy were beginning to be printed while the unclean remained taboo is a curious little symptom of the decline of the sacred. Nor is it a mere figure of speech to use the word 'taboo' in this context. That primaeval fear that to name, describe or picture the act which perpetuates the human race can dissolve the social order and plunge us into chaos, a dread deeper than any rational consideration of social benefit or harm, is characteristic of taboo in the strictest anthropological usage. Even when sexual taboo is expressed in superficially moral language the effect, ironically enough, is that the word 'immoral' itself becomes pre-moral, more appropriate to a short skirt than to lying, theft or murder. There is nothing in remote religions stranger to moralistic thinking than the bivalence of such words as Latin *sacer*, which can set apart either as sacred or as abominable; yet it revives in modern man when he loses his temper, in French *sacré* and even, feebly, in English 'blessèd' as a euphemism for 'cursèd'

The obscene in ordinary speech is at its most naked in the violence of the curse. Its purity is in its unsustainable intensity; and provided that the passion subsides as one expects, and the language is formulaic, and it is spoken at an implicitly permitted time and place (in a barracks but not a church), society easily tolerates it. Yet one has only to analyse the formula to see that in intent the obscene assails just what the sacred upholds, the cosmic order itself. To exclaim 'Christ, you fucking bastard!' violates the order of language, both syntactically (there is no sentence) and semantically (neither adjective nor noun expresses a reasonable reproach), to juxtapose the desecrated Saviour with the unnameable act and the breach of the marriage rite which makes a birth unholy. Spoken in earnest, it is an explosion of anger which momentarily strains to dissolve the world in chaos, to confound the orders of the divine, the human and the bestial. However, even the most potent oath is a formula eroded by overuse, and we hear its message, and the pathos of words striving to be deeds, only when a poet finds new words.

> *Duchess of Malfi:* ...I'll go pray—
>   No, I'll go curse.
> *Bosola:* O, fie! .
> *Duchess:* I could curse the stars
> *Bosola:* O fearful!
> *Duchess:* And those three smiling seasons of the year
>   Into a Russian winter: nay, the world
>   To its first chaos.
> *Bosola:* Look you, the stars shine still.[8]

As for the sacred, the concept is now most alive in the dread of undermining foundations. Any rationalized system of ends and means has to start from the goals accepted simply because its sharers do find themselves spontaneously impelled towards them when they seem to themselves most aware. In a metaphorical language, it is not I but God, or Nature, or the It, that wills the directions in which I turn with changing awareness. If someone conservative by temperament regrets the weakening of 'the sacred ties of the family', and refuses to listen to arguments for a rational re-organization of sexual and parental relationships, more is involved than an estimate that the family is too complex a unit to be radically altered or replaced without unforeseeable social consequences. It is rather that the family is too close to the foundations of his whole system of values, and to imagine himself as having grown up against any other background induces vertigo, a loss of identity. For what ends could it be rational for him to reconstruct the very institution which first shaped his ends?

Here the sense of desecration is a fear of tampering with the sources of all that one already finds good. But the shrinking of the ancient awe of the *mysterium tremendum* to a purely conservative worry is one more sign of how the word 'sacred' declines in force. The sacred is fecund, below the roots of life and creativity, it generates those states of high value which could never have been envisaged as ends because one could not know them before having them. A peculiarly modern sense of its violation is in the dread of scientific progress as a juggernaut out of control, which from very early in the nineteenth century, at the most despised level of literary imagination, was shaping the myth of the Mad Scientist, that degenerate Faust first incarnate as Frankenstein ('I collected bones from charnel-houses, and disturbed with profane fingers the tremendous secrets of the human frame').[9] The dread is at its most intense in atom-splitting and genetic engineering; social institutions sanctioned by religion seem in comparison superficial and transient, with a sacredness corrupted by political interests. We find ourselves driven by the automatism of means to disrupt an order in which all living things and their environment are interdependent, and to risk for the political or commercial interests of the moment a nuclear or genetic catastrophe which could destroy it and all its future possibilities, and ourselves with it. The feeling, not merely of fear but of sacrilege, is not so much in risking our own extermination, as in being irrevocably launched on a course by which, through the subjection to means of reasoning of unprecedented beauty and complexity, we are against our wills drying up the sources of life and value. We are constantly being warned by people who should know that our technology threatens an evolutionary catastrophe, not only exterminating species at a rate which could in a few decades compare with the mega-extinctions of prehistory, but also laying waste the tropical rain forests and other teeming eco-systems which have hitherto been most fecund in speciation. Our surrender to an insane rationality may appropriately be denounced in religious language, for example as a deliberate withdrawal from the grace of God, but let us translate that into our own terms, as reason intruding on spontaneity to the point of killing the goose which lays the golden eggs. Human engineering, the science pioneered by the illustrious Frankenstein himself, exhibits its most debasing possibility, self-emasculation of our power to engender new ends. We are ceasing to take for granted all that in limiting has also defined man, that he is mortal, lives on earth, is born of woman, will go on existing into the indefinite future, has one head, two arms and two legs (he might modify that to fit himself to extra-terrestrial conditions); but if he becomes wholly plastic, he can have no ends which were not programmed by the last generation either as repetitions of its own or, worse, as means to them. In the Brave New World, where men are conditioned from birth to will what the state chooses for them, who is to choose the ends for which the conditioners themselves are conditioned? The scientific élite will be condemned for ever to a mechanical reproduction of the ends of the last scientists of the era before the umbilical cord with Nature was cut.

That the springs of intelligence, personality and life ought to be sacrosanct (*ought*, because they are the sources of awareness itself) in no way implies that they are themselves intelligent, personal or alive. On the contrary, sacredness grows in inverse proportion with these properties, which are attributed less and less plausibly the farther and deeper we penetrate, and soon become altogether inapplicable. Even Gaia herself is only a little island in an inanimate universe. The sacred and the obscene well up from as far down in the inanimate as there is anything on which life can be seen to depend, from a darkness beyond the range of subjective exploration. The deeper the level the greater the fear of disturbing the foundations, of touching off a universal disaster to life and consciousness. What objectively is existence on a tiny planet in Pascal's 'silence of those infinite spaces' is subjectively, not isolation in a meaningless universe, but being moved in good directions or bad by forces from unsoundable, incomprehensible depths, in comparison with which I am just a little more than nothing. One may desire to find at the bottom of those depths, at the remotest distance from man, a God who is personal and moral after man's image. But no mere desire can entitle me to deny the testimony of science that I live in a morally neutral universe in which, as far as present knowledge goes, there are no persons more highly developed than man himself. The sacred and the obscene must finally merge in regions farther than ever from, though continuous with, human experience. To shudder with awe at an intrusion of science into the intimate structure of matter, one has only to foresee the possible consequences for vegetable, animal and human of tampering even with the mineral. Seen from this direction, the mineral is basic and the living superficial, a temporary, vulnerable elevation above it, still dependent on it for the air it breathes and the water it drinks, destined to last perhaps only until it becomes sufficiently intelligent to discover the means to exterminate itself, or until the earth cools, or entropy prevails. Consequently, not even the inanimate is to be seen purely as means at the disposal of man. Suppose that voyagers to a distant planet discover that it shares all the general conditions in which life appeared on earth. Life may already have come in forms unimagined on earth, or be about to in the next instant, or not for a million years, or the opportunity may pass without its coming at all; but the travellers have come for some human convenience which would as a side-effect destroy all possibility of life. Without any need to mythologize, a traveller who opened himself to the full awareness of what he was doing would know the full meaning of violation of the sacred.

Any world-order whether scientific or mythic must embrace the structure of my own body, the configuration of my character, the logical order within which I think and the moral order I try to obey. Unless I am to treat myself as a unique exception outside even the theoretical scope of scientific explanation, why I think rationally and why I made this or that miscalculation, why I accept a moral code and why I fail to live up to it, must all in principle be explainable like the orbits and deviations of the planets. My littleness in relation to nature is not merely in measurable size and duration, but in the subordination of all I think best in me; rationality and morality themselves appear as exotic structures, like the society of an ant colony or the colours of the mandrill, thrown off at random by the infinite prodigality of nature. For this reason there is something not merely fallacious but impudent in the classic Argument from Design for the existence of God. To compare the cosmic order with the structure of a house and infer that since the latter requires a human architect the former similarly implies a designer who is superhuman only in having capacities which are not limited but perfect, is subtly false to the impression which the natural order makes on us. The kind of humility which nature demands is not a recognition that God has our own virtues to an absolute degree, but that we are local specializations within an order which, in the teeming thousands of ova scattered in the sea to generate a single fish is insanely wasteful, and in the mating habits of the praying mantis is insanely cruel. 'God' (if we are to choose this name for nature as the object of human awe, wonder, gratitude, terror) is not to be reduced to the idealized form of one of his creatures.

To the extent that one perceives society as shaped, at a deeper level than its rational institutions, by spontaneous interactions within a cosmic order, it too is seen as integrated or disintegrated by sacred and obscene forces. In stable hierarchies these tend to be identified with the upper and lower strata. Even now, somewhere underneath the political and economic institutions of this country, there still lingers a phantom England in which the middle class which embodies the rational, useful and moral keeps its awe-struck distance from the aristocracy as sacred, while shunning the defiling touch of the unwashed working man as obscene. Order in this mythological cosmos emanates through ritual and symbol from the crown and coronets above, to be menaced by the dirt, rudeness and riot down below. Here as elsewhere the sacred and the obscene have a secret affinity, like the Freudian equation of gold and excrement, beyond the borders of the secular. Both extremes of society prefer the thing done for its own sake to the useful, the noble because they value not by practical results but by quality, in luxury, cere- mony, honour, beauty, play, the masses because unless forced by need they are too lazy and short-sighted to forgo self-indulgence. The extremes are likewise respec- tively above and below bourgeois morality, the nobles drinking, gambling, fighting and whoring as their privilege, the masses because they know no better; they are above and below bourgeois reason too, the noble by the mystique of their ungrounded yet inviolable etiquettes and codes of honour, the masses because they are stupid.[10]

Such a localization of the sacred and the obscene implies classes both widely distributed in mode of life and deeply ignorant of each other, so that after social mobility undermines hierarchy only the old-fashioned, sheltered or naive can fully verbalize it without being conscious of its absurdity. But even when there are no longer simple social landmarks for distinguishing sacred from obscene, the distinction reappears wherever in social tendency the spontaneity of ends breaks out for good or ill from the automatism of means which alienates from ends. The affinity underlying the difference shows up again when a movement is described in the rhetoric of the sacred by itself and of the obscene by its enemies, for example Nazism. Early Nazism may be seen as the purest case of a political revolt against, not a class or élite, but the alienated lives of all classes; it is no compliment to say so, for the spontaneity of ends is an insufficient though necessary condition of their being good in themselves. Its ideology promised community rooted in blood and soil, put race before state, honour before profit, myth before reason, it affirmed the heroic virtues against utilitarian calculation and the supremacy of will over all material obstacles. In the long run, like Communism, it got caught up in the mechanics of its swollen state apparatus, and in the organization of its extermi- nation camps achieved the ultimate of alienation, with everyone working with a good conscience at the means to an end for which no one had to admit respon- sibility. But at all stages Nazism is vitalized by the sacredness of the Leader and of the Destiny which works through him, and by the horror of obscene races which defile the blood. Watching today the film of the first Nuremberg rally, *The triumph of the will*, one hears again that harsh ecstatic voice, the most disturbing of all the clashing noises of the twentieth century, and sees the rapt faces of the crowd for whom the new law is perfect freedom. Is it surprising that they think of their delirium as uplifting them, as it floods them with that abundance of fellow- ship, purpose and power denied them by capitalism, democracy and science? The Leader, so undistinguished until he opens his mouth, is as much possessed as they are, the medium of an inhuman force which energizes his rhythms and inflections like—the comparison would not have pleased him—jazz at the peak of improvization. ('I go the way that Providence dictates with the assurance of a sleepwalker'.)[11] Hitler despised the mechanical when it trespassed outside the realm of means, reached down for the roots of vitality and spontaneity in the biological through the obsessive metaphors of health and infection which pervade the imagery of *Mein Kampf*. But the forces which free from the automatism of means are not necessarily sacred. For witnesses of the film at a safe distance, in time now or in space then, the immersion in universal hysteria is the most horrible of obscenities. The verdict of 'Be aware' is unequivocal; this is a surrender to spontaneity which obliterates reason, forgets consequences, blinds to the view-points of strangers, drowns individual judgement in trust in another. To recall Hitler is a giddying reminder that except in choices of means there is nothing whatever to compel us to respect reality if we would rather not, that tremendous energies are available if only we listen to some enchanter who will lift the burden of awareness from our choices of ends.

The roots of the sacred and the obscene are in the consciousness and the inter-pretation of biological relationships. For each person, the body out of which he grew and to which he first clung is the original sacred being, ignorance of parent-hood is the purest experience of uprootedness, and the primal obscenity is to engender incestuously, confounding the classifications of father, mother and child, brother and sister, from which his cosmos of ends began to order itself. I am one organism distinct from others, but there are episodes when the boundary begins, lapses or ends—birth, sexual union, death, not to mention the daily common-places of eating and excreting. At what moment in or out of the womb did I be-come a separate person? When does the food in my stomach or the air in my lungs become myself? For reason, these are minor puzzles. But for experience, birth, orgasm and death are breaches of the fence between self and other, which expose my continuity with cosmos by placing me within the cycles of generation and decay common to all multicellular life. But they also threaten a fall instead of a rise, a dissolution of self in a subhuman chaos, against which the mechanisms of both self and society are on guard. The stability of selfhood depends on an almost vol-untary closure of memory and imagination against the beginning and the end of life. If my own birth were a vividly remembered event I might feel for everything living that oneness of flesh which is manifest in a mother suckling her child. And indeed, if Freud is to be trusted, the memory of having been in the womb still shapes the images of dreams, as does the foreboding of ultimately inevitable death which breaks only intermittently though the defences of consciousness. Social custom likewise hides the physical processes of birth, sexuality and corruption from the public gaze, and establishes rites of baptism, marriage and mourning which constitute them as not obscene but sacred events.

Within the organism we can find the ultimate roots of the sacred and the obscene in the biological processes of life and death. There is something more than a survival of an obselete phraseology in speaking of the 'sacredness of life'. Self-preservation is no doubt one of my rational ends, indeed the one for which I would be most painstaking in the choice of means. Nevertheless, the urge to live is something very different from any ambition, taste or whim which is particular

to myself. It is a force of nature which resists any rational choice of suicide out of
despair or martyrdom in a good cause, and which strains blindly towards a goal
which is wholly impersonal, not my survival but the perpetuation of life itself.
If my life is threatened it exerts energies, and stimulates an alertness and speed of
thought which I did not know I possessed, and which I could never summon up
for any personal project.

Putting myself in another's place, I experience some of the same horror of taking
his life as of losing my own. What inspires a still deeper awe, in the rare moments
when I am compelled or can voluntarily bring myself to full imaginative awareness
of it, is that the generative process which shapes me in due course discards me,
the vital impulse fails in me and yields to a tendency not only independent of but
contrary to my will, through ageing to death and dissolution. The shrinking from
full awareness is not simply a reluctance to face a rational contemplation of death
as a termination of consciousness, a passage from existence into non-existence.
It is a recoil from the obscene, most actual in the dread of the direct reversal of
vital process in bodily decline and decomposition; we shun or hide from sight
a rotting corpse with a horror we do not feel for the newly dead or for a clean
skeleton. As for the external supports of life, the feeling that the food which
revitalizes me is a sacred substance has weakened in the modern world; I cannot
meaningfully say grace before a meal to thank God for frozen peas or pre-sliced
bread if I have come to think of them as manufactured by man rather than generated by nature. However, the sacredness of natural food often becomes real for
people with a taste for fresh vegetables and stoneground loaves; and the current
obsession about poisoning the body with synthetic foods perhaps has less to do
with medical or pseudo-medical evidence of damage than with an obscure need
to distinguish sacred and obscene in the bodily processes which, whenever they
go wrong, force us to acknowledge our continuing dependence on nature. We all
keep the sense of fellowship in communal eating and drinking, being made one
flesh by the same substance becoming part of each of us. We also retain, as strongly
as ever, abhorrence of the obscenity of the decomposed remains of the food
which the healthy body expels, and excrete in secret behind closed doors.

Sexuality obstinately persists in being both sacred and obscene, regardless of
all efforts to rationalize it as a means to the happiness of both parties. It traps us
in insoluble dilemmas, whether to debilitate by taming or submit to a power
which cares nothing for individual or social well-being, aims only at the generation
of new life, can make coupling animals die without defending themselves. It is not
out of goodwill to us that Nature has made it the intensest of our pleasures. It
frets at the restraints, not only of conventional self-interest and morality, but of
the spontaneous altruism which at first it makes a pleasure; the conflicting needs
of faithless polygamous male and loyal monogamous female have deep springs,
perhaps in the genes themselves.[12] If its function were solely biological we could
discipline it like the digestion for rational interests, but in intensifying awareness
of each instant of experience it regenerates value in ecstasies which radically change
us. The spontaneity of love lifts awareness of another person to an unsurpassable
pitch, but illusion as well; and the most intimate, tender impulse eludes voluntary
control as capriciously as the most carnal. We can tame by civilized art the blind

urge to orgasm in the male ahead of the female, and agree as two rational indi-viduals to manipulate it to our mutual advantage. Yet to use sex too judiciously is to remain isolated in self-consciousness through the one respite from the isola-tion of the body between the birth already forgotten and the coming obliteration in death. Can we afford to force it altogether out of the darkness of the sacred and the obscene? Its promise, as much as its risk, is in being overwhelmed by more than we understand. We are caught in the contradiction of both flinching from and thrilling to that dissolution of self which has so often been compared to a death. Within a traditional Christian context, it is sacred inside holy matrimony, obscene outside it. We do not have to draw the line on these or other merely institutional grounds; but it would be a pity to lose the sense that, among the things not to be spoken about to others, the intimacies which come as unforeseen blessings are sacred, and being trapped in an obsessional routine of masturbatory fantasies is obscene.

The crucial point at which I must admit or deny my continuity with nature is death. Shrinking from that continuity, I prefer to think of my body after that moment as having nothing to do with me; I shall become nothing, or else survive as disembodied spirit. But it is hard to cling to these abstractions in the presence of a corpse. The mortician's art may encourage me to believe that it is alive and peacefully sleeping. If that does not convince me, my alternatives are to feel only the horror of being eaten by the worms, or to see farther, into the cycle of decay and engendering by which life will renew itself after my death, and recognize that ultimately Nature is wiser in putrifying me to fertilize the soil than I am in im-moderately clinging to life. Funeral rites, whatever their other purposes, help to guide us past a dangerous crossroads, towards accepting the final dissolution in unconscious process in the calm of surrendering to the sacred, not the horror of being overwhelmed by the obscene. A look of peace on the dead man's face, so precious to his kin, is the sign of taking the right turning. (If one pretends that it means that he is now happy, perhaps at a deeper level one understands better.) The rite of paying my last respects, renewing our affinity within the sacred, beyond and outlasting all human fellowship, very obviously must be performed before the obscene forces are visibly at work. His body lies before me; it is and is not the person I knew, it has become part of nature again, like a rock or a tree, yet the face still has the shape that thought and will and feeling impressed on it. An inhuman power has withdrawn it beyond humanity, and with the passing of thought and passion has imposed a dignity never seen in life. It must not be dis-turbed as it lies, or afterwards thrown away like rubbish; if it is to be treated as a thing, used, this must be as a categorized exception reserved for the secular sphere, for example as a cadaver for the anatomist's table. It is healthy to look now, while it is still at this moment of stasis, but it must soon be hidden away in a tomb, because for a while it will offend all decency.

The life of every organism is nourished by the death of others; man eats animal and vegetable, and leaves his own body to feed the worms and fertilize the plants. The sense of the vitalizing, the sacrificial death, is of all sacred emotions the one which reason most distrusts. It has become easier to forget it, since civilized man does not have to butcher his own meat or even see his vegetables grow. It is indeed a dangerous emotion, separated only by a hair's breadth from sado-masochism. To think of the shedding of blood as vitalizing in itself (even build a culture on it like the Aztecs) is the most disastrous of all man's tricks to make life even worse for himself than it has to be. Yet at every level of civilization the need to exchange life for life arises; the only question is whether to give the exchange the value of butchery or of sacrifice, of means or of end. Nowadays we think of killing for food as butchery, so that the only way to acknowledge kinship with the animals is to be vegetarian; it surprises us to read of peoples that treat the hunting of game and even the reaping of crops as sacrifices. But even in our own world, a church, nation or political party would lose its sense of community if it treated its own dead as mere means to be forgotten now they have served their purpose. When it renews their memory by celebrating them as martyrs, metaphors of blood-sacrifice pervade the rhetoric. Instead of analysing a death and the purpose it served as means and end, in a utilitarian balancing of advantages and disadvantages, the rhetoric synthesizes them as an indissoluble whole, tragic yet rejuvenating. On the other hand the enhanced vitality which many discover in themselves seeing others die (routinely exploited in the violent images of the cinema) is not sacred, since the vitalization depends on the witness separating himself from the dying and momentarily forgetting that he shares their mortality.

On the biological level the most dramatic example of the unequivocally sacred and its nearness to the obscene is childbirth. The sense of the sacred quickens as the fatuous pride we take in achieving fatherhood or motherhood sinks in the recognition that nothing human has a share in it at all. A man who does not habitually say 'God' is watching a woman in labour. He glimpses through the impossibly small slit a patch of skin streaked with hair. The nurse stretches the gap with two fingers to a pink triangle, he sees the crown of a head with a crimson spot in the middle, floating in a swamp of pale watery blood. Forceps grasp the head, the bone gives under the grip, and as the waxy skin below the hair extrudes he does not for a moment recognize its crease and fold as closed eyes and a nose. The forceps twist the head right round, as though to wring the neck, but the shoulders turn with it. In one rush the whole body is out, and dangles limply like a soft doll moulded in violet clay, about to dissolve in the streaming blood. The thought comes that God has a very strong stomach. The features are still only motionless creases. Then the baby wails without opening its eyes, and with a kick springs to life. He is seeing God breathe life into Adam formed of clay. It is suddenly real that this is how he and every living thing began, and for an instant he looks back through this door at the door through which the mother came, up a vista of uncountable generations. Behind the clean geometry and chemical smells of the hospital he catches sight of a scheme of things in which there is no such thing as filth. No such thing as beauty either; the mother's ecstatic smile is beyond it, the shape of the vulva is from before it began. Beauty had served its purpose when it brought him to the door.

We have arrived at a theory of the sacred almost ideally suited to offend both the religious and the rationalistic. The religious find themselves being advised to retreat to something with a startling resemblance to that primitive awe of a pool or grove without even conceptualizing a resident spirit, on which they have supposed the 'higher religions' to be an obvious advance. Nor are rationalists likely to be pleased by the suggestion that the scientific cosmos turns out, when experienced from within, to be one which they too would put below the higher religions. Let us first attempt a reconsideration of Christianity, a religion for which spontaneity raises peculiar problems. I shall sketch in a few pages my position on this complex issue, starting from what is no doubt a highly personal reading of the Gospels.

Jesus inherited from Jewish monotheism an ethical and personal God conceived after the analogy of a human father, whose law must be obeyed, whose anger, when awe of his might compels one to look down on oneself from his viewpoint, is experienced as guilt. But Jesus had a new insight into love as a spontaneous power released by the lifting of guilt, moving men to good and to intensified life without the compulsion of law. It is this insight, the originality of which is not discredited by adducing vaguer pre-Christian recommendations of universal love, which gives the Gospels their luminous air of mankind waking to a new morning. Jesus confronts you with his astonishing 'Thy sins are forgiven'; either the sins fall from you, spontaneous love stirs in the heart, and you rise up to follow him; or else you stand eternally condemned for your hardness of heart. On the then current assumptions, to say 'Thy sins are forgiven' was to claim an authority which belonged only to God, and a man who stood up to say it must be either a blasphemer or else more than a human prophet, must be the Messiah, Christ, 'Son of God'. He was crucified as a blasphemer, and his disciples were left with the new knowledge of the power of spontaneous love, without the single man who could release it by daring to forgive sins, who was therefore in their eyes the Son of God.

But in dying young, Jesus is in an unending tradition of sacrificial and revitalizing deaths. Soon a new significance is read into the death of the Son of God; he suffered as a man to appease the Father's anger against us, and then rose again from the dead. In the rite of the Eucharist the community eats Christ's flesh and drinks his blood, in the form of bread and wine, in order to share in his redeeming death and in the casting off of sin by his resurrection. Thus the community has a myth and a rite in place of the incantatory 'Thy sins are forgiven' of the man who died, to discharge from guilt and transfigure life by the awakening of love. The primal act of Jesus, the calling up of spontaneous love, becomes repeatable through the generations.

The Christian myth which evokes and reorders the spontaneous forces at the roots of morality may be seen, if one thinks of ethical monotheism as a mark of higher religions, as a regress from Judaism, in the direction of the pagan mystery religions of the Roman Empire, which redeem by the blood of sacrificed gods. It declares that before Christ came men lived under the curse of damnation for the innate proneness to sin inherited from their ancestor Adam, who defied God's command in the Garden of Eden. But the Son of God by suffering in their place atoned for their sins, and then after three days was raised by God from the dead. The believer, by reliving through prayer and rite the death and resurrection of Christ, is absolved of his debt of inherited sin, and although his corrupted nature still makes it impossible to resist temptation by will alone, the capacity for spon-

taneous good and an illuminated life is breathed into him by the entry of the
Holy Spirit into his heart. The whole system has the polytheistic tendency natural
to mythologizing, and it was three centuries before it was fully reconciled with
monotheism by the Trinitarian formula which established Father, Son and Holy
Spirit as three persons with one substance.

But now a tension develops between the demands of spontaneous impulse and
voluntary action. The God inherited from Judaism imposes laws which the
believer can voluntarily choose to obey or defy, and rewards or punishes him
according to his deeds. But love cannot be summoned up by will. Christian love is
spontaneous or it is nothing; at the least suspicion that it is forced the preached-at
shrink away. Can a just God reward the loving and punish the hard of heart for
what in the last resort they cannot help? The Gospels have a *naïveté* for which
such theological issues do not yet arise. Christ does save or damn you for the
involuntary motions of the heart; either you respond to his call with the spontaneity of a little child, or he passes you by for ever. But the issue sharpens as the
Church evolves its myth and ritual to loose the knot which its moral demands only
tighten, lift the weight of guilt and free the power of love. Faith in the myth and
performance of the ritual only prepare the ground for the inspiration of Christian
love which, as much as romantic love, or as intellectual or artistic creation, comes
in its own time or not at all. Outside the moral sphere, this capriciousness of the
sacred is taken for granted; the qualities we most value, intelligence, strength,
health, beauty, creativity, may be enhanced by effort, but plainly their possessor
owes them in the first place to the favour of the gods, which has nothing to do with
justice. But in introducing a parallel to the capriciousness of the pagan gods into
moral experience, a terrifying paradox arises. God eternally saves or damns on
moral grounds alone, yet it remains an obstinate fact of experience that he incomprehensibly grants or withholds the grace on which salvation depends. Christianity is not as remote as might seem from the older sense of the sacred as amoral.
Only a faith that the divine will, inscrutable to man's limited intelligence, in the
last resort means him well despite all appearances to the contrary, makes the
Christian cosmos subjectively different from the scientific, in which there is no
such thing as justice outside human society.

We are not denying that to prefer spontaneous love to a willed obedience to
law is indeed an advance in moral sensibility. But its effect, even without a theoretically developed predestinarianism, is to reveal man as almost the prisoner of
his own spontaneity, divided between the pulls of divine and satanic forces, with
at best just enough freedom to side with the former. It also traps the Father in the
mechanically retributive justice which the Son transcends by his 'Forgive thy
enemies', a primitive justice for which crime is inherited in the womb and expiable
only by the blood of the offender's whole race, or by an innocent victim of at least
equal value sacrificed in compensation. The Father has to remain an archaic
thundering Jehovah, the one member of the Trinity who can never be fully Christ-
ianized, because the function of the myth is precisely to release love by dissipating
the terror of the father's wrath, inescapable unless expended on another object,
which is at the deepest and oldest layer of morality in all who grow up in a patri-
archy. The fear and the love, being spontaneous, respond to myth and rite ac-

cording to a mechanics independent of the agent's conscious morality. Paradoxically, the myth inspires a higher morality in man by ascribing a lower one to God; and it is just because the spontaneity genuinely uplifts the believer yet clashes with all human conceptions of the reasonable and the moral, that it impresses as coming from a source other than and higher than man.

It is the independence from man's will that gives the sacred its extra-human kinship with the obscene, so startling in cultures remote from us that anthropologists used to suppose that the savage mind failed to distinguish the two concepts. In Christianity too what is obscene in one context is sacred in another. For a believer in the doctrine of the Real Presence, the eating of Christ's flesh and drinking of his blood is more than a figure of speech; he does partake of the 'substance' of the flesh and blood, even though they have the 'accidents' of bread and wine. That the rite has a family resemblance to cannibal feasts is not just a curiosity of anthropology; the effect of insisting on the dogma, and reconciling it with the evidence of the senses by a semi-Aristotelian formula, is to ensure that subjectively it *is* cannibalism. (Not that it may be called that, any more than, for example, the miracles of Jesus may be called 'magic', for choice of name is crucial to categorization as sacred or obscene.) The thought of cannibalism is one of those which endanger identity in the confusion of one's own with another's flesh. But such a collapse of the walls of personality is bivalent, either a sinking into the obscene or an uplifting by infusion of the sacred. What in another context would be the horror of eating human flesh becomes the awe of oneness with Christ, whose grace enters the spirit while the wafer which is his vitalizing flesh melts on the tongue. In devotion to the crucified Christ there is a similar bivalence in being moved to love by redemptive pain and death. The image of a beautiful and almost naked young man dying nailed by his hands and feet to a cross with women weeping at its foot evokes a very delicate balance of forces, which suspend the spectator only a little above the level of the obscene. Outside the religious context one can hardly conceive another motive for regularly contemplating it than sado-masochistic fetishism, of which morbid religiosity does show the symptoms.

Constant theological disputes over its internal contradictions did not weaken Christianity for some 1,500 years. But in recent centuries it has become harder to tolerate the unending conflict between the myth and faith in the goodness of God. An Aztec god may be as bloodthirsty as he likes, but God the Father has to be at least as good as his worshippers. In the seventeenth century Milton wrote *Paradise lost* to 'justify the ways of God to men', and a little later Leibnitz introduced into theology the term 'theodicy' (vindication of God). Clearly a God whose worshippers start making excuses for him is in serious trouble. Once the issue becomes debatable, all Christian discourse about the love and mercy of God assumes a horrible tone of falsity and special pleading. By the eighteenth century the *philosophes* and then the Romantics are in open revolt against the divine tyranny, and when Joseph de Maistre comes to God's defence in *Les soirées de Saint-Petersbourg* he betrays such relish for the very things seen by others as cruelty and injustice as to give the whole game away. In our own time, quite apart from intellectual objections to the myth, the dissolution of patriarchal authority in the family, as well as the feminist challenge to male dominance, have undermined its psychological foundations. It is possible that these social changes may enable Christianity to disembarrass itself of its pre-Christian Father who rewards and punishes, and reconstitute itself as the religion of spontaneous love inspired by the Holy Spirit to which the charismatic movement in the churches seems to tend. Certainly it would be impertinent to take it for granted that the religious tradition of the West has lost its creative possibilities. What may be doubted however is whether the way to resolve its contradictions is to demythologize itself and commit itself to an unequivocally good and reasonable God; rather, it was the strength of the myth that implicitly it acknowledged what its theology could not, that justice and injustice belong only within human law and convention. A God who reflects a living experience of the sacred must always distribute his favours incomprehensibly, a capriciousness which becomes injustice only when it is insisted that we deserve eternal reward or punishment for being granted or refused his favours. Otto's dislike of a wholly personal and moral conception of God has proved in the course of our argument to be something more than a matter of taste. The Christian myth was born from a struggle with resistant reality to open up the springs of love in a world where the spontaneous order of things is neutral to human hopes and fears. In its prime it was something more than a fantasy that the universe is ruled by a benevolent person, interested in each one of us as a person like himself, who will see that everything turns out right in the end. That however is all that is left of it when it is rationalized to elevate God to human standards of morality. At the same time it loses its psychological depth, and tempts us to the illusion that we can by our own choice, not only obey rules, but become spontaneously loving and caring, a major addition to our already ample motives for hypocrisy and self-deception.

Turning now to rationalism, let us start by distinguishing a kind to be approved from a kind to be deplored.

(A) 'Reason as Guide'. Like the animals, I am an organism which spontaneously senses, analogizes to the already experienced, and tends towards or away. Unlike them, I am self-conscious, can detach myself from spontaneous process in order to analyse and critize perceptions, analogies and reactions, choose ends from my spontaneously emerging goals, choose means to my ends. In becoming self-conscious I require an imperative by which to choose between spontaneous tendencies as they veer with changing awareness, but only one, 'Be aware'.

(B) 'Reason as Master'. In becoming a rational agent, I made an absolute break with my own spontaneity. I choose my means from the spontaneous outside or inside myself, but my ends come from God, reason or a *fiat* of my own. The discontinuity may be conceived as real (I am a soul, mind or Ego distinct from my body) or as a necessary fiction without which I could not think at all, although I know in the abstract that I am identical with my body. On this view, 'Be aware' is irrelevant to choices except in the preliminary collection of information.

Why is it that from first becoming self-conscious we seem predisposed to the 'Reason as Master' position, to the intransigent, the unreasonable claim to an absolute divorce from the spontaneity of the animal? We may find an answer in the subjective experience of thinking, by which anything that I myself decide, in the service of my ends, stands outside the range of causal explanation and prediction by myself. If I fail to see that the incompatibility of decision and prediction by a single agent would not necessarily forbid one agent to predict what another decides, it will seem that there is a difference in kind between things explained causally, by preceding conditions, and things explained teleologically, by ends which they serve. From the seventeenth century teleological explanation, having been banned by science, had to retreat to a realm of spirit inhabited by God and the human soul, declared out of bounds to causal explanation. This move confined the sacred almost to God alone, and the obscene to the Devil as long as he was remembered. Later, when a First Cause was seen to be unnecessary to causal explanation, it became possible to dismiss the sacred and the obscene altogether. There were then no more pursuers of ends except humans, rational and self-contained individuals utilizing as means anything causally explainable, including the spontaneous in themselves. We were thus condemned to think of our spontaneity, not as having its goals sorted and clarified by 'Reason as Guide', but as subjected to serve the ends of 'Reason as Master'. As evidence of the cost in psychic tension of sustaining this attitude, one might point to the *pari passu* advance through the last few centuries, in sophistication as well as in importance, of reason and its subverter humour. The reign of reason has proved intolerable without laughter to ease the strain. Reason fortunately has been able to co-exist with its impudent rival because humour shares its profane spirit, mocks the sacred, unchains the obscene, and by refusing to keep a proper distance from either strips the mystery from them both and forces or licenses them to enter the even light of the secular world. However, there is not only an emotional but a logical tension, for why should I suppose my species privileged to be the unique being still subject to teleological explanation alone? With the thought that the human organism too might in principle be brought within reach of causal explanation, contradictions arise. In every choice I make of a means to my ends I now defy the initial assumption that whatever is transferred from teleological to causal explanation loses its value as end. At the same time I am caught in the intolerable position of still being forced to think in terms of a now admittedly fictitious discontinuity with my body. It is at this stage that the 'Reason as Master' position loses its apparent self-evidence and becomes incoherent.

The attitudes to the sacred and the obscene from the 'Reason as Master' position seem at first sight perfectly symmetrical. The language which excites me to respond to forces as either sacred or obscene is listened to only as long as it is presumed to convey objective information about the divine or diabolic inhabitants of a world of spirit distinct from matter. Once spirit is abolished, there remains room only for objective description of the responses themselves, which become available to me as means. Since the spontaneous in me is conceived as in itself without value, whenever I utilize it as means all the credit is mine for utilizing it. But here an asymmetry arises, that having been reduced to means, what had been classed as sacred becomes an aid to my ends, as obscene an obstacle. A consequence is that, although the obscene is still excluded from myself, the powers formerly revered as sacred are claimed as my own. In a tradition long habituated to 'Reason as Master', one has to unravel etymologies before one notices that a man's 'genius' was once a spirit presiding over his birth and growth, even that his 'gifts' must once have been ascribed to a giver. The great man loses his numinous glow as a person blessed or cursed by powers acting through him, to become an individual utilizing his talents to the best effect. The hardiest survivor among sacred powers is the moral conscience, long identified even within the 'Reason as Master' tradition as the inwardly heard voice of God; but this too comes to be treated as one's own self-admonition. It is admissible for the 'Reason as Master' position that there can be such a thing as a beneficial spontaneity, but assimilated to that of the hand in a manual skill, in which the agent has full responsibility for turning the process on and off in the service of his own ends. Why feel humble or awestruck when the baby is born just as planned? The spontaneity of creative reason itself conspicuously fails to fit the model, being by no means easy to turn on and off, but a discoverer for whom 'Reason is Master' has too firmly bounded a self to think like the prophets or like Rimbaud of his own work as done through rather than by him, must see it as an exercise by himself of his own powers.

The asymmetry of enlarging oneself at the expense of the sacred but continuing to repel the obscene as disruptive of selfhood explains why the former has receded from consciousness so much faster than the latter. Indeed, increasing rationality may heighten the terror of being overwhelmed by obscene forces, until an unevocative language is developed which can deal with them objectively without conjuring them up. Michel Foucault in his *Madness and civilization* called attention to the profound fear of madness behind the advance of rationality since the seventeenth century, the drawing of a sharper line between sane and insane, the driving of madmen off the streets and their seclusion behind the walls of asylums. It had not always been a matter of course that society must reduce the madman to an object, a case for treatment, until by returning to reason he recovers full humanity; it was once possible to relate to him as subject and discern profundities in his folly, intimations of the sacred in his obscenity, as existential psycho-analysis again tries to do, as indeed we all do while we are reading *King Lear*. But although one for whom 'Reason is Master' has to resist and therefore at least tacitly acknowledge the power of the obscene he is embarrassed by this self-betrayal; he is comfortable only if he can wholly disconnect himself, dismiss Sade with a 'I wasn't shocked, I was bored', or condescend to Hitler's incantatory rhetoric as the rantings of a silly man with a funny moustache. This self-distancing from the irrational has something to do with the awful brittleness of rationality in this age of its greatest discoveries; one cannot effectively buttress reason if one does not know how to respond imaginatively to Hitler and Sade, Taoists and Surrealists (and see more than a moral difference between the former pair and the latter). When shutting off subjective awareness of forces that can overwhelm, one is in danger of losing all knowledge of them until an indirect access is found through objective description. A significant part of Freud's appeal is that he proved by his example that language can after all objectivize so much that the 'Reason as Master' tradition could not hitherto risk taking into account: the roots and the deviations of sexuality and violence, the Unconscious, dream and fantasy, the deeper meaning of myth, ritual and taboo. It may not have been pleasant, or even wholly convincing, to hear that you wanted to kill your father and ravish your mother, but it was a relief to find that for the first time for 300 years the West's self-imposed ban was lifted and you were allowed once more to know as much as the people of older cultures about the irrational in yourself, with the security of now feeling equipped to deal with its threats.

In repelling the obscene as foreign to himself the person for whom 'Reason is Master' finds himself in a paradoxical relation with his own biology, with the disruptive power of his sexuality and the irreversible march of the body towards decay and death. The extraordinary intensity of Victorian taboos in the sexual sphere, into which almost the whole meaning of the word 'obscene' has contracted to this day, testifies to the baleful power of the abominable wherever reason is in doubt of its mastery. Victorian prudery was not an anachronistic religious survival, on the contrary it could be shocked by the strong language of the Bible itself. It was a primitive taboo coming to flower at the very height of confidence in science and progress, obsessively reinforced as religious sanctions failed by pseudo-scientific warnings of dangers to health. More recently, penetration of the mysteries of sexuality by objective knowledge and conscious control has emptied it of most of its obscene menace. It has become so manageable in theory that we can disengage ourselves from subjective confrontation even with such an eroticist as Sade himself, the single pure spokesman of the obscene, who unlike the Duchess of Malfi would indeed and in cold blood curse the world to its first chaos, and take in just enough of him to read him as a titillating entertainer, or as one more fearless demolisher of outworn prejudices, or—a characteristically English evasion— to dissipate the tension, and so learn nothing from him, by remembering one's sense of humour. However, the horror of the obscene still remains as strong as ever, transferred from sexuality to cancer, decrepitude, death, abominations of a sort which the Victorians faced much more boldly than moderns do. The mingled attraction and repulsion of obscenity is now less vivid in eroticism than in horror films exorcizing the dread and fascination of bodily and spiritual decomposition, or even perhaps, as far as the dread is concerned, than in the anxiety-ridden fetishism of health foods and exercises now flourishing incongruously among people who have never been so long-lived and healthy.

The shutting off of the rational self from its continuity with nature has to be paid for, in continuing vulnerability to the forces shunned as obscene which will eventually overwhelm it in death. Here we may attempt a restatement of an old accusation of the religious against liberals and rationalists, that in spite of good intentions they lack the sense of Evil. One for whom 'Reason is Master' can condemn an action of his own or of another as wrong, and honestly explore its motives, but only in so far as they are rational, not all the way to those forces disruptive of reason from which his awareness has cut itself off, which he recognizes objectively if at all, as foreign to himself; and when he perceives the continuity in others he shakes his head at man's refusal to listen to reason. I hope I shall not seem to be deriding a great man if I illustrate this point by two accounts of violent rages in the autobiography of Bertrand Russell, who was a model of the strengths and weaknesses of this temperament.

Unfortunately, however, FitzGerald and I had a somewhat serious disagreement during this time.... I came to hate him with a violence which, in retrospect, I can hardly understand. On one occasion, in an access of fury, I got my hands on his throat and started to strangle him. I intended to kill him, but when he began to grow livid, I relented. I do not think he knew that I had intended murder. After this, we remained fairly good friends throughout his time at Cambridge, which however ended with his marriage at the end of his second year.

I became blind with rage, the only time I have been so since I tried to strangle Fitz-Gerald. I pursued the boys with the flashlights, but being lame, was unable to catch them, which was fortunate, as I should certainly have committed murder. An enterprising photographer succeeded in photographing me with my eyes blazing. I should not have known that I could have looked so completely insane.[13]

Many of us recall such incidents in our lives, and may well envy the honesty and clarity of mind which enables Russell to narrate them with such drily humorous objectivity. But what does he feel about them? Shame? That idiotic self-complacency we intellectuals sometimes secretly notice in ourselves when we discover that in spite of all that ratiocination we have strong passions after all? Russell does not tell us, because in spite or because of the lifelong fear of madness which, as he says, 'caused me for many years to avoid all deep emotion, and live as nearly as I could a life of intellect tempered by flippancy',[14] he knows himself subjectively only as a rational man, who in eventually learning to trust his feelings has discovered himself to be passionate, yes, but in the loves and the dedication to social and political causes which his reason approves, so that he knows how to report lapses in self-control only in objective language, as not experience but interruptions of experience. But without information as to how he feels in retrospect, there is an absolute discontinuity with the picture of himself on every other page of the book. In the first episode the outbreak once past is as though it had never happened; in the second, it is only by looking at a photograph of himself that Russell discovers how far he had lost control. But even a person who, as Russell to his credit was not, is content to devote himself exclusively to the most abstract thought, is profoundly mistaken if he thinks of himself as a luminous mind which has occasional lapses. Outside his speciality he will at best be only a little more rational than most.

At the start of this chapter we objected to the doctrine of Original Sin for the inconsistency of ascribing the spontaneous in us to God when it is good and to our own nature when it is bad. The person who submits to 'Reason as Master', whether or not he commits himself to the goodness of human nature, is guilty of the reverse error. When the forces which overwhelm him are creative he takes the whole credit, when they are destructive he feels that he is 'not himself'.

3

THINKERS AT THE LIMITS OF MORAL DOUBT

3.1 Irrationalism and anti-rationalism

No one can by taking thought add one cubit to his stature, says the Gospel.[1] It is a maxim worth bearing in mind, for the man of reason has always been tempted to impose his favourite faculty on problems to which it is unsuited. The tradition called 'Rationalism' in the specialized sense (in contrast with 'Empiricism') hoped to establish the basic truths, such as the existence of oneself and of God, by pure thought independent of observation, but it is no longer embarrassing even to the most rational to admit that one cannot deduce truths *a priori* except in logic and mathematics. Nor do we any longer expect, with the Empiricists, even to find pure observations, uncontaminated by the concepts with which the observer frames his questions, to serve as the irrefragable foundations of knowledge. During the present century, although rational inquiry has in every field of science and technology displayed unprecedented fertility and achieved successes formerly unimaginable, we have become accustomed to hearing from one kind of specialist after another that reason has collided with new limits, in logic at paradoxes of self-reference, in philosophy of science at the failure to validate induction, in sub-atomic physics at the observer's interference with the event observed, in cosmology at the naked singularity.

Such encounters with the angel with the flaming sword crying 'No farther!' do not much worry the man of reason after he has time to get used to them. The longing for a world-view demonstrable like 'two and two make four' belongs to a historical episode which is already past. The Western tradition for a long time could not dispense with absolute certainties, because the salvation of the soul depended on choice of the right faith. In the seventeenth and eighteenth centuries the certainties of geometrical demonstration encouraged it to adopt reason instead of revelation as the opium inducing perfect security, of which it could not yet bear to be disintoxicated. When no longer motivated by the hope and fear of eternal judgement, an insistence on a kind of certainty which no one expects in the issues of ordinary life begins to look like neurotic insecurity. None the less, among the limits at which rational inquiry has come to a stop, there is one to which we cannot be reconciled so easily. Throughout the two and a half millenia of the history of Western philosophy it has been supposed that, once the key is found, it will be possible to establish rationally the ends which man should pursue. But when it became clear that Kant had failed to establish a logically *a priori* imperative, after Hume's separation of 'is' and 'ought' had discredited in advance any ethic based on theological, psychological, sociological or other factual generalizations about actual goals, it became impossible to sustain this hope. Reason can find the means to already accepted ends, and can reconcile or decide between ends, but the ends themselves spring from somewhere beyond its range. This is a concession of quite a different order from abandoning Descartes' *cogito*, or acknowledging the Principle of Indeterminacy or Gödel's Proof. 'How shall I live?' is the question from which philosophy starts and which eternally renews it. It seems that the only help one can now expect from a philosopher is: 'This is how to work out the implications of your choices. As to why you make the choices in the first place, do as the neighbours do, or listen to the poets, preachers, sages, revolutionaries, Hitler —or do the first thing that comes into your head—or despair—but don't come back to me.'

Shall we say that the central question in our lives now passes into the realm of irrationalism? We must begin by admitting that the rationalist's retreat from ends to the implications of ends and to means is not merely a licence to irrationalism; it has put him at a moral disadvantage against the irrationalist. It gives reason in ethics a merely utilitarian, in some eyes a sordid ignoble look. The trouble is that if one's ends cannot be proved to be good in themselves, the only relatively firm starting-points for rational debate will be the means required for the widest variety of possible ends—in the first place self-preservation, necessary to the pursuit of any end whatever, then health, money, power, reputation and so forth. Even if for the foreseeable future my life will not be worth living, it is reasonable to cling to life as a merely potential means, for which I shall be grateful if some end finally emerges to quicken desire and hope. It seems similarly reasonable to cling to money, mindful of its unlimited possible uses, even if in age and ill health I can see nothing left worth using it for. But if I can give reasons for valuing self-preservation or money, but none for judging love or honour good in themselves, is it not reasonable to prefer money to love and survival to self-respect? Thus a rationalistic ethic has a great hole at the centre of it where its ends belong, and it puts us in the false position of being unable to demonstrate their value but well able to whittle away that value by criticism on the level of means.

The most coherent moral codes resist this reduction to systems of means by laying down things which must be done irrespective of all reasons for judging them personally or socially beneficial or harmful. You do not, if you are a Confucian, refuse to give up three years of your career to mourn the death of your father; or if you are an old-time Corsican, shirk avenging the death of a kinsman even if you have to take to the hills; or if you are a liberal and humanitarian, consent to torture a prisoner however urgent it may be to get his confession. One has to draw the line somewhere. It is not that beyond the line values are absolute and universal, but that it belongs to the logic of a code of conduct that its means serve its ends, and if you turn it inside out by sacrificing all the ends to means, you reduce it to nonsense. This logic involves it in a dilemma which may in due course destroy it, that since conflicting codes do not draw the same line there can be situations in which one or the other must either compete at a disadvantage or cease to be itself.

However fully an ethic is rationalized as a system of means, every disadvantage which may be urged against the pursuit of an end may be seen from the opposite direction as a sacrifice to be suffered for it, with the willing acceptance of the sacrifice as the proof of the value of the end for oneself. The man who has ends for which he is ready to die, however irrational or destructive, can throw down the challenge: 'I have something I value for its own sake, have you?'. The limitations of a rationality which is mere prudence in the realm of means are evident even in its criticisms of simple self-indulgences. It appears reasonable to prefer mild diversions to the excitements which might have to be paid for with cirrhosis of the liver, paternity suits or ruinous losses at the tables. But how does one measure a danger against the intensity of a pleasure? The man dedicated to pleasure at any rate has something which he does for its own sake, which gives point to his choices of means, and to the extent that he keeps a clear head about the possible consequences, he confirms by the risks he takes for it the high degree and the genuineness of its value for him. On the other hand the prudent man who thinks it *self-evidently* absurd to risk health or wealth, not for some useful purpose, but for a mere pleasure, raises the question 'But is there anything at all you would do for its own sake?'.

Rationalists have long deplored the continuing revolt against reason which began with the Romantic movement. But since they have themselves discredited their former pretensions to establish ends rationally, an irrationalist might well ask what right they have to complain. We have to find our ends somewhere. To be trapped in the mechanics of means to further means in an infinite regress is a characteristically modern anguish which, to use a slippery word in what is perhaps its most useful sense, is called 'alienation';[2] we should not be surprised at anything men do to escape from it. But the thesis of the present book opens up a prospect of renewing the offensive against irrationalism with a clearer conscience. Certainly ends cannot be deduced *a priori*, but the apparent impossibility of criticizing them except in terms of each other is an illusion of the 'Reason as Master' position. On the 'Reason as Guide' position, inclination spontaneously shifts as awareness expands towards other temporal and personal viewpoints, or contracts to the present and oneself; any goal to which one finds oneself inclining is criticizable as an end by appeal to anything in awareness of which it spontaneously ceases to attract. 'Be aware' is the imperative from which valuation of the spontaneous starts, and reason is the test of awareness. All the limits at which reason has been checked, in logic, philosophy of science, quantum physics, cosmology, just as much as in ethics, confirm its hubris in pretending to be master instead of guide; its function is to decide between alternatives among interpretations of sense experience, concepts, analogies, generalizations or goals, as they are spontaneously formed in the struggle to adapt themselves to circumstances, and the beautiful intricacy and coherence of the relations which it exposes should never tempt us to suppose that it can break free from the spontaneous. On this account, rationality remains crucially important to awareness and therefore to all valuation. But it becomes urgent, when dismissing a position as irrationalism, to distinguish clearly between two separate issues:

(1) the relative importance it allows to analytic thinking and to other resources for awareness:

(2) the yes-or-no issue of whether or not it submits spontaneity to the authority of 'Be aware'.

As for the first point, the relative importance of logical argument and of spontaneous insights and skills in becoming aware is an open question on which there is no need to dogmatize. How far analysis furthers or disrupts artistic creation or appreciation, manual dexterities, insight into other persons, the solution of personal or social problems too complex to be reduced to the simplifications of the proto-sciences of psychology and sociology, are questions full of imponderables to which each finds his own answer. There is nothing irrational, or even anti-intellectual, in admitting that someone may be rigorously logical, yet all in all not very intelligent. There remains always a no man's land which some try to bring within the scope of analysis while others trust to spontaneity. Let us call the former 'rationalists' and the latter, not irrationalists, but 'anti-rationalists' , and since the frontier between them is indefinite and disputable, use both terms quite neutrally. Whether the reader chooses to call the philosophy of this book by one name or the other is his own business.

Wherever the line may be drawn, everyone learns by experience that within a certain range of practical concerns he cannot afford to flout reason, and also that many spontaneous activities are best left to take care of themselves. As long as the rival of rationalism is anti-rationalism, the placing of the boundary is itself rationally testable. How far it is safe for the tightrope walker to analyse his own steps as he takes them can be judged by a strictly objective test, whether he falls off the rope. But we might also have a Nazi who appreciates the importance of calm detached thinking in military strategy or the engineering of gas chambers, yet bursts into hysterical denunciations of barren intellectualism if the same kind of critical intelligence is applied to deciding whether the *Protocols of the Elders of Zion* are genuine or forged. Outside the realm of means, where it cannot be disobeyed with impunity, he refuses to be bound by 'Be aware'; there are no practical disadvantages in unawareness of facts which could discourage his hatred of Jews. Here we need another name, 'irrationalism', not neutral but pejorative. This attitude differs from anti-rationalism in resisting, not only trespasses of analytic thinking outside its province, but any kind of intelligence which might expose its delusions. The touchstone is 'Be aware'; the anti-rationalist claims that in specific circumstances analysing is the wrong way to become aware, the irrationalist can make a virtue of being unaware. One of them acknowledges the obstinacy of fact, the constancy and resistance of external reality, in choices of ends as much as of means, the other does not. The anti-rationalist is a rebel against 'Reason as Master', the irrationalist even against 'Reason as Guide'.

Seen from this perspective, it is not that a rational ethic has an empty hole in the middle where it has failed to master spontaneity, but that without the channelling of spontaneity through that hole it would have nothing to guide. Whether a goal springs from one's own experience, or is borrowed from teachers or poets, or imposed by human or divine authority, it is reason that tests the extent and the neutrality of awareness as one is spontaneously attracted or repelled. We are accustomed to having a plethora of desires between which to choose, and when apathetic are incapable of rational choice until inclination is spontaneously roused; an ethic which is a mere structure of means starting from unsupported ends detached from spontaneity has only the empty shell of rationality. Any thinker who stirs our interest with the promise of new ends has in the last resort selected them from spontaneously evolving goals. Whether he knows it or not, in the origins of his thought, before the asking of critical questions, he was no rationalist. But that is not a reproach to him, provided that we can classify him as anti-rationalist. Indeed there may still be things to learn from him even if he does deserve to be called an irrationalist. A contempt for reason and wilfulness in being aware or unaware may be a positive advantage when it comes to acknowledging the irrational in oneself and others, a field of inquiry in which the rationalist is handicapped. In this single field, which is that of self-awareness, the great irrationalists do obey 'Be aware', sometimes more faithfully than the rest of us.

A qualified commitment to analytic thinking may easily tip us in the direction of irrationalism, and we must take precautions against the danger of going over the edge. There are several points at which the irrationalism we condemn diverges sharply from the anti-rationalism we allow. Since the value of a response depends, we claim, on awareness of its object, we may start by classing as irrationalism whatever reverses the relation and pronounces an object real or unreal because the reactions excited by belief in it are good or bad (the jump, not from fact to value, but from value to fact). Thus faith in a religious or political creed may come to be declared a duty, and doubt a sin, irrespective of the evidence for or against. To think of all contrary evidence as God's trial of my faith, and the conquest of doubt even against reason as a moral victory, is a pure case of irrationalism. So is an appeal to believe in the existence of God or the freedom of the will because otherwise life would lose its meaning, morality its authority, society the bond which holds it together; these may be strong motives for believing, but motives are not reasons. Basic to rationality is an acknowledgement that objective fact is independent of human needs and ideals, that wherever the evidence clashes with my finer feelings it is the finer feelings which are likely to be wrong. This basic condition in no way depends on an old-fashioned *naïveté* as to the solidity of objective fact; even on the most sceptical philosophy of science, a right answer is relative to the conceptual frame of the question, not to the questioner's emotions. If I guide my life by a belief in the superiority of the Nordic race, or, at the other extreme, in some egalitarian ideology of the kind which affirms genetic equality as a fact, and take the risk of colliding with reality by applying objective tests for measuring intelligence, I must be prepared, given the general cussedness of things, to be disappointed in either case. If I then proceed, for example, to denounce intelligence testing, not for methodological flaws, but for getting results encouraging to race, class, or sex discrimination, I fall into irrationalism. The delusion of thinking as though only meanly motivated beliefs are wish-fulfilment, and the grand hopes and aspirations which dignify life somehow guarantee the truth of beliefs they inspire, can lead to worse, to the self-confirming assumption that anyone who weighs the evidence differently from myself is blind, wicked or reactionary. If his soul were as sensitive as mine to man's profoundest needs, how could he resist the will to believe? But if a question is genuinely factual, such as whether Christ was born of a virgin, card experiments confirm telepathy, or all civilizations were founded by the Aryan race, the man who wants an honest answer will do his best to leave his soul out of it. Here we had better make it clear that by irrationalists we understand, not people who after weighing the arguments decide in favour of the existence of God or telepathy, nor those whose emotions sway their judgements (which would include us all), but those who coax us towards intellectual or moral excuses for letting motives outweigh reasons.

Secondly, we count it as irrationalism to put intensity before awareness. This is not to deny that intensity is itself a local enhancement of awareness. Since to feel strongly is to be highly aware of sensations, emotions, desires, thoughts, to choose it will, other things being equal, be a decision in obedience to 'Be aware'. However, excitements and enthusiasms tend to fade with fuller awareness of obstacles and tasks. The temptation then is to shrink from dispiriting reality and be seduced by the value of a vivid local awareness into welcoming some ecstasy unsustainable in fuller awareness of its nature and consequences. The extreme example would be surrender to the death-wish before the possibilities of life are exhausted. The death-wish at its purest, as in the impulse to jump over the edge which makes many people afraid of heights, momentary, meaningless and irreparable in its consequences, is not likely to be romanticized by anyone. But it can enter as a stimulus or as a catalyst into the ecstasies of love and battle, disguised as devotion to an end more precious than life, for which it is reasonable to risk even life (which assumes that one does *not* wish for death). The impulse to a motiveless plunge into disaster and death hidden in the sensibility of romantic love is exposed with a peculiar clarity in one of the Surrealist André Breton's reminiscences of a woman he did not love, Nadja, in whom he recognized

...a principle of total subversion, more or less conscious, of which I preserve as example only this fact. One evening when I was driving on the Versailles—Paris road, a woman at my side who was Nadja, but who might after all have been any woman, even *the* woman, her foot holding mine pressed against the accelerator, hands groping to cover my eyes, in the oblivion won by an endless kiss, wished that we should no longer exist, without doubt for ever, except for each other, and that just like that we let ourselves be swept at full speed to crash into the beautiful trees.[3]

Breton is a little too rational for that, but only because he did not love Nadja.

I am none the less grateful to her for having revealed to me, in that terrible thrill, to what a common recognition of love would have committed us at that moment. I feel myself less and less capable of resisting such a temptation *in all circumstances*. I cannot do less than give thanks, in this last reminiscence, to the one who made me understand the near necessity of it.

Is Breton's idea that the lovers should will themselves to sustain, for the few necessary seconds, an absorption in the rapturous present cut off from the future and the might have been? That would indeed be the purest irrationalism. But Breton, extremist though he is, is a thinker who, as we shall see,[4] remains by our definitions within the bounds of anti-rationalism. We may be sure that he imagines the lovers as driving blindly at full speed in perfect awareness of the consequences, and trusting themselves and each other to sustain until the last moment the ecstasy which they prefer to all future prospects. He is fascinated by Nadja's whim as the purest, most challenging instance of the choice of intensity, however brief, rather than worldly banalities, a choice which is at the centre of romantic love, above all in Surrealist *amour fou*. (The Surrealist would also expect at the peak of intensity to transcend the dichotomy of life and death,[5] but we had better ignore this metaphysical complication.) If it were possible to surrender to the impulse in full awareness, would not the few remaining moments be the greatest in life? Whether it is indeed possible is the consideration which has Breton hesitating between speaking of failure to 'resist the temptation' and of a 'near necessity'. As a matter of fact he loved more than once after this incident, and lived to a ripe old age. Lunatic as the whole idea will seem to almost anyone but a Surrealist, it provides a good test case for the outer limits of rational choice. One cannot on the present argument deny in principle that lovers who are aware of all the disastrous consequences of an impulse, yet act it out, have chosen rationally. The only question would be whether in practice one could accept them as fully aware, not merely dazzled by a silly idea. The offence against rationality would be to save intensity by denying the equality of temporal viewpoints, shrinking back into the present from viewpoints in the future.

Thirdly, it is irrationalism to reject the equality of personal viewpoints. By equality we mean that one person's judgement is not to be preferred to another's except on grounds (intelligence, information, impartiality) for which there are objective criteria, which may oblige me to prefer your judgement to mine instead of mine to yours. It is irrationalism to excuse or encourage theoretically the almost irresistible temptation to assume that my own preferences have universal validity. Thus Nazism, which displays to admirable effect all our three aspects of irrationalism, regards Aryan and Jew as biologically destined to see the world differently, even to develop incompatible Aryan and Jewish sciences, and makes no pretence of having objective tests to judge between them. This position should commit it to relativism, obliging the Aryan, if not to tolerate the Jew as an equal, then to recognize his own Aryan instinct to exterminate racial vermin as no better or worse than the corresponding Jewish instinct to enslave the Goyim to the Elders of Zion. But the Nazi does not renounce the right to moralize the issue between the two races; he treats the superiority of his own to the Jewish, and the right of the higher to rule or extirpate the lower, as absolutes, and denounces relativism as itself a Jewish weapon to demolish the Aryan's certainty of his own rightness. This entitles the Nazi to refuse all appeals to put himself in the Jew's place and become aware of how he feels, which would be self-degrading, with the result that his own egocentric moralizing is incorrigible, self-confirming.

This kind of irrationalism is exhibited most nakedly in its attitude to retributive justice. For approval of an act of vengeance to come within our proposed limits of rationality, anger would have to be the informed reaction, not only of the sufferer, but of any who imagine from his viewpoint in sufficient awareness of his situation. Such an act might be a principled private revenge, or the retribution of society satisfying the communal thirst for the blood of the murderer, or a massacre of oppressors sanctioned by a revolutionary ideal of justice. Whoever approves the retribution is committed to seeing even his own actions from the viewpoint of the witness, and admitting that he too, if he offends, may be justly punished. This is not to deny that one may reasonably be repelled by the thirst for vengeance as always in the last resort a reaction in insufficient awareness, but at any rate the awareness, such as it is, may be neutral as to viewpoint.

In Nazism on the other hand an unbridled destructiveness and its moral justification veer between aggression and suicide without regard for any viewpoint but that attributed to the Aryan race, which each discovers by blinding himself to his own viewpoint to see through the eyes of the Leader. At first the destructiveness turns outwards, against alien and therefore inferior tribes, whose inwardness is unapproachable without self-defilement and in any case finally inaccessible. With these there can be no such thing as abuse of power, and no moral relation other than righteous indignation at being wronged by those who by right should be one's slaves; the passion for vengeance, breeding and in turn fed by obsessive hates, is seen as just, not because independent of personal viewpoint, but because it is intolerable that we, the noble, should be defied by you, the base. Later, in defeat, the destructiveness turns inwards. Hitler immolates himself with Eva Braun, and does his best (with the still rational Albert Speer evading his orders) to take the German people with him. The viewpoint from which he pronounces his absolute judgements has now shrunk to himself alone, with the paradoxical result that for the first and last time he has an objective standard for judging between the races, that of their utility as means to the fulfilment of his personal ideal. He finds himself betrayed by the German people, who have proved unworthy of the sublime hopes he set in them, and acknowledges the historic destiny by which they go down before the stronger power from the East.

A breakdown of accepted standards leaves the individual with nothing but his own authentic response in awareness at its fullest extension from present and self to other viewpoints. Even the most rational is in the end thrown back on the resources of his own spontaneity. But it is his own fault if this disorientates him; if he is wholly out of touch with the spontaneity at the bottom of his own valuations, he was never as rational as he thinks he is, in any sense deeper than being able to manipulate logically standards imposed on him from outside. He can expect no guidance in renewing that spontaneity except from teachers who are aware in other ways besides being logical, and are responsive as well as aware, as were all who have been creative of new values in the past. An empty rhetoric denouncing as irrationalists all objectors to 'Reason as Master' only obscures the line for which we should be ceaselessly on watch, between those who in abandoning all other imperatives still hold on to 'Be aware', and those who discard it with the rest. Let us conclude this book by placing on either side of the line certain of the thinkers who are exemplary in having emerged from the crisis of moral scepticism with values that, whichever side we place them, are coherent and their own. We choose only extremists; moderates would not show up so clearly the distinction we draw.

3.2 Irrationalism

3.2.1 Nietzsche

Since we have been quoting Nietzsche with appreciation throughout this book, it may seem ungrateful to turn round at this late stage and condemn him as an irrationalist. Indeed in one of his aspects Nietzsche is a thinker who puts us all to shame by his uncompromising pursuit of what we least want to be told. Yet he also took pride in being the first to ask the question 'Granted we want truth, *why not rather* untruth? And uncertainty? Even ignorance?'[1] It is a question which, instead of submitting ends to the test of whether or not they survive greater awareness, reduces truth itself to just another of the ends which we may or may not decide to pursue. Is the self-denying reverence for disinterested truth after all as virtuous as it seems? Nietzsche discerns in it a perverted taste for self-torment, and in the 'free spirits' of his time, who in rejecting religion in the name of truth think themselves liberated from its morality, the latest and purest expression of the ascetic ideal.

'These men are a long way from being *free* spirits, because they still believe in truth... When the Christian crusaders in the East happened upon the invincible Society of the Assassins, that order of free spirits *par excellence*, whose lower ranks observed an obedience stricter than any monastic order, they must have got some hint of the slogan reserved for the highest ranks, which ran, 'Nothing is true; everything is permitted'. Here we have real freedom, for the notion of truth itself has been disposed of. Has any Christian freethinker ever dared to follow out the labyrinthine consequences of this slogan? Has any of them ever truly experienced the Minotaur inhabiting that maze?[2]

Nietzsche's questioning of the value of truth is not to be confused with his epistemological doubts as to its meaning and its very possibility. Fascinated though he is by the necessity of distorting reality by fitting it into our own schemas, of accepting 'error as the precondition even of thought'[3] and truth itself as 'the posture of various errors in relation to each other',[4] he knows well enough that such epistemological questions are irrelevant to the practical difference between awareness and unawareness as it forces itself on us in the conduct of life. But in spite or because of his own appetite for dark truths, he has a unique insight into the positive function, not simply of unavoidable error, but of delusion, insensibility, lies, in every man's painful progress towards what he most values, and sees it as in the nature of the great discoverer to be also a great deceiver. His criterion for preferring the true or the false is their vitalizing or devitalizing effects:

The falseness of a judgement is to us not necessarily an objection to a judgement; it is here that our new language perhaps sounds strangest. The question is to what extent it is life-advancing, life-preserving, species-preserving, perhaps even species-breeding.... To recognize untruth as a condition of life; that, to be sure, means to resist customary value-sentiments in a dangerous fashion; and a philosophy which ventures to do so places itself, by that act alone, beyond good and evil.[5]

The conclusion is unexpected, and seems not to follow unless Nietzsche has some inkling of the unity of awareness and morality which we have tried to demonstrate in this book. One would have thought that on the contrary a philosophy which recognizes untruth as a condition of life would allow the deliberate establishment of morality on a 'pious fraud'. Much as Nietzsche despises the 'holy lie', he knows well that he has forfeited the right to object in principle:

Ultimately the point is to what *end* a lie is told. That 'holy' ends are lacking in Christianity is *my* objection to its means. Only *bad* ends: the poisoning, slandering, denying of life...[6]

By far the most important defiance of 'Be aware' recommended by Nietzsche is the refusal of the man who knows himself to be superior to enter into minds which he finds base and debasing. The proper reaction of the higher to the lower is not sympathy but scorn. Nietzsche is quite explicit that he is in favour of a deliberate shutting off of awareness:

Aristocratic valuations may go amiss and do violence to reality, but this happens only with regard to spheres which they do not know well, or from the knowledge of which they austerely guard themselves; the aristocrat will on occasion misjudge a sphere which he holds in contempt, the sphere of the common man, the people.[7]

This refusal of awareness is fundamental to Nietzsche's peculiar combination of pessimism and optimism. He sees misery, waste and impotence as the general lot of man, and the ascetic impulse which has hitherto shaped culture as springing from the need to find meaning in pain if life is to have a meaning at all; yet he also sees a future of infinite promise if the few who are on the ascending line of growth resolutely turn their backs on the blindly suffering mass for whom nothing either should or can be done. The metaphor of disease serves him to show why the natural master of men has to shut off some of his awareness:

Our first rule on this earth should be that the sick must not contaminate the healthy. But this requires that the healthy be isolated from the sick, be spared even the sight of the sick, lest they mistake that foreign sickness for their own.[8]

It is a metaphor which was later to serve the racialist rhetoric of Hitler's *Mein Kampf*. One should not hesitate to acknowledge, so many years after 1945, both the depth and richness of Nietzsche's thought and the plain fact that one of its strands leads directly to Nazism.

For Nietzsche, the self-sacrificing impulses awakened by awareness of the sufferings of the base are to be resisted as temptations to help the inferior at the expense of the superior. Fellow-feeling is admissible only towards equals, and pity (an emotion in which there is a tinge of contempt for the weak who need help) is a biologically harmful kind of fellow-feeling which tends to the benefit of the lower breeds. A point of interest is Nietzsche's implicit acknowledgement that the impulse to sympathy is inherent in all awareness from other viewpoints;

you have to be spared the very sight of illness if you are not to risk mistaking it for your own. Here this most psychologically acute of philosophers agrees with a claim of the present book which readers much less committed than Nietzsche to the innateness of human selfishness may have found highly controversial. He thinks that the pity inseparable from subjective understanding of another's suffering is suppressed only by a supreme effort of the will:

It counts with me as weakness, as a special case of the incapacity to withstand stimuli — it is only among *decadents* that *pity* is called a virtue.... I have, as 'Zarathustra's temptation', invented a case in which a great cry of distress reaches him, in which pity like an ultimate sin seeks to attack him, to seduce him from allegiance to *himself*. To remain master here, here to keep the *elevation* of one's task clean of the many lower and more short-sighted drives which are active in so-called selfless actions, that is the test, the final test perhaps, which a Zarathustra has to pass — the actual *proof* of his strength.[9]

By now it is time to pause and ask what Nietzsche means when he pronounces ignorance and falsehood good if they help to foster life, health, the will to power. To make such a judgement one has to be speaking in the third person, and one might have thought that Nietzsche of all philosophers would deny meaning to what cannot be said with an 'I'. I cannot without self-contradiction say to myself 'This is false, but believe it', 'This is relevant to drawing my conclusions, but ignore it'. I can of course listen to Nietzsche as an objective witness, and perhaps assent when he speaks in general terms of unawareness as necessary to the growth of any code of values. I may even acknowledge in the abstract that he may well discern what must remain undiscoverable by me, that a submerged revulsion from some truth is nourishing and strengthening my own values. But I cannot apply his devaluation of truth to my own case. It is impossible to take conscious advantage of a licence to lie to myself, and in any case Nietzsche seems to ask in practice only for a little deliberately protected ignorance, as when 'austerely guarding oneself' against awareness of the vulgar. What I could do, when reversing the roles of witness and agent, is to renounce the right to condemn Nietzsche's own code of values merely because it depends like any other on insensibility and delusion. Not that, if actual deviations from reality were visible to me, I could be converted to his code myself. Nietzsche would have to be content with my tolerance of his values as admissible in his own case, an attitude which he would probably find rather insulting.

'Nothing is true, everything is permitted' leaves nothing upon which to build a universal ethic. If that were all, Nietzsche's irrationalism would be of too simple a kind to deserve close attention. However, he does find an objective basis for his values, by one of the standard philosophical ploys, the proposal of a psychological generalization about a common end which all men recognize to the extent that they are self-aware. Hedonists, for example, identify it as pleasure; Nietzsche finds it, beyond pleasure, health, life and other approximations, in power, in the individual's capacity to master other men, nature and himself. Such a generalization is of course factually very dubious, and likely to lose all meaning when universalized, but here we are concerned only with the inner coherence of Nietzsche's thought. There is an obvious paradox in rooting his end in a psychological generalization, yet reducing all judgements of true and false to means to these ends. The whole case for deriving his ethic from the will to power rests on the irrevocable authority of 'Be aware', and impresses above all by its air of tough-mindedness in searching human motivation without idealizing. How then can the value of power justify me in closing myself to awareness which might undermine my will to it? The most that can be plausibly claimed is that a local unawareness may be recommendable as an occasional means to power, an end itself justifiable by appeal to 'Be aware'—an emasculation of Nietzsche's claim which sacrifices his neutrality between truth and falsehood. However, let us see how far we can without inconsistency follow Nietzsce on this course.

We may concede, as an inference from 'Be aware', that an end to which everyone sufficiently aware of himself is aware of spontaneously inclining will be an end good from all viewpoints. For example, suppose that a Christian comes to regard his religion as no more than a blind mechanism with the function of attaining, for the deprived and downtrodden of the Roman Empire and of today, some share of pleasure (according to hedonists) or of power (according to Nietzsche), much as pain is Nature's mechanism, often inefficient, corrigible by medical knowledge, for warning against danger to the organism. Then he will find himself obliged to abandon his religion for a more direct means to the goal which is now his conscious end. If that end is pleasure he will now, as a hedonist, value each individual by his personal capacity for happiness even in unfavourable conditions, for example by his lack of inhibitions, peace of mind, ability to extract joy from the little things in life. Similarly Nietzsche, who sees all life as a conscious or unconscious struggle for power, is entitled to grade men by their strength or weakness as individuals, preferring the self-discipline and unthinking authority of the proud aristocrat on the scaffold to the *canaille* who have pulled him down only by their collective power as an incoherent mass. It seems then that, granting the factual generalization about a universal struggle for power, the philosopher can be not only witness but judge, inferring from 'Be aware' to 'Prefer the strong', and can approve in others than himself that desensitization, that retreat into unawareness, which is among the means of becoming strong.

Here we are at a point of equilibrium in Nietzsche's case. The witness obeys 'Be aware', and having become aware that all moral codes serve the will to power, is able also to judge, to grade men as relatively strong or weak. The strong with their restricted awareness think they are the best, but so do the weak; only the witness knows why it is the strong who are the best. What upsets this equilibrium is in the first place that Nietzsche cannot bear to acknowledge the right of the weak, the majority, to think of themselves mistakenly as the best. By no means the philosophical egoist he appears at first sight, Nietzsche approves of selfishness only in the few who are on 'the ascending line of life', and requires the weak and degenerate to respect their betters and serve them altruistically.[10] This amounts to demanding of the average man a self-sacrifice beyond that of Christians, quite without reward. Is the Nietzsche who expects this the realistic psychologist or the 'aristocrat misjudging a sphere which he holds in contempt'? There could be no motive for such a sacrifice without the most difficult kind of awareness, that my oppressors are my superiors in terms of an end in itself, the personal capacity for power, which, against the grain of my prejudices and interests, I supposedly find myself forced to recognize when most self-aware. But if it is the harsh duty, not only of the witness, but of everyone outside the life-advancing minority, to put 'Be aware' before his own interests, the strange consequence follows that only the very best of us deserve the privilege of unawareness.

The demand that the weak acknowledge the strong as their betters is not essential to Nietzsche's case, and could be dropped to avoid this anomaly. But there is the more serious difficulty that his system has after all no place for the philosopher as pure witness. The thinker is himself one of the contestants for power, and treasures his will to truth because knowledge is his special weapon. But in entering the arena the thinker is trapped in an insoluble dilemma, whether to extend the demand for awareness from himself to the few he judges highest, or to stultify himself by trying to join them in their insensibility. To start with the first alternative, his knowledge gives him an advantage only because everyone on occasion needs to borrow from it, and has to bow to the expert who knows best. An intellectual élite can exert power only because its imperative 'Be aware' is acknowledged reluctantly and in varying degrees, by everyone. Moreover this élite, like any other, will in achieving a distinctive code of values be claiming superiority for itself. How can it fail to despise a noble caste stupider than itself? And how can it be satisfied to watch the good and the bad rise and fall blindly, like species in the Darwinian struggle, without ever giving a conscious direction to the better by showing them why they are better?

Following this line Nietzsche is driven to extend the authority of 'Be aware' even to the noble, who are thus drawn within the rule of reason. He enters altogether within the scope of rational discourse, which by our classification is to shift his ground from 'irrationalism' to 'anti-rationalism'. Thus in his *Genealogy of morals* he achieves a degree of detachment towards the healthy Teuton innocently exulting in his power and the downtrodden twisted subtle Jew. It may seem at first sight that Nietzsche prefers without reserve the exuberant barbarian who sees the world as it is, and freely accepts its inherent injustice because he benefits by it, to the Jew who as a victim of fortune consoles himself with the sickly vengeful delusions of religion, which will pull the noble down into the masses if they betray their instincts by being converted. The Nazis, who saw only the irrationalist side of Nietzsche, did impose this simplification. But Nietzsche approves the blond beast only partially and by the principle of awareness, for his brutal unselfconscious realism; at the same time he scorns him as stupid, and appreciates the sharp intelligence which the tormented envious Jew has tempered as a weapon in the weak man's struggle against the strong. His ideal aristocrat of the future, as described in *The will to power*,[11] has as much of the sophisticated Jew in him as of the savages who sacked Rome. (Nietzsche, who detested anti-semites, can hardly mention Jews and Germans in the same sentence without deriding the latter: 'What a blessing a Jew is among Germans!')[12] But if the superior become aware of why they are superior, the imperative 'Prefer the strong' to which they have given unthinking allegiance becomes dependent on 'Be aware', a mere inference from 'Be aware that all values express the will to power', and is pulled within the scope of critical debate. In his last work, the autobiographical *Ecce homo*, Nietzsche writes

> How much truth can a spirit *bear*, how much truth can a spirit *dare*? that became for me more and more the real measure of value.
>
> This ultimate, joyfullest, boundlessly exuberant Yes to life is not only the highest insight, it is also the *profoundest*, the insight most strictly confirmed and maintained by truth and knowledge. Nothing that is can be subtracted, nothing is dispensable.[13]

But if 'nothing can be subtracted', how is the noble spirit to justify that effort of will to shut himself off from the viewpoints of most of humanity which alone saves him from being dragged down into the universal morality of the masses? Nietzsche's thinking, whatever may be urged against it, was never simplistic, and in pondering the victory of Christianity and democracy ('Why did life, physiological well-constitutedness, everywhere succumb?') he could ask himself the question:

> Suppose the strong had become master in everything, and even in moral valuation; let us draw the consequences of how they would think about sickness, suffering, sacrifice! Self-contempt on the part of the weak would be the result; they would try to disappear and extinguish themselves. And would this be *desirable?* — and would we really want a world in which the influence of the weak, their subtlety, consideration, spirituality, *pliancy* was lacking?[14]

The other choice in Nietzsche's dilemma is to move in the opposite direction into unawareness, and obliterate the witness in a universal irrationalism. The thinker who discovers that his passion for truth is only a blind psychological mechanism serving his instinctive urge to power will be obliged (like the Christian discovering the true function of his 'slave morality') to seek a more direct route to becoming strong, and yield to some of those temptations to flight from reality which in obedience to 'Be aware' he had thought it his duty to resist. It is this second Nietzsche who can say 'Once and for all, there is a great deal I do *not* want to know. . . Wisdom sets bounds even to knowledge', or 'About certain things *one does not ask questions:* first imperative of instinct'.[15] He cannot of course tell us when he is himself perpetrating some pious fraud for the good of his irreligious soul, but about the deliberate refusal of awareness he is frank enough. He invites us to trust blindly to that impulse of a healthy manly pride to think 'We are better than you', which segregates the noble, matures their distinctive codes of value, and saves them from the debasement of seeing through the eyes of their inferiors, so that judgement is withdrawn from all critical comparisons and becomes self-confirming. The peculiar moral thrill of reading Nietzsche is at least in part the vertigo of this surrender to pride, of a courting of self-delusion like his own in the brilliantly lucid yet megalomaniac self-portrait in *Ecce homo*, where one hardly knows whether to see the radical disproportion in his view of himself as a symptom of his coming madness or as a practical consequence of the philosophy.

The Assassins' 'Nothing is true' has indeed led Nietzsche into a labyrinth, but with no centre and no Minotaur. One result of his dilemma is a very peculiar relation to the reader. It is no surprise to notice that a great thinker is losing sight of the difference between the arguments for his philosophy and the rhetoric with which he preaches it, or has weak places in his thought behind which one suspects dishonest motives (Nietzsche himself had a very sharp eye for the latter). But it is not so common to meet one who cannot allow himself to differentiate the truths of his philosophy from those bracing fictions, so much more life-advancing than insipid truths, with which on the authority of the philosophy he fosters noble values in himself. It leaves the reader with the task of segregating the philosophy from those flat bullheaded statements of personal prejudices about women or the masses in which Nietzsche seems to be announcing 'Blond beasts, look, I can be as stupid as the best of you'. Nietzsche himself can exhibit the difference only unconsciously, through his style. To read him seriously, as with all thinkers who are aphorists rather than reasoners, one has to listen all the time for the ring of sincerity, which in the best of *Genealogy of morals* or *Beyond good and evil* is indeed peerless in its clarity, and take warning whenever the phrasing is inflated and over-emphatic, as in the reference to Zarathustra's temptation which we quoted above.[16] (Although *Also sprach Zarathustra* used to be accepted as Nietzsche's masterpiece, the mere mention of the old fraud's name should be enough to put one on guard.) Why does Nietzsche so dramatize Zarathustra's battle against pity? Because it always embarrasses him to have to explain why proud martial aristocracies have let themselves be undermined by a Christian morality which serves the will to power of the rabble. He has to protest that, in spite of man's ineradicable egoism, on which he more usually insists, pity is a nearly irresistible temptation which only the strongest can vanquish. He is trying to conjure away the simple fact that we feel at least as powerful drives to shut out each other's distress, or to take a cruel, envious or malicious pleasure in it, so that his strong man's choice on the same side as these drives could just as well be taken as a self-deluding surrender to them. It is not that compassion is inherently hard to resist, but that it is harder to resist the more we are aware from the sufferer's viewpoint. Nietzsche's difficulty is that he cannot permit himself an indiscriminate awareness without his whole ethic falling to the ground. He cannot reconcile, or finally choose between, the conflicting currents of his thought: on the one hand, a dauntless will to awareness however painful, unwelcome, value-transforming: on the other, the pressure (to which it is irrationalism to yield) to hold fast to the ends sanctioned by his instincts, even in the knowledge that fuller awareness would dissolve them —his archaic, aristocratic, heroic ends which, as he sees everywhere in the decadent world around him, do in fact dissolve in the awareness from other viewpoints fostered by Christianity and democracy. To some extent the conflict is disguised by a rhetoric which lulls us into assuming that he is closing himself only to the short-sighted sympathies which distract from far-sighted ends, like a surgeon whose callousness protects his efficiency. But the surgeon's end, to heal, would remain unaltered if he did let himself heed the pain he inflicts, while Nietzsche's objection to pity is precisely that it changes your ends, turns you into a decadent, a liberal, a humanitarian; unlike the surgeon, he is clinging to ends which are vulnerable to greater awareness.

Nietzsche is a reactionary who harks back, not to the security of traditional beliefs, but to the authenticity of the innocent selfishness, and of the spontaneous sympathies with each other and antipathies to outsiders and inferiors, of the closed clans and élites of the past. He perceives that, as modern man is drawn farther into expanding circles of social interactions, the gap widens between what he authentically feels and what he thinks he ought to feel, *would* feel if he could sustain awareness from the viewpoints of all the multifarious strangers and underdogs of whom he can no longer be complacently ignorant. With the usual parallelism of personal and temporal viewpoints, the same gap opens between the deep-rooted impulse to violence and the shallow and precarious preference for settling differences peacefully which endures only as long as we succeed in holding in mind the increasingly destructive consequences of rending the intricate fabric of modern civilization. Nietzsche is the most intelligent of the tempters who encourage us to shrink from the strain of a too complex effort of imagination from other viewpoints, back into the assurance of our deepest prejudices. But we must insist that it is no objection to the newer reactions on the outskirts of expanding awareness that inevitably they are frail and sickly compared with the sturdy health of the older and more basic, which were shaped in one's own or in society's relatively ignorant past. Nazi Germany's catastrophic rebound from a painfully stretched awareness into the blindness of tribal instinct would have appalled Nietzsche, but he has his place in the German irrationalist tradition which prepared the way for it. No, we must answer him, we shall *not* 'austerely guard ourselves' against an inconvenient excess of awareness.

3.2.2 Sade

The thinker who by the middle of the twentieth century was superseding Nietzsche as the most extreme irrationalist influence is Sade. In his first significant work, the brief *Dialogue entre un prêtre et un moribond* (1782), Sade is still a true rationalist, the most radical of the *philosophes*, an atheist and hedonist who seeks happiness by fulfilling the sexual and other desires instilled in him by nature while protesting that

...reason, — yes, my friend, reason alone, should inform us that to do harm to our fellows can never make us happy, and our own hearts that to contribute to felicity of theirs is the greatest for ourselves that nature has accorded us on earth.[1]

If his radicalism had stopped there it could have been said by the 1960s that we are all Sadeans now. His later *Justine* and *Juliette*, with their crimes and orgies and philosophical discourses in defence of them, may seem to differ from the *Dialogue* only in degree, in pushing the rationale of hedonism to the point of justifying the pure egoist, who

...will feel that the utmost multitude of injuries to another, none of which he will himself experience physically, has no weight against the lightest of the joys bought by that unheard-of accumulation of crimes.[2]

But one does not have to read far into these books to recognize that they are different in kind. Egoism as the terminus of his thought has been left behind in a voyage into a boundless malevolence. Our argument that philosophical egoism, which seems an invulnerable position, is not a coherent one at all,[3] is well illustrated by the easy transitions by which the apparently self-centred desires of Sade's heroes become disinterested, even self-sacrificing. His chemist Almani, who can destroy a city by an artificial earthquake (let no one say that Sade lacks contemporary relevance) ruins Messina for the amusement of a friend and tells him, when offered payment, that he takes money only for the useful and does harm to mankind for nothing.[4] Amélie, excited by watching Borchamps flay his wife alive, makes him vow some day to make her his victim too: 'to become, in expiring, the occasion of a crime is a thought which makes my head reel'.[5] Juliette, planning her escape from Minski, is reluctant to put an end to so great a menace to mankind, and at some risk decides 'to let this man live who is so indispensable to crime'.[6] In the movement of his thought towards some absolute beyond egoism, we no longer have the impression, as in the *Dialogue*, of a thinker organizing a rationally coherent case. Of course Sade offers innumerable reasons for his rejections of moral demands, some of them individually very interesting, seeming to anticipate Nietzsche, Freud, Proudhon's 'Property is theft', Women's Liberation, the Permissive Society, but arbitrarily, indiscriminately, with an air of parody and mockery. He will argue that one should care only for self or deny oneself in the service of evil, that crimes do no harm or that one should commit them for the sake of doing harm, that all desires are legitimate because natural or all the sweeter for being unnatural, that Nature cares nothing for good and evil, or demands sufficient evil to balance good, or desires only evil, claims which he repeats endlessly from book to book without ever pretending to reconcile them. It is not that Sade's thought is confused but that his regular practice, which the reader soon takes for granted, is to exploit any usable argument without regard for its logical relations with any other. It is as though he cannot submit to coercion even from the obligations of reason, and is determined that his choices be seen as finally gratuitous, pure expressions of his sovereignty. The current on which his philosophizing rides is his own eroticism. He treats reason as the plaything of desire; and for him the more voluptuous alternative is always the one which by current standards is is the more immoral.

Must we conclude that after the *Dialogue* Sade destroyed himself as a thinker? Even as a spokesman of irrationalism he does not, like Nietzsche, explicitly defend unreason, he simply exhibits it, to a degree which to his contemporaries seemed to justify confinement in a madhouse. Before deciding, we may notice a similar anomaly in his status as a writer. The once common judgement that Sade had no literary talent overlooked both how well he writes when he wants to and the conflict between literary values and his deepest concerns. Sade as novelist, in his drive to find an extreme beyond every extreme, turned his back on his prospects of becoming a literary artist, at any rate if we demand of the artist that he submerge his own intentions in a fully impersonal artefact. He did achieve the impersonality of art in one relatively early work, *Les 120 journées de Sodome* (1785), which has shape, development, characterization, the swift terse style of the best of his letters, and in the earlier and milder episodes (his solidest contribution to psychopathology) even the flavour of anecdotal truth. In this one book the atrocities, even at their most fantastic, impress as demonstrations of the most terrible possibilities of human nature, with a psychological validity which transcends the author's motives in imagining them; it is a story which hangs a dead weight on the heart like the newsreel of Belsen, perhaps the only fiction for which one could risk such a claim. But it poses a dilemma for Sade, that although restraint and impersonality intensify his effects they also allow the work to slip out of his control and assume meanings contrary to his intentions. This exclusion of himself is intolerable to Sade. In *Justine* and *Juliette* events which if objectively realized would agonize us are reduced to fantasy so thin, monotonous and protracted that all our attention centres on the mind manifested through its transparency. To develop character or drama would by acknowledging other viewpoints mar the self-sufficiency of his own, it would take away his freedom to be as aware or unaware of others as he pleases. What matters to Sade is that we be moved, not by the story, but by the vertigo of confronting its author and the desires and disgusts he arouses in ourselves.

The point is well illustrated by his rewriting of the grand climax of *Justine*, in which the virtuous heroine dies struck by lightning. In the versions of 1787 and 1791 the message, that Nature cares nothing for human virtue, is left unstated but implicit in the parody of a moral conclusion, which has Mme de Lorsange illogically converted by the terror of Justine's end and taking a Carmelite's veil. It is the conclusion of a writer still thinking in terms of rounding off a work of art, but it does not satisfy Sade; he is driven to a cruder climax which will push his intention to the foreground. In *Juliette* (1797) the libertines drive Justine out into a storm, confident that Nature in its wrath will punish her obstinate persistence in virtue. She is struck by lightning through the mouth and out through the vagina, the libertines rejoicing in this proof of Nature's hatred of goodness sodomize the charred corpse, and her sister Juliette masturbates as she looks on. Thus in place of the implausible happy ending loved by moralists Sade puts, not reality, but his own happy ending, the immoralist's, not merely implausible but insolently defiant of possibility. Through the ruins of literary art Sade directly confronts the reader: 'This is the world as *I* desire to see it.' We might go as far as to say that in his stories as in his thought nothing is real except the author and the desires. The shaping of the narrative is naked wish-fulfilment, following the conventions of the novel of entertainment rather than of art, indulgent as in a thriller even to the most unrealistic wish of all, to think as though death happens only to other people. With the usual exception, the *Dialogue entre un prêtre et un moribond*, his fictions, like the popular cinema, shrink from death except as murder, as enjoyable spectacle; the heroes with whom he identifies die off stage if at all.

However, the author and the desires are real indeed. It is time to pause and remind ourselves that this irrationalist and fantasist exposed to the light a range of experience which, however congenial to himself, was an almost unacknowledgeable reality to his earlier readers. Since his works became publicly available in the middle of the present century his importance, although variously interpreted, has hardly been doubted by anyone with the stomach to read him with attention.

Sade put together two thoughts of which neither the Church nor the Enlightenment had dared to face more than one, and which we have never since been able to pull apart, that there is no God and that the evil in man lies at least as deep as the good. Nor is Sade simply an atheist who rediscovers Original Sin. Original Sin had been conceived as a natural proneness to rebel against divine and human authority. It included of course cruelty to one's fellow men, but as a comparatively unimportant excess not very clearly distinguished from a righteous pleasure in punishing. (It takes quite a search of the sins in the *Summa theologica* of Aquinas to find the brief discussion of *crudelitas*, defined as 'immoderation in punishing', and *saevitia*, in which 'one does not consider any fault of the person punished, only a pleasure in torturing'.)[7] The Enlightenment, to the extent that it tended to judge human nature good, did not so much ignore old knowledge as revalue disobedience as a just demand for freedom. It is Sade who initiates a modern pessimism centred on man's proneness to disinterested cruelty, which is the sin against not authority but fraternity. But how did Sade make his contribution to our changed conception of man? Hardly through his philosophizing, rather through the legend of his life, through the clandestine novels which (unlike mere pornography) force the reader to think about the lusts and revulsions they arouse in him, and through nineteenth century poets haunted by the life and the novels. He called attention to the obsession which now bears his name, and discredited the purely physiological explanations of sexual stimulation by flagellation current in the seventeenth and eighteenth centuries, not by analysing the desire but by indulging it unequivocally, in life, in fantasy and in the wanton dislocations of his thought. He does not, like a pornographer, say implicitly 'It's all in good fun, afterwards we go back to the real world', he never lets us doubt that he **is** wholly in earnest. Nor does he hide under the old moral disguise still today maintained by moralists over-enthusiastic about hanging and flogging, he is faithful to the anti-moral direction of the impulse he shares with them and follows it through to the end. It is this which distinguishes him from another great irrationalist, his Catholic brother-under-the-skin on the opposite side in the French Revolution, Joseph de Maistre, who let his theology be shaped throughout by an unacknowledged pleasure in imagining universal but *deserved* suffering, and is useless for our purposes because he lacks the self-awareness of Nietzsche and Sade.

But although Sade has cruel truths to tell, the point is in the cruelty, not the truth. If he has any preference at all for his truths over his lies, it is because a lie loses its sting when exposed but a truth is a barb not so easily dislodged from the flesh. The centre of his interest in relation to 'Be aware' is in a total refusal to subordinate ends to awareness. In thought and imagination he drives towards an end in the service of which he treats reality as wholly fluid, starting and stopping any logical chain where he pleases, reducing persons to puppets with enough inwardness to suffer for his amusement but not enough to become (as in reality, including the reality of Sade's life as we find it in his letters) independent presences exerting moral pressures. Unlike Nietzsche, who in questioning the value of truth wanders in an endless labyrinth, Sade disdaining truth aims straight at some personal absolute. But what is this end which for Sade outweighs 'Be aware'?

Since Guillaume Apollinaire in 1909 acclaimed Sade as 'the freest spirit which has yet existed',[8] it has become common to read him as the apostle of absolute liberty. At first sight this interpretation seems absurd, and not only in the trivial form offered by readers who see only a rebel against outmoded sexual taboos. On the face of it, it would seem proper to identify the ideal of Sade as not liberty but pure Evil, as did his nineteenth century readers. Sade is a rebel, not against the repression of the individual by society, but against every bond between man and man except complicity in crime. He can conceive no freedom except an unrestricted despotism over others; he loves prisons, statutes, constitutions, only provided that the end they serve is an institutionalized injustice. One may illustrate this point from the black humour of his parody of a revolutionary pamphlet, *Français, encore un effort, si vous voulez être Républicains* (1795),[9] which literal-minded readers have taken quite seriously as his programme for a libertarian republic. Here Sade argues in detail that all crimes, theft, murder, incest, sodomy, deserve to be encouraged rather than punished by society. The functions of the state should therefore be reduced to such essentials as military defence, the persecution of Christianity, the punishment of women who refuse to submit themselves to any man who desires them, and—an urgent matter on which Sade descends from generalities to a concrete proposal—the establishment of public brothels in which 'all sexes, all ages, all creatures, will be offered to the caprices of the libertines who come there for amusement, and the most complete subordination will be the rule for the individuals put at their disposal; the least refusal will be punished at once and at his own discretion by whoever suffers it.'[10] This Utopia of perfect freedom is in its essentials identical with the unsubvertable tyranny planned by the minister Saint-Fond in *Juliette*.[11] Both programmes suppress Christianity and replace it as the basis of education by the principles of nature; both set up a pagan cult, the former to nourish the spirit of freedom, the latter because even an anti-Christian despotism cannot dispense with superstition and priesthood to support its authority; both abolish all sexual restrictions, the former to liberate man's natural desires, the latter because 'to the extent that the subject gangrenes and enfeebles himself in the delights of debauchery, he does not feel the weight of his chains'; both license the crimes of libertinage and institute brothels for the indulgence of every caprice, the former because everyone has the right to satisfy all his desires, the latter as privileges of the free minority forbidden to the enslaved multitude. We see that Sade's procedure is to imagine the policies which by current standards would be most immoral, and then as a pure intellectual game weave them into either a libertarian or an authoritarian programme, arguing with equal facility from either point of view. Neither policy has anything to do with his active politics in the French Revolution, in which he favoured a constitutional monarchy and Parliament with two chambers on the English model,[12] and was nearly guillotined for his moderation.

However, on closer inspection one begins to see the point of claiming Sade as a prophet of liberty rather than of unmotivated evil. A Sadean hero when triumphing over some helpless victim will lecture her on the biological and anthropological proofs that Nature has created women for slavery, when seducing an innocent to libertinism will teach her to defy her parents and claim the same rights as men, and the reasons for either position will be equally plausible; since by prevailing standards both are immoral, both are deserving of support. But the immoral, as the socially forbidden, does not coincide with evil, understood as the pure will to hurt others. Reading Sade after nearly 200 years of changing mores it is curious to notice that in his eyes arguments in favour of homosexuality, which we now find entirely reasonable, and of murder, which we would still reject, have exactly the same status; no moralist was ever better content with the code of his time, which he inverts without altering. Should not a thinker whose prime motive is love of evil for its own sake choose a course, not because it happens to be disapproved by his contemporaries, but because he believes it truly harmful? Yet one move which Sade could not conceivably make is to defend publicly a conventional position which he privately thinks does more harm than good, with the secret motive of taking pleasure in the suffering it causes. The love of evil is one of his passions, rooted in his sexual constitution, but whether his positions are actually harmful or not is in the end a secondary consideration; what matters to him is that they are commonly believed to be, and that he is publicly seen to hold them. The philosophizing and fantazising of his novels have no meaning except as social acts, as obsessively repeated gestures in a lifelong stance of defiance.

That the strongest thrust in Sade's thinking is towards rebellion rather than pain and destruction may be demonstrated from another direction. The natural mythology for a cult of pure cruelty would centre on the Devil or an evil God. But Sade is an uncompromising atheist, materialist, scorner of superstition. He does have one theistic hero, Saint-Fond, who bashfully confesses that, thwarted by the impossibility of prolonging the pain of his victims after death, he has persuaded himself to believe in a malevolent God and in a secret ceremony to contrive their eternal damnation.[13] (Here Sade, that stripper of moral disguises, takes a course like Maistre's but without the hypocrisy.) His friends sympathize but gently chide him for the betrayal of atheism, and advise him to console himself by increasing the number of his victims. His faith in hell is refuted in a long passage remarkable as one of Sade's few examples of consistently sustained and rigorous argument.[14] Yet the attraction of Saint-Fond's temptation for Sade is apparent in *Les 120 journées*, where the last and culminating passion of the series is the one called 'infernal', in which every fortnight fifteen victims are tortured to death in a cellar by executioners masked as demons. The libertine in command precedes his entertainment by a brief retreat (as did Saint-Fond): 'no one knows what he does in this moment of solitude'. Here Sade, faithful to his atheism, contents himself with a simulation of hell and the faint hint of the libertine's backsliding, and even yields to reality by stopping at the number 15, apparently the largest he thinks plausible. But after 120 days of progressively intensified atrocity, this is an anticlimax. Sade's drive towards a theoretically conceivable absolute, the most evil possible thought, has no terminus short of a pleasure open only to the God of Saint-Fond, the gratuitous damnation of the entire human race. Why has Sade halted, frustrated? Not because it would involve willing his own eternal torment, a possibility which Sade discerns in the case of Saint-Fond ('You would rather', he is told, 'incur yourself the eternal damnation of which you speak than renounce the delicious pleasure of terrifying others with it.').[15] An insane thought, no doubt; but why would Sade, whose importance as a thinker is that he stops at nothing, and whose beliefs and denials are wholly in the service of his desires, submit to any check at all to his imagination? Because for him it is anathema to admit the existence of any power with a right to tell him what he ought to do, whether the God against whom a Satanist affirms his freedom by doing what he ought *not*, or a malign God who commands only what the libertine desires. There can be no God because Sade, who can reluctantly admit an insuperable barrier to his desires, if only in their own contradiction, can admit none to his rebellion. Of God he writes: 'The thought of such a chimera is, I confess it, the one wrong I am unable to forgive mankind'.[16]

What then is the terminus of Sade's thought? The fullest answer is in *Juliette*, his dramatization of the moral evolution of a Sadean heroine. Juliette, who has been in the habit of committing crimes only when moved by passion, is trained by her friend Clairwil to discipline herself to disdain any pleasure which she has not chosen in cold blood in the knowledge of committing crime. (She later poisons Clairwil misled by a false accusation, and afterwards loves the accuser Durand for deceiving her into murdering without reason.)[17] This requires a long ascesis to deaden the sensibility, eradicate love and pity, and attain a perfect indifference to everything which Nature or man can do to her, which Sade sometimes calls by the Stoic name of 'apathy'.[18] In this apathy all joys spring from the consciousness of a strength which can do or suffer anything. The pride of ordinary men depends on the approval of others, that of the Sadean hero on proving to others that he has escaped all dependence on them. His sovereignty is absolute and his distinction from common men is one not of degree but of kind. When Juliette, still in her apprenticeship, is told by Saint-Fond of his plan to starve to death two-thirds of the population of France, she fails to suppress an involuntary start. It betrays that she is not yet one of the elect, he turns silently away, and she has to flee for her life.[19] It would be a mistake to think that in conceiving so aberrant an end in life Sade can no longer have anything to teach us about ourselves. A symptom of modern alienation is that with the fading of the sense of spontaneous communion we can find ourselves left with the alternatives of professing what we no longer feel or protecting integrity by emotional disinvolvement. Emotional invulnerability has a powerful attraction, as long as we can find some moral disguise for it; an example is the fascination, for a certain kind of intellectual in flight from sentimentality, of political ideologies which justify unfeeling acts by a ruthless logic. The spell of Communism for rational and high-minded people was never more hypnotic than in Stalin's time, without any consciousness of playing Juliette to Soviet Clairwils and Durands. The freedom to stop at nothing, because one feels nothing, paradoxically combined with a duty to sacrifice everything, is for some temperaments an irresistible combination of attractions. The archetypal case is the anarchist Bakunin's confederate Nechaev, whose avowed principle of treating even his closest comrades as mere means to the Revolution, to be deceived, blackmailed or murdered at his discretion, became a suicidally consistent end in itself. Even so, Nechaev fell short of a perfect invulnerability by preserving in theory a single precarious lifeline with humanity, the persuasion that in the last resort he was working for a better world. Sade cuts that lifeline (as no doubt in his secret heart did Stalin).

But the Sadean hero proves his independence not only by the magnitude of his crimes but by his indifference to humiliation and punishment. He achieves the ideal approached by the tough guy of the old Hollywood crime film, who can take it as well as dish it out. This is not a frivolous comparison, for the lasting popularity in entertainment of the kind of hero architected in the 1920s by Dashiell Hammett (later a Stalinist), amoral, emotionally unreachable, never too much in love with a woman to send her to the electric chair, is the plainest testimony to the wide appeal of a Sadean apathy, as long as we can be spared its cost in moral isolation by just a little social approval, if only for the loner's bravery and integrity. Here again, Sade shocks by showing an undercurrent in ourselves without disguise; he strips the hero even of that virtue of the tough guy almost indispensable to sympathy with the wicked, physical courage. Other rebels against morality count on our reluctant admiration, the Sadean does not deign to notice us. The immeasurably proud Saint-Fond does not mind in the least being known for his cowardice (a weakness which he claims to be an advantage, sharpening his appreciation of the terror of his victims), than which there could be no more insolent proof of his indifference to anyone else's opinion of him.[20] He also surprises Juliette by 'a very curious mania, he had me soil the very things in which he found his strongest motives for pride', and explains after wiping her with his *cordon bleu* that it is to show that 'these rags made to dazzle fools do not impose on the philosopher'.[21] When friends of his victims waylay, thrash and sodomize him he is roused to sexual ecstasy by the humiliation.[22] He tells Juliette

...the humiliation in certain acts of libertinage serves as nutriment to pride.[23]

Here Sade intervenes in a footnote:

That is easily understood; one does what no one else does; hence, one is unique of one's kind. It is on this that pride feeds'.[24]

Clearly this explanation has a personal significance for Sade, who in his life met with far more humiliations than triumphs. In *Les 120 journées*, on the 23rd day, the point that the criminal can take pride and joy in the punishment intended to deter him is illustrated by an anecdote about the 'Marquis de S***' being roused to orgasm by the news that the magistrates had decided to burn him in effigy. (This did happen to Sade.) Here we are at a point in the progression of Sade's thought which is beyond the love of crime. He puts himself above us by withdrawing beyond reach of our judgement, by choosing, with equal indifference, to do the things which for *us* are crimes, suffer the things which for *us* are punishments. He has withdrawn into a terrible solitude, but always aware of our eyes looking on. He indulges the fancy that a new Archimedes will invent a machine to pulverize the world,[25] yet universal destruction, like universal damnation, is beyond the reach of his desires; he might not hesitate to destroy himself too in an apocalyptic orgy, but what meaning could he give even to the supreme crime if it left no witnesses?

With the concept of apathy Sade leaves immorality behind for a pure amorality, the essence of which, as ever, he exposes quite nakedly. On the 'Reason as Master" position amorality is a rational, perhaps the only rational, approach to ethics; what successful proof has there ever been that I *ought* to forget the unbridgeable, gulf between my Ego and other persons? Yet amorality does not, like immorality, release pent-up spontaneity in myself, it is a frigidly calculated self-divestment of whatever spontaneously bonds me to others; we have already explored this self-impoverishment at length.[26] It requires the deliberate dismantling of a bridge which is already there; how it can be there is unintelligible on the 'Reason as Master' position, demands the shift to 'Reason as Guide', but Sade is well aware of its existence. When writing as immoralist he claims consistently that man cannot go wrong as long as he acts on the impulses instilled in him by Nature. But Juliette's progress towards amorality is a resolute struggle against spontaneous inclination, hindered by temptation and backsliding.

But little by little your mind will be fortified; habit, that second nature which often becomes more powerful than the first, which succeeds in annihilating even those natural principles which seem the most sacred...will dull remorse, silence conscience, put to scorn the promptings of the heart.[27]

The amoral, like the moral, summons up its own kind of Original Sin, which is after all only nature resisting the imposition of any consistent principle whatever, 'pity like an ultimate sin' assailing Nietzsche's Zarathustra,[28] Huckleberry Finn failing in his duty to betray his friend the runaway slave. The sternly principled life of *Les 120 journées* is desolating in its lack of spontaneous joy; the four libertines, two of them nearly impotent, every expression of their pleasure extravagantly insincere, bound like their victims by elaborate regulations enforced on themselves by fines, inflicting unlimited suffering for a residue of pleasure on the verge of loathing, wring the impulse of pride and power which rouses them to orgasm from the consciousness of their strength in being invulnerable to love and pity, untouched by the horror, contempt or disgust of others. What makes Sade indeed different from a pornographer is that he consistently pushes beyond spontaneous desire, taboos normal coition like a puritan, repels even fellow sadists by his coprophilia, dares us to join him in the willed breach with humanity which would make us his equals. He wills an isolation eerily lacking in an essential dimension, the anguish of solitude. Any writer submissive to psychological truth (to take a remotely comparable case—all comparisons with Sade are remote—Lautréamont in *Les chants de Maldoror*) does acknowledge that anguish. But Sade wills that it be otherwise; to suffer would be to have failed to cut his last bond with vulnerable humanity.

The Sadean rebellion then, which begins in the passions revolting against law and morality, finally concentrates in the individual will freed from subjection to the passions. The appeal of apathy is in release of self from being pulled to and fro by hopes and fears; it promises, not victory for the rationally approved drives over the disapproved, but a final liberation from them all, as pure Ego isolated from and impassively manipulating the spontaneous, intervening from beyond at some geometrical point at the centre of the vortex. Yet is not this detachment of the Ego which Sade vainly strives to realize concretely the same from which as an abstraction Kant or any other rationalistic moralist thinks that he can start? Is it perhaps only by tracing the route of Sade that one discovers its full meaning and its cost? It implies that 'Be aware' cannot engage with spontaneity to generate values; the moral philosophers try vainly to elude the nihilistic consequences, Sade revels in them. Our claim throughout this book has been that the autonomous Ego in final detachment from spontaneity is a fiction of the 'Reason as Master' position. Sade himself cannot fully reconcile it with his materialism and determinism. His pride cannot in the end tolerate the thought which in argument he never ceases to use as one of his throwaway objections to morality, that it is Nature that makes the sadist, that it is not by his own free choice that he is what he is. His chemist Almani hates Nature and studies her secrets in the hope, which he knows to be vain, of outraging her by being wickeder still.[29] Another libertine speaks of the anguish of knowing it impossible to act against Nature's will:

> In all that we do, it is only idols and creatures that we offend, not Nature, and it is her that I would like to outrage. I would like to derange her plans, block her march, halt the course of the stars, overturn the spheres that float in space, destroy what serves her, protect what harms her, exalt what irritates her, in a word insult her in all her works, suspend all her grand effects; and that I cannot do.[30]

The absolute to which Sade aspires remains beyond his reach, because the point outside Nature to which he is trying to retreat does not exist.

With the concept of apathy Sade appears to give definition at last to that true philosophical egoism which at first seemed a simple matter of releasing his nature from social obligations, but in the later stages of his thought has turned into a remote ideal approachable only by a self-lacerating effort of pride. But one spontaneous emotion still joins him to other men, the promptings of the pride which requires them as witnesses. He is proud because alone among men he and his like have the strength to make the declaration of independence, not from society only, but from mankind. 'Do you really think of yourselves as human?' asks Juliette, upon which Saint-Fond remarks: 'She is right; yes, we are gods'.[31] It would seem that Sade's right to that pride has been recognized in our collective unconscious, at the level where sacred and obscene are one, for a startling epithet has always clung to him, 'the divine Marquis'. But it is all that remains to him, for in the apathy at which he arrives in thought he has left behind everything else, even liberty. The free man, however we define him, has his own desires, tastes, goals, does not merely make a primary choice to negate those of others. The Sadean hero on the verge of his perfected egoism has emptied himself of selfhood to become the inverted image of his society, the counterpart of the perfect conformist who does not know what he wants unless society prescribes it to him. The sole difference is in terms of pride; the conformist humbles himself, Sade aggrandizes himself. By measuring himself against us all he escapes the insignificance of the individual submerged in the multitude. He would even, if he could, extend the scope of his revolt from society to Nature and transcend the littleness of man before the vastness of the universe.

Sade like Nietzsche changes the normal relation between author and reader, but more radically. The supreme misunderstanding of him—injustice to him— is to suppose that in the last resort he has our good at heart. Since he cares for truthfulness no more than for any other virtue, and for the reader no more than for any other potential victim, the ordinary conditions of communication are wholly subverted. He makes no secret of this. Rather, it pleases him to hint that his writing is a sadistic act at his reader's expense. In *Justine* a virtuous character refers in passing to

...those perverted writers whose corruption is so pernicious, so active, that their sole end in printing their frightful systems is to go on adding when their lives are over to the sum of their crimes; they can do no more themselves, but their accursed writings will make others commit them; and this sweet idea, which they take with them to the tomb, con- soles them for being obliged by death to renounce evil.[32] (To take in the full meaning of these words, recall that readers of *Justine* since Sade's death include Ian Brady of the Moors Murders.)

Similarly when Clairwil longs to commit a crime everlasting in its effects, Juliette suggests 'what may be termed moral murder', the propagation of libertine prin- ciples through counsel, writing or action.[33] But if Sade's books are indeed depraving and corrupting me, does it not follow that I should distrust their message, and also that by warning me Sade has reduced his prospects of harming me? Certainly, and through the paradox one sees again that for Sade the actual harm he does matters less than his self-display as a being invulnerable to reason who goes an unpredictable way which endangers mankind. In *La philosophie dans le boudoir* he achieves a work of which the whole structure fulfils this design, with the philo- sophizing in defence of one crime after another dramatized as itself a sadistic act, the seduction of a convent-educated girl by 'the most corrupt, the most dan- gerous of men'.[34] A convert to Sade's thought would have to reverse the relation- ship. One has a sense of incongruity whenever an admirer pays a conventional tribute to him as a great thinker, as though he were just another seeker after truth like the rest of us. A genuine disciple would be capable—let us try to achieve a truly Sadean thought—of revealing to Sade on his deathbed that his lamented masterpiece *Les 120 journées* (lost in the storming of the Bastille) has after all survived, and then burning the manuscript before his eyes. Not that he would bother to do it, since the master, if true to his own teaching, would exult in being unreachable even by that blow. There is a paradoxical harmony between Sade's heroes who, each locked in his own solitude beyond help or harm, occasionally murder each other out of self-interest but not (as they would the rest of us) for the mere pleasure of it. There is also a paradoxical justice in his world; since apathy alone has objective value, you can never either wrong or be wronged, because it is a man's own fault if he lets anything hurt him.

Clearly the practical outcome of such a public defiance must be that, whatever your hopes of doing harm to future generations, in the short term at least you injure society much less than it injures you. Sade convinced the world for a century or more that he had lived by the philosophy of *Justine* and *Juliette*. But if he had a practical philosophy it was always the rational hedonism of the early *Dialogue entre un prêtre et un moribond.* The philosophizing by which he won his uniqueness in the history of thought, by refusing to be bound by the limits of what is commonly recognized as sanity, was the provocative act of a sane man who, never mind the sexual excesses which got him into prison, did when not philosophizing have a genuine concern for the well-being of other people. Here is Sade writing to his lawyer Gaufridy on 3 August 1793, while active in revolutionary politics, and excellently placed to realize his murderous fantasies and also destroy the hated family of his wife, the Montreuil:

I'm finished, done for, I spit blood: I mentioned I was president of my section: my tenure has been so stormy I can't stand any more! Yesterday, the usual thing, after being obliged to excuse myself twice, I found myself forced to hand over the chair to my vicepresident. They wanted to make me put to the vote a horror, an inhumanity. I never would. God be thanked, I'm out of it. Goodbye, think of me a little; I trust you more than ever to look after my affairs: I think fondly of you.

While I was president I let the Montreuil on to a list of the exonerated. If I had said a word they would have been in trouble. I kept quiet; just look how I avenge myself!

Can the author of that letter really have meant what he wrote in his clandestine novels? We seem to have the strange case of a thinker taking enormous risks to propagate an ethic by which he wishes to live only in fantasy. But whether Sade *believes* what he writes is never a relevant question. The writing is of a piece with the life because it is one of the many provocative gestures in that life. Every word is wholly in earnest, in that no consequence either for mankind or for himself could have deterred him from writing it. His dream of liberation from the burden of being human is attainable only in the act of writing it down; he writes obsessively, interminably, oblivious of the petering out of communication in boredom, because at the moment of laying down his pen his freedom will lapse and he will become again the same mixture of good and evil as the rest of us. His books may not in fact have added, all in all, to the sum of human misery, but there is no disputing the cost of his provocations to himself. He was many times imprisoned, twice condemned to death, once executed in effigy; although clinically sane he died confined by the state in a madhouse, his name was taken by later psychiatry to label a perversion, and although his orgies seem never to have done anyone lasting physical injury he has hardly yet lived down his reputation as a Jack the Ripper. All his life Sade persisted in this desperate bargain, and one is bound to ask why. Can the masochism which accompanied his sadism, in his debauches as well as in his writings, be the whole explanation? It is as though it is only in the experience of resisting suppression that he feels himself to be free, as though it suits him to trade the imperfect freedoms of the real world for a liberty without bounds which is only of the mind. That in his case the act of defiance is primary and the choice of evil secondary, no more than the most defiant choice, can be seen in his letters, where one goes on discovering with amazement Sade as a social being. Here he fs writing to his wife from the prison of Vincennes at the end of November 1783.

Either kill me or accept me as I am, for devil take me if I ever change — I told you the beast is too old — there's no more hope — the most honest, frank, sensitive of men, the most tender-hearted, the kindest, idolater of my children, for whose happiness I would throw myself in the fire, pushing even to extremes the scruple of wishing neither to corrupt their morals nor taint their minds nor make them adopt in anything my systems, adoring my kinsfolk — (my own you understand) such friends as I have left and above all my wife, whom I aspire only to make happy, and with whom I have the greatest desire to make up for a lot of the imprudence of my youth — because after all *one's own wife shouldn't be brought into all that*, it is a truth which I felt and told her, more than six months before entering here: she can witness to it. So much for my virtues — as for my vices — domineering rages — an extreme hot-headedness in everything, an imagination the most licentious there has ever been, atheist to the point of fanaticism, in a few words there I am and I say it again kill me or accept me like that, for I shall not change.

All the reality behind his endless sophistries and fantasies is concentrated in those words 'I shall not change'. That ring of personal truth, and of what one might call normal calculation and self-deception, is scarcely heard outside the letters. But there are places where he displays himself as he would like to be seen, as in the personal reference we noticed in *Les 120 journées*.[35] Was he really excited to orgasm by the news that he had been burned in effigy? It is enough that he wishes us to believe it. Of especial interest is Sade's last will and testament. Here, as in the letters, he is a social being, and grateful to those who stood by him in his troubles; the image of himself as a monster scornful of all human loyalties has fallen away. But it is in this document that he finds the subtlest expression for the naked impulse to defy which is at the root of both the writer and the man.

The ditch once covered over it will be strewn with acorns, in order that in course of time, the ground of the said ditch being overgrown again and the copse as thick as before, the traces of my grave may vanish from the surface of the earth, as I flatter myself that my memory shall be effaced from the minds of men....

Sade has convinced us that he can dispense with our approval, but has never ceased to need us as witnesses to his infamy. Here, preparing for death, he professes to break this last bond of dependence on mankind. It is the apotheosis of the Divine Marquis, his transfiguration by absolute freedom. He is lying to us again of course; he knows very well that we shall remember him, and why, if he does not need us, does he have to tell us, in the most solemn of legal documents, in such memorable words? But with Sade what matters is not truth but the meaning of the pose. In this final, most deliberately prepared gesture, he disdains to be immortalized by our memory, *flatters himself* that we shall not remember him.

In Nietzsche one is always conscious of the tension between the rational and the irrational man, which is why in spite of his treachery to reason one accepts him as a philosopher. In Sade there is no such tension, only a mocking dance of reason on the surface of irrationality. That in no way reduces his importance: it is what makes him the greatest, the most instructive, of irrationalists. He has followed through to the end the consequences of that 'No!', for no other reason than another's 'Thou shalt', which is after all the first stirring of the consciousness of freedom in the childhood of all of us. Sade's importance is as an indispensable witness, the single man who in imagination completed the journey from there to one of the ultimate poles of thought and experience, and was brave and wicked enough to tell the tale.

3.3 Anti-rationalism

3.3.1 Chuang-tzŭ

There is more than one reason for letting Chuang-tzŭ, a Taoist of the late fourth century BC, author of the nucleus of a heterogeneous book bearing his name, intrude into the company of Western and comparatively recent irrationalists and anti-rationalists. The first is personal, his direct influence on myself. I began to think on present lines in course of working on Taoism in my professional capacity as a sinologist, prepared this book simultaneously with translating him from the Chinese,[1] and first tried out the basic idea in papers on Chinese philosophy.[2] Secondly, he will serve to illustrate the possibility that the present approach to reason and spontaneity can be of general help in relating Eastern traditions of thought to our own. Western philosophy, which is no longer the 'love of wisdom', as an academic discipline is reluctant to recognize the Orient, as a guide to life is in danger of abdicating to the Orient. This is not merely an unsatisfactory but a perilous situation, and there is an urgent need of some kind of conceptual bridge, without which thought outside our own tradition remains neither seriously usable nor criticizable by us. Thirdly, Chuang-tzŭ is the profoundest sceptic in an age when doubt was as deep as in our own, and the strongest enemy of rationalism at the moment when China seemed on the point of making the same commitment to logic as Greece, but did not. His viewpoint, so remote from our own in culture, time and place, offers an unfamiliar perspective down which to look at ourselves.

   Chinese philosophy in general may be said to accord with the approach of this book in assuming both that the springs of action are spontaneous, and that to evaluate requires only knowledge, awareness, wisdom. Although Taoists are exceptional in directly recommending spontaneity, even Confucians think of self-improvement as adjustment of spontaneity to measure, harmonizing the passions and letting oneself be moved to no more nor less than the proper degree. As for the deliberated act in accord with measure, the Chinese language does have normative verbs of the type of English 'ought' and 'should', but the tendency is to prescribe, not what one ought to do, but what the sage, wise man or gentleman actually does. If we return to our original instance of the child afraid of being sick,[3] and to the question whether its lesson would be more naturally formulated as 'One ought not to eat too much' or 'Sensible people don't eat too much', the Chinese answer can be found in the words of Confucius himself, 'The gentleman in eating never seeks repletion'.[4] It was not of course that the Chinese thinkers had already solved the problem of fact and value, 'is' and 'ought', but that it had not arisen for them; they were not at the level of logical sophistication at which one starts forgetting that one is choosing between spontaneous inclinations which veer with awareness of the situation, and gets caught in a vicious circle of verbal formulae detached from experience and dependent only on each other. Before the conception of 'Reason as Master', they could know only 'Reason as Guide'.

The great creative phase of Chinese thought lasted from Confucius (551–479 BC) to the 'Burning of the Books' in 221 BC. It was a period of accelerating social, political and technological change, and of a breakdown of accepted standards which could look extraordinary even from a viewpoint in the first half of the present century. 'It is hard for us today', wrote Arthur Waley in 1934, 'who live in societies, like those of France and England, which despite a surface of moral anarchy, are in fact rooted upon Christian ethics, to imagine such a state of chaos as existed in China in the fourth and third centuries'.[5] In Chuang-tzǔ's lifetime the main contenders were two moralistic schools, the Confucians who defended, clarified and refined the traditional code, and the Mohists who subjected standards to the utilitarian test of whether they did in fact benefit or harm. The habit of controversy had sharpened interest in defining terms and strengthening argumentation, and recently sophists had emerged who studied logical puzzles for their own sake. Chuang-tzǔ sets himself against both the moralists and the logicians. He denies all formulated rules of conduct, and in his stories and dialogues delights in putting his thoughts in the mouths of spokesmen who openly violate the rites of mourning, or flaunt the chopped foot which is the punishment for a petty crime. He denies too that moralists or sophists can ever settle their differences by logical demonstration that—to choose the closest convenient English equivalents for the Chinese formulae of assent or denial—'That's it' or 'That's not'.[6]

You and I having been made to argue over alternatives, if it is you not I that wins, is it really you who are on to it, I who am not? If it is I not you that wins, is it really I who am on to it, you who are not? Is one of us on to it and the other of us not? Or are both of us on to it and both of us not? If you and I are unable to know where we stand, others will surely be in the dark because of us. Whom shall I call in to decide it? If I get someone of your party to decide it, being already of your party how can he decide it? If I get some-one of my party to decide it, being already of my party how can he decide it?...[7]

Disputation is a waste of words, because the parties use the same names to pick out different things as 'it', as in the conflicting Confucian and Mohist definitions of the basic moral terms. Why should the sophist Kung-sun Lung go to the trouble of trying to prove that 'a white horse is not a horse', when all he has to do is name something else 'horse', so that what has commonly been called a horse will no longer be a horse?[8]

Saying is not blowing breath, saying says something: the only trouble is that what it says is never fixed. Do we really say something? Or have we never said anything? If you think it different from the twitter of fledgelings, is there proof of the distinction? Or isn't there any proof?... What is It is also Other, what is Other is also It. There they say 'That's it, that's not' from one point of view, here we say 'That's it, that's not' from another point of view. Are there really It and Other? Or really no It and Other? Where neither It nor Other finds its opposite is called the axis of the Way. When once the axis is found at the centre of the circle there is no limit to responding with either, on the one hand no limit to what is *it*, on the other no limit to what is not.[9]

13

Even if everyone did agree on something I would not *know* it (it would only be that they all happen to call the same thing by the same name); even to know what it is I do not know is a contradiction (or so Chuang-tzŭ thinks, like Meno in Plato's dialogue the *Meno*), and to find a rockbottom of scepticism in 'I know that no thing knows anything' is to contradict myself again.[10] Confucius in 60 years 60 times changed his mind; how do I know of anything I now affirm that I shall not deny it 59 times over?[11] Does the organ which thinks—which for the ancient Chinese was not the brain but the heart—control the body at all? Isn't it rather that the body is a system in which the organs take charge in turn, in accord with that ultimate patterning of things which is the *Tao*, the 'Way'?[12] In any case we all have hearts, and if each of us, wise or foolish, takes his own as the final authority, how can we ever agree?[13]

Chuang-tzŭ's scepticism and relativism are not in themselves unfamiliar to a modern reader, far from it; what is perhaps strange to him is that there is no vertigo in the doubt, which pervades the most rhapsodic passages of a philosophical poet who seems always to gaze on life and death with unwavering assurance. But there is anguish in ethical scepticism only if one feels bound to choose without having grounds to choose. For Chuang-tzŭ, to pose alternatives and ask 'Which is beneficial, which harmful?' or 'Which is right, which wrong?', and try to formulate the Way as a set of rules for ordering empire, family and individual, is the fundamental error in life. People who really know what they are doing, such as cooks, carpenters, swimmers, boatmen, cicada-catchers, do not go in much for analysing, posing alternatives and reasoning from first principles, they no longer even bear in mind any rules they were taught as apprentices; they attend to the total situation and respond, trusting to a knack which they cannot explain in words, the hand moving of itself as the eye gazes with unflagging concentration. The many stories about craftsmen in *Chuang-tzŭ* are always especially illuminating to a Westerner grappling to understand Taoism. He learns from them that the Taoist art of living is a supremely intelligent responsiveness which would be undermined by analysing and choosing between alternatives, and that grasping the Way is an unverbalizable 'knowing how' rather than 'knowing that'. As the wheelwright in one 'School of Chuang-tzŭ' story tells Duke Huan,

> If I chip at a wheel too slowly, the chisel slides and does not grip; if too fast, it jams and catches in the wood. Not too slow, not too fast; I feel it in the hand and respond from the heart, the mouth cannot put it into words, there is a knack in it somewhere which I cannot convey to my son and which my son cannot learn from me.[14]

The analogy of the craftsman to the Taoist sage has the limitation that the sage, instead of putting his unthinking dexterity in the service of ends, is spontaneous from the very centre of his being, he responds to things as immediately as echo follows sound or shadow shape. In terms of the traditional Chinese dichotomy of 'man', who thinks and chooses, and 'Heaven', which is responsible for everything independent of man's will, his motions derive not from himself as man but from Heaven working through him. Shall we say then that in discarding all traditional imperatives Chuang-tzŭ has substituted a new one of his own, 'Be spontaneous'?

That has long been a common interpretation of Taoism. But with spontaneity the question always arises of which kind is being recommended. Western romanticism extols intensity of spontaneous emotion however much it distorts reality by subjectivity, Taoism the spontaneous incipience of the act when reflecting the situation objectively as though in a mirror. The Taoist is no different from the Confucian in assuming that action starts from spontaneity and is guided by wisdom, but instead of laying down rules by which the wise man adjusts his spontaneity to measure, he reduces wisdom itself to its essence, the dispassionate mirroring of things as they objectively are.

The utmost man uses the heart like a mirror; he does not escort things as they go or welcome them as they come, he responds and does not store.[15]

The sage does not use the heart, the organ of thought, to plan ahead, only to reflect the situation as it objectively is before he responds. Like a mirror, it reflects only the present, does not 'store' the past experience which traps in obsolete attitudes; the sage perceives and responds to every situation as new. The metaphor of the mirror is further developed in later strata of *Chuang-tzŭ*.

> Within yourself, no fixed positions:
> Things as they take shape disclose themselves.
> Moving, be like water,
> Still, be like a mirror,
> Respond like an echo.[16]

The first couplet relates the sage's perfect flexibility to the objectivity of his vision; the external situation as it takes shape presents itself from moment to moment as it objectively is. He is as fluid as water which is unimpeded because in moving it adapts to the contours of the ground, his response is as immediate as the echo to the sound.

When the sage is still, it is not that he is still because he says 'It is good to be still', he is still because none among the myriad things is sufficient to disturb his heart. If water is still, its clarity lights up the hairs of beard and eyebrows, its evenness is plumb with the carpenter's level: the greatest of craftsmen take their standard from it. If mere water clarifies when it is still, how much more the stillness of the quintessential-and-daemonic, the heart of the sage! It is the reflector of heaven and earth, the mirror of the myriad things.

Emptiness and stillness, calm and indifference, quiescence, Doing Nothing, are the even level of heaven and earth, the utmost reach of the Way and the Power; therefore emperor, king or sage finds rest in them. At rest he empties, emptying he is filled, and what fills him sorts itself out. Emptying he is still, in stillness he is moved, and when he moves he succeeds.[17]

The essential point here is that the sage's heart is not subject to the agitations which obscure the common man's clarity of vision, to which Chuang-tzŭ himself is represented as confessing in one anecdote: 'I have been looking at reflections in muddy water, have gone astray from the clear pool.'[18] The sage does not even exert his heart to 'sort' things into categories and grades; he keeps the heart empty and lets the external scene fill it, sort itself out in its own objective relations, and then 'move' him. His heart has the 'evenness', the neutrality to all human goals, of the universe itself. Having achieved this mirror-like lucidity he no longer has to evaluate, even to judge that 'It is good to be still'; it is enough that he does *not* value anything in the universe above his own clarity of vision ('None among the myriad things is sufficient to disturb his heart'). His response in unclouded illumination of his situation is perfectly apt to the goal to which at that moment he spontaneously tends; 'when he moves he succeeds'. His 'Power', aptitude, knack, is at its height, his act coincides exactly with the Way.

Looking back, we find two stages in Chuang-tzu's thought.

(1) All principles for grounding rules of conduct are themselves groundless.

(2) At the rockbottom of scepticism there remain spontaneity and a single imperative to guide it, 'Mirror things as they are', equivalent to our 'Be aware'.

We can now identify the profound difference from Nietzsche and Sade which has led us to categorize Chuang-tzŭ as not irrationalist but anti-rationalist. For him, no end however highly valued can outweigh 'Be aware'. He accepts without question that we have to take the world as objectively it is, denies only that analytic reason is the way to find out about it. What the thinker distinguishing and formulating alternatives is trying vainly to pin down in words is objectively there, the wood which the wheelwright is chiselling, the famine or rebellion which confronts the ruler; in the stillness of the sage's heart it shows up as plain and undistorted as a face in calm water, and at any one moment, for any one individual who reflects it clearly, there can be just one response. He may name things as he pleases, and his descriptions will alter with the naming; but if he *sees* things as he pleases, lets the passions blur the mirror of perception, his spontaneous move will no longer accord with the Way.

Chuang-tzŭ differs from Nietzsche and Sade also on another issue which we take as critical in distinguishing anti-rationalism from irrationalism, the neutrality of viewpoints which forbids me to give preference to my own. He rejects the dichotomy of self and other with all other antinomies, and declares that the sage is without self.[19] It appears from one obscure sentence that in submerging in spontaneity, ceasing to decide and simply 'being about to', the sage thinks of other people as 'I'. To explain the mystery of a man who has become famous as a mourner without feeling sorrow, he says,

When another man wails he wails too; it is simply that all the way up from that which they depend on to be-about-to-be, he is with him in recognizing him as 'I' [Chuang-tzŭ immediately adds: 'How would I know what it is I call recognizing as "I"?'].[20]

Whatever is to be made of this, there is no doubt that the sage ruler mirroring the empire is conceived as responding on behalf of all.

The benefits of his bounty extend to a myriad ages, but he is not deemed to love mankind.[21]

Or, according to a later writer in the book, the sage does love mankind but does not know it until others tell him, as a beautiful woman knows she is beautiful only after seeing herself in a mirror.[22]

Granted that Chuang-tzǔ does not believe in any ultimate rational grounding either of truths or of values, how does he regard the ordinary practical use of reason without which we would be not human but animal? Drawing the traditional distinction between Heaven and man, he thinks of himself as at his best when he surrenders and lets Heaven act through him, at his second best when he behaves as a thinking man, and he recognizes both courses as necessary.

To know what is Heaven's doing and what is man's is the utmost in knowledge. Whoever knows what Heaven does lives the life generated by Heaven. Whoever knows what man does uses what his wits know about to nurture what they do not know about. To last out the years assigned you by Heaven and not be cut off in mid-course, this is perfection of knowledge.[23]

My body is born, grows, decays and dies independently of my will, as Heaven works through me; but I, as a thinking man, have to assist the process by feeding my body and taking care of my health. Similarly I nurture a spontaneous skill by the thought and effort of apprenticeship, and sagehood by Chuang-tzǔ's own philosophizing. But in formulating the distinction between Heaven and man Chuang-tzǔ has to remind himself that it is an artificial division made only while reasoning as man, obscuring a fundamental continuity, and returns to the questions he had raised about the arbitrariness of naming.[24]

However, there's a difficulty. Knowing depends on something with which it has to be plumb; the trouble is that what it depends on is never fixed. How do I know that the doer I call 'Heaven' is not the man? How do I know that the doer I call the 'man' is not Heaven?[25]

There can be no discontinuity between the spontaneous and the thinking person. At the centre of himself the sage is spontaneous, belongs wholly to Heaven, does not yet make any distinction between benefit and harm, self and other, even Heaven and man ('For the sage, there has never yet begun to be Heaven, never yet begun to be man').[26] At the periphery he is a thinking man, finding means to the goals towards which Heaven moves him, and collecting the information to which he is moved to respond. On this periphery he does make distinctions, although only as provisional and relative, and deliberately pursues what he likes and avoids what he dislikes. We have here the exact opposite of a Western rationalist's conception of himself as reasoning Ego exploiting his own spontaneous tendencies, aptitudes and temperamental strengths in the service of his ends.

The True Men of old used what is Heaven's to await what comes, did not let man intrude on Heaven... Hence they were one with what they liked and one with what they disliked, one when they were one and one when they were not one. When one they were of Heaven's party, when not one they were of man's party. Someone in whom neither Heaven nor man is victor over the other, this is what is meant by the True Man.[27]

As for the state of possession by Heaven, Chuang-tzŭ belongs to that older world in which selfhood was still experienced as indefinite and transitory, or that future one in which more efficient psychologies will have dissolved once more the habit of assuming one's perfect separateness. Here we had better try to avoid generalities about mystical oneness and get as close as possible to his own conceptualizations. He thinks of himself in terms of a then current psychology or physiology—no line was drawn between mind and body—which is more foreign to us than the philosophy itself. He experiences himself as vitalized by *ch'i*,[28] energizing fluids which rhythmically expand and contract, called Yang in the active phase and Yin in the passive, recognizable at every level of organization from the alternation of breathing out and in up to the overall cycle of the body's gradual growth and decay. He cultivates tranquility of mind and health of body in the first place by controlled breathing, about which he gives no details, presumably something like yoga.[29] Its effect is to refine and rarify the *ch'i* to perfect tenuousness (at which stage the word is conveniently translated simply as 'energy'), so that it circulates freely through the relatively dense and inert which it activates. When preparing to act, you 'fast the heart', empty it of all thoughts, ends and principles of conduct, contemplate the object, and wait for the now perfectly attenuated fluid to respond and move you in one direction or another. One dialogue represents Confucius as telling his disciple Yen Hui:

> Unify your attention. Rather than listen with the ear, listen with the heart. Rather than listen with the heart, listen with the energies. Listening stops at the ear, the heart at what tallies with the thought. As for 'energy', it is the tenuous which waits to be roused by other things. Only the Way accumulates the tenuous. The attenuating is the fasting of the heart.[30]

In renouncing control of the energies the self dissolves; yet paradoxically in ceasing to distinguish myself from what all the time has been acting through me, I become for the first time the true agent of my actions. It is by grasping this point that Hui convinces Confucius that he understands:

> When Hui has never yet succeeded in being the agent, a deed derives from Hui. When he does succeed in being its agent, there has never begun to be a Hui.[31]

At this ecstatic height, when the distinction of self and other does not yet arise, I cannot affirm even that 'Everything is one', merely not yet begin to distinguish even between the one and the many.[32]

Heaven, as the power controlling the universe, is not conceived as a personal God, but does have a strong numinous resonance. 'Personal' and 'impersonal' would in any case be another false dichotomy, and Heaven may be presumed to fit neither of these names. Similarly, although Chuang-tzŭ does not personify the influences from Heaven as gods, he does think of the undeliberated yet perfectly apt move as prompted by daemonic forces[33] which condense in him as something like the *daimonion* of Socrates, not quite personal yet wiser than himself. Even the effortless grace with which Cook Ting carves an ox comes from the daemonic in him:

Nowadays I am in touch through the daemonic in me, and do not look with the eye. With the senses I know where to stop, the daemonic I desire to run its course. I rely on Heaven's structuring, cleave along the main seams, let myself be guided by the main cavities, go by what is inherently so. A ligament or tendon I never touch, not to mention solid bone. A good cook changes his chopper once a year, because he hacks. A common cook changes it once a month, because he smashes. Now I have had this chopper for nineteen years, and have taken apart several thousand oxen, but the edge is as though it were fresh from the grindstone. At that joint there is an interval, and the chopper's edge has no thickness; if you insert what has no edge where there is an interval, then, what more could you ask, of course there is ample room to move the edge about. That's why after nineteen years the edge of my chopper is as though fresh from the grindstone.

However, whenever I come to something intricate, I see where it will be hard to handle and cautiously prepare myself, my gaze settles on it, action slows down for it, you scarcely see the flick of the chopper—and at one stroke the tangle has been unravelled, as a clod crumbles to the ground.[34]

It is in experience of the continuity of the spontaneous in oneself and in the world outside that Chuang-tzŭ finds his solution to the problem engagement with which most intensifies his writing, that of death. He expects no personal immortality, but is satisfied that in the dissolution of the body he will remain what at bottom he has always been, the constantly transforming continuum out of which the body condensed and into which, proceeding on that inevitable course which is the Way, it will disperse to assume new forms. He will not be reincarnated as a person (an idea which entered China with Buddhism considerably later), but will still be alive in the living who come after him. The conduct of mourning, especially sacred for the Chinese, provides him also with the most dramatic illustrations of his defiance of all formulated rules.

Soon Master Lai fell ill, and lay panting on the verge of death. His wife and children stood in a circle bewailing him. Master Li went in to ask after him.

'Shoo! Out of the way!' he said. 'Don't startle him while he transforms.'

He lolled against Lai's door and talked with him.

'Wonderful, the process which fashions and transforms us! What is it going to turn you into, in what direction will it use you to go? Will it make you into a rat's liver? Or a fly's leg?'

'A child that has father and mother, go east, go west, go north, go south, has only their commands to obey; and for man the Yin and Yang are more than father and mother. Something other than me approaches, I die; and if I were to refuse to listen it would be defiance on my part, how can I blame him? That hugest of clumps of soil loaded me with a body, had me toiling through a life, eased me with old age, rests me with death; therefore that I found it good to live is the very reason why I find it good to die. If today a master swordsmith were smelting metal, and the metal should jump up and say "I insist on being made into an Excalibur", the swordsmith would surely think it metal with a curse on it. If now having once happened on the shape of a man, I were to say "I'll be a man, nothing but a man", he that fashions and transforms us would surely think me a baleful sort of man. Now if once and for all I think of heaven and earth as a vast foundry, and the fashioner and transformer as the master smith, wherever I am going why should I object? I'll fall into a sound sleep and wake up fresh.'[35]

In Taoism, the most sceptical of philosophies in an age as deeply in doubt as our own, we hit a rockbottom where just two things remain unquestioned—that in spontaneity one should prefer the reaction when perfectly mirroring things as objectively they are, and that no viewpoint has privileged status. Not of course that these assumptions are conceptualized in the terms in which we have posed the issue; it has taken a long process of reason ramifying in detachment from sponta- neity to bring us to the impasse from which the insights of a logically less sophis- ticated tradition can help us to retrace our steps. These ramifications are the great Western contribution to awareness, and initially might have been impossible without the stance of taking 'Reason as Master'; but no addition to them can be evidence that reason should indeed be our master, and none of them has to be abandoned in returning to 'Reason as Guide'.

3.3.2 *Three modernisms: Futurism, Dada, Surrealism*

Those who see the twentieth century as an age of material progress and spiritual decline, of proliferating means to ends which have lost their foundations, generally seek regeneration through old or new philosophical, religious or political creeds. But there is another tradition which, instead of seeking objective truths overlooked by the sciences, tries to recover the sense of living in a subjectively intelligible cosmos through the symbolisms of the arts. Within this tradition there is neither demonstration of truths nor appeal to sacred authority, instead an undisguised attack on the nerves and senses, and a preoccupation with experimental techniques designed to alert us to the changes of the times and shock us into new adjustments to them. It is an enterprise which seems to assume that spontaneous reorientation in heightened awareness and responsiveness needs no further justification. For many this assumption is irrationalism, for us not; it is among revolutionaries in the arts that we would look, not of course for a new creed, but for the most instructive models for any modern exploration of the possibilities of anti-rational- ism. Here, as in Taoism, we recognize the instinct, when all standards of value are discredited, to return to the roots, to rediscover the authentic response and make a new start from the single imperative which it is supremely irrational to doubt, 'Be aware'.

Let us then examine certain modernist movements of which the declared aim was to put the arts in the service of life. Earlier in the century there was an apos- tolic succession of such movements: Futurism, which originated in Italy in 1909: Dada, which took the lead in Switzerland in 1916 when Futurism lost its momen- tum: Surrealism, founded by former Dadaists in Paris in 1923. In the proliferation of modern art movements the distinctiveness of this tradition is easily missed. These were not, like such 'isms' as Impressionism, Cubism, Imagism, revolutions in the technique of a single art lacking wider applications. They were attempted proofs of the possibility of enjoying the unprecedented gifts of the twentieth century without their turning to Dead Sea fruit in our mouths. Futurism, Dada, and Surrealism all claim to revolutionize life, not for ever like a new religion, but for that short decisive interval when an *avant-garde* makes its mark before the trend turns in another direction. All begin in poetry, and have as theoretician and impresario a poet (Marinetti, Tzara, Breton) whose manifestos attract more attention than his verse, but they soon spread to painting, theatre, cinema, and in the case of Futurism to architecture, music, dance, dress, cuisine (but not philosophy, in contrast for example with Existentialism, which begins in philosophy and spreads to literature). The wider public always misunderstands them as primarily fashions in painting. The Second World War submerged this tradition, but in America, to which it was carried by European artists in exile, it blended with indigenous influences, the right in the constitution to life, liberty and the pursuit of happiness, the bohemia of the hipster, jazz and marijuana, to generate at the carefree height of post-war prosperity the most widespread and recklessly daring of all collective experiments in renewing the springs of twentieth-century life, the Counter-culture of the late 1960s. Each movement passes as swiftly as a fashion in dress and appears as superficial; yet much as the basic ideas on which the civilizations of the Old World have been living so long were thought once and for all by wise men in Greece, Israel, Iran, India, China, within a few centuries on either side of 500 BC, so it seems that we have never yet made fundamental additions to the adaptations to a desacralized and technologically revolutionized world first announced by restless and brilliant minds during a few years after 1909.

Throughout the history of this tradition, although it is through the arts that the message is transmitted, faith in the work of art as having a value in itself is more and more openly disowned. The Futurists scorn the hope of eternal fame, from Dada onwards it is respectable to forget one's own expendable productions and call them anti-art, and by the 1960s there is no longer any pretence that to enter Bohemia you have to profess an art at all; that is only one of the ways of doing your own thing. The arts are seen merely as tools in successive attempts to restore us to an inhabitable cosmos, by the subjective rediscovery of the world which science and practical pressures habituate us to objectivize. The last of the movements, Surrealism, is of especial interest to us as the most intellectually stimulating of all modern challenges to the intellect. We could no doubt find wiser mentors (including greater artists who remained outside fashionable sects), but that is not the point. For present purposes what matters is that as schools of writers and painters, self-conscious and adventurous in experimentation with symbols, they expose to full view the mechanics of a process which in religious, philosophical and political thinking disguises itself as the discovery of abstract truths.

At first sight the movements from Futurism to Surrealism may seem to have nothing in common other than a taste for outrage and excess. But there are generalizations which apply to all of them, and to more recent modernisms and postmodernisms as well. Let us list some items, without regard for which of them one finds silly or dangerous and which might have lasting value. The whole tradition rejects both orthodox religion and the nineteenth century hope of putting science in its place. It loathes a materialism in which ends recede from sight beyond vistas of means to further means, but proclaims that the realm of ends is within reach wherever you can burst through the accretions of habit and good taste to discover your own authentic response. It is at home with technology, the city, the media of publicity certainly, scientific cosmology, but in the conduct of life is anti-rationalistic, dismisses fixed standards whether moral or aesthetic, distrusts analytic thinking as damaging to immediate awareness and responsiveness. Indeed, although not itself irrationalist by our definition, it is always open to irrationalist influences, Nietzsche from the beginning, Sade increasingly towards the end. It derides the bourgeois (as had every *avant-garde* since far back in the nineteenth century) as the prisoner of obselete and sterile attitudes, who is unaware of the new world in which he lives, who must be shocked out of his sleep by insults, outrages, a sensationalism which offends his delicacy and stirs the sexual and violent urges which frighten him. It dogmatically affirms new values, as though they were self-evident to anyone with senses fully open to the concrete and transient and nerves alert to stimulation. If it ever looks back, it is to the primitive still latent in civilized man, never (as in nineteenth century Romanticism, and in many individual modern poets and artists outside the movements) to religious or political institutions of the past. In its celebration of spontaneity it is impatient of social and moral bounds to personal freedom; but another consequence, only superficially incompatible, is that it belittles the merely personal, is bored by the exploration of character in novel and drama, cares for no psychology except depth psychology, but delights in the spontaneity at the roots of selfhood which unites the individual with his fellows and with the non-human. It no longer thinks of society as maintained by the interactions of reasoning and choosing individuals. It sees the individual in the modern city less as choosing than as carried along for better or worse by impersonal trends, whether swept forward by accelerating progress (as it believed up to 1914) or trapped in the mechanics of a self-destructive civilization which can be revitalized only by the mythopoeic powers of spontaneous imagination and dream. It insists on intensity of life in a dispiriting world, demands revolt not resignation, can welcome horror yet detests tragedy, melancholy, pathos, would rather a cruelty which exhilarates than a pity which depresses. When it laughs, it is with a humour for which nothing is sacred, the sublimest thought, the profoundest feeling. It is inspired to risk breaching the barriers to chaos less by a Rousseauist faith in the goodness of human nature than by a Nietzschean insight that mankind owes as much to the impulses it calls evil as to those it calls good. Politically, it has a hunger both for liberty and for community deeper than can be satisfied within liberal institutions. It yearns for revolution and inclines to anarchism, but is highly unstable, because in practice its only options are a self-destructive surrender to Fascism or Communism, or else a grudging admission that its own existence is after all a luxury possible only within liberal democracy. It is in its destiny that in opening up the prospects of renewal it also, in its wilful, almost willed shallowness, helps to undermine what remains of the moral and political defences of civilization. Finally it is characteristic of such a movement that it teems with men of talent or genius who are attracted in youth, are shaped by it, and then go their own way. You gain by joining, but if you continue to grow cannot afford to stay long in that dehumanizing atmosphere of extremist rhetoric. In these laboratories for trying out stimulating and dangerous simplifications the only still-developing persons who can afford a prolonged confinement are the leaders, strange creatures who do not quite fulfil themselves either as poets or as human beings.

Up to the year 1900 artistic vanguards, as though the dying century were more than a chronological fiction, liked to think of themselves as decadent and *fin de siècle*. With the hypnotic date safely passed, Futurism wakes to the new century with a fresh appetite, eager to discover positive value in everything 'passéists' find superficial or vulgar, in science, the machine, speed, noise, sport, record-breaking, tourism. The Futurists are the first unreserved admirers of science who come fully to terms with the fundamental difference between the problems it solves and the problems of life. They proclaim that, although analytic thinking is necessary to the designer of an automobile (that supreme Futurist symbol, of which Marinetti is already writing ecstatically in the original *Futurist manifesto* of 1909), in the conduct of his life man is in the driver's seat, and survives by the speed of his reflexes. Marinetti's central insight is that the man of the new century has to orientate himself in space expanded by ease of communication but in time contracted by the acceleration of change. Futurist man no longer has leisure to analyse causal relations in sequence and so perceive events as ordered, he is driven forward at a momentum which cuts him off from the past and plunges him into a scramble of disconnected fragments in chance juxtapositions, like the scene through the windscreen of a car. The pattern of our information is that, not of a history book, but of 'the great newspaper (synthesis of a day in the world's life)'.[1] In the remarkable list of 17 significant novelties in modern sensibility in Marinetti's *Destruction of syntax—Imagination without strings—Words-in-freedom* (1913), he starts from and more than once returns to these themes.

1. Acceleration of life to today's swift pace. Physical, intellectual and sentimental equilibration on the cord of speed stretched between contrary magnetisms. Multiple and simultaneous awareness in a single individual.
. . . .
15. The earth shrunk by speed. New sense of the world. To be precise: One after the other, man will gain the sense of his home, of the quarter where he lives, of his region, and finally of the continent. Today he is aware of the whole world. He little needs to know what his ancestors did, but he must assiduously discover what his contemporaries are doing all over the world...
16. A loathing of curved lines, spirals and the *tourniquet*. Love for the straight line and the tunnel. The habit of visual foreshortening and visual synthesis caused by the speed of trains and cars that look down on cities and countrysides. Dread of slowness, pettiness, analysis and detailed explanations. Love of speed, abbreviation and the summary 'Quick, give me the whole thing in two words!'[2]

How does the Futurist choose the course which he steers so adventurously through the chance conjunctions of the moment? While he is acting it is no doubt too late to think, since high speeds demand 'the intuitive synthesis of every force in movement' and only sluggards can indulge in 'the rational analysis of every exhaustion in repose'.[3] But in intuitively synthezising he is on course towards a goal, and how has he chosen it in the first place?—a question which the Futurist would impatiently brush aside. Although Marinetti speaks often of 'will' he means, not a Kantian exertion of the rationally choosing mind which directs the body, but a Nietzschean will, a focusing of biological forces, 'the concurrence of energies as they converge into a single victorious trajectory'.[4] The Futurist has only to concentrate attention and respond, and since that is to guide spontaneity by 'Be aware' we shall not quarrel with the logic of his position. Marinetti is as fond of the word 'instinct' as of 'will', and even calls on playwrights to 'dramatize all the discoveries (no matter how unlikely, weird and antitheatrical) that our talent is discovering in the subconscious'.[5] One might say that if Marinetti's ideal man thinks of himself as an autonomous and conquering individual, it is because he finds it healthy to gaze unwaveringly ahead; if he were so morbid as to look back into his subconscious, as with the shattering of confidence by world war the Dadaists and Surrealists were soon to do, he would perceive it as the channel through which he is moved by powers from beyond him. But the sense of the individual as self-commanding is obligatory for Marinetti, of the Beyond as sacred absolutely alien to him; he presents as No. 4 of his 17 novelties in sensibility:

Destruction of a sense of the Beyond and an increased value of the individual whose desire is *vivre sa vie*.[6]

Among Marinetti's later writings is an allegory of the conflict and mutual dependence of instinct and thought, *The untamables* (1922), the symbolism of which he explained in an open letter to a critic.[7] This story differs from the other sources we are using in that, as one would after all expect, Marinetti's thinking as imaginative writer is richer than, even conflicts with, his theoretical pronouncements. The Untamables are brutal criminals imprisoned in a burning desert in sight of an oasis, chained together and banded with spikes so that they cannot move without goring each other, guarded by Negro warders whose faces are locked in steel muzzles ('Both are instinctive, primordial, cruel, unconscious forces'). Their masters are the Paper People, who are cones of written-over paper with a light inside ('symbols of ideas and hence of the Book that confines but does not master the instincts'). Messengers in paper ships have been bringing them the commands of the Great No One, but now merely open their mouths to the shape of an O and sibilate the word 'Zero'. Each night both jailers and prisoners are freed by the Paper People to rest in the oasis, but in the morning never remember what they have seen. On the night of the story, after finding their way to the oasis, they plunge into the cool lake ('Lake of Poetry', 'Lake of Goodness'), and join in a dance to the music in the leaves, soothed, peaceful and loving. The Paper People judge them worthy, now that they have 'discovered the great rhythm', of admission to the city, where their own race is born as pages which fly off twirling from enormous luminous books standing in the streets. Off the thoroughfares of the brilliant city the Untamables find dark factories, where they sense that something new is happening. They hear the noise of riot, a paper revolutionary calls for the demolition of the dam blocking the river which strains to flow to the Lake of Poetry. Among the books the pages of which keep on turning into Paper People, Rousseau's *Social contract* is already at its last page, but the Futurist manifestos are generating paper poets who fly up and write blazing messages in the sky. The chief of the Untamables perceives that the times demand a leader, and steps forward. Watched with detachment by the Futurists in the sky, crowds of lighted Paper People and half-lighted humans fall in behind the opaque Untamables.

Perhaps because they had become used to their own steady light, those lamps had forgotten their strength. Perhaps those blind coals, precisely because they were blind, had absolute creative insight.[8]

Here we are at the rise of Fascism, with which Marinetti was in general sympathy, although in 1922 he had temporarily left the movement. Does he approve the abdication of reason at this historic moment? No, unless as contributing in the long run to the liberation of instinct, for the immediate results are disastrous. Ignoring the warning of a wise old paper revolutionary that without enlightenment the river cannot be guided to the Lake, the Untamables tear down the dam, are themselves nearly overwhelmed by the flood, and as the sun rises blazing in the sky flee back with relief to the desert and their familiar chains. But this time their leader remembers the oasis. (Another difference: he has killed the chief jailer.) The Untamables, instead of boasting as they used to about the wanton crimes for which they were imprisoned, listen quietly as he tells the tale.

It was finally the superhuman cool distraction of Art that caused the metamorphosis of the Untamables.[9]

In this story Marinetti's neatly plotted allegorizing has not killed a mythopoeic impulse released on a course of its own by images from his childhood in Egypt. The oasis of peace, of love, of 'the only truth, the only force: Goodness', sacralized by religious language, whether explicit ('God is waiting for you on the lakeshore') or embedded in metaphorical description ('A timid confession of humble stuttering light against the confessional grating of the leaves'), with its 'Lake of Goodness that cancels diversity', to be left behind for the city only because there can be no final satisfaction in 'stasis even if happy, nor unconsciousness even if divine',[10] is as though from another mind than the author of the manifestos. If we are to draw the full implications from the symbolism of memory and oblivion, Marinetti, or rather his myth, is saying that the function of art is to make us dream wide awake, bring to consciousness a paradise of instinctive fulfilment into which we submerge in sleep, guide us out of the vicious circle of repression and rebellion towards the freeing and harmonizing of desires. The founder of Futurism, when his intellectual guard is down, is already in sight of Surrealism.

In recognizing the instinctive sources of the will, Futurist man recovers that unity with nature which his committal to science seems to deny him. He has already escaped that impasse in which, we have argued, Jacques Monod remains trapped.[11] Futurism thrives on the thought that the brain is a machine and 'every human activity is a projection of nervous energy';[12] one manifesto even proposes, a little prematurely, to replace art critics by professional 'measurers' who will fix the market price of a work by estimating mathematically the quantity of cerebral energy expended in producing it.[13] But Marinetti understood that this kind of claim requires as its converse that, if I am to use the pronoun 'I' and say 'I will' without losing sight of my continuity with the rest of nature, I must explore the affinity subjectively as well as objectively.

Deep intuitions of life joined to one another, word for word according to their illogical birth, will give us the general lines of an *intuitive psychology of matter*.[14]

Not of course that I may, like passéist poets, see nature after the analogy of myself.

Be careful not to force human feelings on to matter. Instead, divine its different governing impulses, its forces of compression, dilation, cohesion and disaggregation, its crowds of massed molecules and whirling electrons. We are not interested in offering dramas of humanized matter. The solidity of a strip of steel interests us for itself; that is, the incomprehensible and nonhuman alliance of its molecules or its electrons that oppose, for instance, the penetration of a howitzer. The warmth of a piece of iron or wood is in our opinion more impassioned than the smile or tears of a woman'.[15] (D. H. Lawrence, stimulated to define his own emerging preference for the 'non-human in humanity', objected to the last sentence that 'what is interesting in the laugh of the woman is the same as the binding of the molecules of steel or their action in heat; it is the inhuman will, call it physiology or like Marinetti psychology of matter that fascinates me'.)[16]

Marinetti sees the affinity of man and machine as more than theoretical, he is impressed by the mysterious sympathies between the driver and his car, the mechanic and the machine he tends, and includes as No. 12 of his 17 points:

New mechanical sense, a fusion of instinct with the efficiency of motors and conquered forces.[17]

Hence we must prepare for the imminent, inevitable identification of man with motor, facilitating and perfecting a constant interchange of intuition, rhythm, instinct and metallic discipline, of which the majority are wholly ignorant, which is guessed at by the most lucid spirits.[18]

From this development, and from the favourability of the modern city to impersonal, amoral organizers, Marinetti finds reason to hope that mankind in further progressing will blend with the machine to evolve into a 'nonhuman and mechanical being, constructed for an omnipresent velocity'.[19]

For Marinetti, then, there is no need whatever for modern man to pity himself as a lost orphan in the alien universe of physics. He can discern in natural and mechanical automatisms precisely the value which he finds in the spontaneity of human instinct and will. Fascinated by the motions of mechanical pianos and cinema projectors, he remarks,

These are likewise motions of matter, outside the laws of intelligence and *therefore* [my italics] of a more significant essence.[20]

However, that unity of the human and the non-human which can be analysed in scientific language is directly communicable, as he explains in technical discussions of his poetics, only by a stretching of poetic language to its limits, to break down syntax (in order to avoid imposing a logical order), elevate the infinitive verb (in order to dispense with the 'I' of the human observer), metaphorize the most remote analogies without personifying, to 'penetrate the essence of matter and destroy the dumb hostility which separates it from us'.[21]

The imagination without strings, and words-in-freedom, will bring us to the essence of material. As we discover new analogies between distant and apparently contrary things, we will endow them with an ever more intimate value. Instead of *humanizing* animals, vegetables and minerals (an outmoded system) we will be able to *animalize, vegetize, mineralize, electrify* or *liquefy* our style, making it live the life of material. For example, to represent the life of a blade of grass, I say 'Tomorrow I'll be greener'.[22] (His example is rather feeble, but we shall soon be quoting a fine piece of mineralizing by Tzara.)[23]

When 'the poetry of cosmic forces supplants the poetry of the human',[24] it will show man his proper place in the physical universe. It is a very modest one.

The traditional narrative proportions (romantic, sentimental and Christian) are abolished, according to which a battle wound would have a greatly exaggerated importance in respect to the instruments of destruction, the strategic positions and atmospheric conditions... In fact I observed in the battery of Suni, at Sidi-Messri, in October 1911, how the shining, aggressive flight of a cannonball, red-hot in the sun and speeded by fire, makes the sight of flayed and dying human flesh almost negligible.[25]

Marinetti, always stimulated by the frigid thrill of the inhuman and amoral, here betrays a touch of false aestheticism. We may grant that he himself might, like a detached observer, judge his own death of negligible importance compared with the outcome of a battle, but hardly with the splendour of a cannon-ball red-hot in the sun. However, in the exhilaration of writing he must have assumed that he would, or at any rate should, would if he could take in the scene with sufficient detachment; this is not the violation of the equality of viewpoints which would be a lapse into irrationalism.

In politics Marinetti believed that the trend of the future was the disengagement of nationalism and militarism from reaction and their mergure with an 'anarchic individualism'. He supposed that Mussolini, then a socialist inclined to anarcho-syndicalism, shared his vision, and worked in close alliance with him from 1915 to 1919, when he made the mistake which eventually ruined him, of committing himself to Mussolini's nascent Fascist Party. He withdrew almost at once, when Mussolini came to terms with Church and monarchy, but later compromised and ended up as an academician honoured and ignored by the Fascist dictatorship. Yet Fascist ideology was at first so fluid that in his *Beyond Communism* (1920) he declares himself delighted to learn that the Russian Futurists are all Bolsheviks, and for his own country still anticipates an 'anarchic paradise of absolute freedom', which will 'free Italy from the Papacy, the Monarchy, the Senate, marriage, Parliament', and 'abolish standing armies, courts, police and prisons'.[26] Marinetti grounds his nationalism on the estimate that the nation is 'the greatest manoeuvrable mass of ideals, interests and private and common needs fraternally linked together', big enough to transcend the selfishness of individual and family, not big enough to become an abstraction ('To say: "I'm not Italian, I'm a citizen of the world" is equivalent to saying: "Damn Italy, Europe, Humanity, I'll think of myself" ').[27] Like so many of the most forward-looking in the years before 1914, he is weary of the interminable peace unbroken in Western Europe since 1871. He extols political violence as regenerative of the nation's manhood, whether as the anarchist's bomb-throwing or as 'war, the world's only hygiene'[28]. 'Marinetti himself', we are told, 'always carried a few grenades in his pocket and gave them away to his friends like cigars. Mussolini used to keep these unwelcome gifts in the stove (and a pistol on his desk) and was nearly blown through the roof one morning when a new porter tried to light the stove without clearing it'.[29] It may be noticed that although his nationalism and militarism look very passéist nowadays, the concerns of which they are the outward and temporary dress—anarchy, communal solidarity, the mystique of violence—eternally reappear in the unworldly politics of the *Avant-garde*. Indeed nearly all that Future imagined by a few brilliant Italians in the years after 1909, from the architect Sant'Elia's designs for megalopolis to Russolo's 'art of noises' (ancestor of electronic music) and the simple, loose-fitting, quickly disposable dress in brilliant colours of Balla's *Futurist manifesto of men's clothing* (1913), in some form remains a presence for better or worse in the last quarter of the century.

The first *Futurist manifesto* professed 'scorn for women', but in this as in other matters Marinetti's thought quickly developed. The movement, unlike Dada and Surrealism, always remained a male preserve, flamboyantly virile, with women as occasional honorary members, such as the Marchesa Casati, complimented by Marinetti on 'her languid jaguar's eyes, which digest in the sun the cage of steel which she has devoured'.[30] But by 1913 he had recognized as No. 7 of his symptoms of modernity

Semi-equality of men and women and a lessening of the disproportion in their social rights.

No. 8 is 'disdain for *amore*', not only by men but by women, who with greater erotic freedom are nowadays (Marinetti is not quite sure that he likes this) more excited by their dressmakers than by their lovers. As for physical desire, Futurism recognizes it as healthy and stimulating as long as it is unconfined by marriage and uncontaminated by love. 'We must strip lust of all the sentimental veils that disfigure it' says the *Futurist manifesto of lust* (1913), the only one of the manifestos written by a woman, the dancer Valentine de Saint-Point. [31] Another characteristic twentieth century attitude certainly, except perhaps that even the purely carnal is allowed little significance. Lechery as well as romance has for Marinetti the enervating taint of the *fin de siècle*.

The Futurists, who delighted in imagining the giant battles of machines which they expected soon to make life much more exciting, eagerly welcomed Italy's entry into the war in 1915, and emerged uncowed at the armistice, not yet aware that their time had passed. That hope and trust in the coming war, of some of the best of the young before 1914, has in retrospect an extraordinary pathos; yet the same urge to renew the spontaneity of ends by a regeneration of instinctive springs through violence, and the same dilemma that by accelerating the progress of technologies of combat and social control it only deepens subjection to the automatism of means, always returns in new forms, if not war then revolution, or romanticized crime. With the unfolding of the First World War an unqualified faith in the twentieth century, science and the machine was no longer sustainable without the hope of profound social change, to which the Russian Revolution at first gave substance. That faith passed from Futurism, increasingly compromised by Fascism, through Russian Constructivism and the German Bauhaus to the eventual realization of the Futurist megalopolis in design, architecture and town-planning after the Second World War, and the proof by experience that it is uninhabitable. But our present interest is in the subjective aspect of Futurism, as a fresh response to a civilization from which meaning is draining away. In this, as in manifesto-writing, adventurous typography and public outrages, the successor of Futurism is Dada.

The German and Rumanian exiles led by the poet Hugo Ball who in 1916 in neutral Switzerland founded Dada at the Cabaret Voltaire in Zurich detested nationalism and militarism and cared neither for mechanical progress nor for social revolution. A manifesto by Tristan Tzara read at the very first Dada demonstration mocks the automobile and declares itself 'definitely against the future'.[32] Dada rejects tomorrow for the moment, and instead of the shaping of will by convergence of spontaneous energies on a project prefers a fluid spontaneity with its source in the unconscious, even in that Beyond which Futurism categorically denies.

The Dada which at the end of the war in 1918 became an international movement may be seen as a nihilistic game acclimatizing to unmeaning and chaos, as may the independent tendencies centred especially in New York (of Duchamp, Picabia, Man Ray) which merged into Dada after Picabia's visit to Zurich in 1918. But Zurich Dada during its wartime isolation seems rather to be a collective plunge into a spontaneity which risks chaos in the hope of discovering a profounder order. Picabia's wife Gabrielle Buffet, contrasting Zurich with New York, noted that 'the Dadaists displayed an attitude less egotistical, more mystical and naive, a desire to appeal to automatic, primitive, collective forces, rather than individualistic exasperation'.[33] Ball, a temporarily lapsed Catholic who still detested the whole secularizing trend of Western civilization since the Renaissance, conceived the entertainments at the Cabaret Voltaire as rites to summon up the irrational powers of the subconscious, dramatise and exorcise the chaos of the present, and recover the 'supernatural', the 'world of archetypal images', which lies hidden in man below the level of reason.

The primaeval strata, untouched and unreached by logic and by the social apparatus, emerge in the unconsciously infantile and in madness, when the barriers are down; that is a world with its own laws and its own form; it poses new problems and new tasks, just like a newly-discovered continent. The levers to pry this stale world of ours off its hinges are in man himself.[34]

14

He describes the excitement of the mediumistic effect of masks designed by Marcel Janco:

We were all there when Janco arrived with his masks, and everyone immediately put one on. Then something strange happened. Not only did the mask immediately call for a costume; it also demanded a quite definite, passionate gesture, bordering on madness. Although we could not have imagined it five minutes earlier, we were walking around with the most bizarre movements, festooned and draped with impossible objects, each one of us trying to outdo the others in inventiveness. The motive power of these masks was irresistibly conveyed to us. All at once we realized the significance of such a mask for mime and for the theatre. The masks simply demanded that their wearers start to move in a tragic-absurd dance.[35]

For Ball the Dada rites have no formulable meaning. It is not simply that he dismisses all verbalizations of the Truth as false or as inadequate; he believes that the reorientation of life demands not the correctness of propositions but the force of images and rhythms. In his 'phonetic poems' he experiments at a language without syntax and vocabulary, rid of its parasitic function of affirming and deny-ing, freed to act directly on the nerves through sonorities, rhythm and the images suggested by elusive resemblances of its phonemes to known words. He wants to rediscover 'the evangelical concept of the "word" (logos) as a magical complex image'[36] The name 'Dada' itself is primal noise with meanings beginning to emerge out of it, 'Yes, yes' in Russian and Rumanian, 'geegee, hobbyhorse' in French babytalk (there were no English Dadaists to understand it as a recall to infantile trust in the authority of the father).

Adopt symmetries and rhythms instead of principles.[37]
We are now trying to find this origin and womb of things. The origin of symbols, where each image just illumines the next, and where it does not matter what assertions are made—because the assertions group together, because they come from a common centre, if only the individual himself has an axis.[38]

At one moment in 1917 he seems to be in sight of this ultimate source.

Seek the image of images, the archetypal image. Is it pure symmetry? God as the eternal surveyor?[39]

However, Ball was already on the point of leaving Dada and finding his way back to the Church. By 1917 he was coming to regard the forces of the subconsci-ous as demoniac, the worship of symmetry as mere aestheticism, and Dada itself as a nostalgia for the 'natural paradise' which did not satisfy his hunger for a reality beyond nature. The new impresario of Dada was Tzara, who rather than leading floated on the surface of the movement (and later went on to Surrealism). The attitude of pure irresponsibility, to win invulnerability to universal disaster by refusing to take life or art seriously, which has come to seem the distinguishing characteristic of the wartime tendencies recognizable as Dada, still took some time to define itself. Tzara's Dada, before his departure from Zurich to Paris in 1919, is rather a provocative mixing of sublime and absurd, the sublime being a vision like Ball's of universal structure branching from a common centre, but without his Christian-Manichaean distrust of nature. He insists on order in poetry, but the same spontaneous order he finds in nature.

Nature is organized in its totality, rigging of the fabulous ship tending to the focal point, in the principles which rule crystals and insects in hierarchies like the tree...The organism is complete in the mute intelligence of a nervure and in its look.[40]
Rhythm is the jogtrot of heard intonations; there is a rhythm which one neither sees nor hears, radiation from a grouping within towards the constellating of order... But the poet will be stern towards his work, to find the true necessity; from this asceticism order will flower, essential and pure.[41]

Even when Tzara has the expected Dada tone of reckless indifference one notices that for him a cosmic order beyond good and evil, and the spontaneity which unites man with the non-human, are *divine*.

...nothing is sacred, everything is of divine essence.[42]
...but not all flowers are holy, fortunately, and what there is of the divine in us is the awakening of anti-human action.[43]
... abolition of memory, DADA; abolition of archaeology, DADA; abolition of prophets, DADA; abolition of the future, DADA; faith absolute indisputable in each god immediate product of spontaneity, DADA; elegant and unprejudiced leap from a harmony to the other sphere; trajectory of a word thrown like a gramophone record a cry; respect for all individualities in their madness of the moment...[44]

Tzara conceives creative spontaneity as an uprush of images from the depths of the organism continuous with physical nature (that 'awakening of anti-human action'); and by devices inherited from Futurism he forces language to preserve the continuity, defying punctuation, squeezing together and fusing organic, mineral and mechanical metaphors.

We seek the force direct pure sober unique we seek nothing we affirm the vitality of each instant the anti-philosophy of spontaneous acrobatics...
Prepare the action of the geyser of our blood—submarine formation of transchromatic aeroplanes, metals cellular and ciphered in the leap of images... above the regulations of the Beautiful and its supervision[45] (We omit with a bad conscience the typographic devices marking the relative prominence of words).

Criticizing a novel of Pierre Reverdy for the traditional failing of putting the human characters at the centre of things instead of on the same level with the rest, Tzara writes

To art for art's sake, Reverdy opposes art for the sake of life. To which *we* oppose art for the sake of cosmic diversity, of totality, of the universal, and we wish to see as innate in that the slow life which exists and sleeps even in what one is accustomed to name 'death'. But theories and formulae are relative and elastic—from the angle of the absolute, they would become narrow dogmas and fanaticism—and we don't want to go in for that.[46]

Here we may notice the direct descent from Marinetti's 'the poetry of cosmic forces supplants the poetry of the human' (and anticipation of the Surrealist doctrine of the unity of life and death), but also Tzara's implication that whatever he says in

14*

opposition to Reverdy has only a relative validity, and that beyond the sayable there is an absolute. In his *Dada manifesto* of 1918 Tzara illustrates by the picture of a pointing hand the sentence 'Dada does not mean anything'. He conceives every verbal statement which specifies and defines as having, like a picture projected in linear perspective, only relative validity, depending on the angle from which one views the cosmic structure, but in the symmetry of the structure itself Tzara like Ball discovers the absolute.

Painting is the art of making two lines geometrically declared parallel meet on the canvas before our eyes, in the reality of a world transposed following new conditions and possibilities. This world is neither specified nor defined in the work, it belongs in its innumerable variations to the spectator. For its creator, it has neither cause nor theory. *Order = disorder; self = not-self; affirmation = negation:* supreme radiations of an absolute art. Absolute in purity of cosmic and ordered chaos, eternal in the globule the second without duration, without breath, without light, without control.[47]

Every revolt against rationalism is implicitly a questioning of the superiority of Greece and post-Renaissance Europe over other periods and civilizations. It is in Dada that one first notices the tendency, which has become very obvious since the migration of modernism to America, for the revolt in recognizing its allies else-where to polarize towards, on the one hand the mystic Orient with its immemorial wisdom reducing multiplicity to the One, on the other the Negro, savage symbol of an untamed spontaneity. These interests, still strange to Futurism, have proved to be something more than exoticism. By now our civilization has assimilated from both quarters practices which at the beginning of the century still seemed utterly alien to it: Zen and yoga techniques of meditation to suspend will and conceptu-alization and recover psychic spontaneity serve as aids to health and relaxation even to those little interested in self-enlightenment; the dance to an orgasmic rhythm yearning after collective trance, that African institution accidentally imported by slave-traders into America, has become central to the sub-culture of the young. Tzara, who so often sounds like a Taoist—'Dada is not a doctrine to be put into practice', 'Dada is a quantity of life in transparent effortless and gyratory trans-formation'[48]—is himself fully aware of his affinity to our archetypal anti-rational-ist Chuang-tzǔ. His *Zürich chronicle* under December 1918 has 'Chuang-tzǔ the first dadaist',[49] and in the *Lecture on Dada* (1922) at the very end of the movement his illustration to show that there was nothing new in Dada is 'Chuang-tzǔ was as dada as we are'.[50] The other great Taoist, Lao-tzǔ, was, with Jacob Boehme, the inspiration of Hans Arp's thinking.[51] Even more obtrusive than its orientalizing is Dada's passion for the African sculpture which had already fertilized Cubism,[52] for the 'negro rhythms' Richard Huelsenbeck drummed out in the Cabaret Vol-taire,[53] and for primitive poetry—Tzara's 79 *poèmes nègres*[54] are genuine versions or adaptations of translations taken from the anthropological literature.[55] Not that Dada pretends to escape from Western civilization:

DADA remains within the European frame of weaknesses, it's still shit, but we want henceforth to crap in diverse colours, to adorn the zoo of art with all the flags of the consulates.[56]

The Zurich attitude differs in principle from the nihilism of others in New York and elsewhere classed retrospectively as Dada, Duchamps, Picabia, Jacques Vaché, for whom the one thing meaningful in a meaningless universe is to transcend it by mocking its futility, demonstrate that you know there is no reason for doing anything but don't care. Vaché in particular is remembered (almost exclusively through his influence on Breton), not for any works but for the gestures, culminating in an enigmatic and elaborately staged suicide, by which he distinguished himself as a personage confronting 'the theatrical (and joyless) uselessness of everything'.[57] On this course too all valuation finally reduces itself to its essence, the preference for awareness, for a last residue of value is found in one's own superiority to the unaware incapable of recognizing the emptiness of life (Hans Richter on Duchamp: 'Vanity he regards as a basic human characteristic ('otherwise we should all kill ourselves')—it is his only concession to humanity').[58] To strike the pose of nihilistic Dada it is necessary, *not* to surrender to spontaneity, but to make one's own choices, fortuitous of course, to exhibit oneself as a sovereign individual who sees through and derides the pretensions of reason. This is to retain without question the 'Reason as Master' position while abandoning reason, as does Sade; it keeps the assumption of a self isolated from nature which ZurichDada has already undermined.

The golden period of Dada, as recalled by Richter,[59] was in 1917 and 1918, when the Zurich artists felt themselves lifted to the height of creativity by a common trust, not only in spontaneity and the unconscious, but in external chance—Hans Arp tearing up a failed drawing and seeing its fluttering scraps settle on the ground in the perfect layout which his strivings had missed,[60] Tzara composing poems by cutting words out of a newspaper and shaking them up in a bag.[61] 'Chance became our trademark' says Richter, 'we followed it like a compass'.

This experience taught us that we were not so firmly rooted in the knowable world as people would have us believe. We felt that we were coming into contact with something different, something that surrounded and interpenetrated *us* just as we overflowed into *it*. The remarkable thing is that we did not lose our own individuality. On the contrary, the new experience gave us new energy and an exhilaration which led, in our private lives, to all sorts of excesses.[62]

By appealing directly to the unconscious, which is part and parcel of chance, we sought to restore to the work of art something of the numinous quality of which art has been the vehicle since time immemorial, the incantatory power that we seek, in this age of general unbelief, more than ever before.'

But he continues.

Proclaim as we might our liberation from causality and our dedication to anti-art, we could not help involving our *whole* selves, including our conscious sense of order, in the creative process, so that, in spite of our anti-art polemics, we produced works of art. Chance could never be liberated from the presence of the conscious artist. This was the reality in which we worked, notwithstanding all Tzara's press-cutting poems and Arp's fluttering scraps of paper.[63]

Beginning from 1917 the Dadaist creates by exploiting the riches of chance as, according to Monod's Neo-Darwinian account, does Nature herself. New species appearing by fortuitous mutation sustain a consistent direction, not by purposive striving, but by natural selection sparing only the mutations which accord with the organism's structural orientation. Similarly the Dadaist at his creative moment does not, as in practical life, look out for opportunities to get what he already wants, but spontaneously selects from the fortuitous what in retrospect will be seen to fit the trend of his own line of growth. Not that Dadaists bother about evolutionary theory, but they are already at the point of view, to many still unintelligible, from which Darwinian mutation allows a value to new forms of life which Lamarckian purpose degrades to utility;[64] they would be grateful to discover in nature the gratuitous prodigality of the artist rather than the purposeful constructiveness of the bourgeois. But the Dadaists in 1917 have also the faith in the positive beneficence of chance which is indeed rewarded when the trend in the interactions of self and circumstances is towards integration, mutual support within a temporarily emerging system, encouraging the sense of luck running one's way and of living in a cosmos within which the coincidences of simultaneous events compose an a-causal order. In Dada, as in any rising and declining political or cultural movement, or love affair, when the orientation shifts temporarily or permanently towards disintegration and conflict, luck runs down and the vision of order dissolves in chaos.

The turning point is already reached in Tzara's chopping of a newspaper article, in contrast with Arp's tearing of a too-contrived drawing. Whether the Arp story is apocryphal or not, we have it on his own authority that during the Zurich period he and Sophie Taeuber experimented with the simplest forms 'arranging the pieces automatically, without will', with the result that 'since the disposition of planes, the proportions of these planes and their colours, seemed to depend only on chance, I declared that these works were ordered "according to the law of chance", as in the natural order, chance being for me merely a restricted part of an ungraspable *raison d'être*, of an order inaccessible in its totality'.[65] In the formation of a sea shell or a flower, the integrative process of nature reveals its affinity to the artist's; at certain moments the two processes meet, as in the rhythm of the hand which did the drawing tearing along the line of least resistance in the texture of the paper, and in the integration of gusts in the air depositing the pieces where, if he had not been pushed off course by the interference of will, the artist would have placed them; and the intelligence of Arp discriminates such moments. But in Tzara's game with fortuitously dislocated words there is neither natural structuring nor intelligent selection, nothing to distinguish his act from a nihilistic gesture to declare that poetic order and chaos are one and the same.

Tzara exploited the same chance factors as did Arp, but while Arp made conscious use of his eye and brain to determine the final shape, and thus made it possible to call the work his, Tzara left the task of selection to Nature. He refused the conscious self any part in the process. Here the two paths Dada was to follow are already apparent.

Arp adhered to (and never abandoned) the idea of 'balance' between conscious and unconscious. This was fundamental to me as well; but Tzara attributed importance exclusively to the Unknown. This was the real dividing line. Dada throve on the resulting tension between premeditation and spontaneity, or as we preferred to put it—between art *and* anti-art, volition *and* non-volition, and so on. This found expression in many ways and was apparent in all our discussions.

Whatever may have been going on at the same time in New York (and later in Berlin and Paris), in the euphoria induced by the discovery of the spontaneous, we in Zurich saw Dada as a means of attaining what Arp called 'a balance between heaven and hell'. We wanted to stay human!

As this tension between mutually necessary opposites vanished—and it ended by vanishing completely in the Paris movement—Dada disintegrated. In the resulting general tumult and chaos personal relationships disintegrated too, and so did the image of Dada in the memories of our contemporaries.[66]

Surrealism emerged in 1923 as a recall to seriousness by André Breton's Paris group of ex-Dadaists, who for several years had been seeking a new balance between reason and spontaneity through psycho-analytic theory and quasi-scientific experiments in automatic writing and collective trance. The worthlessness of current existence, which Dadaists braved out by striking nonchalant poses, confronted the more earnest Surrealists with nothing less than a choice between the attraction of suicide and a desperate hope of renewing the sources of life by poetry, love and revolution. The discovery which encouraged them in that hope was the quality of the 'Marvellous' in illogical sequences of images without conscious control, a practical demonstration of Freud's claim that the Unconscious is the source of poetry and myth. The first organ of the movement, *La révolution surréaliste* (1924—1929), which had the format not of an art but of a science journal, published unrevised automatic texts, unadorned reports of dreams, inflammatory proclamations ('Open the prisons, disband the army!'), symposia in answer to questionnaires ('Is suicide a solution?', 'What sort of hope do you put in love?'), not many art reproductions at first. The extraordinary fertility in poetry and painting of successive generations of Breton's circle—for with the shift to Paris the vanguard of anti-rationalism was for the first time attracting the newest talents in the capital of vanguardism in the arts—tends to distract attention from a message which is in any case hard to decipher in the turmoil of Surrealist activity in the twenties and thirties. But during his exile in America (1940—1945) Breton, who had something of the system-building instinct, had time to put his thoughts in order (not that in the Existentialist Paris to which he returned there were many who still listened). Here we are not concerned with the merits of the writing of Aragon or Eluard, the painting of Ernst, Dali and Magritte, Giacometti's sculpture, Buñuel's films, Artaud's proposals for the theatre, any more than we were with the inferiority in painting of Futurism to its Parisian contemporary, Cubism. Our concern is with Surrealism as an original and daring experiment in regenerating life. For this enterprise, Breton's theorizing has the great advantage that it is singularly free of preconceptions derived from the many disciplines on which it touches, the arts, philosophy, religion, occultism, the scientific positivism of Freud and the dialectical materialism which he professed from his temporary entry into the Communist Party in 1927, and that the borrowing of the word *surréal* 'super-real, more than real' (an already current coinage

by Apollinaire) releases him from both philosophical and common-sense presuppo-
sitions as to whether, and how much it matters whether, something is to be classified as 'real'. His still astonishing synthesis, a practical realization of his denial of
all antinomies, has an inner coherence which fuses the seemingly contradictory,
atheism and the sense of the sacred, moralism and libertarianism, modernity and
primitivism, science and esoterism, revolutionary politics and the private abandon
to love, poetry and dream, untrammelled fantasy and meticulousness in autobiographical fact. By a historical accident the English language took over the French
word *surréal* instead of translating it, and then let it be coloured by superficial
impressions made by Surrealist painting; we had better regularly translate by
'super-real', but keep 'surrealism' as the name of the movement in general, with the
capital 'S' to mark the orthodoxy of Breton's own circle.

The 'new mode of pure expression' called 'super-realism', conceived as a psychic
mechanism for 'the solution of the principal problems of life' (only incidentally
for throwing off poems and paintings) is defined in the first *Surrealist manifesto*
(1924).

SUPER-REALISM, n. Pure psychic automatism, by which it is proposed to express,
whether verbally, in writing or by other means, the real functioning of thought. Dictation
of thought in the absence of all control exercised by reason, outside all aesthetic or moral
preoccupations.[67]

We put off to later[68] the question why the flow of 'thought'—that is, free analogizing in its rawest state in automatic writing, dream and trance—seems to Breton
to carry him not away from but deeper into and beyond reality. For the moment
we note only that he is not turning his back on the information of science or common experience. Breton borrows techniques of automatism and trance from the
spiritualist séance, but rejects in principle the possibility of communication with
the dead,[69] and takes no interest in the queer physical phenomena of mediumship
about which the superficially more scientifically-minded Martinetti betrays credulity.[70] At first he assumes that the poet in analysing the mechanism of his own
inspiration will no longer hold it in awe as 'sacred'.[71] In his later writings however,
although still fiercely anti-religious, he does interpret poetic automatism as an
invasion from beyond, inspiring a dread of the unknown, even reviving 'the possible claims of the "sacred", disengaged from the degenerate ritualisms which
conceal it'.[72] He writes of the Gnostic Valentinus of Alexandria

But in the thought of Valentinus what deserves to be retained is rather the share it
allows to that sacred terror which seizes hold of the artist in the presence of his work
created 'in the name of God', in other words of a higher, unknown principle...All the
artist's will is powerless to reduce the resistance exerted against his own ends by the
unknown ends of nature. The feeling of being set in motion, not to say *played with*,
by forces which exceed our own, will not cease, in poetry and in art, to become more
acute, more overwhelming—'It is false to say "I think", what should have been said is
"I am thought" ' (Rimbaud).[73] Since then there has been full scope for the question:
'What we create—is it ours?'[74]

Psychic automatism is seen by Breton as the recovery of that absolute freedom in a timeless realm shaped by omnipotent desire which psycho-analysis declares to be the condition of the Id

Granted that automatism can come to terms, in painting as in poetry, with certain premeditated intentions, one runs a strong risk of departing from super-realism unless automatism is still going on, underground at least. A work has a claim to be super-realist only to the extent that the artist strives to reach the entire psycho-physical field (of which the field of consciousness is only a small part). Freud has shown that in the 'abyss' of these depths there reigns an absence of contradiction, the shifting of emotional blockages due to repression, timelessness, and the replacement of outer reality by the psychic reality subject only to the pleasure principle. Automatism leads us directly to this region.[75]

For Freud, this absolute freedom is something to outgrow, to be remembered only in myths of a lost paradise, as the maturing man becomes reconciled to the reality principle. Breton does not think we should outgrow it. He is an intransigent of the Romantic revolt, which in the nineteenth century saw itself in terms of the Christian myth as Lucifer's rebellion against God. Restated in psycho-analytic terms, it is revolt of the Id against Super-ego and Ego as well, to return reason to the status of assistant, not repressor, of primordial desire. 'What Surrealism has always made the first article of its programme' is

...the imperious need to be finished with this fatal dissociation of the human spirit by which one of its constituent parts has succeeded in winning for itself full licence at the expense of the other.[76]

Breton shares with Taoism, Dada, anti-rationalism in general, a distrust of the dichotomizations of analytic thinking; but he is exceptional in regarding all dichotomies, not simply as illusory or as relative, but as imprisoning, enslaving the spontaneous process of thought:

It is only by the exclusive appeal to automatism in all its forms that we can hope to resolve, outside the economic plane, *all* the antinomies which, having pre-existed the form of social regime under which we live, are only too likely to outlast it. These antinomies demand that we work to abolish them, because we smart under them as implying another servitude, profounder and more definitive than the temporal one, and because this suffering no more than the other should find man resigned. These are the antinomies of waking and sleep (reality and dream), of reason and madness, the objective and the subjective, perception and representation, past and future, sociality and love, even life and death.[77] (It may be noticed that unlike Tzara he does not mention 'self' and 'not-self'.)

Breton's way of thinking about dichotomies and their resolution belongs to the legacy of Hegelianism, and when his interest widens from personal to social revolution he finds the key to a synthesis of Surrealism and Marxism in their common ancestry in Hegel.[78] But the social revolution to overcome the contradictions of class society can for him never be more than a step towards a total liberation by the spontaneous imagination pushing a dialectic of logically clashing images towards that 'point in the mind from which life and death, the real and the imaginary, the past and the future, the communicable and the incommunicable, the high and the low, cease to be perceived as contradictory'.[79] The images which crystallize from primordial desire are not yet distinguished as past or future, as illusion, memory or prefiguring: until one is choosing how to act on them they are neither sane nor mad; if the inorganic fauna in animate landscapes of Surrealist painting depict them truly, they are not even alive or dead. (Behind the Surrealist question 'Is suicide a solution?' is the elusive thought of sinking finally into, not death, but that life-in-death.) That the purpose of resurrecting this vision is, at least in the eyes of the founder of the movement, nothing less than a blow at the antinomies aiming, to cite his own ecstatic language, at 'the annihilation of being in a diamond inward and blind, which is no more the soul of ice than of fire',[80] is easily overlooked by those interested in the Surrealists only as artists. The crucial antinomy, the one which the word *surréal* was adopted to discredit, is the opposition between the imagined and the real:

I believe in the future resolution of these two states, in appearance so contradictory, which are dream and reality, in a sort of absolute reality, of *super-reality [surréalité]*, if one may so speak.[81]

In this passage, which is the original introduction of the term in the first *Surrealist manifesto*, 'super-reality' looks at first sight like a mere rhetorical variation on the absolute reality which is the terminus of the Hegelian dialectic. But the change of name marks a break with the old ambition of philosophy and science to achieve a perfect representation of reality stripped of the veils of illusory appearance. Surrealism is among other things an interpretation of the historically new experience of finding oneself necessarily in interaction with whatever one is trying to pin down as an object of knowledge. We have argued[82] that description of an object will inevitably be shaped either by spontaneous reactions, in poetic language, or by adaptation to deliberate action, in scientific; that the former is relevant to ends, the latter to means; and that there is no point in getting involved in the metaphysical question of which is the truer. But the positivistic do assume an answer to that metaphysical question, that only the world of science is real; and Breton, instead of disagreeing, goes one better and pronounces the world of poetry more than real, super-real. Like all for whom 'Reason is Guide', he thinks of human activity as primarily spontaneous, secondarily guided by reason; but he is distinctive in thinking of spontaneity as disrupted by the Ego's repressive apparatus, so that the object can be experienced as super-real only when psychic automatism has reopened communication with the Unconscious. It is then that one meets the paradox of feeling closest to the object when intensity of sensation and imagination approaches a hallucinated solipsism, an intensity for the evocation of which twentieth century techniques of writing become more and more sophisticated, achieved a generation later in the *Hundred years of solitude* of Garcia Marquez, that perfect fusion of novel and myth, on a larger scale than the Surrealists themselves ever attempted. We shall ignore the ontological status of the super-real, note the genuineness of the Surrealist hunger for a heightened reality. This is quite distinct from the dissatisfaction at being shut out from reality by a paper-thin illusory world which inspires much philosophical idealism, and never more clamorous than in the *Second Surrealist manifesto* (1930), where Breton is fully committed to Marxist materialism. The choice of the word 'super-real' confirms the world of reason as fully real, but merely real, a prison in which the would-be seer desperately hurls himself against 'the impassable wall of silver spattered with brains'.[83]

In what sense does Breton think that he can be freed from the antinomies by surrender to the spontaneous flow? As a frenetic adorer of *amour fou*, who concludes his *Nadja* with the proclamation 'Beauty will be CONVULSIVE or will not be', he certainly does not hope to transcend all distinctions in the peace of a mystical oneness with everything; in any case he is too much of an individualist to renounce selfhood. It is of course a familiar plea to the intellectual that it is time for him to throw off the rigid dichotomies which hinder him from responding sensitively to the variety of experience. But would not a mere retreat into the turmoil of the Id blind me to differences instead of lifting me above them? The proposal however is not to flee into the Unconscious but to drop the barriers which exclude it from the total interaction in which I am closest to the object. When irradiated by psychic automatism the perceived and the imagined are alike super-real; that I do not yet conceptualize the distinction between them does not prevent me from responding to them differently, as spontaneously as the body to heat and cold. If it is dream rather than waking that excels in its incorruptible super-reality, that is because in the depths of the dream I cannot ask 'Am I dreaming or awake?', yet respond fully without (as in hallucination) reaction issuing in deluded action, and because the images reverberate from abysses inaccessible to waking consciousness. If Freud is to be trusted, deeper than all my practical problems soluble by reason is the problem of ordering the reconcilable or irreconcilable impulses springing from the Unconscious, a problem continually solving itself spontaneously in response to the symbols of dream, poetry and myth, until a blockage requires psycho-analysis to shift it; should it not follow then that I come to grips with the real world at a more fundamental level through the distorted images of it in sleep than through perception when awake? No fact could be more important to me than that I shall some day die, but it might be that I am never fully aware of it except in a recurring nightmare of facing a firing squad. The ultimate Surrealist hope, then, would be to live in a super-real world which, wherever a question interrupts the spontaneous passage from impulse to action, divides along a fluid line between real and illusory, which in due course peters out in a reintegration of the super-real.

The denial of antinomies, which in mystical philosophies and even in Dada suggests an ideal of desireless tranquility, becomes, when interpreted in Freudian terms, a passionate act of revolt. The Surrealist discovers himself to be everywhere starved and thwarted, would like to feel every impulse which a despotic order has repressed from his consciousness; he excludes none as in principle illegitimate, even the most destructive. Within the constrictions of present society, he finds scope for the primal freedom in dream, in love, in humour (the subversive 'black humour' which has been one of the movement's most durable legacies), in the poetic flow, and in those conjunctions of 'objective chance' when the real perfectly coincides with the desire it brings to consciousness, experiences in which imagination or perception is transfigured by the impulses strange to himself which give them the quality of the Marvellous. These are local and temporary recoveries of that primordial vision which does not yet distinguish the real from the imaginary within the super-real. In them he discovers that the religions are wrong (and tyrannical) in requiring him to deny himself in submission to the sacred; he learns that to live in perfect freedom is identical with recovering the not yet desacralized world of the child and the primitive. His highest personal hope, for which he might perhaps even betray the Revolution[84] (this was a serious ethical issue for the Surrealists) is of love, the *amour fou* in inevitable collision with social norms and practical prospects, the absolute surrender both physical and ideal to spontaneity in imagination, caprice and act, which reveals to the lovers the Marvellous in each other. The mutual election of lovers, seen by the Surrealists as at its highest unique, instantaneous and lifelong, is the supreme instance of the bounty of objective chance. Futurism, on what is still the dominant trend in this century, had desacralized Eros; Surrealism, which inherits some Futurist attitudes (an untroubled acceptance of the flesh, contempt for bourgeois marriage and dissipation, distaste for homosexuality and its influence in cultural fashions), rediscovers the sacred in sexual love, as in a different way does the psychedelic Counter-culture a generation later. It also corrects the masculine bias of Futurism, by combining a modern acknowledgement of sexual equality with a revival of the archaic wonder of Man at Woman as a being instinctively closer to the mystery of things.

The Surrealist, denying the antinomy of the imagined and the real, does not think of dream as an escape from the world, but as incipient living which solves the fundamental problems of action. He discerns its solutions by listening (as though to an oracle) to the voice which speaks in automatic writing and puts sentences into his head between sleep and waking, by watching (as though for omens) for the sights to which subconscious influences guide his attention when will is suspended. He seeks what Breton eventually identified as 'a certain extra-religious Sacred', wishes 'to penetrate the meaning of the ancient myths as well as to rediscover the secret of their gestation'.[85] He would like to restore modern man to his place in the world by images as archaic, amoral and pre-rational as that of Kronos eating his children, metropolitan myths in contemporary dress such as the disjointed dreamlike stories of the surrealist films *Un chien andalou* and *L'age d'or*. If it was Freud who discovered how primordial insights can be recovered by translating them from mythological into quasi-scientific language, it is the Surrealist who explores how they can be relived. Even in action what matters to him is not the sterile if inescapable manipulation of means to pre-established ends, but an undirected wandering of the streets of Paris on the alert for objective chance. The unforeseen which by touching off submerged desire evokes the Marvellous, such as the 'found object' picked up on the seashore or in the flea-market, plunges him back like the dream into the super-real, which is neither the merely real envisaged in advance as a goal nor the merely unreal towards which conscious wish-fulfilment guides him in fantasy. But his haunted landscape is unpeopled by gods. Surrealism offers itself as successor, not of religion, nor of mysticism (which denies selfhood), but of magic; it conceives poetry and love as a sorcery which, without claiming the supposed practical effects of traditional magic, wrests from the Unconscious its secrets and endows the magus with its powers. Nor is there any question of the super-real deriving its value from a mystery beyond it; the super-real image is appreciated for itself and not as a symbol, and the Marvellous is conceived as a luminous quality of immediate experience, wholly manifest in it. The Surrealist even in his primitivism is post-Renaissance in his commitment to an individual liberty which would be betrayed by recognizing any power to which man must bow down. The name of Faust, central to the self-image of the West, is missing from Breton's mythology but is superfluous, because he himself is Faust, with an ambition nourished by the same alchemists and dedicating his soul to the angel of revolt, the Lucifer who as morning star brings illumination from the depths of night at the end of his *Arcane 17*. It is true that Breton, like Marinetti and the whole modernist tradition, thinks of man as dethroned by scientific cosmology from supremacy in the universe, and in his *Prolégomena à un troisième Manifeste du Surréalisme ou non* (1942) even reawakens the primitive dread of superhuman forces by offering his myth of the *grands transparents* to undermine our conceit as a species. However, the Great Transparents are not objects of worship but creatures higher in the evolutionary scale whose perfecting of natural camouflage has made them imperceptible to our senses, influences behind nature's cyclones and humanity's wars, 'who show themselves to us obscurely in fear and the feeling of chance'. Their super-reality, by the way, is established by an adroit toppling of antinomies:

A new myth? These beings, should we convince them that they issue from mirage, or give them the opportunity to disclose themselves?[86]

For Breton an actual found object is on the same level of super-reality as the book which he once dreamed of seeing in an open-air market, with a white-bearded wooden gnome as its back and pages of heavy black wool; he considered having it fabricated, to try out the effect of the image on other people.[87] But to be super-real the found object must, like the dream image, correspond only to the unique desire which it discloses in its instant of revelation. If one has consciously projected something similar, it is the difference between the discovery and the anticipation which uncovers the authentic impulse behind the latter.

I must admit to having desired to see constructed a very special object, answering to a certain poetic fancy. This object, in its material, in its form, I more or less foresaw. Then it happened to me to discover it, no doubt the unique one to be manufactured. There could be no mistaking it, although there were differences on every point from what I had foreseen...In such cases however the pleasure is a function of the very dissimilarity between the object intended and the *find*. The find, whether artistic, scientific, philosophical or of as commonplace utility as you please, in my eyes takes away all beauty from what fails to be *it*. In it alone is it given to us to recognize the marvellous precipitate of desire.[88]

The external becomes super-real also when the subconscious transforms it into a vehicle for its own messages.

I am intimately persuaded that any perception registered quite involuntarily, as for instance of words spoken off stage, bears in it the solution, symbolic or otherwise, of some difficulty one has with oneself. It is simply a matter of knowing one's way about the maze. Delirium of interpretation begins only when the ill-prepared man takes fright in this *forest of signs*.[89]

An especially striking instance is a message which Breton himself originally failed to read. In 1927, as he tells in *Nadja* (1928), Louis Aragon pointed out to him a hotel sign, MAISON ROUGE, of which seen from a certain angle the first word vanished and the second became POLICE. This optical illusion did not interest Breton until a few hours later he happened to see a trick engraving of a tiger which from the left turned into a vase and from the right into an angel. Breton seems helpless to explain satisfactorily why he thinks this sequence of events worth reporting: 'I call attention to these two facts because for me, under those conditions, it was impossible not to associate them, and because it seems to me quite out of the question to establish a reasonable correlation between them.'[90] But read in the light of later events it has a divinatory significance which can hardly be missed. By what subconscious influence would the alternative readings of the hotel sign attract the attention of two libertarians who that very year joined the French Communist Party? Surely there was something at the bottom of them which had noticed that seen from a certain angle dedicated members of a revolutionary party look very like policemen, an insight which they were not yet ready to acknowledge. One can understand too that the tiger which looks so different from left and from right would stir confused political or anti-political thoughts which might reactivate the submerged sense of danger in the optical illusion previously dismissed as trivial. It is indeed no simple matter to impose the antinomy of real and illusory on the super-real. The subconscious, wiser in these matters than the conscious, points through the hotel sign at the issue which will break up the friendship of the two poets, when in 1931—3 the contradictions between Surrealism and Stalinism drive Breton to settle for the former and Aragon for the latter. In a later edition of *Nadja* Breton added a footnote to say that he recognized the meaning of this incident only at the time of Stalin's great purge.[91]

Breton by no means confines his curiosity to queer events which allow a psychological explanation. He does not hesitate to expose himself to the suspicion expressed by Trotsky when they met in Mexico: ' "I am not sure you aren't interested in keeping open"—his hands described a diminutive space in the air—"a little window into the beyond" '[92] Even when he uses the mocking anagram AVIDA DOLLARS for SALVADOR DALI it is as though it were more than a joke, as though through it objective chance magically strips Dali's innermost nature. There is a strange moment in one of the poignant haunting monologues of the waif Nadja (insane, as it later turns out) whom Breton met for a few weeks in 1926:

As the dessert arrives, Nadja begins to look around her. She is certain that a subway passes under our feet, coming from the Palais de Justice (she shows me from which spot in the Palais, a little to the right of the white steps) and circling the Hotel Henri IV. She is troubled at the thought of what has already happened in this square and of what will happen in the future. Where at this moment only two or three couples are fading into the dark she seems to see a crowd. 'And the dead, the dead!' The drunkard is still making his lugubrious jokes. Nadja's gaze is now travelling over the houses. 'Do you see that window over there? It is black like all the others. Take a good look. In a minute it will light up. It will be red'. The minute passes. The window lights up. It does in fact have red curtains. (I am sorry, but there is nothing I can do about it, if this perhaps passes the limits of credibility. However, it is not a matter on which I would wish to take sides : I confine myself to *acknowledging* that from black this window did change to red, no more.) I confess that at this point I am frightened, and Nadja is beginning to be frightened too.[93]

Breton's fine balance between credulity and scepticism is crucial to his fascination with the conjunctions of chance. A striking coincidence interests him because it pulls one forcibly back into the spontaneous analogizing at the roots of thought and perception, much as when, for example, a phantom green face emerges from a chance configuration of the leaves over which one's gaze is idly playing. The close likeness of the realized to the anticipated event compels attention like the semblance in the leaves, even if one thinks precognition, like the vegetable face, physically impossible; both loom as super-real, stirring an uncanny emotion, because one is no longer distinguishing unreal prevision from real succession, the unreal face from the real greenery. In such experiences one recovers the open prospects which the fixing of a conceptual scheme has closed, whether they would have led away from or still nearer to reality (in Kuhnian terms, to let the mind dwell irrationally on such coincidences *might* start a paradigm-shift which would make precognition explicable and verifiable). But Breton is not one of those who collect recurring coincidences in the hope of discovering an a-causal law.[94] The whole atmosphere of the Marvellous would dissipate if he asked Nadja to do it again. Before the fall of France in 1940 someone circulated a numerological calculation that the war would end on 11 April 1946, based on a striking coincidence in the dates of the Franco-Prussian and First World Wars. Breton's comment in 1941 on the impression made by this prediction was a curt 'Just see how much the irrational had gained at the expense of the rational'.[95]

The Surrealists inherit from the Romantic Agony a fascination with the beauty of evil. Their interest however is no longer in evil for its own sake, but in the taste for forbidden fruit as a motive to revolt. Since their aim is to liberate all desires, and the good ones are free already, it naturally follows that the more we are attracted to evil the better.

The problem of evil is worth raising only as long as we are not yet quit of the idea of the transcendence of a certain good which could dictate duties to man. Until then, the exalted representation of innate 'evil' will keep the greatest revolutionary value.[96]

Good and evil belong then among the antinomies which dissolve in the super-real, although not included in the lists of them we have had occasion to cite. The Devil, beloved by Romantics and Decadents, has no more place in Surrealist mythology than God; the Lucifer, morning star of revolt, introduced at the end of *Arcane 17*, is evidently conceived as transcending the distinction between

mad in their delusions. Religion nauseates Breton as the putrefaction of the super-real, enslaving man to the products of his own imagination, mortally dangerous because its securities tempt our cowardice to a self-betrayal in which freedom and creativity dry up. He denounces religion as though its dividing line from surrealism were the single antinomy exempt from criticism. But is the super-real as 'extra-religious Sacred' quite discontinuous with the 'numinous' which Otto divined as still potent behind the rationalizations and moralizations of theology? And could it be kept perpetually fluid without subjecting us all to the sterile modernist imperative to unending novelty? Breton as he grew older became conscious that free imagination needs a focus in commonly shared and relatively stable myth. Such a myth would have to crystallize, without being credited with the authority of the real, from super-real images already active at the submerged roots of col-lective thought, leaving us free to discover the real in and through it, and would evolve and in due course die without ever fossilizing as a religion. This guided spontaneity he sees as not a hindrance but a help to rationality, which will be secured not by dismissing or rationalizing myths, but by acknowledging the differ-ent functions of science and mythopoeia.

Scientific knowledge of nature can have value only on condition that *contact* with nature can be re-established through the paths of poetry and, may I say it, of myth.[104]
   In humanity mythic thought, in constant becoming, never ceases to run parallel with rational. To refuse it an outlet is to render it dangerous, with the result that it irrupts into and disintegrates the rational (delirious cult of the leader, cheapjack messianism).[105]

The myth to which he looks forward is of course not conservative but revolution-ary, drawing among other sources on the cosmos-building side of Fourier and other Utopians neglected since the ascendancy of 'scientific socialism'.[106] In his *De la survivance de certains mythes et de quelques autres mythes en croissance ou en formation* (1942),[107] a little album of enigmatic montages each juxtaposing one quotation with two photographic reproductions, he stimulates the reader to explore the significance of 15 myths selected as still or already alive, for better or for worse, in collective imagination and action. The series begins with old favour-ites (the Golden Age, Orpheus, original sin, Icarus, the philosopher's stone, the Grail), but continues with the artificial man, interplanetary communication, the Messiah, the execution of the king, the silence of Rimbaud, the Superman, the Androgyne, and the triumph of science, to which he optimistically adds his own Great Transparents. Breton's most ambitious effort in this direction was the erec-tion at the Surrealist Exhibition of 1947 of 12 altars to beings supposedly endowed with mythic life, this time drawn exclusively from the iconography of the Sur-realists themselves and their favourite poets. But it only confirmed that the private imagery of these very individual poets and artists never did cohere in a collective myth valid even for their own circle.
   The liberty to which Surrealism aspires, despairing and uncompromising, is perhaps the only new absolute presented for us to measure ourselves against in this relativistic age. To what extent can we place it in our scheme of things as a coherent ideal? It would be dedication to profoundest impulse independent

either of egoism or of morality, impulse which proves its authenticity by seeming foreign to me while challenging me to deny that it is mine, discovered at the root of the desires which impel but are distorted by my projects, springing up without reason although requiring to be guided by practical and moral considerations. From the 'Reason as Master' position it seems to betray a basic contradiction. A principle of absolute liberty cannot be reconciled with moralism except on the assumption that human nature is in some sense good, that at bottom we all want each other's benefit; but no one could be farther than the Surrealists from the Rousseauist faith in natural benevolence. The lesson which many would draw from their idols Sade and Lautréamont is that the absolute liberation of desire is self-contradictory, since men desire to enslave each other. Neither of them, probably, would have disagreed; for Sade, freedom's essence is the licence to tyrannize, and Lautréamont's two contrasting books seem designed to present the human condition as an insupportable dilemma of which the horns are self-knowledge which uncovers vitalizing but mutually destructive passions (*Les chants de Maldoror*) and a sterile order demanding a cultivated ignorance of ourselves (*Poésies*).[108] Does not the Surrealist rebellion lead precisely to this dilemma? One could see *L'age d'or* itself, against its maker's intention (and what are conscious intentions to a surrealist?) as not a call to revolution but just that anguished vision of mankind trapped between intolerable alternatives, a barren order and empty gestures of revolt.

However, Breton's position is not 'Reason as Master' but 'Reason as Guide'. From there, one is concerned neither to realize nor to conquer human nature, understood as the older and more basic drives consolidated in relative ignorance, but to choose the direction in which one spontaneously inclines when most aware. To bother about whether the inclination is sufficiently constant to have a regular label, and if so whether it is innate or learned, would be beside the point. Admittedly it might still be the case that the better we understand ourselves and each other the further we shall be drawn into irreconcilable conflict; but if so, the conclusion from this position would be, not that man's nature is evil, but that his destiny is tragic. In practice our anti-rationalist tradition, without refusing some place for inevitable conflict, assumes without intellectual justification that to the extent that we understand each other we do recognize our fundamental solidarity, an assumption which in our second chapter we decided does have an intellectual justification. In Marinetti's *The Untamables* the hope of escape from the vicious circle of licence and repression is found not in the goodness of nature but in the protean fluidity of desire, which moves from conflict towards harmony with greater enlightenment. In *L'age d'or*, a much stronger work in impressing with the psychological inevitability of its shifts, Eros is similarly in constant transformation as the hero gropes towards awareness of his lusts and of the social and religious restrictions which frustrate and pervert them; libido, maturing in true Freudian fashion from mother-centred infantilism and excremental curiosity to genital love, is defeated at last by social pressures, turns to hatred of woman and of life itself, blazes as a godless sadism, and finally, when sadism too exposes itself as no more than desire twisted by religion (in the climactic scene of the Duc de Blangis revealed as Christ), settles on love's counterpart, revolt. Breton does not,

any more than other anti-rationalists, think of freedom in terms of fulfilling the
ineradicable desires of a static human nature. Violence and cruelty, fundamental
as they may be, are not treated as needs which, like a concentration camp guard,
the healthy man may satisfy without inhibition, but as blind urges which social
and political awareness clarifies and directs. Moreover the awareness which guides
them cannot be mere canniness about one's own interests in society, because
'the accent has been displaced from the Ego, always more or less despotic, towards
the Id, common to all men':[109] the release of the impersonal forces of the Unconscious opens vistas beyond the self-centred awareness of a rationalistic individualism. Nothing could be more foreign to Surrealism than to find calculations
of self-interest at the bottom of the human heart—a point exemplified by Breton's
distaste for La Rochefoucauld and preference for Vauvenargues among the
French moralists. [110] The activities of the Surrealist circle were a collective enterprise, not for mutual assistance to pre-existing personal ends, but for self-discovery
through experimentation, alert to the view from each others' eyes, awaiting without
preconception the creative contacts of interacting spontaneities. Its politics was
a communism in which the dismally utilitarian 'to each according to his needs'
became the derationalizing, revitalizing 'to each according to his desires'.[111]
Surrealism in no way differs from a rationalistic liberalism or communism in its
scorn of prejudices of race, sex or class, those unimpeachably authentic and spontaneous tendencies which Nietzsche licenses us to indulge, and which are held in
abeyance only by a sustained awareness from other viewpoints; this is a crux at
which Nietzsche reveals himself as in our terminology an irrationalist, Breton an
anti-rationalist. A sense of the weakness of human nature may of course revive
with an acknowledgement of our overwhelming resistance to the transient impulses of our most aware moments. Granted that we are permanently changed by
stable gains in awareness, there must always be further heights and breadths of
awareness which we fail to sustain. Breton like Nietzsche has his personal combination of optimism and pessimism, in his case a vision both of man's possibilities
if he throws off externally imposed laws and of his ignoble failure hitherto.
But it remains the highest duty of the Surrealist to side at whatever cost with,
not the supposed nature, nor the practical prospects of man, but with whatever
quickens the best of life in him. In every creative moment of love, poetry or revolt,
'the imperishable secret is inscribed once more in the sand'.[112]

In the poise, or swing, between extremes of hope and despair, in Surrealism
and later in the Counter-culture, we may measure a shift in expectations which
has resulted from the technological changes of our century. To be equally aware,
while all standards of conduct are crumbling, on the one hand of the prospects
opened up by increasing material abundance and by political freedom, on the
other of the sterility of experience degraded by the automatism of means, and the
terror of uncontrollable acceleration in the means to universal destruction, breeds
a quite new combination of unlimited demands on life and unappeasable hatred
of things as they are. To ask so much of existence, not in another world but here,
has a 'spoiled brat' look by which earlier generations would have judged and
condemned it. Of the three immediate precursors acknowledged by Surrealism,
Rimbaud gave up—grew out of—his poetry at 19, Lautréamont died at 24,

Jarry's Ubu plays began as schoolboy lampoons on his physics master; something had changed radically when a whole movement in their spirit could be founded by mostly very strong-minded men in the neighbourhood of 30, of whom the leader continued into old age maturing without ever compromising. Breton however, disgusted by a faith in progress proved hollow by the First World War, never appreciated that he was himself one of the new men of a technological age. He sees himself as living at the end of a civilization vitiated from the start by Greek philosophy and Hebrew religion. He discards most of Europe's past, to nourish himself on its rebels and heretics and also, but circumspectly, on cultures which have escaped the double curse of Christianity and rationalism. Along the line we have traced from the *Futurist manifesto*, it has taken a mere 15 years to pass from eulogies of the machine to the rhapsodic appeals to the East to overthrow or redeem the declining West characteristic of the first years of Surrealist propaganda.[113]

Right at the beginning of the movement the Surrealists tried unsuccessfully to enrol René Guénon, author of a systematically developed theory that the West is decaying because it has disconnected science from the metaphysical knowledge on which all civilizations depend, which survives within Islam as Sufism, in China as Taoism, and is preserved at its purest as the Vedanta in India.[114] This superbly reactionary defender of order, hierarchy and immutable spiritual truth was almost the only outsider thus courted, and Breton never lost interest in him.[115] But in agreement with Guénon, who held that a civilization can recover the true metaphysic only through its own resources, not by syncretistic borrowings from others, Breton does not seek external support in Asian parallels to his own denial of the antinomies, and allows that for us the Orient can have 'only a symbolic value'.[116] What fascinates him is the subterranean resonance in the soul of the sick West of the *word* 'Orient', which signals a direction by concentrating in super-reality everything the Occident obscurely misses in itself.

This word which in fact like many others plays on a literal sense and several figurative senses, with of course any number of misreadings as well, has been pronounced more and more over the last few years. It must correspond to a disquiet particular to this time, to its most secret hopes, to an unconscious prevision; it ought not to recur with this insistence absolutely in vain... Why, in these circumstances, should we not go on claiming the Orient for ourselves, even the 'pseudo-Orient', to which surrealism consents to be no more than a homage, as the eye inclines towards a pearl?[117]

As for the real Orient and its philosophies, Breton has in any case no personal use for thought detached by translation and cultural remoteness from the living voice of the thinker. Like D. H. Lawrence, who in despairing of European civilization made off for Australia and the United States, this nearly monolingual Frenchman never comfortable abroad has in practice a deep reserve about borrowing from alien traditions. To congratulate a surrealist on his sense of balance would be an inept compliment, but without his instinct for the assimilable he could never have synthesized the diverse trends which meet in Surrealism. His caution may even be said to have temporarily held at bay the extra-European influences on the *Avant-garde* which in Dada had already polarized as the mysticism of the East and the rhythms of the Negro. These did not exert their full force until a generation later, when the Counter-culture discovered in rock music, together with an Indianizing mysticism aided by hallucinogenics, its most potent agencies in revolutionizing life. Breton attended to other cultures only to the extent that he could respond to the look and touch of their artefacts or to the sight of their rituals. But the influences which came to him through the senses twice affected the course of the Surrealist movement. He and his friends were the first to recognize the virtue which Lévi-Strauss has since, in comparing the distinctive strengths of the world's cultures, identified as characteristic of the Melanesians: 'the talent they show for integrating into social life the most obscure products of the mind's unconscious activity'.[118] Breton testified in a later essay on Oceania to the obsession with living surrounded by ritual objects from the Pacific which so deeply marked their visual imagination; 'the surrealist enterprise, in its beginnings, is inseparable from the seduction, the fascination they exerted on us'.[119] During his wartime exile in America his strongest stimulation came from the artefacts and rituals of the Zuni and Hopi Indians, from black surrealist poets he visited in Martinique and Haiti, and from witnessing in Haiti 'the phenomena of "possession", which have always been one of the poles of interest for surrealism'.[120] It was from these, and from the Martiniquan Jules Monnerot's *La poésie moderne et le sacré* (1945), that he came to recognize the affinity of the super-real to the sacred.[121]

For all his early ventures into the perilous depths, Breton soon discerned the line which separates anti-rationalism from irrationalism. The temptation of Surrealism, as of the psychedelic Counter-culture later, was to suppose that free imagination once loosed from rational restraints is a magic to which external reality is malleable. 'Nothing is true, everything is permitted' wrote William Burroughs at the beginning of the psychedelic era, borrowing the slogan Nietzsche coined for the Assassins.[122] Breton came to think that Surrealism at the start did err in that direction, until the brutal fact of the Moroccan war of 1925 shocked it out of its 'intuitive' into its 'reasoning' epoch.[123] His ban on the use of drugs, those treacherous aids which in heightening some kinds of awareness also delude, was one protection against the danger. Another was his commitment, not to the anarchism which might seem the natural politics of the movement, but to a disciplined Marxism, even to the Communist Party until the consolidation of Stalinism, thus enforcing acknowledgment of an objective social reality which can be changed only by concerted action. (Revolutionary socialism, which lifts some into the clouds, is just what surrealists need to keep them within reach of earth.) Breton always remained in some aspects the traditional French rationalist, an atheist and for much of his life a materialist, a believer in Liberty and (less enthusiastically) in Equality, with a positive taste for the intellectual rigours of the Marxian and Freudian systems, and an admirably lucid, detached and controlled style when he chose to use it. A certain ponderousness even in his imaginative writing reveals him as less a visionary poet than a thinker who turns to poetry because, having recognized that his vision is shaped by pre-rational forces, he wants to experiment with them to make himself see better. The problem of the false relation between author and reader which we noticed in both Nietzsche and Sade,[124]

and which is perhaps characteristic of true irrationalism, does not arise with
Breton, any more than with Chuang-tzŭ, Marinetti, Ball or Tzara. There is even
a sense in which he might be said to push the demand for reality farther than
what is called realism in the novel. He pursues the super-real in the life of everyday,
and demands the meticulous first-hand report, whether of the chance encounter
or of the dream; his dislike of the novel as a literary form is rooted (as he shows
at the beginning of the autobiographical *Nadja*) in contempt for what is neither
reality nor imagination but fiction, the futile rearrangement and adornment of
personal experiences better left to speak for themselves. He may permit himself
a few questionable divagations into astrology or crystal-gazing, but in spite of the
dangerous ground he treads he nearly always avoids collision with orthodox
science. One of the lasting lessons of Surrealism has been that one can resacralize
this world without postulating another beyond it, that the hunger for the Marvellous neither demands nor will be appeased by intellectual proofs of the existence
of God, experiments in telepathy or reports of flying saucers.

Breton in person, self-disciplined, averse to intimacies and informalities, guiding
the progress of the movement with intimidating authority, the supervisor of controlled chaos and violence, from which some of the weaker fell away into madness
or suicide, permitted the full surrender to the Unconscious only in a spirit of
experiment. For a while he committed himself without reserve to automatic writing, with notable success in the fluent incandescent *Poisson soluble* (1924),[125]
but became alarmed by 'disturbing tendencies to hallucination from which I had
to pull myself together at once',[126] also soon came to recognize that the unarticu-
lated voice of the subconscious loses its inspiration when it has learned what
tricks are expected of it, and reduced the technique to the status of a preliminary
exercise, dispensable once you have learned to stay in touch with the spontaneous
flow without loss of critical consciousness. The experiments in 1922–3, when the
movement was first taking shape, in collective trance, in which Breton's temperament inhibited him from directly participating, as fascinating and at a sufficient
distance as outrageously funny as the Counter-culture's in psychedelic drugs, he
discontinued altogether as too dangerous.

I remember especially a seance consisting of about thirty guests at Picabia's friend
Madame de la Hire's place. Enormous house, discreet lighting; try as we would to avoid
it, around ten of them, men and women, by no means all acquainted, were in trance
at the same time. As they came and went vaticinating and gesticulating for all they were
worth, it was not much different you can imagine from the spectacle presented by the
convulsionaries of Saint-Medard. Around 2 o'clock in the morning, worried by the disappearance of several of them, I finally discovered them in the cloakroom, almost too dark
to see, where as if by common consent and fully equipped with the necessary rope they
were trying to hang themselves from the coatrack.—Crevel, who was one of them, seemed
to have put them up to it. We had to give them rather a rude awakening. Another time
after a dinner at Eluard's in a Paris suburb it took several of us to overpower the sleep-
walking Desnos, who brandishing a knife was running after Eluard in the garden. As you
can see, the suicidal ideas present in Crevel in a latent state, the muffled hatred which
Desnos felt for Eluard, took under these conditions an active and extremely critical
turn[127] (René Crevel did commit suicide in 1935).

The anti-rationalism of Breton, whatever its other sources, on the intellectual level starts from a determination to recover the unconscious motives behind conscious projects, and from the implicit question: 'If the end is rational, would it not be even more rational to act on the impulse farther back, as far back as it can be traced?' The psychic process by which, according to Freud, the Ego coheres, takes over some archaic tendencies and represses others, and so lays down the foundations of my current ends, is the crude operation of an ancient mechanism which in case of neurosis has to be corrected by psycho-analysis, and which I have every right to criticize radically; why not, as far as I can, rediscover the unconscious motives of my actions and do the work of comparing, reconciling and selecting over again?

Taking this line Breton, far from defying reason, is pressing the thought of Freud to its logical conclusion (which if you like is unreasonable). Granted our position that ultimately all rational choice is between spontaneous inclinations, the deeper he plunges into the spontaneous the more will be brought within the scope of 'Be aware'. Is his rejection of such antinomies as the real and the imaginary a retreat into self-delusion? We have already argued that it is not, that he breaks the habit of dichotomistic thinking to restore the creativity of free analogizing, in his own words 'to wrest thought from its ever harsher servitude, put it back on the path of total comprehension, restore it to its original purity'.[128] Or might one say that Surrealism is irrationalist in the gross disproportion of its demands on awareness? One could say as much of all the modernisms, if not of all philosophies of life which do not elevate balance and proportion as positive virtues. Of course Surrealism is *unreasonable*.

Two issues which will serve as test cases of Breton's respect for reason are his attitudes to Sade and to the occult tradition. Since we have chosen Sade and Breton as the West's purest spokesmen of irrationalism and anti-rationalism respectively, our categorical distinction would be in danger if we fail to account for Breton's unqualified admiration for his infernal predecessor (whose sexual orientation by the way he did not share).[129] Here a distinction is necessary. Sade has a rightful place among Surrealist heroes as the supreme rebel, whose life and writings have transfigured him as the most potently super-real of subversive idols, the 'Divine Marquis' beyond good and evil who by exciting indiscriminately the whole range of forbidden desires forces us, when it comes to real action, to revise but not abolish the bounds of the permissible. This is in general Breton's approach, fully rational and moral, and in theory would be quite compatible with recognizing the total irrationality of Sade's thought, as appropriate to a rebel against the very conditions of existence. At one corner of the super-real landscape there is a place fillable only by the ultimate outlaw who, if his finger were on the button of the Doomsday Machine, would have nothing in his head which would inhibit an impulse to push it. Breton however, less discriminating here than with the word 'Orient', confuses the super-real Divine Marquis with the real man, and has to convince himself that the Sade he adores would *not* push the button. He wants to think that Sade's revolt, like his own, is on behalf of truth and human dignity. It is this refusal to look straight down into the abyss of Sade's thought which reduces most Surrealist writing about him to vapid rhetoric eulogizing the freest man who ever lived. Bataille, Breton's superior as atheistic explorer of evil and the sacred, was rightly scornful of the frivolity of the Surrealist cult of Sade.[130] Although the movement contributed much to drawing attention to him (as to many neglected or execrated figures), a serious understanding of Sade began with Bataille and others outside the circle, and not until the late 1940s.[131] The comments with which Breton introduces Sade in his *Anthologie de l'humour noir* (1939) are of an insipidity astonishing in so original and perceptive a critic of writers he admires. 'Thanks to M. Maurice Heine, the immense range of the Sadean *oeuvre* is today beyond controversy; psychologically, it has claims to be the most authentic forerunner of that of Freud and of all modern psychopathology; socially, it looks forward to nothing less than the establishment, deferred from revolution to revolution, of a true science of morals'.[132] How curious to see Breton trying to hold Sade within the bounds of reason! He concludes by quoting with approval an extraordinary piece of sentimentality by Eluard: 'Since virtue brings its own happiness with it, he strove, in the name of everything that suffers, to degrade and humiliate it, to impose on it the supreme law of unhappiness, against all illusion, against all deception, so that it could aid all those it reprobates to construct on earth a world to the immense measure of man'.[133] The Surrealists, at the climax of the modernist adventure on the edge of reason, meet true irrationalism with incomprehension.

As for the occult, Breton's fascination with coincidence interested him in horoscopes, and the often startling successes of blind co-operation in surrealist games inclined him to admit the possibility of some kind of pooled consciousness. At the time of the *Second manifesto* he was sufficiently impressed to propose a serious inquiry into astrology and telepathy. But his approach remained that of the open-minded man of reason, demanding 'the minimum of necessary distrust', 'a precise, *positive* idea of the calculus of probabilities' (unobtainable, he admits, in the present circumstances of Surrealist experiment)[134] and he betrays no emotional involvement in buttressing his view of life by proving facts rejected by current science. His lifelong and developing interest in the literature of alchemy and magic is of a different order, and has nothing to do with curiosity about queer happenings. He rejected the pretensions of occult lore to be an immutable secret science handed down from antiquity, but valued it as the West's only stock of cosmos-building symbols independent of Christianity, a treasury on which poetry, in alliance with sociology, may draw to generate new myth.[135] He was impressed by the extent to which his immediate predecessors, the subversive poets and Utopian thinkers of the past century, had nourished their imaginations from occultist rather than Christian mythology.[136] He never intruded his personal symbolism into the official programme of Surrealism; in that crucial respect, he was no magus. Nor, although he once proposed the 'occultation' of Surrealism to protect it from the curiosity of the profane,[137] did he ever treat his coterie as a secret society for initiation by degrees into his own doctrines; the movement remained a collective exploration, with himself of course as the dominant—the awesomely dominant—influence. One of his last works, *Arcane 17* (named after the 17th card of the tarot) gives a peculiarly lucid and self-aware account of what attracts him to occult philosophies:

Esoterism, all reservations granted as to its very principle, at least offers the enormous interest of sustaining in a state of dynamism the system of comparison, unlimited in scope, at man's disposal, which supplies him with the relations capable of linking the objects to all appearances farthest apart, and reveals to him something of the mechanics of universal symbolism.[138]

There is one point of collision with reason in Breton which is not directly relevant to our argument because it is special to himself. His language is pervaded by the sense of a primal wrong, deeper than any injustice of human society, to which it is an unforgivable betrayal ever to be reconciled.

Absolutely incapable of reconciling myself to the lot assigned to me, touched in my highest conscience by the denial of justice which is in no way excused in my eyes by original sin, I take care not to adapt my existence to the derisory conditions, *down here*, of all existence.[139]

It is as though he were a fallen angel, no, as though we were all angels inexplicably cast out of heaven. This is from his *Confession dédaigneuse*, written in 1923 just as Surrealism was emerging from Dada. In 1944, in *Arcane 17*, almost his last poetic work, his purest and noblest testimony to his faith in the dignity of man, during war and exile, awaiting the turning point to renewal from the bottom of despair, he proclaims with the same intransigence the rejuvenating power of rebellion 'even and above all in presence of the irreparable', compliments his future wife Elisa, whose child has been killed in an accident, on having remained unresigned to 'the unsurpassable wrong which has been done to you' and scornful of the 'miserable priests' who tried to console her, and discovers in the myth of Lucifer the message that 'It is revolt itself, revolt alone, which is creator of light'.[140]
    It would be pointless to dwell on the self-contradiction of an atheist making moral judgements outside the human sphere, speaking of an 'injustice' to man and of his 'wrongs', and elsewhere of the antinomies of thought as a 'servitude' to which he ought no more be resigned than to social oppression.[141] In the black rage against the whole order of things, and the pride of defiance, in Breton tightly controlled, one touches that indissoluble core of unreason which may be divined at the bottom of individuals who exert a troubling and unaccountable personal power. It is his true affinity to Sade, and to Vaché, who impressed him more than any other person he met. But although it motivates his subversive thinking he is too rational to let it shape either the philosophizing or the personal myth. Even in adapting the Romantic myth of Satan, he resists the temptation to invent for himself a Jehovah or Demiurge for the sake of defying him; and in place of the name of the devil he chooses 'Lucifer', for the light born of intensest darkness at the point where 'the high and the low cease to be perceived as contradictory'.[142]
    Surrealism is the culmination of the movement which began with Futurism, and to some extent it has escaped the rapid obselescence which is the destiny of an *avant-garde*. It remains alive not only as an influence in the arts but in the subversive spirit most eloquent in the exhilarating or frightening graffiti which spread over the walls of cities from Paris after May 1968, 'Imagination takes power!',

'Take your desires for realities', 'Crime is the highest form of sensuality', 'Society is a carnivorous flower'. It even resembles a religion in having followers in each new generation with the inclination to organize like Breton's circle, define an orthodoxy, denounce heresies, indulge self-righteousness and righteous indigna- tion. Its durability need not surprise us, for it brought something new with which it seems that we shall not be able to dispense. Surrealism has shown that it is still possible to locate ourselves subjectively in that cosmos of ends from which the objectivizing language of science had seemed to exile us, without either reviv- ing an obselete or borrowing from an alien tradition. It is a laboratory in which one may watch the seeds of morality and of the sacred, which seemed dead, sprout again displaced from their traditional soil, in unprecedented and to some eyes monstrous forms. Like Taoism in ancient China, it carries us to that extreme of thought where to direct our spontaneity no imperative remains except 'Be aware', and instead of ending everything begins again.

NOTES

NOTES TO CHAPTER 1.1

1 R. M. Hare, *The Language of morals*, Oxford 1952, I.3.2.
2 J-P. Sartre, *Being and nothingness*, trans. Hazel E. Barnes, London 1958, p. 462.
3 cf. pp. 67–72 below.
4 F. Nietzsche, *Beyond good and evil*, trans. R. J. Hollingdale, Harmondsworth 1973, § 17.

NOTES TO CHAPTER 1.2

1 cf. p. 5 above.
2 Jean Piaget, *The child's conception of the world*, London 1951.
3 cf. Ch. 1.5 below.
4 cf. pp. 6, 9, 13 above.
5 I reproduce these paragraphs from a premature attempt to develop my anti-egoist argument in *The Problem of value* (Hutchinson's University Library), London 1961, pp. 57–9.
6 cf. p. 16 above.
7 cf. p. 17 above.
8 F. Nietzsche, *The will to power*, trans. Walter Kaufman and R. J. Hollingdale, New York 1968, § 372.
9 Richard Dawkins, *The selfish gene*, London 1978.
10 *ut supra*, p. 30.

NOTES TO CHAPTER 1.3

1 G. E. Moore, *Principia ethica*, London 1903.
2 cf. p. 2 above.
3 cf. p. 30 above.
4 cf. pp. 10, 11 above.
5 cf. p. 12 above.
6 *Beyond good and evil*, § 229.
7 cf. pp. 22, 23 above.
8 For this slogan, cf. section 3.3.2 n. 122 below.
9 cf. p. 1 above.
10 I was never able to come fully to grips with this difficulty in the premature formulation of my anti-egoist argument in *The Problem of value*, pp. 47–60.
11 cf. p. 6 above.
12 *Beyond good and evil*, § 39.

NOTES TO CHAPTER 1.5

1 cf. Ch. 1.2 above.
2 Ludwig Wittgenstein, *Philosophical investigations*, Oxford 1953, § 65–7.
3 Thomas S. Kuhn, *The structure of scientific revolutions*, Chicago 1970, p. 63.
4 Kuhn, pp. 117f.
5 Karl S. Popper, *The logic of scientific discovery*, London 1959.
6 Donald A. Schon, *The displacement of concepts*, London 1963.
7 Schon, p. 172.
8 cf. p. 187 below.
9 Gilbert Ryle, *The concept of mind*, London 1949.
10 Kuhn, p. 77.
11 Kuhn, p. 122.

12 S. Le Gall, *Le philosophe Tchou Hi* (Variétés sinologiques 6), Shanghai 2nd ed. 1923, p. 30.
13 Joseph Needham, *Science and civilization in China*, Vol. 2, Cambridge 1962, pp. 557–62.
14 Fritjof Capra, *The Tao of physics*, London 1976, pp. 224f.

NOTES TO CHAPTER 2.1

1 cf. pp. 45, 46 above.
2 cf. pp. 47–52 above.
3 cf. Ch. 2.3 below.
4 cf. E. R. Dodds, *The Greeks and the irrational*, Berkeley and Los Angeles 1951, pp. 80–2.
5 This selection of standards is more fully discussed in my *The problem of value*, pp. 93–118.
6 cf. Ch. 1.4 above.
7 *Poetics*, viii, 32–4.
8 cf. Ch. 1.3 above.
9 cf. Ch. 1.3 above.
10 *Collected papers of Charles Peirce*, Harvard, 1931ff., 5.2, 8.33.
11 cf. pp. 45, 46, 65 above.
12 cf. Arthur Koestler, *The case of the midwife toad*, London 1971, 47f.
13 John Taylor, *Black holes*, London 1973, pp. 27–30.
14 John Keats, letter to J. H. Reynolds, 3 May 1818.
15 cf. pp. 56, 57 above.
16 cf. Charles Fort, *The book of the damned* (lst ed. 1919), London 1979, pp. 17–28 *et passim*.
17 My information on SHC is from Michael Harrison, *Fire from heaven*, London 1977.
18 Letter to Fliess, 15 October 1897.

NOTES TO CHAPTER 2.2

1 Jacques Monod, *Chance and necessity*, London 1974.
2 cf. pp. 61, 62. 75–8 above.
3 Monod, p. 144.
4 Monod, p. 146.
5 cf. p. 198 below.
6 D. H. Lawrence, *St Mawr*.
7 cf. Ch. 1.2 above.
8 Rudolf Otto, *The idea of the holy*, Oxford 1925.
9 *Revelation*, 1:14–16 (Revised Standard Version).
10 J. E. Lovelock, *Gaia*, Oxford 1979, ix.
11 *Gaia*, p. 4.
12 *Gaia*, p. 146.
13 *Gaia*, p. 11.
14 cf. pp. 83–5 above.
15 Monod, p. 24.
16 Monod, p. 115.
17 Monod, p. 110.
18 Monod, p. 137.
19 cf. pp. 205–7, 211–15 below.
20 cf. p. 96 above.
21 Ernest Jones, *The life and work of Sigmund Freud*, ed. and abr. Lionel Trilling and Steven Marcus, London 1964, pp. 316f.
22 Breton collected other examples in *Le pont suspendu* (in his *Perspective cavalière*).
23 Monod, p. 158.
24 Monod, p. 160.
25 Monod, p. 30.
26 Monod, p. 158.
27 cf. p. 90 above.

NOTES TO CHAPTER 2.3

1 cf. pp. 63–7 above.
2 cf. p. 81 above.
3 cf. n. 14 below.
4 Michel Gauquelin, *The cosmic clocks*, London 1973, pp. 83–6, 117–21, 156–71.
5 Karl Marx, *Economic and philosophic manuscripts of 1844*, Moscow n. d., p. 75.
6 It is notorious that 'alienation' is a dangerously mobile word, allowing one to speak of institutions as going a way of their own alienated from the wills of those caught up in them, or of the individuals as alienated from themselves if they submit to them or from society if they do not. Marx developed this originally Hegelian concept in successive reworkings of his fundamental ideas unpublished in his lifetime, *Economic and political manuscripts of 1844*, in which man in capitalist society is seen as alienated from his own 'essence': *The German ideology* (1845–6, in collaboration with Engels), in which he drops the concept of a human essence (apparently shamed out of this metaphysical abstraction by Max Stirner) and avoids the previously overused abstract noun for the simple adjective 'alien': and the *Grundrisse* (1857–8), which more cautiously revives the abstract usage. The political pamphlets and technical economic studies published in Marx's lifetime seldom draw upon his fundamental theorizing, but alienation occasionally surfaces even in *Capital* (cf. I. Mészáros, *Marx's theory of alienation*, London 1970, pp. 221–6). Although it used to be supposed that in *The German ideology* Marx abandoned the concept, his temporary self-discipline in writing of the rise of religion, the state and the market only as institutions independent of and alien to men's wills, to be dissolved eventually in the voluntary co-operation of communism, makes the *Feuerbach* chapter of this book his clearest exposition of alienation. It is in a manuscript note of the same period (1845-6) that Marx for the first time succeeds in clearly formulating the question he had been struggling to answer: 'Individuals always started, and always start, from themselves. Their relations are the relations of their real life. How does it happen that their relations assume an independent existence over against them? and that the forces of their own life overpower them?' (*The German ideology*, London 1965, p. 658).
7 Claude Lévi-Strauss, *La pensée sauvage*, Paris 1962.
8 cf. the observation of Breton cited on p. 226 below.
9 Mircea Eliade, *Myth and reality*, New York 1963.
10 cf. pp. 96–7 above.
11 *New Larousse encyclopedia of mythology*, London 1968, p. 441.
12 cf. pp. 96–100 above.
13 cf. pp. 83–5 above.
14 The poem *The sun beneath the coral*, with its submerged myth of evolution stopping and starting again, the death and rebirth of the sun, and a city of coral which accretes in the night out of the sea and is destroyed by lightning, grew out of lines thrown up in experiments in automatic writing, or noted down on a pad by my bed as they came into my head on the verge of sleep, during a period when I was fascinated by Surrealism. The myth as it took shape from the pattern of involuntary images disturbed me by a pessimism about the present world which was at that time (1966–7) foreign to my conscious thought, although I have since moved rather nearer to it. I reproduce this text as a practical demonstration of the cosmos-building process in its raw state, without making any claims as to the value either of the poetry or the myth.

NOTES TO CHAPTER 2.4

1 cf. section 3.3.2 below.
2 Georg Groddeck, *The unknown self*, London 1951, p. 39.
3 cf. p. 12 above.
4 cf. pp. 75–8 above.
5 cf. pp. 47–52 above.
6 F. Nietzsche, *Genealogy of Morals*, trans. Francis Golffing, New York 1956, pp. 241–3.
7 cf. Ch. 1.2 above.
8 John Webster, *The duchess of Malfi*, act 4, scene 1.

9 Mary Shelley, *Frankenstein*, in *Three Gothic Novels*, Penguin English Library 1968, p. 315.
10 This paragraph is strongly influenced by Georges Bataille's *La structure psychologique du fascisme*, in his *Oeuvres complètes*, vol. 1, Paris 1970, pp. 339–71.
11 Hitler's speech at Munich on 14 March 1936, after reoccupying the Rhineland.
12 cf. Richard Dawkins, *The selfish gene*, pp. 176f.
13 *Autobiography of Bertrand Russell*, New York 1969, vol. 1 p. 47, vol. 2 p. 186.
14 Russell, op. cit., vol 1 p. 106.

NOTES TO CHAPTER 3.1

1 *Matthew* 6:27; *Luke* 12:25.
2 cf. p. 108 above.
3 Andre Breton, *Nadja*, Paris 1945, p. 20 note.
4 cf. section 3.3.2 below.
5 cf. pp. 209–10 below.

NOTES TO SECTION 3.2.1

1 *Beyond good and evil*, trans. R. J. Hollingdale, London 1973, § 1.
2 *Genealogy of morals*, trans. Francis Golffing, New York 1956, p. 287.
3 *The will to power*, trans. Walter Kaufmann and R. J. Hollingdale, New York 1968, § 544.
4 *The will to power*, § 535.
5 *Beyond good and evil*, § 4.
6 *The Anti-Christ*, trans. R. J. Hollingdale, London 1968, § 56.
7 *Genealogy of morals*, p. 171.
8 *Genealogy of morals*, p. 261.
9 *Ecce homo*, trans. R. J. Hollingdale, London 1979, pp. 43, 44.
10 *The will to power*, § 373; *Twilight of the gods*, trans. R. J. Hollingdale, London 1968, pp. 85, 86.
11 *The will to power*, Book 4. cf. the suggestion in *Beyond Good and evil*, § 251 that the German aristocratic officer caste might be the better for a little Jewish blood: 'It would be interesting in many ways to see whether the genius of money and patience (and above all a little mind and spirituality, of which there is a plentiful lack in the persons just mentioned) could not be added and bred into the hereditary art of commanding and obeying.'
12 *The will to power*, § 49.
13 *Ecce homo*, pp. 34, 80.
14 *The will to power*, § 401.
15 *Twilight of the idols*, pp. 23, 95.
16 cf. p. 166 above.

NOTES TO SECTION 3.2.2

1 *Dialogue entre un prêtre et un moribund*, Paris 1949, p. 27.
2 *Justine, ou les malheurs de la vertu*, Paris 1950, p. 49.
3 cf. Ch. 1.2 above.
4 *La nouvelle Justine*, Paris 1978, p. 479.
5 *Histoire de Juliette*, Paris 1976, vol. 2, p. 258.
6 *Juliette*, vol. 2, p. 258.
7 Aquinas, *Summa Theologica*, 2/2, q. 159.
8 Guillaume Apollinaire, Introduction to *L'oeuvre du Marquis de Sade*, Paris 1909, p. 17.
9 *La philosophie dans le boudoir*, Paris 1976, pp. 187–252.
10 *La philosophie dans le boudoir*, p. 218.
11 *Juliette*, vol. 1, pp. 399–402.
12 Letter to Gaufridy, 5 December 1791.
13 *Juliette*, vol. 1, pp. 419, 460ff.
14 *Juliette*, vol. 1, pp. 464–92.

15 *Juliette*, vol. 1, p. 501.
16 *Juliette*, vol. 1, p. 39.
17 *Juliette*, vol. 3, pp. 295–305.
18 *Juliette*, vol. 1, pp. 343–53 and elsewhere.
19 *Juliette*, vol. 2, pp. 183, 184.
20 *Juliette*, vol. 1, p. 308.
21 *Juliette*, vol. 1, p. 293.
22 *Juliette*, vol. 1, p. 307.
23 *Juliette*, vol. 1, p. 271.
24 *Juliette*, vol. 1, p. 507 note 1.
25 *La nouvelle Justine*, p. 366.
26 cf. pp. 23–4 above.
27 *Juliette*, vol. 1, p. 427.
28 cf. p. 166 above.
29 *La nouvelle Justine*, p. 481.
30 *La nouvelle Justine*, p. 679.
31 *Juliette*, vol. 1, p. 301.
32 *Justine*, p. 198; *La nouvelle Justine*, p. 367.
33 *Juliette*, vol. 2, p. 151.
34 *La philosophie dans le boudoir*, p. 46.
35 cf. p. 178 above.

NOTES TO SECTION 3.3.1

1 Chuang-tzŭ, *The seven inner chapters and other writings from the book 'Chuang-tzŭ'*, London 1981.
2 'Taoist spontaneity and the dichotomy of "is" and "ought"' in *Experimental essays on. Chuang-tzŭ*, ed. Victor H. Mair, Honolulu 1983; *What was new in the Ch'eng-Chu theory of human nature?*, paper presented at the International Conference on Chu Hsi, Honolulu 1982.
3 cf. pp. 4–5 above.
4 *Analects of Confucius*, 1/14.
5 Arthur Waley, *The way and its power*, London 1934, p. 70.
6 For the choice of these equivalents, cf. *Chuang-tzŭ* (as n. 1 above), pp. 10, 33, 34 n. 21.
7 *Chuang-tzŭ*, p. 60.
8 *Chuang-tzŭ*, p. 53.
9 *Chuang-tzŭ*, pp. 52, 53.
10 *Chuang-tzŭ*, p. 58.
11 *Chuang-tzŭ*, p. 102.
12 *Chuang-tzŭ*, p. 51.
13 *Chuang-tzŭ*, p. 51.
14 *Chuang-tzŭ*, p. 140.
15 *Chuang-tzŭ*, p. 98.
16 *Chuang-tzŭ*, p. 281.
17 *Chuang-tzŭ*, p. 259.
18 *Chuang-tzŭ*, p. 118.
19 *Chuang-tzŭ*, p. 45, cf. p. 150.
20 *Chuang-tzŭ*, p. 91.
21 *Chuang-tzŭ*, p. 91.
22 *Chuang-tzŭ*, p. 141.
23 *Chuang-tzŭ*, p. 84.
24 cf. p. 185 above.
25 *Chuang-tzŭ*, p. 84.
26 *Chuang-tzŭ*, p. 111.
27 *Chuang-tzŭ*, p. 85.
28 I leave this Chinese term untranslated because I have already had occasion to discuss it, see p. 57 above.

29 *Chuang-tzŭ*, pp. 48, 84, 97.
30 *Chuang-tzŭ*, p. 68.
31 *Chuang-tzŭ*, pp. 68, 69.
32 *Chuang-tzŭ*, p. 56.
33 The use of the easily misunderstood word 'daemonic' as translation equivalent is discussed in *Chuang-tzŭ*, p. 35 n. 72.
34 *Chuang-tzŭ*, pp. 63, 64.
35 *Chuang-tzŭ*, pp. 88, 89.

NOTES TO SECTION 3.3.2

1 *Futurist manifestos*, ed. Umbro Apollonio, trans. Robert Brain, R. W. Flint, J. C. Higgitt, Caroline Tisdall, London 1973, p. 96.
2 *Futurist manifestos*, pp. 96–8.
3 Marinetti, *Selected writings*, ed. R. W. Flint, trans. R. W. Flint and Arthur A. Coppotelli, London 1972, p. 95.
4 *Futurist manifestos*, p. 154.
5 Marinetti, p. 128.
6 *Futurist manifestos*, p. 96.
7 Marinetti, pp. 161–245. Marinetti's explanation of the symbolism of *The untamables* is given on pp. 246–8.
8 Marinetti, p. 234.
9 Marinetti, p. 245.
10 Marinetti, pp. 202, 247.
11 cf. Ch 2.2 above.
12 *Futurist manifestos*, p. 136
13 *Futurist manifestos*, pp. 135–50.
14 Marinetti, p. 88.
15 Marinetti, p. 87.
16 D. H. Lawrence in letter to Edward Garnett, 5 June 1914.
17 *Futurist manifestos*, p. 97.
18 Marinetti, p. 91.
19 Marinetti, p. 91.
20 Marinetti, p. 88.
21 Marinetti, p. 88.
22 *Futurist manifestos*, p. 100.
23 cf. p. 203 below.
24 *Futurist manifestos*, p. 155.
25 *Futurist manifestos*, pp. 155ff.
26 Marinetti, pp. 153ff.
27 Marinetti, p. 149.
28 *Futurist manifestos*, p. 22.
29 Unattributed quotation by R. W. Flint in Marinetti, p. 34.
30 Caroline Tisdall and Angelo Bozzolla, *Futurism*, London 1977, p. 156.
31 *Futurist manifestos*, p. 73.
32 Tristan Tzara, *Oeuvres complètes*, Paris 1975, vol. 1, p. 357.
33 Gabrielle Buffet-Picabia, 'Some memories of Pre-Dada' in *Dada painters; an anthology*, ed. Robert Motherwell, New York 1951, p. 266.
34 Hugo Ball, *Flight out of time: a Dada diary*, ed. John Elderfield, trans. Ann Raimes, New York 1974, 8, viii, 1916.
35 Ball, 24. v. 1916.
36 Ball, 18. vi. 1916.
37 Ball, 12. iii. 1916.
38 Ball, 18. iv. 1917.
39 Ball, 7. v. 1917.
40 Tzara, pp. 395ff.

115 *Entretiens*, pp. 111, 289; *Perspectives cavalières*, pp. 127–9; Thirion, pp. 159–61, 192f.
116 *Point du jour*, p. 28.
117 *Point du jour*, pp. 47f.
118 Claude Lévi-Strauss, *Structural anthropology*, vol. 2, trans. Monique Layton, London 1977, p. 343.
119 *La clé des champs*, p. 215. To prefer African sculpture to Oceanian, for its stronger formal relationships, was disdained as an obsolete Cubist taste (pp. 213f.). Breton's interest bypassed the Negro until his visit to Martinique in 1941, celebrated in his *Martinique charmeuse de serpents* (1948). His self-confessed insensibility to music obscured from him what was very soon obvious to sympathizers outside his immediate circle, that the plainest example of psychic automatism in the culture of his time was improvised jazz. In the 1920s jazz was one of the tastes which distinguished the outer circle in the Rue du Château from the inner circle of the Rue Fontaine (Thirion, pp. 93, 95).
120 *Entretiens*, p. 204.
121 Monnerot had joined Breton's circle and introduced him to black poets as early as 1932. Thirion notes that Monnerot at this period 'anticipated the changes in Surrealism after the forties' (Thirion, p. 320); he was already treating Surrealism as a revival of primitive thinking and re-invention of sorcery in a contribution to *Le surréalisme au service de la révolution*, May 1933. He did not, however, yet use the word 'sacred', presumably borrowed later from Bataille (cf. n. 72 above), to whose *Acéphale* he contributed in July 1937.
122 William Borroughs and Allen Ginsberg, *The Yage letters*, San Francisco 1963, p. 60.
   Nietzsche's 'Nothing is true, everything is permitted' (cf. p. 164 above) seems to be adapted from a comment by Joseph von Hammer, that agents trained in the secret antinomian doctrine of the Assassins 'since they consider everything [that is, in religion] a cheat and nothing forbidden, are the best tools of an infernal policy' (Joseph von Hammer, *Die Geschichte der Assassinen*, Stuttgart and Tübingen 1818, p. 56).
123 André Breton, *Qu'est-ce que le surréalisme?*, Brussels 1934, pp. 11f.
124 cf. pp. 170, 181 above.
125 That *Poisson soluble* is a case of true automatic writing without afterthoughts is said to be confirmed by the state of the manuscript (Anna Balakian, *André Breton, magus of surrealism*, New York 1971, pp. 64, 65). The 'soluble fish' of the title is a phrase thrown up by automatism which frightened Breton, who recognized it as referring to himself, born under the sign Pisces, and swimming and dissolving in the stream of his thought (Manifestes, p. 49).
126 *Entretiens*, p. 95.
127 *Entretiens*, p. 96.
128 *Manifestes*, p. 134.
129 Apart from the evidence of his imaginative writings, we have Breton's report on his sexual tastes in the 'Researches into sexuality', in *La révolution surréaliste* No. 11 (1928), p. 40.
130 cf. the manuscripts (drafted soon after the *Second surrealist manifesto*) published in Bataille's *Oeuvres complètes* vol. 2, Paris 1970, pp. 51–109.
131 Pierre Klossowski (of Bataille's circle), *Sade mon prochain*, Paris 1947; Maurice Blanchot, *Lautréamont et Sade*, Paris 1949; Bataille, preface to Sade's *Justine*, Paris 1950.
132 *Anthologie de l'humour noir*, p. 39.
133 *Anthologie*, p. 42.
134 *Manifestes*, pp. 181, 182 n.
135 *Entretiens*, pp. 268, 278, 285.
136 *Entretiens*, pp. 266, 267, 276.
137 *Manifestes*, p. 181.
138 *Arcane 17*, p. 105.
139 *Les pas perdus*, pp. 7, 8.
140 *Arcane 17*, pp. 108, 121.
141 cf. 209 above.
142 Quoted p. 210 above.